ISLAM & SLAVERY

John Andrew Morrow

ISLAM & SLAVERY

John Andrew Morrow

Academica Press
Washington~London

Library of Congress Cataloging-in-Publication Data

Names: Morrow, John Andrew (author)
Title: Islam and Slavery | John Andrew Morrow
Description: Washington : Academica Press, 2024. | Includes references.
Identifiers: LCCN 2023950285 | ISBN 9781680536379 (hardcover) |
9781680536386 (e-book)

Copyright 2024 John Andrew Morrow

"What will make you know what the steep path is? It is the freeing of a slave" (Qur'an 90:12-13).

Contents

Foreword xiii

Words of Support xv

Disclaimer.. xvii

Trigger Warning... xvii

Notice xix

Terminology & Philosophy xxi

Preface xxiii

Introduction 1

Chapter One
Tell Me Something I Don't Know.................................... 3

1.1 Introduction... 3

1.2 The Curse of Ham 3

1.3 Islamic Law Supports Slavery 9

1.4 Opposing Slavery is Hypocrisy, Apostasy, and Infidelity 10

1.5 Free the Slaves 13

1.6 Muhammad, the Slave Master?.................................. 13

1.7 Muhammad, the Abolitionist 16

1.8 Conclusions.. 17

Chapter Two
Mariya the Who? 19

2.1 Introduction.. 19

2.2 There is Something About Mary................................. 19

2.3 Conclusions.. 24

Chapter Three
Thou Shalt Have Sex with Slave Girls **25**

3.1 Introduction... 25

3.2 Married Women as Sex Slaves 28

3.3 The Covenants of the Prophet
Prohibit Sexual Coercion and Forced Marriages 32

3.4 Possessed by the Right Hand 33

3.5 Taking Captives as Concubines 36

3.6 No Concubinage in Islam 36

3.7 Conclusions... 37

Chapter Four
That Booty is Booty: Women as Spoils of War **39**

4.1 Introduction... 39

4.2 Women as Spoils of War 39

4.3 Thou Shalt Crave a Sex Slave... 40

4.4 Humanizing Sex Slaves 42

4.5 Questioning Qur'anic Misinterpretation 43

4.6 Conclusions... 47

Chapter Five
Opposing Abolition **49**

5.1 Introduction... 49

5.2 Jews, Christians, and Slavery 49

5.3 Aggressive *Jihad* 50

5.4 Freedom is Not a Human Right in Islam 54

5.5 Islam is Submission, Subjugation, and Slavery: Not Freedom 56

5.6 Conclusions... 57

Chapter Six
Snake Oil Salesmen and Merchants of Religion.. **59**

6.1 Introduction... 59

6.2 Prime Swampland for Sale 59

6.3 Emancipatory Islam 67

6.4 Conclusions.. 68

Chapter Seven
Salvaging Scripture from the Slave Master.................................... 71

7.1 Introduction... 71

7.2 Jewish and Christian Responses to Slavery 71

7.3 Muslim Jurists Fully Embraced Slavery 72

7.4 Conclusions... 73

Chapter Eight
Slave Master Imams or Abolitionist Imams? 75

8.1 Introduction... 75

8.2 Will the Real Hasan Please Stand Up? 75

8.3 Ain't no John Brown in this Town 77

8.4 Imam 'Ali 79

8.5 Slave Master Imams?... 80

8.6 Imam Ja'far al-Sadiq: Between Fact, Fiction, Fantasy, and Forgery 81

8.7 The Schizophrenic *Sunnah* 86

8.8 Perpetuating Sexual Debauchery 90

8.9 Support for Slavery from Shiite Religious Authorities................ 95

8.10 Conclusions... 99

Chapter Nine
Religious and Racial Reckoning 101

9.1 Introduction... 101

9.2 Facing Reality 101

9.3 Between a Rock and a Hard Place:
From Sunnism to Shiism and Beyond 101

9.4 Convert Clowns, Muslim Pimps, Players, and Hojabis 103

9.5 Conclusions... 108

Chapter Ten
No Means Yes, No Means Tie Her UP, NO Means Smack Her Up 109

10.1 Introduction... 109

10.2 Speak of the Devil... 109

10.3 Idyllic "Islamic" Slavery: A Muslim Man's Utopia?............................... 114

10.4 Sex and Violence 114

10.5 Facing the Music.. 116

10.6 The Worst of People 118

10.7 The Duty to Think.. 118

10.8 Conclusions... 119

Chapter Eleven
No Real Abolitionist Movement Emerged in Islamic Civilization **121**

11.1 Introduction.. 121

11.2 Sexual Slavery as Misogyny 121

11.3 Collective Culpability 122

11.4 Conclusions... 124

Chapter Twelve
I Own You: Your Ass is Literally Mine **125**

12.1 Introduction.. 125

12.2 Old Enough to Bleed.. 125

12.3 Islam: A Pimp's Paradise? 126

12.4 Thou Shalt Emasculate Boys 127

12.5 Booty Boys 127

12.6 And Boys will be Toys:
The Eunuch as an Essential Component of Islamic Civilization 128

12.7 Castrated Cold-Blooded Killers and Concubine Hunters 128

12.8 Conclusions... 131

Chapter Thirteen
The Moral Conundrum of Slavery **135**

13.1 Introduction.. 135

13.2 Reforming, Dismantling and Eradicating Slavery 135

13.3 Conclusions... 140

Chapter Fourteen
The Illusion of Abolition in the Muslim World **143**

14.1 Introduction.. 143

14.2 Slavery is Alive and Well in the Muslim World 143

14.3 God Does Not Change the Condition
of a People Until they Change Themselves 147

14.4 Conclusions 168

Chapter Fifteen
The Horrors of "Islamic" Slavery 169

15.1 Introduction 169

15.2 The Blind Following the Blind 170

15.3 The "Islamic" Slave Trade 176

15.4 Comparing and Contrasting 179

15.5 Conclusions 182

Chapter Sixteen
The Islamic Basis for the Abolition of Slavery 185

16.1 Introduction 185

16.2 Islamic Abolitionism 185

16.3 Conclusions 199

Conclusions 201

Post Scriptum 213

Appendix 1
Grounds for the Prohibition of Slavery and Concubinage 229

Appendix 2
Artistic Depictions of "Islamic" Slavery and Concubinage 255

Appendix 3
Fatwa Prohibiting Slavery and Concubinage:
The Shortest but Most Significant Edict in Islamic History 269

Appendix 4
After Thoughts 271

Works Cited 275

Index 291

Foreword

Edip Yüksel, J.D., Retired Professor of Philosophy;
author, translator, and commentator of the Qur'an

Dr. John Andrew Morrow's groundbreaking work, *Islam & Slavery*, dispels one of the most pervasive misconceptions about the Islam and the Qur'an. This book presents compelling evidence and arguments that refute the historical conspiracy propagated by sultans against the system of peacemaking, known as Islam.

Muhammad, one of history's most transformative leaders, established a federal-secular, multicultural city-state, replacing tribal oligarchy with a just, elected leadership based on a social contract. Under his guidance, women were granted equal status and rights, including the right to vote. The state was prohibited from imposing a specific faith or religion, instead, it was mandated to treat all citizens equally. The traditional claims of superiority based on tribes or colors, men or women, was rejected and the only superiority among the citizens was declared to be based on "righteous deeds."

In the darkness of the medieval Arabian desert, an egalitarian society was born against all odds. This progressive community valued reason, scientific inquiry, liberty, justice, rule of law, freedom of expression, human unity, a free-market economy adjusted by social and economic rights, and global peace. The city that birthed this revolution was fittingly renamed from Yathrib to al-Madinah, The Civilization.

Despite the forces of ignorance and aggression, the liberating message of the Qur'an served as a beacon for humanity for centuries. In just twenty-three years, the teachings of rational monotheism and the system of peacemaking guided Muhammad and his friends far and wide.

Muhammad and his courageous companions fought against a polytheistic, warmongering tribal system that was deeply superstitious, misogynistic, racist, and cruel. However, to reverse these reforms within a few decades, the power-hungry oligarchs who lost their influence fabricated countless *hadiths* and volumes of *tafsirs* and sectarian jurisprudence.

As discussed in *Manifesto for Islamic Reform* and *Qur'an: A Reformist Translation*, the claim that the Qur'an did not reject slavery is one of the greatest falsehoods in human history. According to the Qur'an, enslaving another person is not just a major sin and crime, but the cardinal sin and crime: it is polytheism.

The Qur'an frequently reminds us of Moses's struggle against the Pharaoh and his government, a story of freedom against slavery. The Qur'an refers to Moses by name one hundred and thirty-six times, almost twice as often as the second most repeated name, Abraham, who is mentioned sixty-nine times. The Sunni and Shiite clergymen, using countless *hadiths*, distorted the meaning of key words and verses in the Qur'an. To claim that Muhammad and his monotheist friends practiced slavery is akin to declaring them Pharaohs who claimed to be lords besides the only Lord.

Dr. Morrow explores the complicated relationship between Islam and slavery in this thought-provoking study. This book delves into the historical, religious, and socio-cultural aspects of slavery within the Islamic world, offering a comprehensive analysis that is both enlightening and balanced. The author, a diligent scholar, navigates the complexities of this topic with sensitivity and scholarly rigor, providing readers with a refreshing understanding of a subject often shrouded in controversy. *Islam & Slavery* is an essential read for anyone seeking to deepen their knowledge of Qur'an, Islamic history, and its intersection with the historical phenomenon of slavery.

Words of Support

"Dr. John Andrew Morrow's book counts on my unconditional support." **Biram Dah Abeid,** Mauritanian politician and president of the Initiative for the Resurgence of the Abolitionist Movement (IRA)

"I wholeheartedly endorse Dr. John Andrew Morrow's *Islam & Slavery*. This important book will generate a necessary debate on taboo issues in Islamic cultures. Morrow provides a fascinating critique and constructs a compelling argument against an edifice of legal fictions such as concubinage and slavery in Islamic law. One must read the entire book to understand the poignant point he wishes to convey. This book critiques scholars who have been cowed into silence and those who have volunteered their services to reactionary causes. It will certainly receive praise and criticism. The book's approach and conclusions will encounter some resistance from certain corners, but it will be accepted by people whose core principle is justice. It is a fantastic and wonderful book. The topic it tackles is horrible. However, it is the naked truth." **Dr. Chouki El Hamel**, Professor of History in the School of Historical, Philosophical and Religious Studies at Arizona State University, and author of *Black Morocco: A History of Slavery, Race, and Islam*

"This is a thorough, exhaustive, courageous, unabashedly honest, and tragically painful book. The horrific scourge of slavery afflicts humanity in our age more than at any other time in history. It is a well-known fact that there are more slaves in the world today than when slavery was legal. Yet, as you learn from Dr. Morrow's book, there remain Muslim scholars who are effectively moral apologists for the institution of slavery. With unflinching moral clarity and awe-inspiring scholarly rigor, Dr. Morrow exposes the incoherence and amorality of these apologists. This deeply profound and transformative book should become the standard work on the subject of Islam and slavery for decades to come." **Dr. Khaled Abou El Fadl,** Omar and Azmeralda Alfi Distinguished Professor of Law UCLA School of Law

"Dr. John Andrew Morrow has convincingly refuted Dr. Jonathan A.C. Brown's thesis in his book *Slavery & Islam*. Anyone who reads Islamic scriptures without an innate prejudice and is acquainted with Islamic history cannot but see that Prophet Muhammad, the Holy Qur'an, and the *Hadith,* oppose the practice at every step and in every possible way short of dismantling this important pillar of the economic structure of the society which continued to be the case in many parts of the world in different forms until the nineteenth century CE. That in the seventh-century CE, a religion endeavored to abolish its sanctity from the hearts of its followers is nothing short of revolutionary. Dr. Morrow's book is a must-read for all those interested in the subject. Even critics of Islam should keep it as a companion volume to Dr. Jonathan A.C. Brown's book." **Sultan Shahin,** Editor of *New Age Islam*

"Professionally written with the highest academic standards, *Islam & Slavery* provides a valuable and desperately needed resource in the English-language. As Dr. Morrow details, those who took over Islam after the death of the Prophet Muhammad were concerned primarily with profiting from the religion rather than spreading its message of peace, freedom, and co-existence. They lied and misinterpreted the Qur'an to serve their worldly agendas. This resulted in the so-called 'Islamic conquests' with all the atrocities they brought to the world, including, slavery, which was abolished by the Qur'an." **Amin Refaat,** *Executive Vice President, International Qur'anic Center*.

Disclaimer

No John Brown was harmed in the writing of this book.

Trigger Warning

Reading this work may cause psychological, physical, and spiritual trauma. If you are a Muslim who is troubled by slavery and concubinage, it may save your faith and your mind. Timely, powerful, and provocative, it is a work of righteous rage and indignation and an Islamic Emancipation Proclamation.

Notice

For the sake of concision and style, titles, honorifics, and pious invocations are avoided. No offense is intended by their exclusion. The Prophet Muhammad and the Imams, as portrayed in Islamic sources, are treated like literary figures, as opposed to historical ones. The statements attributed to them are allegations in the best-case scenarios. Most of the material consists of myths, legends, and lore. Whenever it is written that "Muhammad said" or "Ja'far al-Sadiq said," it should be implicitly understood that these are claims made by compilers, collectors, and concoctors of traditions, who lived centuries after the passing of the subjects they supposedly cited.

This work does not criticize the Prophet and the twelve Imams. No disrespect is directed towards them. On the contrary, it defends them from their detractors, and it condemns all the sayings that were falsely attributed to them over the ages -- by parties of all persuasions -- that contradict the Qur'an, reason, morals, ethics, and common sense. For many Muslims, the Prophet and the twelve Imams were pure, immaculate, infallible, and sinless. Anything that is unbecoming cannot be attributed to them.

Those who disrespect religious sanctities and sentiments are those who attribute evil to God, the Prophet, and the Imams. This is not a work of Islamophobia but of Islamophilia and theophilia. Just like it is not anti-Jewish or anti-Christian to oppose slavery, it is not anti-Islamic to be an abolitionist. In fact, it makes them better Jews, Christians, and Muslims. After all, "God is with the righteous" (9:123).

Finally, just as I hold others accountable, I hold myself accountable to an even higher degree. Although I act with the best of intentions, in all sincerity, and exercise due academic diligence, including a rigorous peer-review process, I am not infallible. I have radically revised my views on many subjects over the course of the past half-century as a result of acquiring more knowledge, experience, and maturity. Hence, any errors, omissions, or shortcomings remain my own. With the exception of citations from other authors, the views expressed in this book are mine alone. It is the work of a *faqih*, literally, "one who seeks to understand" by analyzing, deconstructing, synthesizing, and reconciling the sources; a *mujtahid*, an interpreter of Islamic law, a *muhaddith*, a traditionist, a *mufassir*, an exegete of the Qur'an, a *mu'arakh*, a historian, a *mutakalam*, a theologian, and a *mufakir*, an intellectual, with over forty years of Islamic studies.

Terminology & Philosophy

As Voltaire (1694-1778) said, "If you want to converse with me, define your terms." Consequently, I acquiesce to his request. In some contexts, the term "concubine" can refer to lower status wives or sexual partners in polygynous societies. This is the case in much of the Bible. In other settings, the word can refer to mistresses and common-law sexual partners. There is a dramatic difference between a lower status second wife, brought into a family to produce an heir, a mistress who is seen on the side for the sake of fleeting pleasure, and a long-term live-in sexual partner in a committed relationship.

In this work, however, which focuses on the "Islamic" world, the term "concubine" refers to enslaved women who are exploited for their sexual services. They were generally captured in wars and slave raids. Some were sold by their fathers or families. They were trafficked, sold, bought, owned, and used for their labor. In some cases, many, or most, were born free. Others were the children of enslaved women. They were not lower status or common-law wives. In theory, more than practice, concubines could be emancipated after the death of their masters if they bore them a child. However, this was only the case if their owners stipulated so in their wills.

Although some concubines were forced into prostitution by their owners who made their living as pimps, these women were not courtesans. With the exception of those who were compelled to sell their bodies in brothels, concubines in the Muslim world were typically cloistered by their owners whereas courtesans often had independence and freedom and catered to a higher-class clientele.

As for slavery, it is the ownership of a person as property. Slaves were owned by individuals, tribes, organizations, or states. They were compelled to obey their masters. Their labor was unpaid. They were entitled to food, clothing, shelter, and protection. Avenues for emancipation were available to some of them.

Male slaves, many of whom were eunuchs, worked as servants, guards, agricultural workers, laborers, cooks, porters, miners, and bureaucrats. In many parts of the Muslim world, there were entire armies of enslaved men, many of whom were emasculated. Young boys were often used by men as sex slaves or molded into "Islamic" warriors and concubine hunters. Slaves were subjected to corporal punishment. In some cases, they were worked to death or killed by their masters without consequence.

Female slaves worked as laborers, maids, cooks, nannies, nurses, singers, dancers, and entertainers. The most attractive ones were reserved for sexual services. The younger they were, particularly prepubescent girls, the more they were prized. That being said, masters had the right to have sex with any of their female slaves. In other words, they could have their way with their cleaning staff, babysitters, and housekeepers. Some concubines of wealthy men could aspire to a higher standard of living than those who worked on plantations in the scorching sun from dawn to dusk; however, their plight remained pitiful, demeaning, degrading, and humiliating. In some cases, their situation was even more brutally traumatizing. What is worse? Backbreaking physical labor? Or being raped and beaten on a daily basis?

Conditions varied greatly. Concubines were at the mercy of their masters. Some were abused less. Others were victimized, brutalized, and even murdered with impunity. However, an enslaved and enchained woman remains an enslaved an enchained woman. They were physically and psychologically devasted to different degrees. To be deprived of freedom and movement, whether it is in prison, behind bars, or behind walls, without any hope for liberty, produces permanent mental and emotional scars. In some cases, the cage was made of gold. However, it still remained a cage.

Unlike Jonathan A.C. Brown, who holds that "moral condemnations of slavery are… not reflections of eternal moral realities," (5), this work operates under the premise that slavery, ancient and modern, in all of its forms, is immoral and unethical, irrespective of its legal status. It is founded on moral absolutism, namely, the view that actions are intrinsically right or wrong, and moral universalism, that is, the view that ethics apply universally. It is rooted in a rejection of moral nihilism and moral relativism. It also grounded on a repudiation of fideism, the theory that faith is independent of reason, which is shared by Protestants, as well as many, but not all Muslims, but which is rejected as heretical by the Roman Catholic Church and repudiated by Islamic rationalists.

Preface

Dr. Jonathan Andrew Cleveland Brown (b. 1977) is the author of several interesting works, including *Misquoting Muhammad*, which I thoroughly enjoyed. When *Slavery & Islam* was released, I was eager to read it hoping I would find it equally engaging. The work is well-written and well-researched. That is a given. I would expect nothing less from an academic like Brown. However, I must admit that I found the arguments advanced unconvincing, unpalatable, and unacceptable. As a Western Muslim of indigenous, French Canadian, Irish, and Morisco ancestry -- bloodlines that make me bound to fight for freedom -- I was always flabbergasted to meet Western Muslim converts of African ancestry who defended slavery and concubinage. Most of them presented themselves as militants, radicals, and revolutionaries who idolized Malcolm X (1925-1965) and his role in the black liberation movement while simultaneously supporting "Islamic" slavery, namely, the slavery practiced by Muslims in the name of Islam, and viewing it as morally acceptable. They were paradoxes personified and classic cases of cognitive dissonance. They had PTSD and battered slave syndrome. They were people in a psychological state of stupor. In this case, rather than a black Muslim convert defending slavery in defiance of morality and rationality, we have a white Muslim convert defending slavery and sexual bondage. Go figure. As he put it himself, "As a white American man and a Muslim, I am twofold the slaver" (11). This work, which started as a concise review of *Slavery & Islam* for an academic journal, has turned into a full-size book. However, it is not a comprehensive survey and condemnation of slavery and concubinage in Islam nor it is a complete overview of Brown's book. Rather, it is a refutation of some of the most salient arguments made by Jonathan A.C. Brown in his apology for "Islamic" slavery and sexual servitude.

Introduction

In *Slavery & Islam*, Dr. Jonathan A.C. Brown, the Alwaleed bin Talal Chair of Islamic Civilization at Georgetown University, devotes over four hundred pages to support his conviction that slavery and concubinage are permissible according to the Qur'an and the teachings and practice of the Prophet Muhammad (570-632) (2020: 70, 96). He is adamant that God and His Messenger allowed, condoned, and supported them (2020: 7, 9, 202). In his words, "the permissibility of slavery and concubinage is undeniable in the Qur'an" (Brown 2020: 196).

Rather than abolish sexual slavery, Brown asserts that Muslim jurists embraced the practice fully and took it to its maximum (2020: 81, 82). He admits that "the number of concubines taken by Muslims jumped dramatically with the early Islamic conquests" (Brown 2020: 114). Brown also stresses that, in Islamic law, "consent for sexual relations was assumed or irrelevant" (2020: 96, 281). Not only does he argue that sex slaves played a central role in Arab and Ottoman slavery, but he goes as far as to trivialize the age of consent (2020: 278-281). Moreover, he argues that freedom is not a fundamental human right in Islamic law (Brown 2020: 299-302; Clarence-Smith 2006: 22) and treats serial polygamists, who had hundreds of sex slaves, as moral exemplars (Brown 2020: 82).

Brown equates opposition to the institution of slavery and sexual servitude as opposition to the Messenger of God (2020: 196, 199-200). He considers those who oppose slavery but refuse to condemn the Prophet to be hypocrites (Brown 2020: 96). When faced with dissenting views on the disputed subject of the legitimacy of slavery in Islam, Brown's strategy is to respond with a loaded trick question and a theological trap: "Did the Prophet Muhammad commit a grave moral wrong?" (2020: 196). For Brown, a Muslim does not remain a Muslim if he or she answers in the affirmative. Consequently, he provides a jurisprudential justification for the practice of *takfir*, namely, the ex-communication of so-called heretics and apostates (Brown 2020: 198, 393, note 205; 405), and provides ample evidence that Muslims have a long history of enslaving other Muslims who do not share their ideology (Brown 2020: 106-109; 303-307; 370: note 24; 406, note 31 and 32; see also Clarence-Smith 42-45).

Brown may claim to believe that "slavery is wrong," however, he makes an important disclaimer: "as a Muslim myself, I cannot condemn it as grossly, intrinsically immoral across space and time. To do so would be to condemn the Qur'an, the Prophet Muhammad and God's law as morally compromised" (275). However, rather than support Islamic abolitionists, he assumes the role of the

Devil's Advocate, devoting an inordinate amount of time in his book to dismissing, debunking, and repudiating their arguments as violating the Qur'an, the *sunnah*, and the *shari'ah*. If one rejects the views of Muslim scholars who spurn slavery, is one an opponent or supporter of this evil and abominable institution? In fact, Brown wonders whether slavery is in the DNA of Islam (204). In his words, "we cannot pretend it is not part of our religion" (Brown 4).

Brown's entire work is an ideological defense of Slave Master Islam. That it comes from a white American Muslim is even more abhorrent. This is the product of a conscious choice. His work is not simply a survey of historical opinions on the permissibility of enslavement, human bondage, sexual captivity, subjugation, and violation. It is a validation of those views. Alternative interpretations of Islam, which are abolitionist and emancipatory, are amply available. He is perfectly familiar with their arguments and evidence, namely, that sexual relations are only permissible in wedlock and that the Prophet Muhammad stated that slave traders were the worst human beings (Brown 392, note 199; 237). Brown, however, has deliberately decided to denounce them.

The fact remains that there is not a single verse in the Qur'an that commands slavery. The verses that touch upon the topic are descriptive. They deal with a temporal socio-economic reality. Slavery is neither an article of faith nor is it a religious obligation. In fact, the Qur'an encourages and even requires Muslims to emancipate enslaved people (2:177; 47:4, 24:33). As far as the exponents of Islam's spiritual, moral, ethical, and egalitarian tradition are concerned, the Qur'an, the Prophet, and Islam introduced a system that would reform the practice of slavery and abolish it entirely and forever. Rather than select the sharp and narrow path, Brown has selected the wide and shallow one of the classical Islamic *status quo*. And since he likes to confront critics with a question, this introduction ends with a question, not of my own, but one that God poses in the Qur'an: "What will make you know what the steep path is? It is the freeing of a slave" (90:12-13).

Chapter One

Tell Me Something I Don't Know

1.1 Introduction

It takes Jonathan A.C. Brown over four hundred pages to tell educated and informed people what they already know, namely, that Islam and slavery have gone hand in hand for most of its history -- just like Christianity, Judaism, and most other world religions for that matter -- and that Muslims have a long history of racism. As expected, Brown claims that racism "is totally illegitimate in the religion," although several sayings attributed to the Prophet Muhammad support such prejudice and bigotry (2020: 12, see also 120-123). Although many scholars treated them as spurious, as they contradict the egalitarian passages of the Qur'an and other sayings of the Messenger of God (570-632) that are treated as genuine, some leading scholars, including al-Hakim (933-1014), Ibn Hibban (884-965), and Ahmad ibn Hanbal (780-855), did indeed accept them as authentic (Abou El Fadl 249); thereby granting racism a veneer of Islamic legitimacy in the minds of some racist, intolerant, and prejudiced Muslims who rebranded bigotry as piety.

1.2 The Curse of Ham

The Qur'an, the revelation that Muhammad is believed to have received over twenty-three years and which was collected into a book years and even decades after his earthly demise, is adamant that human beings are equal, stressing that "We created you from a single (pair) of a male and a female, and made you into nations and tribes, that ye may know other" (49:13). It also affirms that, "Among His signs is… the diversity… of … your colors" (30:22).

Several sayings of the Prophet Muhammad also insist on racial equality. "Whoever practices racism," states one, "God will cast him in the Fire" (Kulayni, vol. 2, chapter 120: 265). Another affirms that "whoever has racist feelings… God will resurrect him with the Arabs from the Days of Ignorance" (Kulayni, vol. 2, chapter 119: 263). Yet another warns that "you have no superiority over one another with white or black skin, except by righteousness" (Ahmad).

There are many traditions in which companions of the Prophet insulted other disciples of full or partial African ancestry. In one case, 'Uthman (c. 573 or 576-656) called 'Ammar (c. 567- c. 657), a "son of a black slave." The latter complained to the Prophet Muhammad, stating, "We did not enter [the fold of

Islam] in order to be reviled [and insulted]." The Prophet told 'Uthman: "You have removed your Islam, so go away" (Majlisi vol. 30, 125-126). It is also reported that after each of his prayers, the Messenger of God would profess that "all human beings are brothers to each other." Finally, the Prophet stated, "People are equal like the teeth of a comb" (Khattabi).

While this is fine and dandy and comes in handy when presenting Islam as a non-racist religion, several traditions attributed to the Prophet Muhammad express overtly racist sentiments. In one tradition, he states that "Blacks live guided by their private parts and stomachs" (Hindi, Tabarani, al-Khatib al-Baghdadi, Jurjani; see also Azumah 131). This is more literally rendered as "Whenever they are hungry, they steal, and whenever they are full, they fornicate" (Diakho 76-77). In another, the Prophet warned people not to marry them (Hindi, Jurjani, Minawi, Kulayni, Nu'man vol. 2: 178; Azumah 137). One tradition, cited by Bukhari, predicts that blacks will destroy the Kaabah and trigger the end of the world (Azumah 131; Diakho 77). In another, categorized as authentic by some traditionists, an Ethiopian woman tells the Messenger of God: "You Arabs excel us (blacks) in all, in build, color, and in possession of the Prophet." She asks him whether, if she believes, she will be with him in Paradise. He reassures her that "the whiteness of the Ethiopian will be seen over a stretch of a thousand years" (Azumah). Whether one treats this tradition literally or metaphorically, and accepts it as genuine or not, it implicitly confirms the superiority of light-skinned Arabs over blacks.

In one racist tradition, which is sick, but comical, by some standards, and blasphemous by others, the Prophet Muhammad, on the authority of Ja'far al-Sadiq (702-765), shares the stereotype that blacks have humongous penises. An African man comes to the Prophet Muhammad and tells him that he has a big problem -- his penis is so massive that no woman can bear it -- and so he asks for permission to have sex with a camel or a donkey. The Prophet does not even blush. He does not warn him against bestiality. He basically tells him to find a big black woman. There is no mention of marriage. The man leaves but returns shortly after that, thanking the Messenger of God and instructing him that he found a woman in whose vagina his penis could finally fit (Mahajjah). The tradition, titled "Allah, Most Blessed, Most High, Has Created for People Similarities," reads:

> Abu 'Abd Allah [Ja'far al-Sadiq]... has said that once a man came to the Holy Prophet ... and said: "O Messenger of Allah, I carry the largest thing that [a] man [can] carry, [let me know] if I can make use of the animals that I own, like a donkey or she-camel, because women cannot bear what I have." The Messenger of Allah said, "Allah has not created your thing without creating what can match your thing." The man went and very shortly came back to the Messenger of Allah and repeated what he had said before. The Messenger of Allah... said: "Why do you not look for black women with tall necks and healthy bodies?" He went and very shortly came back and said, "I testify that you are the Messenger of

Allah in all truth. I searched for what you commanded me to do and found her to be of my kind and match, and I am satisfied." (Kulayni, vol. 5: 304)

An alternate translation reads:

A man came to the Messenger of Allah ... and said, "O Messenger of Allah, verily I have been extremely well-endowed as no other man has been, so would it be permissible for me to satisfy myself with a camel or donkey, as no woman can bear what I possess?" The Messenger of Allah ... said, "Verily Allah did not create you except that He has also created your equal capable of enduring you." So, the man left, but it was not long before he returned, making the same request. The Prophet said: "Have you not approached the African ladies with long necks?" So, the man left, but it was not long before he returned, saying, "O Messenger of Allah, I testify that you are truly the Messenger of Allah. I sought what you instructed and found one capable of enduring me, and she has satisfied me." (Mahajjah)

The words of the Prophet were *suda' al-'antanatah* or blacks with long necks. There is nothing about healthy bodies. This tradition appears to refer to Ndebele women who wear neck rings to symbolize wealth and status. They are a Bantu people from parts of South Africa. Such slaves were found in Arabia at the time of the sixth Imam: not during the time of the Prophet. In the seventh century, the relatively few slaves that were to be found in the *Hijaz* came primarily from Ethiopia, Byzantium, or Persia. In any event, I am inclined to believe that the earliest form of this spurious tradition did not speak of black women with long necks, but rather, of black women with wide hips and big buttocks.

How Kulayni (864-941) could collect this racist and sexist tradition, and treat it as genuine, as he believed it was, says much about him and the trustworthiness of *al-Kafi*, which is widely considered the most valuable and comprehensive collection of Twelver Shiite traditions. Treated as entirely authentic by some scholars, others admit that eighty percent of its content is weak. Obviously, the tradition is no reflection of the sixth Imam any more than it is of the Prophet Muhammad. Despite their humanity, and their participation, as actors, in human history, falsehood and obscenities should not be attributed to religious figures whether or not one considers them infallible, sinless, impeccable, and immaculate.

The narrator of this tradition, Burayd ibn Mu'awiyyah ibn Abi Hakim al-Kufi (d. c. 765), is considered one of the consensus companions, namely, one who had direct contact with an Imam and whose traditions are accepted without question. According to some accounts, he received lavish praise from both Muhammad al-Baqir and Ja'far al-Sadiq. In another tradition, however, he was cursed by Ja'far al-Sadiq, who asked God to destroy him. The Imam sent a message to him warning that "every innovation is misguidance," to which Burayd responded, "I will never retract what I have said ever" (Mahajjah). He was a bold, insolent, and defiant liar. No wonder the sixth Imam said: "May Allah curse Burayd" (Tusi qtd. Mahajjah). Like all the others, this last tradition shows every sign of being a forgery. Since the word of the Imam was final, a simple scholar was weakly positioned to reject a *hadith* based on personal opinion. Claiming that it was false based on content was not a viable option. One option for refuting the tradition was by weakening its chain of narrators. The other option was to use another saying of the Imam, authentic or not.

The Twelver Shiites may claim that the Sunnis follow forged traditions while they follow the true teachings of the Prophet Muhammad as preserved by his "purified, immaculate, and infallible progeny." The fact remains that a considerable number of racist traditions are attributed to the Imams of the Household of the Prophet. "Beware of marrying blacks [*zanj*]," 'Ali reportedly said, "for they are an ugly and deformed creation [*khalq mushawwah*]" (Kulayni, vol. 5, chapter 28: 320 and Nu'man, vol. 2: 178). "Do not marry blacks," Ja'far al-Sadiq said, "for their wombs are unfaithful" (Kulayni). In another tradition, he is quoted as saying that "the sweetness of faith will never enter the hearts... of black people [*zanj*]" and placed them in the same category as people who were born of adultery (Saduq).

In his "Supplication for the People of the Frontiers," Zayn al-'Abidin (659-713), the fourth Imam, comes across as a staunch supporter of Arab-Islamic imperialism, invoking the curse and wrath of God upon His enemies "in the regions of the lands, the Indians, the Byzantines, the Turks, the Khazars, the Abyssinians, the Nubians, the *zanjis* [blacks], the Slavs, the Daylamites, and the rest of the idol-worshipping nations" (Chittick 97). Since the Byzantines and the Abyssinians were Christians, they cannot be categorized as *mushrikin* or polytheists. They were monotheists. The Prophet Muhammad had specifically issued directions concerning the protection of non-belligerent Christians (Morrow 2013, 2017, 2021, 2023; Considine 2020, 2021; Zein and El-Wakil 2023). Since the Negus of Abyssinia had protected the early Meccan refugees, the Prophet Muhammad had commanded his followers never to wage war against them unless they were first attacked.

Many of the Slavs or *saqabila* mentioned in the supplication were still pagans during the life of 'Ali ibn al-Husayn; however, some of them were Christians. They were evangelized in waves from the seventh century until the twelfth century. The animosity directed toward the Daylamites seems entirely out of order, as well. In fact, it was among them that many early 'Alids or partisans of 'Ali (600-661) found safety and shelter from Umayyad persecution, and where they gradually started to convert the population to Shiism. In fact, Daylam soon became home to several Zaydi, 'Alid, emirates.

After the 652 conquest of Egypt, general 'Abd Allah ibn Abi Sarh, who served from 646-656, concluded a treaty with the Christian kingdom of Nubia, known as the *baqt*. This treaty, which lasted for seven hundred years, decreed that the Arabs and the Nubians would not attack one another, that immigration and settlement would not be allowed, that free trade would be permitted, that the Arabs were not required to protect the Nubians from third parties, that the Nubians would return any runaway slaves or Muslim rebels, and most importantly, that the Nubians were to provide three-hundred-and-sixty slaves per year to Egypt in exchange for staples such as wheat and lentils. The slaves were supposed to be of the highest quality and a mixture of males and females.

Inciting Arab Muslims to attack, conquer, slaughter, subdue, degrade, and humiliate Nubians, Christians or otherwise, as Zayn al-'Abidin did in his "Supplication for the People of the Frontiers" is not in keeping with the principles of the Qur'an, the promises made by the Prophet Muhammad, and the treaty of 652 that was made during the early Arab conquest of Egypt. It seems inconceivable that a man whose family suffered under Umayyad hegemony and whose mother was allegedly a victim of the Arab conquest of Persia would laud their wars of imperial aggression and conquest.

Some apologists may claim that the Prophet Muhammad and the Imams only opposed marrying the *zanj*, namely, a group of Bantu-speaking East African blacks, because, at the time, they were infidels hostile toward Islam. They may also claim that some of the people who quoted these traditions, like Ahmad, would be viewed as blacks or Afro-Arabs today, which is comical. This is imposing modern American concepts of race on medieval Arabs. Dark-skinned or not, of partial African ancestry or not, Arabs viewed themselves as Arabs. They did not view themselves as blacks or Africans. What is more, the term *zanj* was applied to blacks in general. Today, it describes blacks from all walks of life, including black Africans and Africans from the Americas. However, the question that begs to be asked is this: When did the *zanj* ever attack the Arab Muslims? On the contrary, they were attacked by Arab Muslims in false *jihads*, not to convert them, but for the specific purpose of enslaving and selling them. These were the infamous razzias, or slave raids, of the Arabs, which appear to be praised by Zayd ibn 'Ali when he asks God to "send out the Muslims of every region on raids against the idolaters" (96-97). Some of the populations he targeted as enemies of God were Christians, and even if they were pagans, the Arab Muslims had no right to wage wars of aggression to slaughter and enslave them.

Even if we admit that Arab Muslims viewed Africans as belonging to distinct ethnic groups, such as the Sudanese, the Abyssinians, and the *zanj*, the racist nature of these traditions, which treat the Bantu people as ugly deformed creatures, cannot be cast aside. Some Bantu women are gorgeous according to any standards of beauty. That being said, it is essential to note that these racist, bigoted sayings stand in stark contrast to others in which the Prophet Muhammad insisted upon racial equality and the oneness of humanity. Rather than defend these traditions, they should be debunked and discarded. Regrettably, some Muslims still quote them to justify their anti-black racism. And shamefully, many converts to Islam continue to struggle to integrate into such segregated and endogamous communities where interracial, intertribal, and intercultural marriages are both taboo and anathema. They should show some pride and step aside.

While the curse of Ham, the son of Noah, is not found in the Qur'an, "Arab culture would adopt the racial aspect of the Hamitic curse in a manner that associated race with slavery" (El Hamel 64-65). The belief that blackness is a malediction and that blacks were condemned to slavery by God does appear prominently in the works of early Muslim scholars, and others were all the more willing to follow suit. They claimed that Noah cursed Ham, and his offspring, asking God to "darken their skin and make them servants and slaves of the descendants of Shem" (Diakho 76). In one of his sermons, 'Ali praised God for turning the lineage of Ham into slaves (Majlisi v. 25: 40). Even the tenth Imam, 'Ali al-Naqi, taught that all blacks, wherever they may be, are the children of Ham who are cursed to be slaves until the Day of Judgment (Majlisi 74; vol. 11: 308; vol. 59: 353). This tradition is also found in Majlisi's *Hayat al-qulub* in "An Account of Nuh."

As much as Muslims speak of Islam's racial equality, their cultures testify against them. In Turkish folklore, blacks are symbols of wickedness and barbarity (Azumah 134). In Arab and Persian Muslim writings, "blacks are depicted as stupid, untruthful, vicious, sexually unbridled, ugly, and distorted, excessively merry, and easily affected by music and drink" (134). In some works, they are stereotyped as cannibals, infidels, and enemies of God at war against Muslims (134). For Sa'id al-Andalusi (1029-1070), blacks were "more like animals than men" (Azumah 135). Ibn Sina (980-1037) viewed them as inherently inferior and slaves by nature (Azumah 135). For Nasir al-Din Tusi (1201-1274), "the ape is more capable of being trained than the Negro, and more intelligent" (Azumah 135). And for Ibn Khaldun (1332-1406), blacks are "closer to dumb animals than to rational beings" (Azumah 135; Segal 49). Out of fairness, these are the same views one finds in the literature of other cultures of the period, including those of Europe. No people have been treated as poorly as black Africans.

The racist traditions attributed to the Prophet Muhammad and some of the twelve Shiite Imams were accepted as authentic by many jurists over the ages. They were used, and continue to be used, to pass racist rulings. Whether these traditions are authentic or not is immaterial. Their impact is entirely material. There is, therefore, no question that there is, as tenuous it may be, a theological and jurisprudential basis to racism in Islam, not in its primordial inspired form but as a religion interpreted and fashioned by racist and sexist men, and one that was exploited to enslave and sexually exploit human beings. Since people are flawed, fallen, and frail, it would seem that Muslims of all sects share in the sins of racism and slavery. Let him, without sin, cast the first stone.

What is more disturbing of all, however, is the suggestion and possibility that the traditions attributed to the Messenger of God, the racist and anti-racist ones, as well as the woman-hating and woman-loving ones, were manufactured by opposing parties (Azumah 132; Osman 172). In the view of Bernard Lewis (1916-2018), the sayings placed in the mouth of the Prophet Muhammad "clearly reflect the great struggles in the early Islamic Empire between the pure Arab conquistador aristocracy, claiming both ethnic and social superiority, and the converts among the conquered, who could claim neither ethnic nor family advantage" (Azumah 132). Consequently, the positive depictions of black Africans were dismissed as dubious, including, saying such as "Emulate the blacks, for among them are three lords of the people of Paradise, Luqman, the Sage, the Negus [Emperor of Abyssinia], and Bilal the Muezzin" (Ware III 13).

"If the Prophet characterized black people as exemplars of knowledge, justice, and piety" (Ware III 13), how could any faithful Arab or Berber Muslim slaughter them, enslave survivors, and force black women into sexual slavery? Is this how one honors and respects black people? As Ware asserts, "Islamic and African Studies need to take African Muslims seriously as bearers and interpreters of forms of Islamic knowledge and embodied practice with powerful claims to scriptural authority and Prophetic precedent" (14).

If the Messenger of God indeed foresaw that "the people of the West will keep triumphantly following the Truth until the Hour arrives," and this applies to West Africa, as Rudolph T. Ware believes (237, 243), how could any God-fearing and Prophet-loving person enslave Africans? *Ittakhadhu al-sudan*, namely, "emulate the blacks," excludes the possibility of enslavement. Be that as it may,

> Under the Umayyads, the descendants of Quraysh, some of Muhammad's bitterest enemies, the world conquests of the Arabs unfolded. By the seventeenth century, blacks were probably a majority of the slaves in the lands of Islam. By the nineteenth century, they were nearly the only slaves left, and they were more numerous than ever before. Blackness, slavery, and unbelief were now all collapsed in together in unprecedented ways. (Ware 29)

If we discard the *ahadith* as a literature of lies, which might contain an occasional kernel of truth, and are left only with the Qur'an, the revealed word of God according to Islamic dogma and doctrine, the theological, jurisprudential, and sociological basis for racism in the Muslim world dissipates. Any claims of racism would hold no water. After all, noted Ahmad Baba (1556-1627), a Sanhaja Berber jurist from Timbuktu, who belonged to the Maliki school of jurisprudence, "even if we admit that Ham is the ancestor of black people, God is too generous to punish millions of human beings due to the sin of one of them" (Diakho 29; see also Freamon 1998: 56). Ironically, though he opposed enslaving black African Muslims, he was not against slavery.

1.3 Islamic Law Supports Slavery

Like most Muslim scholars throughout history, Jonathan A.C. Brown operates on the foundational premise that the Qur'an permits slavery and allows Muslim men to marry four wives and take countless women as concubines (70, 96). For him, this is ground zero, the starting point, and an absolute fact that cannot even be questioned by any believing Muslim. In his words, "the permissibility of slavery and concubinage is undeniable in the Qur'an itself, a historically intact scripture, and Islam's ultimate bedrock" (Brown 196).

A more cautious scholar would have formulated that sentence in the following way: "for many or most Muslim scholars, the permissibility of slavery and concubinage is undeniable in the Qur'an itself." On this we could all agree. It is not, however, an absolute fact that the Qur'an endorses slavery and concubinage. These practices were not universally accepted. They were not unchallenged. Likewise, it is not undeniable that the Bible validates and mandates human bondage and sexual servitude.

As Bernard Kenneth Freamon (b. 1947), a black American convert to Islam and a professor of Islamic law, admits woefully, "slavery" does indeed have "a great deal of support in Islamic legal history" (2019: 465). As Elizabeth Urban, an American academic focusing on early Islam, notes, "classical Sunni lawyers considered concubinage a perfectly legitimate form of sexual relationship and means of producing children" (7). The days of deception and denialism are done.

The claim that "slaves in Muslim lands were often better treated than elsewhere" and that they were treated as part of the family is dishonest and duplicitous (Saeed, Gould, Duderija 131). Consequently, the purpose of this study is not to paint a Pollyanna portrait of the Prophet Muhammad or some fanciful fantasy Islam. Its goal is to diagnose the disease without confounding it with the patient. Treating an illness is not an attack against its host. The part is not the whole. The foreign invader is not the organism. The body of Islam is beautiful but the wart of slavery must be burned off.

Undoubtedly, the Qur'an, the *hadith*, and the *shari'ah* have been used and abused to justify horrors of all kinds, not the least of which are slavery and concubinage. What must be questioned, however, is whether their interpretations have a scriptural basis. Many Muslims refuse to believe that they do, not because of blind faith but because of a close reading of the Qur'an. Where is the evidence? "Produce your proof, if you are truthful" (27:64). It simply is not there. If we study the Qur'an, we can see that the case for "Islamic" slavery and concubinage was built out of thin air. In the words of Jesus, "Woe to you, scribes and Pharisees, hypocrites!" (Matthew 23:13-36).

1.4 Opposing Slavery is Hypocrisy, Apostasy, and Infidelity

Like dogs on a leash, lemmings leaping into the ocean, and startled bison stampeding over cliffs, many Muslims are mindless, devoid of a moral compass, and obstinately opposed to logic and reason. They desperately hold onto the interpretations of misogynistic and mentally challenged medieval men as if their spiritual lives depended on them. Tragically, notes Nimat Hafez Barazangi (b. 1943), a Syrian American scholar who focuses on feminism, gender, and sexuality, "the majority of today's Muslims are not willing to abandon the centuries-old representations of Islam that are misleading and unjust, and replacing them with the egalitarian intention of Islam as outlined in the only divine and binding source, the Qur'an" (10).

When anyone questions, criticizes, or condemns slavery, Jonathan A.C. Brown quickly turns the tables on such critics by answering them with ambush questions like: "Did the Prophet Muhammad commit a grave moral wrong?" (2020: 196). Or, as he told a questioner at his lecture on February 7, 2017: "He had slaves, there is no denying that. Are you more morally mature than the prophet of God? No, you're not" (Strauss). Wow. What a reaction. That seems to have struck a nerve. However, for Nathaniel Matthews, a historian of modern Africa, "the Prophet Muhammad's attempt to protect the enslaved and grant them protections and rights, without abolishing slavery, was not a moral failing, but the advancement to the limits of what was possible to envision in his era." However, as Muhammad Diakho, a Muslim jurist from Senegal, stresses, "protecting slaves does not mean protecting slavery" (136). Likewise, the fact that the Prophet protected the People of the Book does not imply that he promoted disbelief (136).

"According to the consensus of Muslim scholars across fourteen centuries," asserts Brown in absolute fashion, "stating that the Prophet had committed a grave sin (*kabirah*) or unambiguously belittling his moral judgment would be unbelief (*kufr*) that removed someone from Islam" (2020: 198). He then quotes Ibn 'Abidin (1784-1836), the Syrian jurist, who claimed that merely viewing concubinage as morally repugnant places one in danger of committing *kufr* or disbelief (Brown 199). The very premise of Brown's statement is founded on falsehood. He believes that slavery and concubinage are part and parcel of the Qur'anic worldview. He is convinced that they form an integral part of Islam. He treats slavery as a matter of faith. He believes that God and His Prophet blessed such binding practices. This is not the argument made by Muslim scholars who oppose slavery and concubinage. They do not accuse the Prophet Muhammad of committing a major sin. They believe that the message of the Qur'an and the Prophet was betrayed.

In Brown's mind, people who ask him to condemn slavery while refusing to condemn the Prophet, are hypocrites (2020: 196). In fact, he goes out of his way to provide evidence supporting the practice of *takfir* or the ex-communication of Muslims (2020: 393, note 205; 405). As Brown puts it quite plainly:

> According to the entirety of the Islamic tradition… the Prophet's moral infallibility and unmatched moral excellence in no way clash with his morality and humanness… Attributing the gross, intrinsic wrong of slavery to the Prophet comes along with an equally consequential corollary: presumably, he would not have knowingly committed such a wrong. So, he was not even aware of the wrong he was committing. This would be a dramatic assertion indeed. It would, in effect, overturn the Islamic theology and moral epistemology entirely.

The foundation of Islamic doctrine and law rests on the premise that the Prophet's authoritative precedent (*sunnah*), to some degree or another provided the context, application, and explanation of God's message in the Qur'an... Suppose that a Muslim today was able to travel back to Medina during the time of the Prophet and arrived there the day after he had been given Mariya, the Coptic slave girl, as his concubine. What would this Muslim say to the Prophet? "What you are doing is a profound moral evil, O Messenger of God?" That is not a conceivable statement for a Muslim to make and remain Muslim. (2020: 199-200)

In short, it could be argued that Brown shares the very same position as the radical Islamists, namely, that "denial of the right of a man to take a concubine is a denial of Qur'anic text and, in this sense, an act of apostasy" (Hammoudi). Despite claims to the contrary, this is not a fringe position among Muslim jurists. After all, Nasr Abu Zayd (1943-2010), the Egyptian professor, was declared an apostate by the Egyptian court in 1995 and forcibly divorced from his wife, despite the opposition of the couple, for denying the lawfulness of sex between a man and the enslaved women he purchased for his sexual pleasure (Hammoudi).

Not only do we have to contend with machine-gun totting discontents riding around in Jeeps and killing so-called apostates to their hearts' content, but we have state-supported legal institutions in the Muslim world that also agree that opposing sexual slavery is apostasy. As Haider Hammoudi, the Iraqi American Muslim jurist, notes, the only disagreement revolves around who can justifiably be enslaved and sexually used and abused. The last time I checked, Christ and Muhammad warned against doing to others what you do not want them to do to you. For Brown, it would seem, some people deserved to be enslaved, and some women deserved to be taken as sex slaves. It is the will of God, His divine decree, and a reward for the believers.

If that were not bad enough, Brown also documents that Islamic extremists have a long history of enslaving other Muslims who do not share their ideology (2020: 106-109; 370: note 24; 406, note 31 and 32). In some cases, like Morocco, free Muslims were enslaved because they were black (El Hamel 9). In theory, notes Azumah, the enslaving of Muslims by Muslims was prohibited under traditional Muslim law. In practice, he points out, "this was hardly the case... both in Muslim Africa and in the heartland of the Islamic world" (126). Case in point, "The Oghuz Turks... reduced many Muslims to slavery. Similarly, Muslim khans of Iran enslaved fellow Muslims... while Sunni lawyers in Ottoman Tukey and Central Asia declared it legal to enslave Shi'is" (Azumah 126).

Let us tell it like it is. As interpreted by most Muslim scholars over the ages, Islam is and has always been, a religion of slavery that justified, promoted, and enshrined this abominable institution. For them, the practice of slavery is supported by the Qur'an and the *hadith*, was practiced by the Prophet Muhammad, his companions, the caliphs, Imams, sultans, and shahs of Islam, and thereby forms a fundamental part of the *shari'ah*.

While it is a historical fact that slavery has been central to Islam since the time of its early conquests, which took place after the passing of the Prophet Muhammad and was only ultimately and definitively prohibited as a result of Western Christian and secular pressure, many Muslims beg to differ that the Qur'an and the original teachings of the Prophet Muhammad support slavery and concubinage. Forgive us for holding God and His Prophet to a higher moral standard and placing them on a more elevated ethical plateau. When it comes to ideals, we should reach for the sky, seek to improve ourselves, and move forward, not reach down, and backtrack. We were all made to evolve morally.

1.5 Free the Slaves

For morally, ethically, and intellectually grounded Muslims, incipient and emergent Islam was emancipatory. The Qur'an told Muslims to free slaves. The Prophet Muhammad freed his slaves. He told his followers to free their slaves. The Messenger of God warned that, on the Day of Judgement, he would testify against those who enslaved and sold free human beings (Bukhari and Ibn Majah). He categorically asserted that slave dealers were the worst of people (Kulayni). As Aslam Abdullah, an Islamic scholar, Imam, author, editor, and activist, notes,

> The companions of the Prophet competed with each other in setting slaves free. The Prophet personally liberated as many as seventy-seven slaves. The number of slaves freed by his wife 'A'ishah was sixty-seven. His uncle 'Abbas released seventy. The son of the second caliph 'Abd Allah ibn 'Umar liberated one thousand, and another companion 'Abd al-Rahman [ibn 'Awf] purchased thirty thousand and set them free. How is it possible that those liberating and freeing slaves would buy new slaves against the dictates of the Qur'an?

Critical thinkers, some labeled rationalists, modernists, Qur'anists, neo-*ijtihadists*, moderates, or secularists, do not believe that slavery is moral and ethical. They do not believe that the Qur'an commands it. They do not believe that the Prophet promoted it. They believe it was prohibited, or a plan was set in motion to phase it out or allow it to wither out. They are not accusing the Prophet of any sinful or immoral behavior. They refuse to accept that he had sex with slave girls without emancipating and marrying them beforehand. They also refuse to believe that a man of his moral magnitude had sexual relations with a nine-year-old girl. They are not accusing the Prophet Muhammad of any sin. They refuse to accept that he committed some of the actions attributed to him by bitter enemies who assumed power after his passing.

1.6 Muhammad, the Slave Master?

To defend the theological and jurisprudential legitimacy of "Islamic" slavery, Jonathan A.C. Brown insists that Muhammad had slaves (Strauss). This is a half-truth. He reportedly owned slaves; however, he liberated them, including Barakah, an enslaved Ethiopian he owned as a child. In the company of his grandfather 'Abd al-Muttalib, the young Muhammad went to the Kaabah and proclaimed:

> This is Barakah. I, Muhammad, the son of 'Abdullah, with the support of my grandfather, hereby declare Barakah from this moment forward to be free like the wind, no longer weighted down by the yoke of bondage. O people, bear witness and let those present inform those who are absent. (Jebara 48)

When Muhammad married Khadijah, she gave him Zayd (c. 581-629), a sixteen-year-old slave, as a bridal gift. Muhammad freed him immediately and encouraged him to return to his biological family. Zayd, however, insisted on remaining. "Standing on the steps of the Kaaba, Muhammad raised Zayd's right hand and declared, 'This is Zayd. From this day forth, he is my son, all that is mine is his'" (Jebara 107).

As Freamon notes, "Muhammad's emancipation of Zayd, although prior to the advent of Islam, is probably the first historical example of his soon-to-be prophetic conduct in furtherance of a behavioral ethic encouraging the emancipation of slaves" (2019: 90). Muhammad's emancipatory ethos did not stop at Zayd. As Jebara writes,

> Upon marrying Khadijah and joining her household, Muhammad technically became a co-owner of slaves. As his liberation of Barakah and Zayd demonstrated, Muhammad reviled the institution of slavery, which represented to him the ultimate example of forced stagnation...
>
> Khadijah's slaves, of course, belonged to her -- and could be freed only with her consent. When Muhammad became her business partner, he began to subtly sow the seeds of liberation in her mind. He treated the enslaved members of her household with consideration unheard of in Meccan society. He helped them load camels, gave them rest breaks and time off to recover from illness, dressed them in fine linens, shared his perfumes with them, and paid them for doing exceptional work.
>
> One day on his way to work, Muhammad saw a master ruthlessly whipping his enslaved servant. On the spot, he offered the owner double the man's worth and purchased his freedom. With Khadijah's slaves, Muhammad took an alternative approach. He chose to sit on the ground and eat with them from the same serving platter. He learned that most had been abducted as young children... They not only knew what it was like to be free but had endured the trauma of abduction and dehumanization.
>
> Recognizing that Khadijah's enslaved workers had free minds inside their bonded bodies, Muhammad encouraged them to voice their opinions and, in the process, restored their sense of dignity... Muhammad began to demonstrate to his wife that they did not need forced labor... Khadijah... was inspired by his example.

After al-Qasim's birth, Muhammad felt the time had come to ask his wife to liberate her household. Khadijah did not need much convincing. Yet she and Muhammad recognized that publicly freeing over a dozen domestic slaves in front of the Ka'bah would spark an uproar.

Because slavery was such a widespread practice, Muhammad understood that trying to eradicate it at once would infuriate masters who relied on slave labor for their livelihood. Instead, Khadijah organized a private ceremony in her warehouse with Ibnu Jud'an, 'Atiq, and Barakah, as witnesses. The enslaved listened with astonishment as Khadijah officially liberated them with the declaration: "You are now all free, like the birds of the sky, and like the wind, to wander where you please." (109-111)

Muhammad's emancipation of Barakah proved providential, as she was the one who would lead his followers to safety in Abyssinia (Jebara 151-153). What is more, she and her nurses saved the life of Muhammad at the Battle of Badr in the year 624 (Jebara 236). She was one of two women with whom the Prophet entrusted his master plan after the Treaty of Hudaybiyyah (Jebara 243). True it is that there were "at least twelve slaves around the Prophet Muhammad at various stages in his life" (Freamon 2019: 96). However, "all were emancipated, and all played important roles in the emergence of a new Islamic polity" (Freamon 2019: 96). As Abdul Malik Mujahid (b. 1951), the Pakistani American imam, producer, author, and leader, notes,

the Prophet Muhammad launched an anti-slavery movement in which he personally liberated all of his slaves, and even promised prisoners of war their freedom if they taught ten Muslims how to read. The Prophet's companions followed his example, freeing tens of thousands of slaves of their own volition. To the Prophet and his companions, liberating slaves was not merely one specific good deed out of a long list of potential opportunities for good; rather, it was one of the ultimate means of reaching moral and spiritual excellence. This is why his wife, Khadijah, and his ... companion, Abu Bakr, both wealthy businesspersons, became almost penniless buying slaves their freedom.

It was because of this anti-slavery movement that most people who accepted the Prophet's invitation to believe in One God and join his peace movement were slaves. It was this core message of the equality of all human beings as explained in Surah 49, Verse 13, "People, We created you from a male and a female and made you nations and tribes so that you may know one another. The best among you in the sight of God is the one who is most mindful of God. God is All-knowing and All-Aware," that attracted Malik El-Shabazz (Malcolm X), Muhammad Ali, and Kareem Abdul-Jabbar, among hundreds of thousands of African Americans, as well as former untouchables in India, to Islam.

While Mariya the Copt, the concubine, who supposedly died in 637, appears to have been a myth, and one debunked in chapter two, the war captives, Safiyyah (c. 610-614- c. 664-672), Juwayriyyah (c. 608-676), and Rayhanah (d. 631) appear to stand on firmer historical ground. In all three cases, the war captives fell into Muhammad's hands. Rather than taking them as concubines and sex slaves, he emancipated and married them, setting an example for other Muslim men (Diakho 158). It would seem, however, that the tale of Mariya the Copt was concocted to overturn these precedents, thereby granting libidinous men a prophetic justification to take prisoners of war as sex slaves.

That being said, the point is not that Muhammad had slaves, males, and females, at some point in his pre-prophetic life. The point is that he freed them all and encouraged others to do the same with those they held in bondage. That is the *sunnah*. That is the model that pious and God-fearing Muslims must emulate, not freeing slaves only to hypocritically re-enslave others, creating a perpetual cycle of servitude, subjugation, oppression, and exploitation. The Prophet was sent to solve a societal problem, not entrench, and perpetuate it in his name and the name of God. He called upon people to become the slaves and servants of the one God: not the bondmen and bondmaids of human beings. As Zafar Bangash (b. 1950), the Pakistani Canadian editor, journalist, Imam, and leader, asserts, the Prophet and Messenger of God "never kept any slaves, nor encouraged his companions to do so" (268, note 62).

1.7 Muhammad, the Abolitionist

The Prophet Muhammad surfaced in a society and world in which slavery existed. He attempted to moderate the evils of the institution. Speaking of slaves, he told his followers to "feed them from the same food you eat and clothe them from the same clothes you wear" (Bukhari). He demanded that enslaved people be treated with dignity: "None of you should say: 'My slave," for all of you are the slaves of God. Rather, you should say 'My boy.' The slave should not say: 'My Lord' [*rabbi*], but rather he should say: 'Sir" (Muslim).

If a slave were struck in the face by his master, the Prophet Muhammad would command the master to set him free (Muslim). He prohibited Abu Bakr from cursing his slaves and warned him, "Do not do it again" (Bukhari). "Whoever strikes his slave without limit or slaps him," the Prophet Muhammad said, "then the expiation for the sin is to emancipate him" (Muslim). "He who mistreats his slaves," said the Messenger of God, "will not enter Paradise" (Ahmad).

The Messenger of God said, "none of you strikes his slave unjustly except that the slave will be granted retaliation on the Day of Resurrection" (Bukhari). He describes slaves as family members,

> Your slaves are your brethren upon whom Allah has given you authority. So, If one has one's brethren under one's control, one should feed them with the like of what one eats and clothe them with the like of what one wears. You should not overburden them with what they cannot bear, and

if you do so, help them (in their hard job). (Bukhari)

The Prophet Muhammad also warned that, "whoever falsely accuses his slave will be flogged on the Day of Resurrection" (Bukhari).

Despite assertions to the contrary, the Messenger of God did not view slavery as a permanent institution. He provided the enslaved with rights and protections, encouraged their integration into families and societies, and provided them pathways to emancipation. These provisions, found in the Qur'an, and provided by the Prophet Muhammad, were aimed at people currently enslaved. They were introduced as a means of eliminating slavery incrementally. Had he witnessed the crimes committed by Muslims -- the slaughter, enslavement, exploitation, violation, and torture of millions of human beings -- in his name, the name of the Qur'an, the name of Islam, and the name of God, he might have recoiled in horror and cited the words of Krishna from the Bhagavad Gita: "I am become Death, the destroyer of worlds."

1.8 Conclusions

As far as morally minded critical thinkers are concerned, the traditionists, Qur'anic commentators, jurists, and scholars who advocate slavery, concubinage, and sex with pre-pubescent children, including toddlers and newborn babies, are the ones who attribute gross, intrinsic, moral wrongs to the Messenger of God. They are the ones who attribute evil to God and His Prophet. As Aslam Abdullah states,

> The prevalence of slavery and the concubinage system in the Muslim world until 1969 does not justify them. Scholars' silence in denouncing it and preventing the traders from engaging in this trade does not sanctify it. The practice of having concubines for one's pleasure by rulers, traders, and even scholars does not support it. Slavery was wrong, and those who were engaged in slave trades were against the fundamental teachings of Islam that built its ethics on the idea of the dignity of human beings.

If Christianity has failed to penetrate the hearts of Christians for two thousand years, Islam has failed to humanize the hearts of Muslims for fourteen hundred years. Just like Christians failed to become Christ-like, Muslims have failed to live up to the message of God and Muhammad. As Malek Chebel (1953-2016), the Algerian philosopher and anthropologist of religions, has noted, the Qur'an is not the main obstacle to abolishing slavery but rather the official position of Muslim jurists at the service of the Islamic Establishment (26). The few scholars who may have been reticent to accept slavery subjected themselves to self-censorship (27). As a result, from dynasty to dynasty and from century to century, slavery became a fact of the Muslim reality (27). Islamic morality ceased to operate (28).

Neither God nor His Prophet can be blamed for the evils of slavery and sexual servitude. They are, and have always been, abhorrent to God and His Messenger. The blame falls squarely on the heads and souls of the men who permitted, tolerated, condoned, justified, legalized, regulated, and enshrined it as part of Islamic law. They held low standards when it came to human behavior and sexual ethics. They viewed Muslims by their limitations as opposed to their potential. They made life easy for them and even an earthly paradise for some, while they subjected their fellow beings of other racial and religious origins to hell on earth. As the Qur'an warns, "whoever commits evil will be rewarded accordingly, and they will find no protector or helper besides God" (4:123).

Chapter Two

Mariya the Who?

2.1 Introduction

When confronted with the moral dilemma of sexual slavery, Jonathan A.C. Brown, like other apologists, Islamists or otherwise, is quick to invoke the image of the mythological Mariya the Copt, a supposed sex slave of the Prophet Muhammad who was allegedly gifted to him by Muqawqis, who was purportedly a Christian governor of Alexandria during the Persian occupation. Her story certainly poses a problem for the morally minded and ethically elevated. Fortunately, it also has a simple solution in the minds of some sources: she was his spouse. Brown, however, rejects the views of all the scholars who argue that Mariya was indeed a wife of the Prophet as opposed to a concubine (Brown 75-76, 163, 197, 265-266, 294-298, 392 note 199).

If presented with a set of traditions and sources that claim that she was a wife, a more dignified station, and another set that stipulate that she was a sex slave, which is the most honorable to accept? And since the Qur'an and the Prophet encouraged Muslims to free enslaved women and marry them (2:222; Bukhari), "how could the Prophet go against his own words?" (Abdullah). Was the Messenger of God a hypocrite? Did he fail to practice what he preached? Is Islam, marketed as a religion of freedom, really a religion of subjugation, sexual servitude, and slavery? While some scholars claim that Mariya the Copt was a concubine, and others assert that she was a wife, the most recent research suggests that she never existed. She was a foundational myth and a literary figure created to legitimize concubinage.

2.2 There is Something About Mary

The story of Mariya the Copt is suspicious to any rigorous scholar and serious historian. She is viewed by some sources as a concubine and by others as a spouse. Rather than opt for the latter, Jonathan A.C. Brown opts for the former, which is a poor choice indeed. Assuming she existed, Mariya, the Copt is the sole case used to justify the claim that the Prophet had a concubine (Diakho 158). As Diakho notes, the sources indicate that he did not treat her as a slave and gave her the same visitation rights as his other wives, not half as would be expected of a concubine (Diakho 161). Viewing her as a wife is a sound and proper Islamic position that upholds principles of chastity as opposed to endorsing extra-marital sexual license. As Leena El-Ali (b. 1966), a Lebanese-British-American author, asserts, "it is unthinkable that Muhammad would have disregarded God's command that bondwomen / slaves not be treated as concubines, but be honored through mutually agreed marriage before sexual relations took place" (167).

Not only does Jonathan A.C. Brown reject morally sound solutions that come from within the Islamic tradition, but he also discards the theory of Kaj Öhrnberg (b. 1943), the Finnish Arabist, Islamologist, and historian, that suggests that Mariya the Copt was a literary construct (Brown 297). As Brown summarizes,

> A Syriac Christian chronicle from circa 670 states that the Sassanid Persian shah had two wives, one named Shirin (a Persian) and one named Maria (a Byzantine)... Since Hagar came from Egypt, and since the standard reports about Mariya being given to the Prophet by the patriarch of Egypt mention that her sister Sirin/Shirin was given along with her, Öhrnberg proposed that Muslims combined personages and narratives in an act of historical "transposition." (296)

Brown's rapid rebuttal of Öhrnberg's "fascinating theory" (2020: 297) does little justice. Readers should study the complete work: it relates how Muslims felt the conscious need to fill in the gaps and embellish the meager facts of the Prophet's life; how Muslims wanted to make Muhammad the equal of other worldly leaders; how Muslims appropriated the traditions of subdued people; and how Muslim converts tried to establish parallels between the Qur'an and the Bible as well as between Muhammad and biblical figures (297-298). In his short but insightful study, Öhrnberg concludes that,

> The whole story of the Prophet's Egyptian concubine Mariya and their son Ibrahim is just a transposition of the older story of Abraham, Hagar, and Isma'il, with additions in the form of the names of the Sasanian Shah's two Christian wives from the pseudo-historical literature of Persia, to give the story more standing. (8)

Brown rejects such "revisionist" historical explanations as they require us "to believe in complex conspiracies of collective fabrication... that were supposedly being forged with such miraculous unanimity" (2020: 297). However, as religious historians have amply demonstrated, this is precisely the process that took place as Muslim scholars weaved stories to explain the meaning of the Qur'an and the life of the Prophet, drawing from a vast body of works. Islamic sources are saturated with Christian and Jewish lore and influences from other religions.

When surveying the traditions regarding Mariya the Copt, Brown focuses on their reliability according to traditional, namely, antiquated, faulty, and obsolete, Sunni *hadith* methodology. However, simply because they are rated "authentic" by traditionists who lived over a thousand years ago does not mean they are true and historically sound. As Gabriel Said Reynolds (b. 1973), the American academic, historian of religion, and Qur'an scholar, notes, "it is quite possible that they transmitted the story because they believed in its authenticity and that the story is nonetheless inauthentic" (516: note 14). Religion, however, is not about history. It is about sacred history that men construct.

According to David S. Powers (b. 1979), the American academic who specializes in Islamic Studies, the story of Ibrahim, Muhammad's son with Mariya who died in infancy, was invented to reinforce the idea that he died without a male heir and so that he could fulfill his role as "seal of the Prophets" (Urban 239; Powers 2009). In his words,

> The Islamic narrative is a creative reformulation of Gen. 17. In the Islamic narrative, Mariya is Hagar, and Ibrahim is Ishmael. Both women were Egyptian slaves, and both were given to men who had no son. Hagar was a gift from Sarah to Abraham; Mariya was a gift from Muqawqis to Muhammad. Both women aroused the jealousy of the wives of their respective masters, and both women produced a male child. Whereas the biblical Ishmael became the founder of a great nation -- the Ishmaelites -- Islam's Ibrahim died in infancy. In II Sam. 12 God punished King David for his sin by causing the first son borne to him by Bathsheba to die in infancy. However, Zaynab did not give Muhammad a son. In this instance, the motif was transferred to Mariya the Copt, whose son Ibrahim died in infancy. (274, note 82)

Similarly, Guillaume Dye (b. 1974), the French Islamologist, believes that Mariya the Copt was not a historical character but a literary fiction and a myth (Azaiez 293). For Claude Gilliot (b. 1940), the French Islamologist and Dominican friar, "the figure and 'story' of Mariya al-Qibtiyyah are loaded with legendary and mythical traits" (107). As far as Jan M.F. Van Reeth (b. 1960) is concerned,

> Christian Cannuyer has definitively demonstrated that the account is a legend. Mariya and her sister Sirin (perhaps even her son Ibrahim) never existed... Pointing out anachronisms... implausible aspects and the fact that the story only appears late in the tradition... Cannuyer also succeeded in identifying the source... namely, the story of Mary the Roman and S[h]irin the Aramean who became the wife of the Persian king Chosroes = Kusraw II Parviz... (1132)

As far as Cannuyer (b. 1957), the Belgian historian of religion, is concerned, Muqawqis is identified as Cyrus of Alexandria, the Melchite patriarch Heraclius appointed in 631 (20). Ibrahim, the son of Mariya and Muhammad, is said to have died in June of 631 at the age of sixteen to eighteen months (20). Hence, he must have been born in early 630, and his mother must have been offered to the Prophet nine months earlier, not before the spring of 629 (20). Moreover, the Prophet's letter to Heraclius was supposedly sent in 628 (20). However, at that time, Egypt was under Persian rule (20). In fact, it was conquered in 619 (20). For Cannuyer, this chronological incoherence suggests that this story was forged at a much later period when the biographers of Muhammad could not verify if Muqawqis, who ruled over Egypt at the time of the Muslim conquest of 639-640, had been in power in 628 (20). Moreover, there is no mention of any contact between Muhammad and Cyrus of Alexandria in Byzantine sources (Cannuyer 20).

Cannuyer stresses that Mariya is not mentioned in the Qur'an and only appears in Islamic sources in the ninth century (22). He also insists that Sirin, the sister of Mariya, could not possibly have been Coptic (23). As he notes, the name is a Persian one (23). And while Persia briefly occupied Egypt between 619 and 629/630, there is no record of a single Coptic Christian girl bearing the name Sirin before Islamic times (23). He also argues that Mariya and Sirin were literary avatars of the Christian wives of Chosroes II (23). Finally, he stresses that Islamic sources confuse Mariya the Copt, Maria the Jewess, Mary, the mother of Jesus, Mary, the sister of Moses, Mary Magdalene, and even the Queen of Sheba and Cleopatra (25). For Cannuyer, Mariya al-Qibtiyyah belongs to the same body of legends (25). Even Elizabeth Urban admits that "Mariya's story was modeled after Hajar's to some extent" (228).

What escapes these scholars, however, is the convenient reasons for the creation of Mariya the Copt. "Muhammad's relationship with Mariya the Copt," writes historian Kathryn A. Hain, "provides the basis for the religious sanctioning of sexual enjoyment of slave women" (327). Moreover, "Men born of concubines, who aspired to rule, used the concubines Hajar and Mariya the Copt to assert legitimacy and right to rule" (327). Islam is what Muslims do with it. In this case, they wanted to have sex with enslaved women.

As much as some Muslims argue that Islamic concubinage is no different than Jewish concubinage, the two institutions were distinct. In the Old Testament, concubines were girls sold by their fathers (Exodus 21:7) or gentiles captured in war (Deuteronomy 21:10-14). They could also include free Hebrew women who offered themselves as second wives. A concubine (*pilegesh*) usually refers to a secondary wife, a common-law one who was taken without a legal ceremony, one who did not receive a dowry, and one who could not inherit. They were typically acquired to produce a male heir when the primary wife was barren. Most of the concubines in the Islamic world were Muslims or converts to Islam. If they produced a child, they could not be sold, and would be emancipated upon the death of their masters. The Romans also had two types of marriage: "in hand," and "out of hand" in which the rights of wives varied.

In Islam, a concubine was not offered by her father to a man in a lower form of marriage. In Islam, concubines are not wives. They are sex slaves. Some families did sell their children, the Circassians for example; however, Muslims with a conscience viewed the practice as both abhorrent and prohibited. In Islam, a free woman did not offer herself as a concubine to a man to flee poverty, secure sustenance, obtain protection, and avoid the risk of falling into prostitution. In Islam, virtually all concubines were captured in wars and slave raids as part of the booty or they descended from enslaved women.

Concubinage in Islam cannot be considered a form of secondary or common-law marriage. Neither the woman, nor her father, as was customary in such cultures, provided consent. It was not a condition that was entered into freely. How Islamic jurists could authorize concubinage, sex with captive women, coerced or otherwise, while prohibit sex outside of marriage shows ethical inconsistency. Sexual union in a committed, long-term, common-law relationship, taking a mistress in addition to a wife, or even a one-night stand, is less objectionable morally than having sex with kidnapped, captured, enslaved, and trafficked women. An honorable man would free them, by purchase if that were the only option, emancipate them, and marry them: not exploit them.

As Chouki El Hamel (b. 1962), a Moroccan American historian, notes, "the designation and status of *umm al-walad*," namely, a concubine who gives birth to a child from her master, thereby preventing her from being sold, and ensuring her manumission, "are unknown in the Qur'an -- the Qur'an considers concubinage a prohibited sexual act" (50). In fact, "there is only one *hadith* on which Islamic jurists have made most of their juridical decrees: the story in which the Prophet liberated a slave girl Mariya after she bore him a son" (51).

The story of Mariya the Copt, and her son Ibrahim, was concocted to set a legal precedent, to permit concubinage, and to offer slave girls "a vehicle for upward mobility in the system of slavery in Islam" (51). According to accounts written over a century to a century and a half after the fact, al-Mansur, the second 'Abbasid caliph, invoked the story of Mariya the Copt to prove that he was worthy of the caliphate despite being the son of a concubine (Urban 225, 230). While there might be a glimmer of truth to this claim attributed to al-Mansur, it may very well have been back-projected to him by jurists and traditionists who lived generations later. As Elizabeth Urban notes,

> the men who called on... Mariya had a vested interest in showing that the children of *umm walads* could have noble genealogies and legitimate political authority... The slave status of ... Mariya was thus *useful* for the political aims of powerful men. (238)

If the 'Abbasids tried to give the slave mothers of their caliphs a higher status, the Shiites also attempted to create noble lineages for the slave mothers of over half of their Imams (see Dann 244-265). It was claimed that their concubine mothers were of noble stock and that some were princesses or descended from Christian saints like Peter (d. c. 64 CE), the Apostle of Jesus. As Matthew Pierce has shown, the historical Imams are hopelessly lost in the lore and legends that accumulated around them (2, 8, 21, 40, 45, 81, 88, 92, 93, 149, 152). As far as historians are concerned, the Imams, as portrayed in some Shiite literature, are imaginary. This position is supported by many traditions attributed to the Imams themselves in which they insist that they were ordinary human beings and in which they denounce the exaggerators who exalted them beyond bounds. Many Twelver Shiite scholars share the same view.

2.3 Conclusions

As can be appreciated, the claim that the Prophet Muhammad had a concubine named Mariya the Copt is dubious. It appears to be a myth constructed to set a legal precedent, one that supported the sexual bondage of women and one that attempted to improve the social status and standing of concubines. Since most of the caliphs and sultans of the Sunnis were the sons of slave girls, as were the mothers of seven of the Imams of the Twelver Shiites, both Sunni and Shiite scholars seem to have deployed the same strategy, a veritable public relations campaign, and propagandist effort, to redeem the genealogy and ancestry of their leaders. It was no longer shameful to be illegitimate sons of sex slaves. It was a matter of honor. Rather than be suppressed or outlawed, the use of enslaved women for procreation was to be encouraged.

In modern times, the same strategy has been employed to normalize prostitution and pornography, turning the women in question into sex workers, as opposed to sex slaves, and presenting them as liberated, empowered businesswomen, celebrities, and stars, as opposed to victims of sexual exploitation at the service of pimps, pornographers, human traffickers, and organized crime. If the Prophet Muhammad did not take a sex slave and concubine, the jurisprudential precedent permitting enslaving women for sexual purposes crumbles apart, as do the rulings and laws based on it. This explains the resistance to abolition on the part of many Muslims past, its defense by some Muslims present, and continued attempts to reinstate it by bands of Islamists present and future.

Chapter Three

Thou Shalt Have Sex with Slave Girls

3.1 Introduction

One of the most controversial verses in the Qur'an is 4:23-24, interpreted by most exegetes and jurists as sanctioning sex with captive women, whether married or not. It reads: "Prohibited to you (for marriage) … (are) women already married, except those whom your right hands possess." Even Abdullah Yusuf Ali (1872-1953), the Qur'anic translator and commentator, argues that "formal hostility dissolves civil ties" (187, note 537).

According to a tradition related by Muslim, Abu Dawud, Tirmidhi, and others, this verse was reportedly revealed at the Battle of Hunayn in 630 CE. After overcoming the Bedouins of Qays, the Muslims captured enormous spoils, including women. The companions of the Prophet were reportedly reticent about having sexual intercourse with married female prisoners of war while their captive husbands were within earshot.

In one tradition, Abu Sa'id al-Khudri (d. 682/683/684/693), a companion of the Prophet, claims: "On the Day of Awtas, we captured some women who had husbands among the idolaters. So some of the men disliked that, so God, Most High, revealed: 'And women already married, except those whom your right hands possess'" (4:24) (Tirmidhi). In another version, Muslim reports:

> Abu Sa'id al-Khudri reported that at the Battle of Hunayn God's Messenger sent an army to Awtas and encountered the enemy, and fought with them. Having overcome them and taken them captives, the companions of God's Messenger seemed to refrain from having intercourse with captive women because of their husbands being polytheists. Then God, Most High, sent down regarding that: "And women already married, except those whom your right hands possess" (4:24).

The verse in question was reportedly revealed to reassure them that they could force themselves upon married captive women. According to some sources, they did, despite the cries of the women in the dark and the rage and despair of their humiliated husbands.

It should be noted that the context of revelation, and commentary of this verse, produced many different interpretations. With the rare exception of a modern commentator, all others concluded that this verse permits Muslim men to have sexual relations with the wives of defeated tribesmen as either concubines or wives (Nasr 200-201). In his biography of the Prophet Muhammad, Waqidi (c. 747-823) reports that,

> The Muslims took two female prisoners at that time. They detested taking them for they were married women. They asked the Prophet about that, and God revealed: "[Forbidden to you] are married women except those who your right hand possesses." The Messenger of God said at that time: "Pregnant women among the prisoners may not be 'trampled' until they are delivered. As for the prisoner who is not pregnant, wait until she menstruates. (Faizer 451)

According to this account, the right to rape married women who were prisoners of war was revealed regarding two individuals, not a large number of them; however, the number is immaterial. It also qualifies that they can only be "trampled" or taken by force after they have given birth, if they are pregnant, or after they have menstruated, if they are not pregnant. No such preconditions are placed in other sources. These are jurisprudential rules from the time of Waqidi.

Time and again, Waqidi presents Muhammad as distributing women as prizes of war to his warriors, treating them like common chattel. When trying to enlist fighters to participate in the Battle of Tabuk, the Messenger of God reportedly used female booty as an incentive. As Waqidi reports,

> The Messenger of God said to al-Jadd b. Qays, "Abu Wahb, when you come out with us for this battle, perhaps you might bring back Byzantine girls with you?" Al-Jadd replied, "You grant me permission, but you do not tempt me. Surely my people know there is none with a greater vanity about women than I. But I fear that if I saw a woman of the Byzantines, I would not be patient about them." The Messenger of God turned away from him and said, "I grant you permission." (Faizer 486)

Permission to do what? To remain or to rape Byzantine prisoners of war without respecting their waiting period?

For many Muslims and non-Muslims, the deity depicted in these traditions seems demonic. What sort of a God allows warriors to have sex with enslaved married women whether they consented or not or whether their husbands were there? What sort of a messenger of God would recruit warriors by promising them female booty? What sort of a prophet would require his warriors to wait for enslaved women to have one menstrual cycle or give birth before forcing themselves upon them? And what sort of a messenger of God would give a man an exemption to the waiting period for intercourse with captives due to his lustful impatience? In other words, give him the green light to rape these white Christian Byzantine women on the spot? What sort of a prophet would permit such a thing? What sort of an example would he be? And who would follow such a person? Moral leaders lead by moral example.

Although many of these traditions are treated as authentic by Sunni traditionists and jurists, they are rejected as weak by Twelver Shiite ones. The accounts of Waqidi, while supported by some Sunni scholars, were largely rejected by others. What is more, the sordid account of the raping of married women at Hunayn contradicts those that were transmitted by historians such as Ibn Sa'd (784-845), Ma'mar ibn Rashid (714-770), and al-Tabari (839-923), who reported that the Messenger of God did not distribute the captives, kept them in custody, and waited for a delegation to come to ransom them (Karim). As Diakho points out, Bukhari, along with most traditionists and historians, writes that a delegation from Hawazin came to the Prophet asking for the liberation of their captives, both women and children, and he returned all six thousand of them (155). As Ma'mar ibn Rashid relates,

> On that day, the Prophet took six thousand women and children captive, whom the Messenger of God then handed over to Abu Sufyan ibn Harb.... When the Hawazin came back before the Messenger of God, they said, "You are the most upright and faithful in honoring bonds of kinship, but our women and those in our care have been taken captive, and our wealth seized."
>
> The Messenger of God replied, "I patiently bided my time for you, and with me are those you see. To me, the most preferable speech is the most honest. So choose one of the two, either the property or the captives." "O Messenger of God!" they replied. "As far as we are concerned, if you force us to choose between property and honor, we shall choose honor." Or they said, "We esteem honor above all else." Thus they chose their women and children. (67-68)

The Prophet then addressed the Muslims and asked them to return the women and children that were held captive (68). "Whoever wishes to act so magnanimously, let him do so; and whoever wishes to demand compensation... let him do so" (68). The Muslims answered by saying that "the judgment is good" (68). Since the leaders accepted the agreement, "God's Messenger returned the women and children" (68). He also granted women in the care of some Muslim men from Quraysh the choice to remain with them or return to their families (68). Both chose to return to their families (68-69).

According to Anas, however, the verse was not revealed after the Battle of Awtas but after the Battle of Khaybar, casting doubt on the other version of events (Diakho 155). In fact, one account speaks of two women while the other speaks of six thousand women and children. This further supports the claim that traditions like these were invented by jurists and presented as evidence in support of their edicts. We are faced with three options: an immoral account, a moral account, or a rejection of both accounts. Either way, notes Diakho, verse 4:23-24 is not explicit and cannot be used to issue laws permitting the taking of married captive women as sex slaves (154).

3.2 Married Women as Sex Slaves

Based on the Qur'anic verse in question (4:24) and traditions explaining its revelation, most Muslim jurists concluded that a woman's marriage was invalidated upon enslavement. Nawawi (1233-1277), Qurtubi (1214-1273), al-'Ayni (1361-1451), and others ruled that Muslim men could not have sex with polytheistic women through ownership. However, they certainly permitted sex with enslaved women from the People of the Book. Most jurists, however, ruled that men could have sex with their slave girls irrespective of their religious identification. Even if the pagan or polytheistic religion of the women posed a problem, their masters would force them to convert to Islam as was commonly done. According to Muslim jurists, only Jewish and Christian women had the right to retain their religions if they so willed.

Although Muslim men believed that having sex with a married Jewish or Christian woman was lawful, as her marriage was annulled upon enslavement, this was not the case according to Byzantine and Christian law. In the eyes, mind, and heart of a Christian woman, and according to the laws of her religion and her land, she was still married to her husband. When coerced to have sex with her Muslim slave master, a Christian woman could only conceive of that action as rape and sexual assault and a violation of the sacrament of marriage. "While concubinage is licit from the male owner's perspective," writes Elizabeth Urban, she claims, in a remarkable understatement, that "it is unclear from the enslaved woman's perspective" (29). Really, now?

'Ali, however, appears to have understood the concerns of enslaved married women who were in limbo between chastity and unchastity. After learning that a slave girl given to him as a gift was married, he returned her to the donor (Freamon 2019: 127). As Bernard K. Freamon points out, "his refusal to have sex with a married slave also tended to establish that a transfer of ownership did not dissolve the marriage" (2019: 127). That being said, another tradition attributed to 'Ali claims that the marriage was only valid if both parties were enslaved in Islamic lands. If the woman's husband was not equally enslaved, having escaped to his country, the marriage was invalidated, and the woman could be used as a sex slave (Nu'man, vol. 2: 239). This tradition poses a problem.

After the Battle of Badr, the Muslims from Medina captured a prostitute named 'Inaq in the Meccan camp. One of Muhammad's followers asked if he could marry her. The Prophet refused, freed her as a civilian, and instructed her to return to Mecca (Jebara 227-228). If Muhammad would not allow one of his warriors to take a prostitute as a prize of war, as a sex slave, or as a wife, how could he allow them to take married women as concubines for their harems?

Except for a few modern commentators, Twelver Shiite commentaries of the Qur'an also endorse the belief that Muslim men can take married non-Muslim women as concubines without them getting divorced or embracing Islam. Obviously, the issue of divorce was moot for Christian women since the Church prohibited it. Some of the rare exceptions of Shiite commentators opposed to

Chapter Three

taking married women as sex slaves include S.V. Mir Ahmed Ali (1902-1976), an Indian Shia Muslim scholar, who argued that,

> those possessed by the right hands refers to women taken captives in wars fought for God's cause... against the disbelievers -- those women of the disbelievers who fell as prisoners of war -- and who embraced the truth, Islam, and who could not be returned to their polytheist husbands -- such women, even though they were not divorced by their husbands, are made lawful to be the wives of Muslims. (370 note 516)

Safi Kaskas, in his commentary on his English translation of the Qur'an, also objects to the disturbing dominant interpretation. As he notes,

> Most commentators speculate that this verse is talking about a married woman captured at war, and they speculate that a female war captive's previous marriage is considered dissolved... All commentators that I reviewed failed, however, to bring one single example from the time of the Prophet backing this interpretation. Hence, our disagreement with the traditional interpretation is based on the saying of the Prophet that "these are your brothers and sisters whom God placed in your trust" (Bukhari). (51)

For many Twelver Shiite scholars, 4:23-24 was revealed regarding another matter altogether: the permissibility of temporary pleasure marriage, not only with free women but with enslaved married ones. When Ja'far al-Sadiq was asked about the meaning of "[Prohibited are] the married ones from the women except what your right hands possess," he explained that "It is when the man orders his slave ... to 'Withdraw from your wife and do not go near her.' Then he withholds her from him until she menstruates, then he touches her. So when she menstruates after his touching her, returns her without having copulated with her" (Hub-e-Ali 4:22-41; Kulayni [Arabic] vol 5: 480; 'Amili vol. 21: 149; Tusi's *Tahdhib* vol. 7: 346); Ayyashi vol 1: 232; al-Saffar).

As terrible as the traditional Sunni interpretation may be, namely, permitting captors to have sexual intercourse with married captives, the Twelver Shiite one is even more disturbing, namely, it allows a slave master to separate his married slave girl from her husband, have sex with her after her waiting period is complete, and then return her to her husband after she completes another waiting period. The psychological and emotional damage such a practice would cause to husband and wife is staggering. This is legal and moral according to some Twelver Shiite Muslim scholars. However, sexual intimacy between two unmarried, but consenting adults, is a sin. If raping slave girls, sharing slave girls, and having sex with several slave girls at the same is not a sin, then "Islamic sexual ethics" is an oxymoron. What sort of morals are these?

If married, consenting couples would share their spouses, that would be adultery, punishable by death. However, a married man, who owns a married slave girl, can command her husband, who is also enslaved, to hand over his wife so that he can have sexual intercourse with her and, when he is done, return her to him. He could do this as often as he wished, so long as she respected the waiting period. However, how many slave masters even respected the forty-five-day *'iddah*? And how many cuckolded slave husbands waited forty-five days before having sex with their wives again?

These good-faith measures to determine paternity were entirely futile. They must have wreaked havoc on entire families. As Matthew Gordon, a specialist in Middle East and Islamic history, has noted in "Unhappy Offspring? Concubines and their Sons in Early Abbasid Society,"

> Concubinage shaped domestic arrangements in Abbasid urban households, providing opportunity to fortunate sons, and leaving others with limited recourse to influence and wealth. It would follow, in other words, that a population of young males was left without proper access to guidance and livelihood. Concubinage could, and often did, have the effect of creating fractured, divided households. The result was the creation of an unruly male element.

In fact, Moulay 'Abd al-Rahman of Morocco (1778-1859) denounced the fact that, "most often, men who buy slave girls, have sex with them the very same day, without legally ensuring the absence of pregnancy," thereby confusing lineages (Diakho 201). Unsurprisingly, the owners of slave girls would sell them off, refusing to recognize their offspring, rightly or wrongly, claiming that they were bastards (201). Some used to breed women like they were cows, boasting that they were even more profitable than livestock (Diakho 201). One degenerate gloated that he would impregnate his slave girl every nine months and sell the children she produced, namely, his very own children, when they were four or five years old (Diakho 201). This was precisely the practice of slave owners on the plantations in the southern United States. They condemned their own illegitimate offspring to slavery.

Man-made Islamic laws do not consider the sentiments of the slave woman, her slave husband, or the wife or wives of the slave master. It is male hedonism made manifest. And when the companion of the sixth Imam asked whether the married slave girl, who was coerced to have sex with her master, was counted among the four allowed wives, he responded that "she is not from the four. But rather, she is hired" (Hub-e-Ali 4:22-41, Kulayni, al-Saffar). Yes, "hired," just like a prostitute. Her body is for rent. She is on loan from her husband.

Can Muslim men take married women as sex slaves? Not according to Edip Yüksel (b. 1957), the Turkish American Qur'anist. As he explains,

> The expression *ma malakat aymanukum* has been translated by most translations as "whom your right hands possess" or "captives" or "concubines." We translated this and similar expressions found in 4:3,24,25,36; 16:71; 23:6; 24:31,33,58; 30:28; 33:50,52,55; and 70:30 as

"those with whom you have contractual rights." These were the wives of the enemy combatants who were persecuted because they acknowledged the message of Islam and sought asylum in the Muslim community (60:10). Since they did not go through a normal divorce process, an exceptional contract allows them to marry Muslims as free women. (101)

As far as Muhammad Diakho is concerned, verse 4:23-24 should not be translated as "Prohibited to you (for marriage) ... (are) women already married, except those whom your right hands possess," but rather as "[Prohibited to you are] chaste women, except those you possess in a legitimate way." In other words, "As for women captured during a *jihad*, and who are married to husbands who were not captured, they are permitted to you in marriage" (233). A tradition from 'Ali appears to support this view. It states that:

> Were a woman from *ahl al-harb* [people at war with Muslims] comes into *dar al-islam* [the land of Islam], seeking refuge, and leaves her husband in that country, her husband has no right over her and she may marry whom she likes without observing *'iddah*. If her husband accepts Islam, he may become one of her suitors. (Nu'man, vol. 2: 238)

The odd thing here is not expecting her to ensure she is free of pregnancy before getting remarried.

The women in question had embraced Islam, some openly and others secretly, yet were trapped in marriages to polytheistic men who were waging war against Islam. This was the case with some female companions of the Prophet who were left behind in Mecca with their idolatrous husbands. The same phenomenon was found in other tribes. This verse aimed to emancipate believing women from disbelieving men and join them in holy matrimony with Muslim men. It also encouraged women who were inclined to Islam to openly profess it and join the Muslim community rather than be ransomed and returned to their heathen husbands. The verse in question was decontextualized entirely by later jurists and deployed to justify the taking of sex slaves in raids and wars.

Despite Brown's claims, abolitionist academics know the difference between the past and the present. They do not try to impose modern views and values on pre-modern times. They can see things through the eyes and minds of people from the period. As much as some black American Muslim scholars may claim that no pre-modern Muslims or Islamic scholars ever objected to slavery, some of them did. When it comes to war, rules must be in place to deal with captives. Instead of "kill them," the Qur'an commanded Muslims to capture and ransom them. It never said to enslave them and their descendants. Such "slavery" was supposed to be temporary.

Islamic jurists acknowledged that the only legitimate source of slaves consisted of captives of war. However, the wars in question had to be just. They had to be defensive. They could not be offensive. Virtually all the wars waged by Muslims after the passing of the Prophet were imperialistic in nature. Many were declared for the specific purpose of harvesting slaves. As for any people who were legitimate prisoners of war, the Qur'an stipulated their right to earn their freedom through labor and service. In the absence of facilities for prisoners of war, they were housed with families. They had attacked and killed Muslims. A price had to be paid. Reparations were in order. There is nothing fundamentally unfair or unjust about it.

In the case of captive women, there was a real risk that men might take advantage of them. Hence, the Qur'an encouraged Muslim men to marry captive women permanently. To prevent problems with illegitimate offspring, the Qur'an also provided other options. If both parties consented, they could contract a common law, fixed-term or out of hand marriage. This is entirely different from asserting that a Muslim man had a right to have sex with enslaved women without a contract of any kind. What is more, slaves who embraced Islam were supposed to be emancipated. This practice, however, was rarely put into practice. Most slaves in the Islamic world were Muslims and the children of female slaves were destined for slavery as well. Some jurists ruled that an enslaved woman was to receive her freedom after giving a child to her master. However, others stated that she was only be emancipated after the death of her master. And yet others said that this was only the case if a contract of manumission stipulated as much. The Qur'an provided the means for smooth, effective, and permanent abolition. Faithfully applied, its principles would have resulted in the end of slavery in the Muslim world in a timely fashion.

3.3 The Covenants of the Prophet Prohibit Sexual Coercion and Forced Marriages

In contrast to Islamic law, the Covenants of the Prophet with the Christians insist that Muslim men are not to coerce Christian girls and women into sex or marriage (Morrow 2021: 250). In the words of Muhammad,

> They shall not have to suffer anything, such as the marriage of their wives and daughters. Whoever dares such a thing betrays the Covenant of God, the Most High: none of you shall be allowed to marry their daughters or desire the same. (Morrow 2017, vol. 2: 239)

Similar clauses are found in other Covenants of the Prophet as well. If Muslims may not marry Christian women by force, they most certainly cannot fornicate with them by force, commit adultery with them by force, or have sexual intercourse with them by force under the guise of slavery and concubinage.

If that is the case, and Muslim men may only marry and have sexual relations with Christian women with their consent, then 4:23-24 has been misconstrued and misinterpreted by Muslim jurists. It does not permit Muslim men to have sex with enslaved women, much less with married ones. It merely permits them to marry them. Slavery may break marriage bonds. It is also possible that, when it comes to women, embracing Islam, not the condition of slavery itself, breaks the previous marital ties. Either way, viewed in this light, the Qur'anic verse should be interpreted as encouraging Muslim men to marry and free female captives of war, particularly if they embrace Islam. This is a more sensible interpretation than those proposed by scholars past who served at the leisure of women-hating imperialists, war criminals, moral degenerates, mass murderers, slave traders, and human traffickers.

Although the Covenants of the Prophet were intended to protect Christians, the status of *dhimmah* that was accorded to them was notoriously violated to feed the ogre of slavery (Chebel 21). The janissary corps was filled with Caucasians, Georgians, Greeks, and Slavic people who professed the Orthodox Christian faith, and had been captured along the borders of the Ottoman Empire (Chebel 21).

3.4 Possessed by the Right Hand

Another polemical verse regarding sexual slavery is 33:50, which reads: "O Prophet! We have made lawful to thee thy wives to whom thou hast paid their dowers; and those whom thy right hand possesses out of the prisoners of war whom God has assigned to thee."

Commenting on this verse, Michael Muhammad Knight (b. 1977), the American novelist, essayist, and journalist, argues that "the Qur'an mentions slave rape as an allowed sexual practice." It requires quite an imagination to produce such an interpretation. Where does the verse mention rape? Nowhere. Where does it mention slaves? Nowhere. "Possessed by the right hand" is a legal expression drawn from Byzantine law which signifies a "wife" or "spouse."

Knight also argues that Islamic law permits marital rape. For Knight, "slave rape" and "marital rape… might be unpleasant to consider as part of Islamic sexuality, but they are deeply embedded in our established sources." As he puts it,

> Prior to modern objections to slavery, Muslim legal thinkers never questioned the assumed right of a slave owner to rape his female slaves: they only argued over the legality of possible situations, such as two men going halfsies on buying a woman and then both raping her, or a man raping a female slave who was owned by his male slave.

While this might be so, none of these rulings are rooted in the Qur'an and the example of the Prophet Muhammad.

Regarding sex with slave girls, Joseph A. Islam has stressed that "there is no support for such a view in the Qur'an." What is more, "such interpretations are often the result of the disease that can be transmitted by Islamic secondary sources." Knight, at least, does not believe that Islamic tradition is frozen in stone and that the study of Islam should not be limited to pre-modern texts. He is indeed correct that "every interpretation is a choice."

As for women as prisoners of war, Abdullah Yusuf Ali claims that "the point does not now arise, as the whole conditions and incidents of war have been altered and slavery has been abolished by international agreement" (1121: note 3743). This argument, however, "avoids the difficult jurisprudential problem presented by those who advocate abolition, and it also does not take into account current facts-on-the-ground situations" (Freamon 2019: 144).

As Muhammad Diakho notes, "the meaning of *ma malakat aymanakum* is not established beyond question" (150). The meaning of this phrase is not defined in the Qur'an or the *sunnah* (152). Its interpretation is not beyond a doubt (152). Its translation as "concubines" is based on habit, repetition, blind following, and imitation (151). For Diakho, contextual interpretation categorically denies that it conveys the sense of concubinage (152). After all, *milku al-yamin*, in its official understanding, is not an Islamic institution. It is a pre-Islamic one that was universally found in slave societies (152). For Joseph A. Islam, an independent Qur'anic researcher,

> the term *ma malakat aymanukum* (literally: what your right hands possess) is not gender specific and as an idiomatic expression, applies to "those that one keeps in protection and honor." This can include captives, slave girls, maidens, servants…
>
> It is also apt to note that affluent women would have also been most likely to have possessed men slaves. This is confirmed by the usage of the idiomatic expression *ma malakat aymanuhunna* when used in reference to women's possession. It would be inconceivable to conclude, on the basis of this expression, the permissibility of women to engage in "free sex" with their male slaves or captives. (Sex with Slave Girls)

After examining the verses in which the expression, "those that your right hands possess," is used in the Qur'an, Joseph A. Islam notes that 1) they must be well treated, like parents, orphans, needy people, or neighbors; otherwise, one must release them; 2) they must not be compelled to whoredom; and 3) one may only have sex with them through wedlock (Sex with Slave Girls). His commentary of the following verse is commendable:

> If any of you have not the means wherewith to wed free believing women, **they may wed believing girls from among those whom your right hands possess**: And God has full knowledge about your faith. Ye are one from another: **Wed them with the leave of their owners**, and give them their dowers, according to what is reasonable: **They should be chaste, not lustful, nor taking paramours: when they are taken in wedlock**, if they fall into shame, their punishment is half that for free women. This (permission) is for those among you who fear sin**; but it is better for you that ye practice self-restraint**. And God is Oft-forgiving, Most Merciful. (4:25)

The points he makes are as follows:

> It was better if one practiced self-restraint. But if one couldn't marry free believing women, then the directive was given to **marry** from what their

right hands possessed. Not for prostitution, not for lust, but for wedlock.

Notice here that although one can "marry" a woman from what one's right hands possess; her status is **not** that of a "free believing woman" (as can be seen from the half punishment she can potentially exact'for the same sin). This is the reason why women that form part of those whom your right hands possess are referred to as a separate category. However, they do not form an exception to the marital rule in terms of who is lawful for sex. See 23:6 & 70:30. In other words, they still have to be married.

One logical question bears asking, keeping in view any appetite for carnal desires. If one has wives along with many handmaidens with whom one could potentially have free sex, then what kind of sexual predator and maniac does one have to be to still commit adultery? The Qur'an imparts a consistent message with regards abstention from any unrighteous lust. What is the purpose of having sex with captives if it is not for lust? (Sex with Slave Girls)

Consequently, he concludes, based on this verse, and his findings regarding several other verses, that "scripture has never permitted men to engage in sex outside the institution of marriage whether this is from the category of free believing women, or from the category of what the 'right hand possesses'" (Sex with Slave Girls).

Milk al-yamin does not mean "concubines with whom you have sex" (Diakho 155). In fact, "there is no valid theological basis for such a practice" (153). The Qur'an prohibits Muslim men from marrying women who are already married (154). An exception is made for married women legally captured during combats (154). If the women in question are Muslims or are willing to become Muslims, then Muslim men are allowed to marry them (154). The new marriage would invalidate the former one. The verse does not permit sexual relations with the women, *al-ijma'*, but rather marriage, or *al-nikah* (Diakho 154). As Diakho notes, "the term *milk al-yamin* invariably describes 'legal wives' and 'captive women' and the term *al-sarriyyah* (concubine) never comes into play in the Qur'an and the *sunnah*" (156).

Not only is concubinage in Islam founded on a false doctrine, but it is also "an abhorrent exploitation of the weak by the powerful," signaling that the practice is both "fraudulent and irreligious" (Diakho 156-157). Be that as it may, Qur'anic exegetes and Islamic jurists could not express any idea that contradicted the official line regarding slavery and concubinage (230). Their fourteen-hundred-year-old claim that "Islam permits concubinage" is a serious deviation from the Qur'an, which prohibits forcing slave girls into *bigha*,' namely, prostitution, libertinism, sexual inhibition, lewdness, lasciviousness, sexual immorality, sexual intercourse, fornication, adultery, whoredom, harlotry, and concubinage (24:33).

3.5 Taking Captives as Concubines

As Freamon admits, 33:50 is more difficult to reconcile with abolitionist ideals; however, the solution is in plain sight: "the verse expressly limits itself to the Prophet" (2019: 499). As Freamon notes, Sayyid Qutb argued that "interpretation of the verse so as to confine it to the actions of the Prophet only, which were taken under special circumstances or under conditions that existed then and now no longer exist, is a sound and valid interpretive approach to the verses" (2019: 499-500). As he further explains,

> Verse 33:50, addressed to the Prophet Muhammad, explicitly refers to women whom "thy right hand possesses" as "spoils of war." Commentary indicates that there were two such women in the life of the Prophet, Safiyya bint Huyyay and Juwayriyya bint al-Harith, both of whom were captives of the Prophet, and both were emancipated by him prior to being married to him. (Freamon 2019: 142; see also 122-123)

3.6 No Concubinage in Islam

Since slavery, polygyny, and concubinage are inextricably linked, jurists like Qasim Amin (1865-1908), the father of feminism and the liberator of women, realized that abolishing the former would eradicate the latter. As he noted, the status of women in Islam reflects Arab culture:

> This image we have of women reflects the view of them that has been handed down to us by the Arabs, whose traditional life was one of war and combat, in which booty was the main source of livelihood. It hardly needs pointing out that in a society based on war, women can have no significant place. In such a society, a woman is unable to keep pace with men, and her standing consequently declines. Thus she eventually came to be considered part of the possessions or chattels. The victor took her and counted her among his spoils of war, just as other movable property. And this led to the practice of concubinage and to polygamy. (151)

In his 1913 thesis, Mansour Fahmy (1886-1959), another pioneer of Islamic feminism, also called for the abolition of slavery. Since this was perceived as insulting to the Prophet Muhammad, he lost his position at the university (Clarence-Smith 2008: 18).

In *The Religion of Islam*, Muhammad 'Ali (1874-1951), the British Indo-Pakistani scholar and Lahori Ahmadi, pleads a powerful, compelling, and convincing case against the legitimacy of concubinage in Islam. He admits that "there is a general impression that Islam gives an unlimited license to have as many concubines as one likes" (663). Although concubinage existed before Islam, and slave girls were required to satisfy the carnal passions of their masters, the Qur'anic command to "marry... your female slaves" ended such an evil practice (662-663). "If any master of a female slave kept her as a concubine after that," he notes, "it was against the Qur'anic injunction" (663). Any actions or claims to the

Chapter Three 37

contrary have no value in law (663).

Muhammad 'Ali points out that the verses used to infer that concubinage is permissible (23: 5-6; 70: 29-30) apply to both men and women (664). If they permit free men to have sex with enslaved females, they permit free women to have sex with enslaved men (664). The verses simply call upon believers to protect their private parts, be chaste, and be modest (664). Even if the inference were accepted as true, the two verses in question were revealed in Mecca before the reforms in Medina (665). If there ever was permission to keep concubines, argues 'Ali, it was taken away in Medina when a clear injunction called for all enslaved women to be married (665). Moreover, "neither the Holy Qur'an nor the *hadith*, anywhere speaks of the right of the master to have sexual intercourse with a slave" (665).

While that may hold in Sunni Islam, it most certainly does not in Twelver Shiism, as its sources claim that the Prophet encouraged men to purchase slave women, have sexual intercourse with them via ownership, and seek children with them. "Betake you to the *ummahat al-awlad*, for in their wombs is a blessing" ('Amili). The term *ummuhat al-awlad* is the plural of *umm walad*, namely, the mother of the child, which signifies a slave girl who gives a child to her master. In another such tradition, the Messenger of God tells his followers to "Seek children from the *ummuhat al-awlad* for in their wombs is a blessing" ('Amili). What is more, unlike Sunni sources, that stipulate that a slave girl who provides a child to her master should be emancipated after her death, Twelver Shiite sources state that they should not (Hilali 11). In fact, 'Ali claims that it was an innovation on the part of 'Umar (11).

As critical thinkers and competent scholars and researchers comprehend, these Twelver Shiite traditions are forgeries that reflect 'Abbasid-era sexual norms that were not prevalent during the time of the Prophet Muhammad. It can also be argued that the claim that 'Ali took a slave girl for himself from among the prisoners, as recorded in Mufid's (948-1022) *Kitab al-Irshad*, and echoed in some Sunni sources, was invented to justify sexual slavery (Mufid 111-112). Nobody has been lied about more than the Prophet Muhammad and the People of the House.

3.7 Conclusions

The claim that Qur'anic verses 4:23-24 permit Muslim men to take married non-Muslim women as sex slaves is the product of a perverse, sadistic, and misogynistic misinterpretation of the text. In reality, the verse encouraged Muslim men to marry captives of war who had converted to Islam. Like the case of the mythical Mariya the Copt, the cases of Safiyya bint Huyyay, Juwariyyah bint al-Harith, and Rayhanah bint Zayd -- which were also used by some jurists as precedents -- cannot be deployed to justify sexual slavery and concubinage.

Rather than endorse concubinage, Qur'anic verse 33:50 applied solely to the

Prophet Muhammad or, at the very least, only allowed Muslim men to marry enslaved women after they converted to Islam and were emancipated. The verse did not give Muslim men *carte blanche* to acquire enslaved women and have sex with them. However, it did encourage them to invite enslaved women to Islam, emancipate them, and take them as wives in lawful wedlock. This makes a world of moral difference for those with wisdom and understanding. As Diakho asserts, "having intimate relations with a woman outside of any bonds of marriage, be it *tassari* (concubinage), or whatever other name you wish to give it, is nothing less than a specialized form of fornication" (12). "And come not near unto fornication and adultery. Lo! it is an abomination and an evil way" (17:32).

Chapter Four

That Booty is Booty:
Women as Spoils of War

4.1 Introduction

Jonathan A.C. Brown's claim that women can be treated as war booty, and turned into sex slaves, on the authority of the Qur'an, the *hadith*, and the *shari'ah*, can also be contested on the grounds of culture and custom, as women, in civilized and morally evolved societies, are not viewed as the property of men. In fact, neither 33:50, nor 8:41, nor any other verse of the Qur'an defines spoils of war. Consequently, the interpretation of those verses depends entirely on the morals of the interpreter. Why should the lowest standard be enshrined as law and not the highest? Why should the interpretation of savages and barbarians prevail over that of the righteous and virtuous? And why can't standards vary, evolve, and change? Do we live in the past, or do we live in the present? Should we not strive to improve ourselves and improve our societies? Must we be condemned to live in the perpetual dark ages created by medieval Muslim men?

4.2 Women as Spoils of War

According to traditional Islamic jurisprudence, "women and children are not to be killed in a *jihad* but rather taken and divided as booty… among the victors as slaves." As Muhammad al-Maghili (c. 1140-1505), a Berber Muslim scholar from Tlemcen, now in modern-day Algeria, commanded, "Make *jihad* against the infidels, kill their men, make captive of their women and children, and seize their wealth" (Azumah 126). Simply because Muslims have been doing something wrong for a long time does not make it right in theory or practice.

As Bernard K. Freamon notes, "Eliminating a practice because it is no longer customary among the people is perfectly permissible in Islamic jurisprudence" (2019: 499). Although the claim that the Prophet Muhammad married a nine-year-old girl is contentious, and has been decisively debunked in "The Age of 'A'ishah" (Morrow 2023: 66-127), Freamon uses it to make a point. According to his line of reasoning,

> The Prophet Muhammad was betrothed to Aishah when she was nine years old. This was a common practice at the time. Today it would be

considered child abuse and a form of illegal child exploitation and sex trafficking. Application of interpretations of the *hadith* ... must therefore be determined to be limited to the special circumstances surrounding the Prophet. They cannot, jurisprudentially, morally, or legally be the basis for similar behaviors by Muslim men today. Slavery and slave trading would be in this same category. (2019: 500)

"The argument might be made that those who seek to emulate the Prophet's behavior... should be entitled to hold, purchase, and sell captured women as war booty," notes Freamon (2019: 143). However, "the contrary argument posits that the verse is addressed only to the Prophet and, when he died, the behavior and the treatment of captive women permitted by the verse could thereafter be juridically abolished or severely restricted" (Freamon 2019: 143). In the words of Freamon,

> Jurists must acknowledge... that the customs and usages of war have changed. What constitutes "war booty" is a matter of custom in Islamic law as in other legal systems, and verse 33:50 actually makes no attempt to define the "spoils of war." Putting aside the argument that the verse legislates only the behavior of the Prophet; it could also be argued that Muslim jurists and those who conduct themselves in war might very well have the right and authority to change the definition of what constitutes "spoils." (2019: 143)

If custom played a significant role in the development of Islamic jurisprudence, and jurists could modify their rulings according to local traditions and practices, argues Muhammad Diakho, and all legal systems naturally evolve to address changing realities and circumstances, it is perfectly permissible for Muslim jurists to reconcile Islamic law with abolitionist principles from societies past and present (70).

Claiming that no "innovation" can occur in Islam because it is "perfect" is as preposterous as claiming that no change can take place in physics because it is "perfect." "If jurists maintained the *status quo*," argues Diakho, "it was due to lack of intellectual courage, conformism, or some Machiavellian spirit" (6). In fact, we should be inspired by the example of Ibn Hazm (994-1064), the Andalusian polymath, who "rejected any arguments based on *taqlid*, the blind following of religious and political authorities who present themselves as the exclusive repositories of orthodoxy, and who rejected all pretensions of individual or collective infallibility" (90-91).

4.3 Thou Shalt Crave a Sex Slave

Despite well-intended efforts by Muslim scholars to abolish and eradicate sexual slavery in Islamic law and practice, Brown argues that it is Islamically permissible for Muslim men to have sex with their female slaves outside of wedlock. He seems to share the view that sex with a slave girl, even if it is devoid of consent and is coerced, is better than fornication or prostitution. Others would argue that it is the same as prostitution since most prostitutes are sex slaves owned by pimps and sex trafficking rings and networks. Of course, concubines in Islam were intended to be reserved to a single man. Hence, the situation is similar to prostitution but not entirely the same. They were more like sex slaves owned by a single man.

For the morally minded and the ethically elevated, not only is sex with slave girls an act of fornication, but if the owner is married, it is an act of adultery. And not only that, but it is also an act of sexual assault. While Brown's mythological Muhammad believed in sexual slavery, our Muhammad, the historical and moral Muhammad was mortified by the evil institution. As Mohamad Jebara relates in his poetic prose,

> Young men in Mecca observed what they considered a rite of passage into manhood at fifteen. One day, some youths invited Muhammad to join them for a visit to *al-Hanut* (the shop), a windowless tavern on the outskirts of town. Muhammad innocently assumed the establishment was, as its name suggested, a store. He arrived to find two thuggish men guarding a wooden door covered by a dark blue curtain. After looking the boys over, the bouncers pulled the drape aside and ushered them in. Small olive-oil lanterns provided minimal mood lighting, while shepherd boys played sensual melodies on their flutes. The room had no chairs, and servers, passing among the standing patrons, poured wine from amphorae. In the corner of the room, teenage girls with styled hair, heavy makeup, and cheap jewelry lined up to be ogled, some dancing to the beat of drummers playing animal-skin cylinders.

> The only product sold at *al-Hanut*, Muhammad suddenly realized, were girls, some as young as twelve. When their pimp saw an interested client engage one of his charges, he would approach and negotiate a price. The client would take the girl outside to a nearby sand dune and return once business was concluded.

> Repulsed by the scene, Muhammad dashed out of the tavern, never to return. He understood that the young women were victims, many orphans like himself. Their exploitation angered him, and he determined to oppose the practice. In no uncertain terms, the Qur'an declares: "You shall not force your slave girls into prostitution" (24:33). At the same time, Muhammad recognized that these girls had great potential. One of his most famous sayings would describe such a prostitute, whose pure heart transcended her outcast state. (79-80)

Muhammad was not a mental or moral retard. Whether a master sexually exploited his slave girl or allowed another man, or men, to sexually exploit her, it was equally evil and iniquitous. Whether he reserves the sole right to rape her, or whether he sells her, the slave master and slave dealer remains a pimp and, according to the sixth Imam, "Paradise is made unlawful for a pimp" (Kulayni, vol. 5: 469). As for Muhammad, there is no doubt that he rejected slavery along with the sexual exploitation and repression of women. As Edip Yüksel explains, when the Qur'an states that Muslims should guard their private parts except among those with whom they have contractual rights,

> It refers to those who were concubines before the revelation that prohibited slavery and gave them freedom. Though the Qur'an prohibited slavery for Muslims, at that time, slavery and wars were the reality of the polytheistic world. Prohibited relationships that started before the revelation of the Qur'an, were not asked to be voided, since that would create bigger psychological, economic, and social problems. In other words, the laws of the Qur'an in the sphere of marriage relationships was not applied retroactively (4:22-23). Also, see 4:3,25; 90:1-20. (237)

As Cyrille Moreno al-'Ajami, the Arabist, theologian, and Qur'anic exegete emphasizes,

> The phrase *ma malakat aymanukum* is in the past tense and does not mean "those whom your right hands possess," but rather, "those whom your right hands *possessed*." The meaning is clear. It refers to slaves who were married like free women.

4.4 Humanizing Sex Slaves

Erotic, perverted, sexist, and sadistic fantasies aside, it is ignoble to romanticize concubinage and minimize its trauma. "Female slaves had to endure not only economic exploitation and physical labor," writes El Hamel, "but were also subjected to sexual violence" (11). It was, in practice, "an exploitative act utilizing … the enslaved person's productivity… sexuality and reproductive capacity" (El Hamel 55). As Janet Afary, the American activist and academic who focuses on history, religious studies, and women's studies, notes, "A slave had no right to birth control, sexual satisfaction, or children" (81).

Since they were cheaper than white slaves, in Morocco, black women were preferred as concubines (El Hamel 259), adding another racist element to sexual subjugation. After all, "the price of white females were often higher than black ones" (Akyol 2022: 62). Those who promoted slavery would cite a saying of the Prophet, most certainly spurious, as one can only hope, that claimed that black women never say no: "There is no Negress who would refuse love when it is offered" (El Hamel 259). Speaking of Nubian and Abyssinian women, Muhammad al-Idrisi (1100-1165), the geographer, wrote, "of all black women, they are the best for the pleasures of the bed" (Azumah 156). This reinforces the negative stereotype of black women as being promiscuous and hyper-sexual. However, the descriptions of *zanj* women are so disgustingly racist that they do not deserve to be reproduced (Azumah 157).

In typical hypocritical fashion, these racist men determined that they could copulate with black females but that black men should never be allowed to have relations with non-black females (Azumah 136-137). Medieval Persian literature intimates that "only a whore prefers blacks; the good woman will welcome death rather than be touched by a black man" (Azumah 137). In his study of blacks in the Islamic diaspora, John Owen Hunwick (1936-2015), the British professor, author, and Africanist, found that "the stigma of racial origin was apparent" and that "it would have been unthinkable for an Arab, or a Berber, a Turk, or a Persian, [and one would add, Asian], to consent to his daughter marrying a black African" (Azumah 137).

4.5 Questioning Qur'anic Misinterpretation

"Muhammad Asad," writes El Hamel, "explained that the concubinage system was a form of coercing a slave girl to fulfill her master's sexual desires and is surely prohibited because the Qur'an explicitly describes it as prostitution (*bigha'*)" (26; Asad 602). "Coerce not your [slave] maidens into whoredom," warns the Qur'an, "if they happen to be desirous of marriage" (24:33). As Asad (1900-1992), the Austro-Hungarian born Jewish convert to Islam and Qur'an translator, explains, this "verse reiterates the prohibition of concubinage by explicitly describing it as 'whoredom'" (El Hamel 31; Asad 602). Although sex with slave girls abounded in pre-Islamic Arabia, Islam introduced a moral compass. As El Hamel notes,

> In his study of early Islamic law, Jonathan Brockopp commented that the Qur'an established new ethics by promoting marriage to slaves; it emphasized "sexual intercourse was to be entirely within the marriage bonds." To assert that males are entitled to females slaves' sexuality contradicts the Qur'anic verses 4:3, 24, 25; 23:6; 70:30; and 24:32. I should emphasize here that verse 4:3 means a man who marries a slave must first free her. It is logical then that the concept of *umm al-walad* (literally "mother of the child") and legally a female slave who bears a child for her master) is neither found nor recognized even tangentially in the Qur'an. Therefore, the interpretation of *ma malakat aymanukum* as concubines in most interpretations or exegeses of the Qur'an and implemented in Islamic law does not reflect the language in the Qur'anic message. (26)

Mohammad Ali, the Indian British expert on Islamic law, advances the same argument. He explains that "concubinage was permitted with female slaves and with female prisoners of war" and that "the same custom was followed by some Muslims until the revelation of the Qur'anic verse prohibiting concubinage," namely, "Marry those among you who are single, or the virtuous ones among your slaves, male or female" (24:32). As he notes

> In this verse, we find the same marriage instructions to master and mistress and female and male slaves. Therefore, there is no question of permitting concubinage of [a] master with his female slave as mistresses

are never allowed to have sex with their male slaves. (Ali 33-34)

He also argues that verse 24:33 prohibits Muslims from forcing their handmaids into prostitution. In his mind,

> it is quite clear from 24:32 and 24:33 that if any master of a female slave kept her as his concubine after the revelation of these two verses, he was certainly violating Qur'anic injunctions... However, the unfortunate female slave who is compelled by her master to fornication will receive the mercy of God. (34)

As Qasim Rashid (b. 1982), the Pakistani American author, attorney, and Ahmadi activist, affirms, "Islam does not permit concubinage" and warns that "fornication and adultery trigger the penalty of physical reprimand" (309). Not only did the Prophet Muhammad encourage men to educate slave girls, teach them good manners, and marry them (Abu Dawud), but so did the Qur'an: "marry those whom your right hand possess" (4:26). For Rashid, "Islam has allowed for mutually consenting marriages between masters and slaves -- a union that would automatically lead to the end of the master-slave relationship" (310). After all, the Qur'an reminds people that "you are all one from another" (4:26).

As far as Joseph Witztum, the scholar of the Qur'an, is concerned, "the first part of Q. 4:24 is an independent sentence; that an erroneous reading of it as a continuation of the previous verse led to the replacement of the original meaning of *muhsinat* (chaste women) with married women; and that there is a strong case for understanding the second part of the verse as addressing *mut'ah*" (1). He provides detailed reasons why verses 4:24-25 should be understood, not as "women already married, except those whom your right hands possess" but as "the chaste ones from among the women, but not your female slaves" (14). He insists that "those possessed by the right hand," in verse 25, "clearly refers to potential marriage partners rather than concubines" (10-11).

As Witztum explains, "If v. 24a begins by establishing that one should marry only chaste women (as opposed to slave girls), then it is easy to understand v.24b as permitting sexual relations of a different type... *al-mut'ah*... which signifies temporary marriage" (15-16). For the Qur'anic researcher in question, 4:22-25 gives Muslim men three options when it comes to marriage: 1) permanent marriage to chaste women; 2) temporary marriage; and 3) marriage to female slaves, if necessary (28). If this is correct, then it would seem that Sunni scholars, in their zeal to interdict *mut'ah* marriages, stressed the permissibility of having sex, outside of wedlock, with enslaved girls and women. If so, then the cure was worse than the disease.

As Asghar Ali Engineer (1939-2013), the Indian reformist writer and social activist, and leader of the Progressive Dawoodi Bohra movement, admits, "orthodox Muslims consider it lawful to have sexual relations with women captured in war or purchased in the market" (124). However, as he notes, "many modern scholars and commentators feel that such a relationship is not legal and

Chapter Four 45

has not been permitted by the Qur'an" (124). We should not be subject to the dictatorship of the dead.

Despite all the legal and moral arguments advanced by opponents of sex with enslaved persons, Brown refuses to accept that the Qur'an prohibits "sexual relations with any woman other than one's lawful wife" (Asad 124; Brown 2020: 392, note 199). Referring to 4:24-25, Muhammad Asad notes that "some of the most outstanding commentators hold the view that *ma malakat aymanukum* [those whom you lawfully possess] denotes ... 'women who you rightfully possess [*through wedlock*]'" (123-124). As he asserts, "this passage lays down in an unequivocal manner that sexual relations with female slaves are permitted only on the basis of marriage... consequently concubinage is ruled out" (124, note 26; see also Nasr 201). As Chouki El Hamel elaborates,

> Contrary to most classical exegetes who were of the opinion that *ma malakat aymanukum* means "concubines," ar-Razi (1149-1209), another famous Persian Islamic theologian and part of the Ash'ari-Shafi'i school, who wrote one of the most authoritative exegeses of the Qur'an, was one of those who questioned the moral implications of such interpretations and practices and suggested that *ma malakat aymanukum* should mean "those whom they rightfully possess through wedlock (*an-nikah*)." (25)

In his commentary on 4:25, Malik Ghulam Farid (1897-1977), the Ahmadi scholar and Qur'anic commentator, stresses that "bondwomen should be properly married before conjugal relations are had with them. This is also clear from 2:222, 4:4, and 24:33. Thus Islam has cut at the root of concubinage which was so prevalent in Arab society before its advent."

Increasingly, more scholars and commentators of the Qur'an have come to the same conclusion. Sevim Gelgeç, for example, believes that Muslims must return to the ontological understanding of chastity in their interpretation of *ma malakat ayman*:

> Based on the principle of gradualism, when we follow the course of the verses in which the expression *ma malakat eyman* is included, with this expression, Allah has not approved of a class such as slaves and concubines becoming legitimate. On the contrary, He has transformed this idiom into a pattern... In things that are subject to graduality, there is not an expansion.... There is a contraction and limitation. The Qur'an, whose purpose is to build a mentality, gradually narrows down the issue of slaves and concubines that it finds in its lap and directs people to completely abolish this institution. Based on the last point... we can say that the only way to have sexual intercourse with the concubines, which is a phenomenon of the *nuzul* period, is marriage...
>
> Islam, the last religion, envisaged gradual reform rather than abolishing slavery and concubines immediately, and at the end of this reform movement, it aimed to abolish slavery completely... However,

although it was supported by reason and revelation, people did not consider the abolition of this institution as appropriate because of their interests and their lustful desires. Establishing a human market by becoming deified over slaves and buying concubines by checking their bodies in these markets is contrary to human rights and moral rules like killing someone unjustly, as well as the goals of the Qur'an, and *sunnah* of the Prophet, who passed away by saying *ma malakat ayman* in his last words. At this point, being fairer than other civilizations is not enough to cover up the mistakes of Muslims, nor is it an excuse. In this respect, everything that contradicts revelation is a whim, and following a whim is *haram*. At this point, the final demand of the Qur'an from its addressees is that "minds become Muslims," which we can define as "the main chastity," and to make this a way of life. (1004-1005)

Edip Yüksel, in his commentary of the Qur'an, provides an alternative meaning for the disputed phrase. He argues that,

The word YaMYN means "right hand" or metaphorically "right," "power" or "control." However, its plural form aYMaN is consistently mentioned in the Qur'an to mean not "right hands" but to mean "oaths" or "promises," implying the mutual nature of the relationship (See 4:33 5:89; 9:12; 16:91-94; 2:224-225; 30:28; 66:2; 5:53; 6:109). This unique Qur'anic usage is similar to the semantic difference between the singular and plural forms of the word Ayat (signs) (see 2:106).

The expression in question, thus could be translated as "those whom your oaths/contracts have rights over" or "those whom you hold rights through your contracts," or by reading aYMaN (oaths/contracts) as an object rather than a subject, "those who hold/possess your contracts."

The marriage declaration is a mutual partnership between two sexes and is formed by participation of family members. A married woman cannot marry another man without getting divorced from her husband. However, if a woman escapes and joins Muslims while her husband stayed behind participating in a war against Muslims, she may marry a Muslim man without actually getting divorced from her combatant husband; she will legally be considered a divorcee (60:10). Since this contract is different from the normal marriage contract, this special relationship is described in different words. The same is valid for a man whose wife allies with the hostile enemy. See 24:31 and 33:55. (102)

In *Black Morocco: A History of Slavery, Race, and Islam*, Chouki El Hamel studies all the Qur'anic terms used by jurists to justify slavery, including the expression *ma malakat aymanukum* [those whom you lawfully possess] (29-36). When the Qur'an warns against being sexually intimate with "any but their spouses, that is, those whom they rightfully possess" (23:6), it is not authorizing concubinage; otherwise, it would be contradicting 4:3, "where the subject is clearly about marrying female slaves" (El Hamel 30, note 56). The same goes for

24:32, which urges Muslims to "marry … your male and female slaves as are fit [for marriage]" (El Hamel 35). After examining the thirty-one verses dealing with the subject, El Hamel concludes that the Qur'an condemns concubinage, encourages emancipation, and introduces gradual steps to end slavery (36). As he notes,

> In his commentary on 23:6, which allows Muslim men to have sex with "those joined to them in the marriage bond or whom their right hands possess," Muhammad Asad made the following important observations: "Most of the commentators assume unquestioningly that this relates to female slaves… This conventional interpretation is, in my opinion, inadmissible inasmuch as it is based on the assumption that sexual intercourse with one's slave is permitted without marriage; an assumption which is contradicted by the Qur'an itself (4:3, 4:24-25, and 24:32)" … (579, note 3)

4.6 Conclusions

"Contrary to the popular view and the practice of many Muslims in the past centuries," notes Muhammad Asad in his commentary on 4:3, "neither the Qur'an nor the life-example of the Prophet provides any sanction for sexual intercourse *without marriage*" (118, note 4). Referring to 33:50, Asad asserts, "Islam does not countenance any form of concubinage and categorically prohibits sexual relations between a man and a woman unless they are lawfully married to one another" (El Hamel 31). As Asad explains in his commentary on 2:177, "the abolition of slavery is one of the social objectives of Islam" (46, note 146). Finally, and most importantly, he concludes that "Islamic law has from its very beginning aimed at an abolition of slavery as a social institution, and that its prohibition in modern times constitutes no more than a final implementation of that aim" (Asad 602, note 46). Many Muslims cannot agree with him more.

Chapter Five

Opposing Abolition

5.1 Introduction

As *Slavery & Islam* manifests, Jonathan A.C. Brown is entirely familiar with the writings of Muslim abolitionists and the evidence they presented to oppose slavery and concubinage. Rather than reinforce their views, and strengthen them, out of love and respect for Islam, the Qur'an, the Prophet, and human rights and dignity, the white American academic devotes an excessive amount of time and energy undermining their arguments as un-Qur'anic, un-prophetic, and un-Islamic, in his bulky work. Not only is he on the wrong side of Islam, opponents insist, but he is on the wrong side of humanity along with all those who enshrined evil and immorality and attributed it to the Prophet and God. For critics, they stand with the wicked rather than flee from evil with the righteous. Apologists for slavery and concubinage can be compared to pillars of salt, like the wife of Lot, left behind in Sodom and Gomorrah as testaments to the iniquities they justified.

5.2 Jews, Christians, and Slavery

How many modern and contemporary Jews and Christians justify and promote slavery in the name of religion? How many defend slavery in the name of Moses or Jesus? How many insist that God has ordained slavery and concubinage? On the contrary, their exegetes insist that God never approved such practices. Muslims, it seems, have a lot of moral growing up to do. Yes, indeed, the Bible contains some objectively repulsive content. As the "Good" Book commands,

> When you march up to attack a city, make its people an offer of peace. If they accept and open their gates, all the people in it shall be subject to forced labor and shall work for you. If they refuse to make peace and they engage you in battle, lay siege to that city. When the Lord your God delivers it into your hand, put to the sword all the men in it. As for the women, the children, the livestock, and everything else in the city, you may take these as plunder for yourselves. And you may use the plunder the Lord your God gives you from your enemies. (Deuteronomy 20: 10-14)

What other options did people have at the time? The infidels used to exterminate

50 Islam & Slavery

all: men, women, and children. Killing the male combatants, and enslaving their women and children was a lesser evil, but an evil nonetheless, compared to complete extermination and annihilation. What is more, without men, women, and children were helpless and defenseless. They would have been massacred or enslaved by others. Otherwise, they would have starved to death. So, putting them to the sword would have been viewed as more merciful according to the standards of the age.

From our present vantage point, the Bible is no paragon of morality. Despite the delusions of Christian fundamentalists, Biblical sexuality was not monogamous. Polygyny was normative. Over forty biblical figures had multiple wives, including David, who had eight while Solomon, had seven hundred wives and three hundred concubines (1 Kings 11). Concubinage finds far more support in the Bible than in the Qur'an. In the Bible, God commands the Israelites to slaughter all the non-virgin Midianite women captured in war, with all the male children, keeping only the virgin girls (Numbers 31: 17-18).

While the verses in question make most rational Christians cringe, some extremists and fundamentalists defend the rape and murder of these women as "God's judgment." The problem with "God told me so" is that He tells different things to different people. With rare exception, the "God said so" is "I said so." It is the oldest scam in the Good Book. These criminal commands come not from God but from men with god-complexes. The Muslims, at least, enslaved all captives instead of slaughtering them and took no issue with taking married women as concubines. So, in good faith, we cannot criticize Islam's failings without criticizing the failings of Judaism and Christianity. On the contrary, Muslims must work with anti-slavery activists of all faith traditions and secular ones. Religion may divide, but reason unites.

5.3 Aggressive *Jihad*

Despite the claims of Islamic apologists, like the American scholar Omar Suleiman (b. 1986), for whom "the concept of *riqq* (slavery) in Islam is a condition (as opposed to a status) that dealt with captivity, specifically after a war," Muslims did not limit themselves to enslaving people in defensive wars. They organized aggressive, imperialistic wars and invasions to enslave free people of other races and religions. The early Arab Muslims wanted slaves. They invaded North Africa to capture slaves. They demanded that women and children be provided to them as slaves as a form of taxation. This requirement even applied to Imazighen who had embraced Islam. "Give us your virgin daughters," they demanded, just like the Serbian Chetniks did to Bosnian Muslims. Arab Muslims acted like Pharoah and the worst of infidels.

From its dawn in the seventh century until its decline in the twentieth century, the harvesting of slaves from black Africa, North Africa, Europe, and Asia, was synonymous with Islam. The entire economy of the Crimean Khanate was based on capturing Christian women and children and selling them to the Ottoman

Empire as slaves, concubines, and eunuchs. When will Muslims reckon with their past? As early as the thirteenth century, Alfonso the Wise (1221-1284) admitted that slavery was evil and contrary to natural justice. Unlike other European slave codes, the one detailed in the *Siete Partidas* does not view slavery as God's will or a curse upon blacks. On the contrary, it describes it in the following terms,

> Slavery is the most vile and despicable practice that exists among men. It places man, who is the most noble and free creature among all the creatures that God created, in the power of another, who can do with him as he pleases, even power over life and death. Slavery is so contemptible that the one who falls subject to it loses the power to do as he pleases. Moreover, he lose powers over his own person, only being able to do what his master orders. (89)

Although the Roman Catholic Church played a significant role in slavery, it had the moral maturity to repent and atone. Consequently, it revised its teachings. The *Catechism of the Catholic Church* now asserts that:

> 2414 The seventh commandment forbids acts or enterprises that for any reason -- selfish or ideological, commercial, or totalitarian -- lead to the enslavement of human beings, to their being bought, sold, and exchanged like merchandise, in disregard for their personal dignity. It is a sin against the dignity of persons and their fundamental rights to reduce them by violence to their productive value or to a source of profit. St. Paul directed a Christian master to treat his Christian slave "no longer as a slave but more than a slave, as a beloved brother ... both in the flesh and in the Lord."

The Anglican Church has apologized for its role in slavery. The Dutch Reformed Church, and other South African churches, apologized for creating a theology of apartheid and not opposing it. This is called self-critical faith which is conscious of the danger of particular religious ideas. If Christians have deified Christ, believing that God was made flesh, many Muslims have deified the Qur'an, believing that it was God made book. This compels some of them to follow the Qur'an literally and view all of its content as binding until the end of time, an attitude that many Sunnis apply to the sayings attributed to the Prophet Muhammad.

Religion, however, is not absolute truth. As such, it should be treated as guidelines and not strict rules. As Rachel S. Mikva, the American rabbi and professor, recognizes, "religion consists of humanly constructed responses to what a community understands as divine revelation" (5). It has both the power to harm and to heal (6). Although their inspiration is presumed to be divine by many of their followers, scriptures are human documents (42). They have been used to uphold slavery, discrimination, and other abominations (4). As Mikva notes, every reading is a human interpretation (35). As Shakespeare noted, even "the

52 Islam & Slavery

devil can cite Scripture for his purpose" (35). And so have many men. Jewish, Christian, and Muslim scholars have recognized the danger of specific passages and have attempted to mitigate them (42). The Torah may command that "Both thy bondmen, and thy bondmaids, which thou shalt have, shall be of the heathen that are round about you" (Leviticus 25:44); however, you will not find Jewish rabbis and laypeople calling its implementation.

Rather than follow scripture to the letter, we should focus on its overall spirit. For Mikva, this "self-critical faith does not require that we discard tradition... instead, it recovers the diversity of voices" (8). It recognizes the reality of polysemy and pluralism and the hermeneutical openness of scripture (46-47). In the grocery store of Islam, no lanes are off limits. And we should also feel free to shop from other stores if they offer superior products. The early Muslims absorbed influences from all sources, some good and some bad. As the Prophet Muhammad said, "Seek knowledge even in China" (Bayhaqi, Ibn 'Abd al-Barr, Khatib al-Baghdadi, Tabarsi 338). He said, "Learn wisdom, even from the infidels [*mushrikin*]" (Tabarsi 336). He asserted that "wisdom is the lost property of the believers. Wherever he finds it, he is most deserving of it" (Tirmidhi and Suyuti). After all, God's grace was not limited to the Qur'an. He also gave us *al-hikmah* or wisdom (6:89; 2:119; 2:151; 2:269; 5:110; 17:39). As we read in the Qur'an, "We have granted the Book and the Wisdom" (2:231). Perverted interpretations of Islam are produced by those who try to follow the Qur'an and the *hadith* without relying on logic, reason, knowledge, and wisdom. God, in the Qur'an, calls for critical thinking. Relying on the Qur'an and Wisdom is the *sunnah* of God (33:62). As Hasan Hashmi argues in *Islamic Jurisprudence in Early Islam*, solutions to new issues must not be found in the Qur'an and *sunnah*: they simply must not be against them. As per the teachings of the Prophet Muhammad, Muslims should benefit from the laws of other nations.

Although many Sunnis and Shiites believe in abrogation, the rule was for the more intolerant verses to abrogate the tolerant ones; and the more extreme ones to abolish the moderate ones. Rather than espouse a theory of abrogation, an occasionalist approach is in order, namely, recognizing that certain verses apply in specific times, places, and circumstances, while some apply in others. All too often, people who refuse to accept the literal meaning of a verse, treating it allegorically or as a temporary injunction, are accused of blasphemy, apostasy, and infidelity.

When will Muslims have the moral fortitude to cease making excuses for the crimes of their predecessors and recognize that slavery and sexual bondage were as wrong then as they are now? Most Jews and Christians historicize the Old and New Testaments. They do not follow them blindly and to the letter and recognize the danger of doing so. Jewish rabbis ruled that the laws of the present take precedent over the laws of the past. They realized certain verses could be interpreted dangerously and took steps to prevent that. For Muslims, the time for *tawbah* is long overdue.

Ahmad ibn Khalid al-Nasiri (1834-1897), the Moroccan historian, had the humanity and the decency to oppose slavery and bondage in the nineteenth century. He believed only combatants taken in *jihad* in the time Prophet Muhammad could be taken as prisoners of war (Azumah 153). His treatise against slavery is a plea for God's forgiveness for Muslims because "we have wronged ourselves, and if you do not pardon us and have mercy upon us, we shall be among those who suffer (eternal) loss" (Azumah 153). Not only did he view slavery as prohibited, but it was also a major sin that incurred eternal damnation. He treated the trade in black Muslims as "heinous" and considered it "one of the foulest and gravest evils perpetrated upon God's religion" (Segal 65; Chebel 331).

Speaking of the black African Muslims enslaved and sold in Morocco, Nasiri asked: "How can any man with the least bit of religious scruples acquire such people?" (Chebel 332). Moreover, "how could he have the audacity to take their women as concubines when it is known, according to law, that one should never have intimate relations with women of doubtful condition?" (Chebel 332-333).

"Refreshing as al-Nasiri's views are," notes John Allembillah Azumah, a scholar of Islam and Christianity, an ex-Muslim, and an ordained Ghanaian minister in the Presbyterian Church, "his position was a rare one as far as Muslim attitudes to slavery are concerned" (153). The dominant Muslim view on slavery was shared by the sultan of Morocco in 1842 in a letter he wrote to the British consul general of his kingdom:

> Be it known to you, that the traffic in slaves is a matter on which all sects and nations have agreed from the time of the sons of Adam... up to this day -- and we are not aware of its being prohibited by the laws of any sect, and no one need ask this question, the same being manifest to both high and low and requires no more demonstration that the light of day. (Azumah 153; Lewis 3)

For the sultan of Morocco, the very thought that slavery was wrong or should be abolished was astonishing and perplexing. Manifesting his complete and utter ignorance of history, culture, and religion, he falsely believed that all humans had viewed it as lawful since the dawn of humanity. The consensus was not only Islamic, but it was universal. Hence, the question of the validity and legality of slavery does not arise. Consequently, no evidence is required to prove its permissibility. In the view of the sultan, the lawful nature of slavery was as obvious as day and night.

The fact remains, however, that the case for the Islamicity of slavery is entirely implicit or even imaginary. It is the product of perverse fantasy. No Qur'anic verse explicitly commands or orders the perpetuation of slavery. There are, however, explicit Qur'anic verses that call for emancipating slaves. They supersede the implicit, descriptive, and occasionalist ones and serve as prescriptive and binding ones. Even if the emancipatory verses in question are taken as aspirational, an ideal that society should strive to meet, they negate the

54 Islam & Slavery

view that slavery should be fixed for all times and that Muslims should remain morally stagnant, stuck in cement, frozen, and fossilized.

5.4 Freedom is Not a Human Right in Islam

Not only does Brown argue that slavery is Islamic, prophetic, and Qur'anic, but he insists that freedom is not a human right in the *shari'ah* (299-302). That is strange if one considers the fact that the Qur'an speaks of freedom on so many occasions (2:117; 2:178; 2:221: 4:3; 4:24; 4:25; 4:36; 4:92; 5:89; 9:60; 23:6; 24:31: 24:32: 24:33; 24:58: 24:58; 30:28; 33:50; 33:52; 33:55; 70:30) and actively encourages the emancipation of those deprived of liberty (2:117; 4:25; 4:92; 5:89; 14:31; 24:33: 58:3; 90:1-20) (Freamon 2019: 492-493: note 86; 489: note 76).

As Tahir Haddad (1899-1936) grasped, "Islam is the religion of freedom" and its "highest aim is equality among all God's creatures" (Mir-Hosseini 33). In fact, "the Qur'anic law presumes that all human beings are free" (Freamon 1998: 34). As such, "the concept of freedom in the Qur'an is at once both theological and socio-legal" (1998: 34). It denotes "the absence of slavery" (1998: 34-35). According to the Qur'an, "freedom... is the presumptive and natural state of being, and the preferred mode of action for all humankind" (1998: 40). Most importantly, the Qur'an associates human freedom with justice (1998: 35).

For Cyrille Moreno al-'Ajami, the Qur'an provides ontological freedom, individual freedom, freedom of thought, freedom of belief, as well as civil liberty (2020: 174-177). So central was justice to some Muslims, like the 'Ibadis, the Imamis, and the *mu'tazila*, that they include *'adl* or divine justice in their creeds. The latter, in particular, developed a systematic theology of justice, freedom, and reason (Akyol 2022: 18-21) which, if followed to its logical conclusions, would have resulted in the abolition of slavery. In the mind of Farabi (c. 870- c. 950/951), the Islamic philosopher and jurist, a "virtuous city" or society was founded on *hurriyyah* or freedom (Aykol 2022: 143).

For most Muslims, however, only the People of the Book, under the protection of the Islamic state, had conditional rights. Other non-Muslims from the Land of Disbelief "had no inherent rights thanks to their mere humanity" (Akyol 2022: 59). For Sunni jurists, like Malik (711-795), Muslims had the right to attack non-Muslims outside the Islamic state, slaughter their men, enslave their women and children, and seize their property (Akyol 2022: 271: note 41). How is that for "interfaith harmony" and "co-existence?" As Akyol notes, "Ibn Rushd, along with Ibn al-'Arabi, opposed this view which sanctioned 'the actions of the powerful... without regard to the demands of justice'" (2022: 271: note 41).

If justice must come first, and the *shari'ah* must come second, as the *mu'tazila* believe, immoral and unethical edicts could not prevail. There was always the right, even the requirement, to revoke and reinterpret them. However, for Sunni and Shiite jurists, the law came first, and justice followed. It was for this reason that Mankdim Shashdiw (d. 1034), a descendant of Husayn (626-680), and a student al-Qadi 'Abd al-Jabbar (935-1025), the Mutazilite theologian,

Chapter Five

warned that the exegesis of the Qur'an "should not be done by one who does not have the prior knowledge of the justice of God through reason" (Akyol 2022: 76).

While freedom, as an irrevocable human right, is often traced to Western origins, Nathaniel Mathews notes,

> It has other global, non-Western genealogies that are both Muslim and African. Haitian revolutionaries, among whom were African Muslims, were first among those insisting on this freedom in their struggle to end slavery in the late 1700s. At around the same time, the West African Muslim ruler Abdul Kader Kane sought to abolish the slave trade in his realm, in order to protect his subjects from the French-controlled slave trade at Saint Louis.

In fact, 'Abd al-Qadir Kan (d. 1806) launched an apocalyptic war of emancipation in 1786. As Ware, the historian of West Africa, notes, "some must have thought that the wholesale enslavement of the Muslims and the desecration of the Walking Qur'an were signs of Armageddon's approach" (129). Some surely suspected that he was the Mahdi (129). While "the Moors wanted to ravage everything and take as many slaves as they could," the Peuls, 'Abd al-Qadir's people, wanted to bring them into Islam: "they cried liberty everywhere: they said… they came to set them free" (Ware 129).

In 1882, John Scott, the British jurist, argued in a case heard before the Egyptian Court of Appeal, that "the form of slavery that existed in Africa was not sanctioned by the Qur'an" (Rodriguez 146). In his words,

> Does the Koran, after all, sanction this modern form of slavery? I am inclined to think that the Mahomedan authorities who were consulted in 1877 opined that it did not, and I believe they were right. I have searched the Koran from end to end, and I find that the retention of captives taken in war and not ransomed is the only form of slavery sanctioned by Mahomet (Koran, ch. 47, v. 4 and 5).

> The Prophet would have shrunken with horror from the present system, under which men, women, and children are hurried from their tropical homes, dragged in chains, driven with whips down to the seacoast, or to the river, or to the desert tracks, and finally, a miserable remnant of them sold in the market at Cairo or Constantinople.

> "Show kindness to your slaves" (ch. 4, v. 40), says Mahomet, and again "Alms should buy the freedom of slaves" (ch. 9, 60). But the great doctrine of emancipation itself is preached in one remarkable injunction which might well be printed in letters of gold on the walls of every Mahomedan mosque as a preamble to an Arabic translation of the slave trade convention. It runs thus: "If any one of your slaves asks from you his freedom give it to him if you judge him worthy of it; grant them a little of the goods which God has granted you" (ch. 24, v. 33). (Rodriguez 488)

In *Slavery in Islam* or *al-Riqq fi al-Islam*, a pamphlet published in French in 1888, and in Arabic in 1892, Ahmad Bek Shafiq, the son of a Circassian slave woman, and an associate of Muhammad 'Abdu, insisted that the gradualist abolitionist program of the Prophet Muhammad intended not only to improve the conditions of slaves but also to "dry up the sources of slavery" (Salem 253). Since "the existing slaves of the Muslims could not be shown to have been captured in a just *jihad*," he "recommended the immediate abolition of slavery among Muslims" (Salem 253).

So, is freedom a human right in Islam, or is it not? Ghulam Ahmed Perwez (1903-1985), the rationalist Qur'an scholar, believed that freedom transcended all forms of authority (Kurzman 24). For Malek Chebel, it is an inalienable right in Islam, like in all other civilizations (492). For Mohamed Talbi (1921-2017), the Tunisian historian, it was synonymous with Islam. In his words, "My religion is freedom" (Zouari). "I will never cease to state that Islam gives us the right to freedom," he insisted, "including the freedom to insult God" (Zouari). As he asserted, "terrorism is the negation of freedom" (Zouari).

5.5 Islam is Submission, Subjugation, and Slavery: Not Freedom

As if it were not despicable enough to attack, invade, and conquer sovereign non-Muslim people, massacre their men, enslave their children, transform their boys into eunuchs and turn their girls and boys into sex toys, strippers, and slaves of male lust, lasciviousness, degeneracy, and depravity, Brown proceeds to list the arguments deployed by Sunni jurists to justify enslaving "apostate Muslims or Muslims declared to be unbelievers" which, of course, includes Twelver Shiites (2020: 303-307). Non-Muslims, it would seem, are not safe from Muslims, but neither are the "wrong kind" of Muslims safe from them. "We will kill your men and rape your women." That was, and remains, the moto and war cry of Islamist terrorists and imperialists of all ages. So what has changed? The fact that Western turncoats and traitors embraced Islam, betrayed their countries, cultures, and civilizations, to join the Islamist enemy hordes and defend the Islamic nature of slavery and concubinage?

"The Qur'an," claims Brown, "seems very clearly to permit slavery" (2020: 202). He insists that God and the Prophet Muhammad allowed, condoned, and supported it (2020: 7, 9, 202). "I believe slavery is wrong," claims Brown meekly after writing hundreds of pages justifying and rationalizing it according to the Qur'an, the *hadith*, and the *shari'ah* (2020: 275). However, this apparent double-speak, as critics perceive it, comes with an important disclaimer. "As a Muslim myself," he writes, "I cannot condemn it as grossly, intrinsically immoral across space and time. To do so would be to condemn the Qur'an, the Prophet Muhammad, and God's law as morally compromised" (Brown 275).

If this is the purportedly pious premise upon which Brown operates then, presumably, critics might conclude that he feels the same way when it comes to aggressive *jihad*, polygyny, wife beating, female genital mutilation, and jurisprudentially justified misogyny, as well as sexism, gender inequality, sexual segregation, child marriage, and sex with nine-year-old girls. After all, they all form part of the same patriarchal continuum which is viewed as sacred by paleo-conservative Muslims.

Why were Muslim jurists intransigent in opposing abolition? Only because slavery, concubinage, and polygyny formed the foundation of Islamic family and inheritance law. If slavery were prohibited, feared the jurists, "Islamic" society would collapse. The fact of the matter is that it did not. With the abolition of slavery, however, came the decline, and virtual disappearance, of polygyny in the Muslim world. This is proof positive that these institutions are interconnected.

If we can eradicate slavery without endangering Islam, we can do the same with other problematic practices. Should Muslims beat their "rebellious" wives, as per 4:34? Should husbands lock up their unfaithful wives until they die, as per 4:15? Should they insist upon cutting off the hands of thieves as per 5:38? Should Muslims crucify people "who wage war on God and His Messenger" or cut off their hands and feet on opposite sides as per 5:33?

Are Muslims who question such practices, stressing that they were temporal, metaphorical, or misinterpreted, hypocrites and infidels in the eyes of Brown? Perhaps they are. After all, those who endorse such positions draw upon the Qur'an, the sayings and the actions of the Prophet, the companions, and the successors as proof. They are supported by fourteen hundred years of Islamic jurisprudence. Maybe moderate Muslims are wrong. Maybe the extremist Muslims are right.

If we believe in Brown, critics could argue, that appears to be the case; namely, the Qur'an, the *hadith*, and Islamic law allow or allowed Muslims to attack non-Muslims, slaughter their men, take their girls and women as sex slaves, and rape or "have sex" with them in the name of God and His Prophet. No person of faith and conscience could believe such things. "Exalted be God in His limitless glory, Lord of the Throne, who is far above anything they describe" (21:22).

5.6 Conclusions

As far as morally minded, ethically elevated, and logically thinking rationalist Muslims are concerned; namely, those who believe that Islam must adapt to every age, we should not be the slaves of jurists past. We should live by twenty-first-century laws, not seventh-century ones. Laws are time-bound. They can, do, and should evolve. Only ethical principles transcend time and place. The spirit of the law and not its letter takes primacy. The Qur'an does not say: "Keep us at the same point." It says, "Guide us on the straight path" (1:6). We are not meant to be stationary. We are mean to move, develop, and grow. The straight path is not a precise place. It is a journey. We are meant to walk the path of spiritual perfection. Union with God is the destination. We should not stand still or backtrack.

Slavery and concubinage oppose the spiritual and moral message of the Qur'an and the ethical teachings of God's Messenger. Islam, in the view of moral Muslims, inherently opposes slavery and sexual bondage. Aggressive *jihads* and slave raids violate God's moral laws. Freedom is a fundamental and inalienable human right in Islam. The religion with God is not submission, subjugation, and slavery to other human beings. It is surrender to the Creator and justice, mercy, and compassion toward His Creation. This is the meaning of liberty and the true meaning of "there is no god but God, and Muhammad is His Servant and Messenger."

The so-called *shari'ah*, which is presented as Islamic law, consists of the sole opinions of male interpreters and jurists over the past fourteen centuries and has resulted in injustices against women (Barazangi 2016: 182). "Why," she asks, "has the authority to interpret 'religious texts' been exclusive to male religious elites?" (2006: 113). Since the jurists conceived of God as a Slave-Master, this colored their entire worldview, and they created social hierarchies that mirrored this ontological reality. As Kecia Ali (b. 1972), the American academic who specializes in Islamic jurisprudence, ethics, women, gender, and biography, notes, "slavery … was central to the jurists' conceptual world… it affected how marriage and gender were thought about" (2010: 8).

Since the Qur'an supposedly said that "men have a degree over [women]" (2:228), one of many misinterpreted and mistranslated verses, most jurists concluded that men were superior and that women were inferior. They insisted that one of the degrees of superiority they had over women was the right to take concubines (Shaikh 148). The rise and spread of Sufism and Islamic asceticism was part of a spiritual and social movement of protest against the hedonism that accompanied conquest (Shaikh 42). They responded to sexual excess with sexual satiety (Shaikh 42). They opposed harem culture and sexual degeneracy by practicing and promoting celibacy (Shaikh 42). Even those who married insisted upon chastity and faithfulness.

Unlike the jurists who viewed God as a Supreme Slave-Master, Sufis like Fakhruddin al-'Iraqi (1213-1289) viewed God as Loving, professing that "There is no God but Love." A worldview centered on an eternally Loving God produces radically different legal results and societal outcomes than one centered on a God that is a Wrathful and Deceiving Slave Master. While God is not our biological father, and we are not his biological children, He is our Father, and She is our Mother. The profound imbalance found in many forms of Islam results from losing this equilibrium between the Sacred Masculine and the Sacred Feminine. "Honor your Father and your Mother," commanded God in the Ten Commandments. If the Qur'an commands human beings "to honor and revere the wombs (that bore you)" (4:1), how can a man sexually enslave a girl or a woman, force himself upon her, and sexually assault her? How can a man engage in the sexual trafficking of females? Surely, such a man is neither a man nor a Muslim. To be a Muslim, one must first be human.

Chapter Six

Snake Oil Salesmen
and Merchants of Religion

6.1 Introduction

Many Muslim converts embraced Islam because they were told that it stood for freedom, justice, and equality, that it opposed racism and sexism, that it was committed to social justice, and that it had abolished slavery. According to Jonathan A.C. Brown, it would seem, that was not at all the case. Were they lied to? They were told that Christianity was the religion of the slave master and that Islam was the religion of liberty. Were they sold snake oil? They were told that Islam was a religion of equality. Were they misled? They were told that Islam rejected racism. Were they deceived? They were told that Islam honored women. Were they conned? They were told that Islam was the black man's religion, the religion of people of color, and the religion of all the oppressed of the earth. Were they played? Were they deliberately duped and deceived? Perhaps they were. Then again, perhaps they were not. Religions have many different interpretations. They all have their fundamentalists and extremists. Zionist terrorists do not speak for Judaism. Hindu extremists do not exemplify Hinduism. Buddhist fanatics are not the embodiment of Buddhism. Christian fascists and white supremacists do not represent Christianity. Likewise, radical Islamists and Muslim fundamentalists do not speak for Islam. As Muhammad Diakho has established, Islam and Slave Master Islam are not the same. They are two entirely different entities.

6.2 Prime Swampland for Sale

Although it is calculated that ten to twenty percent of enslaved human beings of African origin in the United States were Muslims -- including abolitionists like Muhammad 'Ali ibn Said (1833-1882), Salih Bilali, Yarrow Marmood, Omar ibn Sayyid (1770-1864), and Abrahim Abdul Rahman ibn Sori (1762-1829) -- and memories of the faith persisted in fragmented forms among some of their descendants, word of Islam reached many Americans and Westerners via the teachings of W.D. Fard, Elijah Muhammad (1897-1975), and Malcolm X (1925-1965). In the words of the Honorable Elijah Muhammad,

> Allah came to us from the Holy City of Mecca, Arabia, in 1930… He came alone… He taught us the truth of how we were made slaves, and how we are kept in slavery by the slave-masters' children. Allah declared the doom of America, for her evils to us it was past due, and that she is number one to be destroyed.

The Islam taught by Master Fard was adamantly anti-slavery. He blamed white Christian devils for destroying black civilization and enslaving black people (Fard). He called for murdering the devil "because he is one hundred percent wicked and will not keep and obey the laws of Islam" (Fard). His was an Islam of "freedom, justice, and equality" (Fard). Elijah Muhammad adhered to this emancipatory Islam, which equated Islam with liberty and Christianity with slavery, exploitation, degradation, oppression, and dehumanization. However, the fact is that Islam did not come to the African continent peacefully, and its spread was primarily the result of coercion as opposed to conviction and voluntary conversion. As far as monotheistic religions were concerned, Christianity and Judaism have far deeper roots in Africa than Islam.

Malcolm X may have mistakenly perceived Islam to be an African religion. The fact is that it was an Arab religion that was spread through the Arabization of Africa. As sad as it is to say, the companions of the Prophet described Islam as *din al-'arab* or the religion of the Arabs. The Umayyads had little interest in disseminating Islam among non-Arabs and treated non-Arab Muslims as second-class citizens in both the Middle East and al-Andalus. As Richard N. Fry (1920-2014), the American scholar of Iranian and Central Asian studies, explains,

> In the first century of the Islamic conquests, ideology reverted in some degree to ancient concepts. The Arab tribes believed that Islam was an Arab religion, restricted to tribesmen and their clients. To become a Muslim meant to become an Arab: to break with one's previous community and faith, learn Arabic, and become a part of the Arab community, the *ummah*. (Morrow 2021: 151)

This Arab chauvinism and racism even found its way into Twelver Shiite traditions. The sixth Imam, for example, is cited as saying that "We are Quraysh, our Shias are Arabs, and our enemies are non-Arabs," as well as "We are the Arabs, our Shias are slaves, and the rest of people are flies" (Majlisi vol. 64: 174, 175, 178). Such Arab supremacy is also found in Sunni sources. In his *Reliance of the Traveler,* Abu al-'Abbas Ahmad ibn al-Naqib al-Misri (1302-1367) ruled that it was detestable for Arab women to marry non-Arab men. As Ibn Taymiyyah (1263-1328) stated,

> Indeed it is the belief of the Ahlus-Sunnah wal Jama'ah that the race of Arabs is superior to the race of non-Arabs, the Hebrews (Jews), the Syrians (Arameans), the Romans (Europeans), the Persians, and others. And indeed the Quraysh … is the most superior among the Arabs. And indeed the Banu Hashim … is the most superior among the Quraysh.

> And indeed the Prophet … is the most superior of the Banu Hashim, for he is the most superior of all creation by his own self, and also the most superior among them because of his lineage (ancestry). (Prima Qur'an)

When Malcolm X broke from the Nation of Islam, he rejected the so-called heterodox and purportedly heretical teachings of the Nation of Islam of W.D. Fard and Elijah Muhammad. However, he continued to conceive of Islam as fundamentally opposed to slavery. He taught that Christianity was the religion of European slave traders and that Islam provided freedom to African people. He appears oblivious that "Islamic traders were themselves engaged in the slave trade in East Africa long before Europeans began acquiring their first slaves" (Rosenberg). Perhaps this was a product of willful ignorance. Perhaps Malcolm X was in denial himself. Perhaps he was trying to reconcile the religious mythology of Islam that he had been taught with the historical reality of Islam.

Although slavery had a basis in the Old Testament, one would be hard-pressed to find support for it in the New Testament. In fact, the early Christians used to free enslaved people. If later Christians engaged in slavery, it was not because of the teachings of Jesus but despite them. Unbeknownst to Malcolm X, or deliberately ignored as an inconvenient truth, "Islamic" slavery was justified based on the Qur'an, the practice and teachings of the Prophet Muhammad, and a vast body of Islamic jurisprudence on the subject. In Christianity, the theological basis for slavery was flimsy. One could not claim that Jesus supported slavery. While much slavery was committed in the name of Christ, "there is, and always has been, something shameful and repugnant about slavery to most Christian minds" (Fregosi 185). In the Christian world, there was a long current of critics who opposed slavery from early times to modern ones.

In Islam, however, the acceptance of slavery was deeply entrenched and only sporadically questioned or opposed. Plenty of so-called proof was presented, claiming that God and His Prophet endorsed it. Slavery did predate Islam and has been practiced in Africa since ancient times; however, "the slave trade had fallen into Arab hands at the time of the Muslim conquests" (Wallbank 356-357). The indigenous African slavery, which included debt bondage, was totally different from the mass slavery that Arab Muslims instituted. As Rosenberg points out,

> Malcolm lightly skips over the connection between Islam and the slave trade of the African East Coast even though, in terms of the slaves transported, its total numbers were greater than the Atlantic slave trade. Which is to say, from the seventh century onward, Islamic slave traders were buying and selling African slaves.

As for the claim that African Americans descend from enslaved Muslims who had their Islamic religion torn from them, it has long been debunked. No more than ten to twenty percent of enslaved Africans were Muslims. The highest estimates conducted by academics suggest that they consisted of thirty percent of enslaved

Africans. However, that is a stretch. It is far from the eighty percent claimed by those involved in Islamic *da'wah*. Moreover, while Europeans purchased them on the West African coast, they were not captured and enslaved by them. Many of them were sold to them by black Africans who had purchased them from Arab and Berber slave traders who professed the Muslim faith. Pretending that Muslims did not play a significant role in the slave trade is like putting lipstick on a pig.

"Far from finding that the ancestors of American black families were descended from Africans practicing a non-slaveholding Islam," notes Roger E. Rosenberg, "historians can attest to the fact that practitioners of Islam bought and sold slaves freely, including Mongolians, Scandinavians, and Africans." Increasing numbers of black American Muslims get their origins traced through genetic testing. Some have traveled to Africa to get a sense of closure from the generational trauma of slavery and to reconnect themselves to Africa and Islam. To their dismay, many learned that their ancestors had been sold into slavery by Muslims and that the practice continues to this day in many parts of the continent. This is a tough pill to swallow. The shock that ensues in such people is hard to fathom.

Malcolm X lambasted and excoriated the white rapist slave master with unbridled hatred. Such behavior, however, was not permitted by the Roman Catholic Church, which prohibited Christian men from having sexual intercourse with their slaves. It was viewed as fornication, adultery, or rape, and the offspring were viewed as illegitimate. The 1685 *Code Noir* of the French stipulated that if a master, who was single, had children with a slave girl, he was obliged to marry and emancipate her, rendering any offspring from such unions both free and legitimate. Later French slave codes prohibited all sexual relations with slaves, including concubinage and marriage.

One can only imagine how shocked people like Malek Chebel were when they found that Islam had its own slave codes, as abhorrent as the ones created by Christians (Chebel 105-109; 339-363; Diakho 114-123). Far from fighting slavery, Muslims spread it wherever they went (Chebel 283). In fact, in all the lands of Islam, there was not a single place where slavery was never practiced (Chebel 72, 283). Millions upon millions of human being, stolen from their homelands, joined the plethora of zombies that worked, under the crack of the whip, in oases, factories, palaces, and quarries (Chebel 283).

As late as the early twentieth century, young, free Muslim girls, were being openly sold as concubines in Ottoman lands (Chebel 282). So ravenous were the Muslim slave traders, and so lust-crazed were harem owners, that they preyed upon young girls of their faith. In fact, as late as 1939, al-Azhar University issued an edict condemning the commerce in Muslim children conducted by Muslims themselves (Chebel 282). This practice continues through matrimonial slavery in which little girls are forced into marriage to older, wealthy, and often senile men, according to "tribal custom" (68). Furthermore, to this day, child slaves, boys, and girls, are sexually exploited in the brothels of Phuket, Bamako, Nairobi, Bombay,

Calcutta, and other large cities, including Arab ones (69). "How many women," asks Chebel, "are forced to provide sexual pleasure for the benefit of a pimp in Muslim Asia, Africa, and the Maghreb?" (67-68). If Islam has prohibited slavery for fourteen hundred years, asks Chebel, why does it remain so widespread in the lands of Islam? (12). He points out that Islam may be presented as a religion of sublime ethics, however, in reality, it is ignored and disdained (290).

Some Muslims claim that Christian soldiers used to rape Muslim women in Islamic Spain. While such crimes were committed in wars, and by all sides, the Spanish Christian laws of the time prohibited sexual assault. It is Islamic law that permitted men to take women captives and to have sex with them with or without their consent.

The situation of slave girls in the Protestant southern United States was similar to that of slave girls in the Muslim world. In the United States, Protestant men were entitled to exploit their female slaves sexually. Sexual abuse, rape, and forced pregnancies were rampant. They were abused by their masters, along with the children and relatives of their owners. They had no legal recourse before the law. Enslaved girls were sold at auctions into concubinage and fetched the highest prices.

Whether Malcolm X knew it or not, and whether he suppressed it, Islam, like southern American Protestant Christianity, permitted slave masters to have sex with their slave girls, irrespective of their sentiments or consent. Some jurists explicitly allowed Muslim men to tie up, rape, and beat their slave girls and their rebellious wives (see Morrow 2020). If their sex slaves gave them children, however, they were treated as legitimate, and their mothers could be emancipated after the death of their masters. Such a practice was present in the early French, Catholic, slave code but was notably absent from the Anglo-Protestant ones.

Islamist apologists may claim that Muslims treated their slaves better than Christians. The Christians, however, did not routinely emasculate boy slaves as did the Muslims. Unlike the Muslims, who prevented enslaved men from reproducing, even with enslaved women, reserving that right for themselves, Christians allowed black men to reproduce. The descendants of slaves in the Muslim world are matrilineal by descent. They are the progeny of Arab/Berber/Turkish/Persian men and enslaved women from Africa, Europe, and elsewhere. The plight of women owned by Muslim men was not measurably better than that of women owned by Christian men. The trauma, cruelty, and inhumanity were all the same. So what if some slave women rose to be concubines of caliphs and Imams. Some slave women rose to be the concubines of Founding Fathers like Thomas Jefferson (1743-1826).

Blacks from the Americas were told that Islam was the religion of their ancestors, only to discover that it was the religion of the slave masters who sold their ancestors to the merchant ships. Some Latinos were told that Islam was the religion of their ancestors when, in reality, it was the religion of the slave masters who conquered their people, killed their male ancestors, and took their female ancestors as sex slaves. Iberian/Spanish Muslims were known as *muwalladun* for a reason. It meant "sons of slave-mothers." They descended from Arab/Berber fathers and Hispanic slave girls.

Blacks from the Americas were told that it was psychologically and spiritually harmful for non-whites to identify with Christianity, which was presented as the religion of the racist oppressor and exploiter: the greatest kidnapper, murderer, robber, rapist, and enslaver on earth. However, black Africans were among the earliest Christians. Christianity was not imposed upon them in Ethiopia and elsewhere. If it is not psychologically and spiritually healthy for blacks to be Christians because the slave masters of their ancestors were Christians, how is it healthy for them to be Muslims when the masters of their ancestors, back in Africa, happened to be Muslims? As John Allembillah Azumah points out,

> Slavery was a very important part of Islamic expansion in West Africa, and in fact in the Sudan, and from the very earliest period of Islamic penetration of Africa. ... Slavery was a very endemic part of Islamic interaction with Africa. And in West Africa, the *jihad*'s period of the eighteenth and nineteenth centuries involved massive slave raiding and slave trading; and many of the slaves that were captured and sold and sent to the transatlantic slave trade [were captured by Muslims]; most of those who were doing the slaving at the time were Muslim communities. (Ibrahim)

As far as critics are concerned, the "Islam" that Brown defends is not what many Muslim converts signed up for. It is the same type of slave master religion that they embraced Islam to fight. They accepted a religion that opposes oppression, not one that condones, perpetrates, and perpetuates it. They placed their faith in a Messenger of Mercy, not a Prophet of Doom. They were presented a man like Moses, who freed the slaves, not a man who promoted imperialism, slavery, and sexual bondage. They were told that "Islam is freedom," only to discover that "Islam is submission." Raised to believe that God was their Father, that they were His children, and that God was Love, they were presented with a God who did not love like a Father and told that their relationship with the Divine was like that of a slave towards a master. This master/slave allegory colored all of Islamic law, even the relationship between a wife toward her husband. For men like Muhammad Farid Vajidi (1875/78-1954), the Egyptian Islamic scholar and Qur'anic commentator, the veil is symbolic proof that for a woman "there is only slavery" and that "she cannot be emancipated from this bondage" (Barlas 60).

Even the Islamic heaven is described as a celestial slave colony. In words attributed to the Prophet Muhammad, "There is in Paradise a market wherein there will be no buying or selling but will consist of men and women. When a man desires a beauty, he will have intercourse with it" (Khatib al-Tabrizi, and Ghazali). Although the Qur'anic description of Paradise and its pleasures are allegorical and tasteful, the *hadith* literature is sexually explicit and even pornographic. Men will have eternally erect penises that will never become limp, soft, and flaccid (Ibn Majah). They will have the strength of seventy to a hundred men (Tirmidhi, Ahmad, Bazzar, Ghazali, Tabarani).

Scores of traditions state that men will have seventy, seventy-two, or even five hundred houris, not to mention four thousand virgins and eight-thousand widows (Ghazali). One tradition attributed to the Prophet Muhammad, and cited by Ghazali, states that each Muslim man will have three hundred and forty-three thousand houris in heaven and enough strength every morning to cohabit with all of them (Islam). According to Majlisi, each man who goes to heaven will have eight hundred virgin girls, four thousand non-virgin women, and two houris to satisfy his sexual needs (Rahnema 114).

One tasteless tradition, attributed to God, promises men palaces containing "seventy thousand rooms" with "seventy thousand tents," each containing "seventy thousand carpets," upon which there are "seventy thousand houris" (Morrow 2015: 209) It seems to me that each man who makes it to Paradise will have sexual access to 1,680,700,000,000, 000,000,000,000 heavenly whores. It seems that heaven is not eternal rest after all. As the *hadith* literature promises, these white women, with transparent skin, perky breasts, and bulging vaginas, will please men perpetually. Many Muslims and converts to Islam want to be at one with the One, not indulge in the perverse sexual fantasies of teenage boys and depraved men who remain permanent adolescents. As Charles Upton (b. 1948), the American Sufi poet and philosopher, writes,

> How much of the spiritual life (it may sometimes be wondered) can be reduced to simple good taste? ... He who says, "not the Garden but the One who planted it! Will inherit the Garden"... He who says, "not pearl, nor coral, nor ruby, nor aquamarine, nor gold, nor silver, but the Owner of them!" will inherit the First Intellect, and the inner secrets of Love... (Morrow 2015: 216)

Fortunately, as Leena El-Ali has noted, the translations and interpretations of the Qur'anic verses that refer to houris have been sexualized by Muslim men (278). In reality, they refer to "purified spouses," both male and female (274, 279). If we return to the Qur'an, as we should, and as we must, we find that,

> the term *hur* is for all companions of paradise and remains genderless. Therefore, the best rendering of this term is "pure companions." This further underscores the doctrine that all rewards of paradise are equally for both men and women... There are no verses in the Qur'an which describe the graphic details found in Islamic secondary sources. The Qur'an furnishes no information as to what the nature of these relationships will entail other than companionship of some kind. (Islam: Sexy Female Virgins)

Patently, men projected their perversions upon the Qur'anic text and let their imaginations run wild when they invented traditions and attributed them to the Prophet Muhammad. The revolting and nauseating sex-slave harem culture of the Umayyads and the 'Abbasids, which was an illicit theft and hoarding of human wealth and potential, was projected onto Paradise, which was depicted in the *hadith* literature as an eternal orgy filled with heavenly harlots designed for the perverted sexual pleasures of men. Human women were designed to be the slaves of their husbands and masters in this life and condemned to be the same in the hereafter.

Even the houris of heaven will be forced to observe *purdah* or sexual segregation as they will be "reserved in pavilions" (55:72) (Sahih International), "guarded in pavilions" (Sherali), "closely guarded in pavilions" (Pickthall), "dwelling in tents" (Sarwar), "restrained in pavilions" (Mohsin Khan), "cloistered in pavilions" (Arberry), "sheltered in tents" (Malik), "reserved in pavilions" (Khattab), or "confined in pavilions" (Shakir) (55:72). Not only are females confined in this world, but they also seem to be confined in the hereafter for the rest of eternity. At least, that is how many Muslim scholars see this world and the next.

However, as Leena El-Ali observes, these translations and interpretations are tainted. The idea that women are confined or restrained "is surely counter-intuitive in the delightful and carefree Paradise the Qur'an describes" (279). "Linguistically," she notes, "the root word at play here is *qasr*, which can mean either 'palace' or 'limitation, restriction'" (279). "Does it make sense," she asks, "to 'restrict' the movements of these female heavenly beings to a particular structure there?" (279). Or "does it make more sense that the verse is saying that they are enjoying these pavilions that are more like palaces?" (279).

As Cyrille Moreno al-'Ajami explains, the "Islamic" paradise is merely the reflection of a sexist and phallocratic world. It is a place of eternal sexual excess where women are made solely to provide pleasure to men. It is one where men are eternally dominant and women are eternally submissive. "If this is heaven," he puts it bluntly, "then it is hell!" As he has shown, the verse that imagines houris "cloistered in tents" awaiting to be deflowered in full sexual segregation reflects the sexual fantasies of the exegetes. In reality, the verse speaks of "pure women resting in the shade" (55:72). It is more the image of women resting under the shade of pavilions on a paradisiacal beach. They are not rewards for eternally lustful men. They are being rewarded for their righteousness in a place of perpetual rest.

Many Muslim converts answered the call of Islam because it was anti-colonial, only to face people who peddle a racist, sexist, imperialistic Islam. They will have none of it! There is a civil war at the very heart of Islam. Its soul is on the line and its very claim to be a divinely revealed religion. An unjust god is no god at all! Muslim converts who are sound of mind and soul are not interested in leaders who enslaved and would enslave their people. They have always longed for liberators, messiahs, and saviors, those who break chains, not those who place

Chapter Six 67

people in them. As the research conducted by the Yaqeen Institute in 2016 has shown,

> the issue of slavery in Islam has become a recurring topic of concern, particularly as younger American Muslims are now more sensitive to the issues of social injustice around them. As one scholar who gave an in-depth lecture on this topic put it, "The 'Islam came to abolish slavery' response is simply insufficient." (Suleiman)

When it comes to addressing the deeply troubling issue of slavery in Islam, Muslims are faced with the "happy slave myth" of Islamic apologists, the Islamist slogan that "slavery is a *sunnah* that must be revived," the self-righteous colonialist paternalism of the Orientalists, and the demonization of Islam on the part of ex-Muslims like M.A. Khan. The few Muslim scholars who have tackled the topic are Westerners and the occasional secular, leftist, Arab. Most Muslims remain in deep denial regarding the magnitude and horror of slavery and concubinage in the "Islamic" world. They deny it outright. Otherwise, they paint a rosy picture. When they are presented with the facts, they accuse academics of exaggerating and ruining the image of Islam and Muslims.

Evading a problem does not resolve it. It has lingered and festered for over fourteen hundred years. The cancer in question has been spreading throughout the organism of Islam. The rot is damaging the structural integrity of the system. Treatment is in order. Amputation is required. Damage control is long overdue. Hence, the emancipatory efforts of Muslim scholars: they are the Bartolomé de las Casas of Islam (1484-1550). In contrast, Muslim supporters of "Islamic" slavery are like the Juan Ginés de Sepúlvedas of Islam (1494-1573), those who support the slave masters, landowners, and statesmen who benefited from the system.

6.3 Emancipatory Islam

Muslims with minds and morals are not interested in Uncle Tom, Jim Crow, or Klansman Islam. Theirs is the revolutionary, liberating Islam of W.D. Fard, Elijah Muhammad, and Malcolm X. Theirs is the Islam of the 1885 Malê Muslim slave rebellion in Brazil that was inspired by emancipatory Islamic teachings. Islam, we must admit, has been part of the problem, and its historical position on slavery has resulted in alienation and even apostasy. However, Islam has also been part of the solution as its teachings "provided the enslaved with resources for resistance and an identity" (El Hamel 10). In West Africa, and elsewhere in the Muslim world, "slaves… drew on Islamic resources to improve their personal situation, to press for reforms, and to critique or try to overthrow the institution as a whole" (Hanretta).

Fighting for freedom from outside of Islam was not feasible. The only practical option was to fight for freedom from inside of Islam, not to undermine, destroy, or alter it, but to fight those that did and who had hijacked the religion, violating its very principles. Islam, like any other religion, is a double-edged

68   Islam & Slavery

blade, a sword of Damocles that can be harnessed for good and harnessed for evil.
It can be invoked for purposes of liberation as well as purposes of subjugation.
Moral and rational human beings have no interest in the religion of the oppressors.
They stand firmly with the religion of the oppressed. As Martin Luther King, Jr.
(1929-1968), proclaimed, "Free at last, free at last, thank God almighty, we are
free at last."

6.4 Conclusions

As a matter of honesty and integrity, Muslims should have enough sense to admit
that their predecessors were right about certain things and wrong about others. As
far as Aslam Abdullah is concerned, "Islam abolished slavery, jurisprudence kept
it alive." Those who claim that the Qur'an endorses slavery are, in his mind, those
"who distort the Book;" those who say "It is from God -- but it is not from God.
And so they attribute lies to God knowingly" (3:78). As he stresses, God makes it
clear in the Qur'an that human beings should be the slaves to God alone and that
it is not befitting to be the slave of a human being (3:79). As 'Ali said, "All people
are born free except for those who (wrongfully) declare themselves to be slaves"
(qtd. Mashayekhi). "Do not be slaves for others," he said, "since God has
established you to be free" (qtd. Mashayekhi; see also Jordac (137).

As far as Edip Yüksel is concerned, "the Qur'an considers slavery to be
polytheism" (4:3,25,92; 5:89; 8:67; 24:32-33; 58:3; 90:13; 2:286; 12:39-42;
79:24) (89), "categorically rejects slavery, and considers it to be the greatest sin"
(3:79; 4:25,92; 5:89; 8:67; 24:32-33; 58:3; 90:13; 2:286; 12:39-42; 79:24) (101).
Far from the *sunnah* of the Prophet Muhammad, Yüksel writes that slavery was
"an evil practice of Pharoah and other polytheists" (103). Hence, "slavery is
prohibited by the Qur'an" (122; see also 153, 237, 347-348). It is an act of
idolatry. Pharoah said: "I am your Lord, Most High" (79:24). So God punished
him and made an example of him (79:25). The only Lord and Master is God.

Three quarters of the Qur'an consists of biblical stories. The story that is
emphasized the most is that of Moses and his struggle to free the enslaved
Hebrews from the yoke of Pharoah. Moses is mentioned one hundred and thirty-
six times in the Qur'an. In contrast, Abraham is mentioned sixty-nine times, Jesus
thirty-five times, and Muhammad, a mere four or five times. Opposing slavery is
a central theme in the Qur'an. Fighting for freedom is a core Qur'anic value. For
Malek Chebel, who witnessed that slavery was alive and well throughout the
Muslim world in the twenty-first century, the Qur'an is conspicuously on the side
of the slave, as opposed to the slave master (17). In his words, "Qur'anic morality
… defends the destitute" (17). When people embrace Islam, they are duty-bound
to emancipate their slaves.

When a man asked Muhammad how to earn heaven, the Prophet answered
without hesitation: "Free your brothers from the chains of slavery" (Chebel 17).
In another authentic tradition, the Messenger of God affirmed that "there is
nothing that God loves more than the emancipation of slaves" (Chebel 10). As

Chebel notes, many Muslims, both Arabs, and non-Arabs, only seem to have been pleased to do the exact opposite of what the Prophet taught (11).

"From a non-Muslim perspective," writes Azumah, "this faceless set of 'true,' 'pure,' and 'original' teaching and beliefs of Islam is not an issue" (234). As he notes, "The issue that concerns non-Muslims is 'Islam' as it is understood and lived by their Muslim relations and neighbors" (234). "It is this Islam," he stresses, "and not the so-called 'true' and 'original' Islam in textbooks, that affect non-Muslims" (234). In other words, Islam is what Muslims do. So, it is time they did the right thing, issued the proper rulings, and righted historical wrongs. They must stop using Islam "as a shield for the actions of past and present generations of Muslims" (177). If blacks wish to seek reparations from the West, states Larry Elder, they should also seek them from Arab and Muslim nations. Islamic civilization was built upon the backs of Africans, Berbers, Europeans, and other enslaved populations who served the empire as agricultural workers, soldiers, guards, domestic workers, entertainers, and sex slaves. The glitter of its "Golden Age" was the product of human servitude and suffering. The Righteous Republic envisaged by the Prophet Muhammad was turned into an Evil Empire.

Chapter Seven

Salvaging Scripture from the Slave Master

7.1 Introduction

If Muslims cannot salvage their scripture from immoral interpretations, how can they expect non-Muslims to do the same? If Muslims cannot reconsider slavery and concubinage, among other iniquities, injustices, and atrocities, then members of other faiths should feel entitled to follow their religious texts literally, even when they advocate abominations of desolation. After all, what is good for the goose is good for the gander. If Muslims wish to lead and inspire, they should do so by example. They should compete with others in deeds of righteousness, not wickedness (2:148).

7.2 Jewish and Christian Responses to Slavery

By failing to "kill both man and woman, infant and nursing child, ox and sheep, camel, and donkey" (1 Samuel 15:3), are Jews and Christians treating the Bible as morally compromised? By refusing to "kill all the boys... and every woman who has slept with a man" (Numbers 31:15), are Jews and Christians committing blasphemy? By failing to "slay ... old and young ... and little children and women" (Ezekiel 9:6), are Jews, and Christians defying the Divinity? If, contrary to the God of the Bible, Jews and Christians do not view the "dashing of little ones ... against the rock" (Psalm 137: 8-9) as a "happy" event, have they become apostates?

When Jews and Christians do not follow the Biblical example of cutting up concubines into twelve pieces (Judges 19:29), have they become unbelievers? When Jews and Christians refuse to heed the call to dash infants to pieces, loot houses, and violate women (Isaiah 13:9-16), are they hypocrites? When Jews and Christians view offering one's daughter as a burned sacrifice, to fulfill an oath, as evil (Judges 11:30-39), have they become infidels? If Jews and Christians refuse to take the Bible's threats of cannibalism and sexual assault seriously (Jeremiah 13: 15-26), are they questioning God? If Jews and Christians do not implement Old Testament law, including the killing of homosexuals (Leviticus 20:13), and the killing of children who curse their parents (20:9), are they waging war against God?

Most Jews and Christians have had the moral decency to "interpret away" certain potentially dangerous Biblical verses. Among Jewish people, "slavery became practically extinct in the Diaspora and was prohibited except insofar the secular laws allowed it" (Jewish Virtual Library). By the rise of Islam, concubinage had long declined among Jewish people, and their rabbis prohibited them from having sex with their female slaves (Robinson 96-97). Although Jewish rabbis were divided on the issue of concubinage in the past, "since more recent times it is unanimously accepted that the taking of a concubine is prohibited" (Jewish Virtual Library). If only that were the case for the *mujtahids*.

Muslims, with any sense of humanity and respect for the Divinity must do the same with any potentially problematic Qur'anic verse or prophetic tradition: not because they disbelieve in the Creator but precisely because they believe in the Creator. For Muslims, who believe in books made by men, as opposed to God, to whom no evil can be ascribed, this is nothing short of *kufr* or disbelief. It is not. The greatest act of disbelief is attributing evil to the One. It is an appeal to conscience. The pure of heart, soul, and mind are called to peer into themselves. They are a book. The world is a book. The universe is a book. Creation is a book. Those who know themselves know God. And they know, in their heart of hearts, in the depth of their soul, that kidnapping, enslaving, raping, selling, and purchasing women is nothing short of Satanic. This principle of appealing to one's heart is found in a tradition attributed to the Prophet Muhammad, which advises people to "ask your heart even if (people) advise you, advise you again, and then advise you again" (Ahmad).

7.3 Muslim Jurists Fully Embraced Slavery

Rather than abolish sexual slavery, Brown admits that Muslim jurists embraced the practice fully (2020: 81). Why, of course, it served their interests and those of the rulers they served. If Jewish and Christian law moved away from polygyny and sexual slavery, treating the offspring of sex slaves as illegitimate, argues Brown, Islamic law headed in the opposite direction, permitting them both (2020: 82).

In a slave society, jurists had two options: prohibit sex with slave girls -- despite abuses and little legal recourse for victims and violators -- or permit and regulate it, providing rights and offering avenues of emancipation. Muslim jurists opted to allow it. However, they could also have availed themselves of a third option: the prohibition of slavery and sexual bondage. Unfortunately, they lacked the moral fortitude to do so. However, the fact is that most of the male jurists who permitted sexual slavery were the owners of sex slaves. As Kecia Ali points out, both Shafi'i and Hanbal had children with sex slaves (2010: 22). Malik purchased three hundred sex slaves and had sex with a different one each night (2010: 22).

Is it conceivable that a slave master with sex slaves would condemn such a practice, thereby incriminating himself? They were hardly objective and impartial. They passed edicts that served their interests. They also served as *fatwa* factories for the obscenely rich and powerful. This should come as no surprise as we have no shortage of rubber stampers in our day and age, namely, Muslim scholars, who sell their souls to petroleum sheikhs, dictators, and despots -- as well as the self-proclaimed caliphs and Imams who feign to rule on behalf of God, the Prophet, and the Mahdi -- and who serve up edicts on demand to support their policies.

The Qur'an says that the color of Muslims is that of God (2:138). That means that Islam was supposed to be the color of Muslims. Rather than acquire the color of Islam; however, Muslims colored Islam according to their culture. Islam was supposed to shape Arab culture, but it was Arab culture that ended up shaping Islam. As Azumah has noted, treating the Arab factor in Islam as "orthodox" and the only vehicle for expressing "true" and "pure" Islam is problematic (239). He also criticizes the fact that "Persian, Indian, and North African elements appropriated in Muslim practice are regarded as "original and unmistakably Islamic" whereas African elements are indiscriminately branded as "pagan survivals" (239).

As Azumah notes, "questions regarding pre-Islamic Arab elements in Islam are, at best, devoid of significance for conservative Muslims, and, at worst, blasphemous" (217). If racist and sexist cultures could impose their negative values upon Islam, such as slavery, patriarchy, and misogyny, what prevents us from integrating our positive, and positively Qur'anic values, such as freedom and equality, into it? Nothing at all. In fact, if we survey the abolitionists of Islam, we find that many of them were ex-slaves or the sons of concubines. To the dismay of the slave masters, and their violent opposition, they became scholars, shaykhs, and leaders, and they reinfused Islam with the morals and ethics it had lost. They did not reject Islam, and they had plenty of reasons to do so. They set out to reform and revive it according to its primordial principles. The slaves of Muslims thereby became the saviors of Islam.

7.4 Conclusions

As Nurcholish Majid (1939-2005), the prominent Indonesian Muslim intellectual, argued, the fact that God sent prophets to all people "implies that truth is everywhere and every time" (Azumah 225). Nobody has a monopoly on truth. There is truth and goodness in every culture (Azumah 225). Therefore, there is "no justification in any implicit and explicit assumption that all other cultures, apart from the Arab one, are nothing but *jahl* or *kufr*" (225). Arab culture is not superior to others. Arab culture does not supersede others. Despite their delusions, they are not the new Jews, or some chosen race. People are only superior in righteousness and justice. They are those who "enjoin the good and forbid the evil" (3:104; 3:110); 9:71; 9:112; 31:17). They are those who oppose slavery; not those who defend, justify, legalize, practice, implement, legislate, spread, and institutionalize it.

Chapter Eight

Slave Master Imams or Abolitionist Imams?

8.1 Introduction

While Islam limited the number of wives to four (according to most, but not all scholars), and reformed slavery, Jonathan A.C. Brown claims that it allowed for an unlimited number of concubines (2020: 82-83). He boasts that "some of Islam's early pious exemplars were serial polygamists with enormous numbers of slave concubines" (2020: 82). He asserts that "the Prophet's grandson Hasan (d. 670) reportedly married around seventy women (no more than four at a time)" -- how reassuring -- "and had more than three hundred slave-concubines" (2020: 82) -- how impressive. Brown treats such allegations as factual, without questioning them when the sources on the contentious subject are controversial and contain a considerable number of conflicting accounts.

8.2 Will the Real Hasan Please Stand Up?

Some Sunni and Twelver Shiite sources claim that Hasan ibn 'Ali married women by fours, divorced them by fours, and had hundreds of sex slaves. He comes across as an unstable and sexually insatiable man who treated women like objects, used them, and discarded them. When conscientious people complained, he claimed it was his divine right to do so. Of course, this is all presented in a positive light in some of the sources. Allegedly, he was "doing the women a favor" by making them related to the Prophet Muhammad.

These lurid accounts uphold the myth that the Imams, like the Prophet Muhammad, were men of unsurpassed virility like Solomon, with his thousand wives and concubines. And yes, some Twelver Shiite traditions even claim that 'Ali went up the pulpit of the mosque in Najaf and warned Muslim parents not to give their daughters in marriage to his son Hasan as he was a habitual divorcer (and an evident womanizer and philanderer according to these accounts). A more balanced and respectful approach would have required Brown to cite the findings of Saeed Akhtar Rizvi (1927-2002), the Twelver Shiite scholar, and others, whether one is convinced of them or not.

Assuming that these salacious traditions are true, and not the fabrications of friends or foes, there is no way, critics will claim, that Hasan was a moral exemplar or, in the Twelver Shiite view, an infallible, immaculate, and sinless proof of God who, along with the Prophet and the other Imams of *ahl al-bayt*, was the very reason for which the world was created. Rather than presenting both sides of the story of Hasan, Brown only presents one. He does not mention the articles and books that refute such allegations which, in the view of their authors, were defamatory and slanderous against the character of the third Imam. He also fails to mention the many stalwarts of Sunnism who maintained harems filled with hundreds of abducted and enslaved women.

Although some scholars, like Ronald Michael Segal (1932-2008), a South African author and anti-apartheid activist, have claimed that Hasan was "all too captivated by the new delight that conquest had brought," leading him to contract and dissolve one hundred marriages," by the age of forty-five, and coming to be called "the great divorcer" (Segal 21) others were not so gullible as to accept these fanciful claims. For example, in his study of the marriages of Hasan, Wilfred Madelung (b. 1930), a German-British scholar of Islamic history, found that the reports that paint a poor image of him are "for the most part vague, lacking in names, concrete specifics and verifiable details, and spun... with a defamatory intent" (385). Some claim he married ninety women in his father's time alone (386-387). As far as Madelung is concerned, all these tales are unreliable (387). It is, therefore, possible that the accounts claiming that many of the twelve Imams had numerous concubines were spun from the same yarn. It is also conceivable that they are correct and lived lives comparable to those of other men during Umayyad and 'Abbasid rule. That would suggest that the Prophet Muhammad and the twelve Imams were mortals and human beings who did not transcend their times. Such is the view of Heather Johnson who claims that,

> Incestuous marriages, slavery, concubinage, and unlimited polygyny were widely practiced. As radical as this may seem to the modern reader, Muhammad and his followers probably did not see anything amiss. As far as they knew, this sort of treatment was entirely acceptable and even condoned by Allah. (575)

Many Muslims beg to differ. Any such person would be unworthy to follow and emulate. The purpose of religion is to raise the moral and ethical bar, not maintain the *status quo* or even lower it. Islam may have banned slavery, argues Muhammad Diakho. What is troubling, however, is the "curious jurisprudential silence on the subject" (30). This silence results from the fact that scholars were sell-outs. The jurists from the second and third generations of Islam collaborated with the ruling powers (21). They brought an end to freedom of opinion (21). These jurists, who served the rich and powerful, fashioned, and codified Islamic law in a definitive form to suit the customs and interests of their masters (21). They then abruptly and arbitrarily declared that the doors of *ijtihad* or independent reasoning were closed and that the last word had been given (21). Since then, Muslims have lived in a world where lies and treason have been erected as religious principles (13). However, as Dietrich Bonhoeffer (1906-1945), the German Lutheran pastor, theologian, and anti-Nazi dissident, who was executed

Chapter Eight   77

by hanging, stated: "SILENCE in the face of evil is itself evil, God will not hold us guiltless, NOT to speak is to speak, NOT to act is to act" (Chesler 420).

8.3 Ain't no John Brown in this Town

If the sources that have been transmitted are true, and that is highly questionable, then the Imams of *ahl al-bayt*, the Household of the Prophet, had many slaves and, in some cases, hundreds of them. When 'Ali died, it is reported that he left behind nineteen concubines (Nu'man, vol. 2: 176). Hasan is said to have had a dozen children with slave girls (Mufid 290). Husayn reportedly had three children from concubines (Mufid 406). Muhammad al-Baqir (c. 676-c. 732) is said to have had three children from slave girls (Mufid 406). Ja'far al-Sadiq (c. 702-765) reportedly had half a dozen children from concubines (Mufid 430).

Musa al-Kazim (c. 745-c. 799) reportedly had thirty-eight children from thirty-two different slave girls (Mufid 457-459). Some sources state that he only had thirty-three children while others assert he had forty or even sixty. How is that for the sanctity of the family? Is that how a saint behaves? Shiite sources claim that Musa al-Kazim was oppressed and imprisoned. However, how can such a persecuted person have the time and resources to have so many children outside of permanent or temporary marriage? These are questions thinking people with critical minds are bound and entitled to ask.

Shiite clerics like Muhammad Rizvi (b. 1957) and Ibrahim Amini (1925-2020) may write about *Marriage & Morals in Islam* and *Principles of Marriage Family Ethics*, pretending Islam promotes monogamy and the traditional nuclear family. However, their vision of the family does not align with the transmitted teachings and practice of the twelve Imams they claim to follow.

From the time of 'Ali to the twelfth Imam and beyond, the norm, in much of the Muslim world, both Sunni and Shiite, was not husband, wife, and children. The norm was the harem: a patriarchal man, a collection of concubines, small or large, and numerous children from different mothers. The master's role was to breed. The role of sex slaves was to be bred. The children had little contact with their father and were often raised by numerous cloistered women. There might be a permanent wife, here or there, who had a higher status than the sex slaves of her husband. However, in many cases, there was no free wife: just concubines. It was a degrading, depraved, demoralizing, and dehumanizing environment for women and children. "The harem," notes Chebel, "was a republic of darkness governed by cruel laws," that traces back, not to Islam, but to Byzantium (115).

So what if some ravishing redhead like Roxelana (c. 1504-1558) occasionally rose from sex slave to chief consort and legal wife of a sultan? Most slave girls were powerless and pitiful. They were objects. Their private parts and whatever they produced were the legal property of their owners. As 'Abd al-Rahman ibn al-Qasim (749/750-806/807) noted in his *Mudawwanah*, "the private parts of the female slave belong to their master. The same applies to her womb (children) and her back (force labor)" (345). The same ruling is found in other "Islamic" Slave Codes, such as the one by Muhammad ibn al-Nujaym (926-969/970) (Diakho 115).

Rather than follow such rulings blindly and foolishly, Muslims should have asked these jurists for evidence. As Diakho asserts, "there is no proof in the Qur'an and the *sunnah* that the private parts of a slave belong to her master" (219). On the contrary, "concubinage is a form of institutionalized fornication, rooted in the customs of uncivilized warriors" (222). Displeased by the Qur'an's prohibition of fornication and adultery, forced prostitution, and a limit of four wives, the jurists played with the Word of God to permit them to have sex with all the women they wanted (233-244). If a man can have sex with countless concubines, the Qur'an's limit of four wives is meaningless. In fact, it makes a mockery of its injunctions. As Diakho notes, chastity and concubinage are incompatible (231). Moreover, "There was never any question of sleeping with anyone in the Qur'an without marriage ties" (232).

Modern-day Muslim apologists can pretend that Islam promotes the nuclear family. They can insist that Islam only allows sexual relations within the confines of marriage. However, that is not what their predecessors preached, much less what they practiced. Permanent wives were a source of status, wealth, family, and political connections. Concubines were sources of sexual satisfaction and the mass production of progeny. The fact that Muslim men could purchase captive women, who were torn from their homes and families through unjust wars, and rape them makes Islamic claims of chastity, purity, fidelity, faithfulness, and family entirely meaningless.

'Ali al-Rida (765/766-818) appears to be the only Imam who remotely approached monogamy with his marriage to Umm Habib, the daughter of the caliph al-Ma'mun. She did not, however, bear him any children. The only child that he had was fathered by a slave girl by the name of Sabika, Durra, Kayzuran, Rayhanah, Sukaynah, Summanah or Sayyidah, a Nubian from Egypt, and purported descendant of the mythological Mariya the Copt, according to some accounts, but most likely a Berber, according to others (Mufid 479-480; Morrow 2021: 55-56). Since he had a single wife, why didn't 'Ali al-Rida become an example? He did, to the 'Alawi-Nusayris, the theological extremists, who deify the Imams, but insist upon monogamy.

Muhammad al-Taqi (811-835) reportedly had four children (Mufid 495). We know next to nothing about their mothers. 'Ali al-Naqi (828-868) had five children (Mufid 506). According to some sources, Hasan al-'Askari (844-874) had some slave girls but reportedly only had one son, Muhammad al-Mahdi (Mufid 522-523). The name of his mother differs according to accounts. The variants include Saqil, Saiqal, Susan, Mariya, Maryam, Nasim, and Narjis (Dann 252). Even her race varies. Some sources claim she was European. Others claim she was a black African (Mirza 98-99). And yet others claim she was the Arab daughter of al-Hasan ibn Zayd al-'Alawi (d. 884 CE) (103), the founder of the

Zaydi dynasty of Tabaristan. Although most sources claim that the mother of Muhammad al-Mahdi was a slave girl, others argue that she was a free woman and a wife (Mirza 102).

Even if we assume that these accounts about the twelve Imams are correct, and there are conflicting ones, they pose ethical problems. It could be claimed that they acted as examples for others as to how slaves should be treated. Some traditions highlight their kindness, patience, and generosity, and how they educated enslaved people and emancipated them. Others, however, paint the Imams, particularly Ja'far al-Sadiq, as defenders and promoters of slavery who treated women like sexual objects. These conflicting images cannot be reconciled. Even if we reject one set of accounts, the other remains problematic. This leaves us with but one option: to reject them all. It is simply not possible that the sixth Imam told the faithful to "buy and sell slaves" (Kulayni) and that "those who buy people are the worst of people" (Kulayni). He could not have encouraged men to have sex with slave girls and condemned slave dealers for doing the same with the women they owned and sold.

There is, however, one plausible explanation to the claims that many Imams had so many children with concubines; namely, the desire of people to claim the status of sayyids by concocting false genealogies tracing them back to people like Musa al-Kazim whose so-called descendants constitute seventy percent of the self-professed *sadat* in Iran. Since Sunni and Shiite sources cannot even agree on how many wives and concubines the Imams had, have conflicting names for some of them, and no names for many of them, how can we be certain of their status? Sure, they could have been sex slaves and concubines. However, they could have had the status of temporary wives, or they could have been enslaved women who were purchased, freed, and married. Such women would not necessarily have been counted among the four permanent wives; a status reserved for free women. What is more, the limit of four wives was routinely violated.

8.4 Imam 'Ali

After he became the fourth caliph, it is reported that 'Ali "banned the enslavement of the womenfolk of defeated foes, except for female slaves captured in the enemy camp" (Clarence-Smith 2006: 55). It is also reported that he freed over one thousand slaves (Mashayekhi; Majlisi vol. 34: 326). That does not change the fact that Sunni and Shiite sources report that he took a sex slave during the final years of the Prophet's mission and that the same sources report that he had anywhere from half a dozen to eight wives, and more than two dozens concubines after the death of his first wife, Fatimah.

Other reports state that 'Ali wanted to take another wife while married to Fatimah and that the Prophet prohibited him unless he divorced his daughter, forcing him to remain monogamous. Why would the Prophet Muhammad protect his daughter from polygyny and not protect other women? If anything, these conflicting narrations reflect differing ideals regarding marriage: some support unlimited polygyny, while others insist on monogamy. Either way, unlike the Imams who followed him, 'Ali had power, albeit tenuous and fleeting. However, in the face of sedition and civil wars, the Imam had more pressing matters: preserving power. If the Prophet Muhammad had intended abolition of slavery, as intimated by his final words pleading people to fear God regarding the enslaved, the fourth caliph did not deliver on the promise. Embroiled in a civil war, freeing enslaved people, however meritorious, may not have been at the top of his socio-political priorities. In fact, it could have been perilous. In search of work, these hundreds of thousands of now unemployed slaves could have been enlisted as paid soldiers in the army of his enemies.

8.5 Slave Master Imams?

According to Shiite sources, the Imams who succeeded 'Ali are also reported to have been opposed to Islamic imperialism. It is reported that Zayn al-'Abidin, the son of Husayn, regularly offered to marry or free his numerous slave girls. He used to liberate the slaves he had been given during the 'Id celebration, while providing them with means of livelihood (Chittick 709). Some contemporary Twelver Shiite scholars claim that he used slavery as a tool of mass education.

As much as Rizvi and other Shiite scholars may claim that Islam introduced a plan to gradually abolish slavery, and emphasize the fact that the mothers of most of the Imams were slave girls, they ignore the elephant in the room, namely, the fact that the Imams themselves were slave-masters who bought and sold slaves and who fathered children with concubines. If the sources in question are historically sound, the Imams were not abolitionists. They were active participants in the slave trade who benefited from it. If they opposed slavery, they did not practice what they preached. The first thing an abolitionist does is liberate his own slaves.

Shiites may claim that the mothers of most of the Imams were *ummuhat al-awlad* or "mothers of children." This merely means that if they provided offspring for their master, they would be freed after his death. This is selling one's body, by force, in exchange for an inherent human right: freedom. It is the exploitation of a woman as a reproductive device. Not only were enslaved girls and women treated like animals, but they were also bred like animals. Certainly, it was a price that many women were willing to pay. It can hardly be considered a free choice, not any more than a rapist asking a woman to decide between "your life or your honor." Under such circumstances, most women resign themselves to being raped hoping to increase their odds of survival.

"What better master could a slave girl get than an infallible Imam and a proof of God for all of creation?" ask Shiites, as if this erased the inhumanity of sexual slavery. The question that ought to be asked is "why would an impeccable saint purchase a sex slave in the first place?" Would not a man of God purchase such victims to free or marry them? This argument is made in *Shi'ism in the Maghrib and al-Andalus*. The work contends that the Imams emancipated or married enslaved women. Such a view is entirely inconsistent with the biographies of the Imams and the traditions attributed to them. Perhaps it is the product of wishful thinking. In fact, according to 'Ali, "marriage with bondmaids is not permissible except for him who fears the commission of sin" (Nu'man, vol. 2: 231).

Although there are pro-slavery traditions attributed to the Imams, and entire chapters devoted to slavery in Shiite sources, there are a few in which they preached against slavery, including one in which Muhammad al-Baqir states that "nothing falls into the hands of the slave dealers except that they spoil it" (Dann 255; Majlisi vol. 48: 10), complaining of the sexual assaults suffered by slave girls, and another in which Ja'far al-Sadiq states that slave traders were the outcasts of humanity (Clarence-Smith 2006: 55; El Hamel 43; Rizvi). According to Syed Ameer Ali, the sixth Imam "utterly reprobated and condemned" "slave-lifting and slave-dealing" (37). He also claims that he "preached against slavery" during the early 'Abbasid period (39).

Although several scholars invoke the tradition as mentioned above, none have cited its source. They all refer back to Syed Ameer Ali (1849-1928), the Indian British jurist who failed to provide a reference (37) or any convincing evidence (Clarence-Smith 2008: 6). However, no such tradition can be found in hundreds of *hadith* volumes surveyed. There are, however, accounts that the slave girls who would become the mothers of the last Imams were purchased to protect them from sexual harassment and assault (Dann 256-257). Such sayings, however, which portray the more brutal aspects of slavery, are few and far between.

Although the sixth Imam's sayings opposing slavery supposedly inspired the *mu'tazila* and the *qaramita* (Ali 39) -- traditions that nobody has been able to locate -- they "were not embraced by the mainstream Shi'a" (El Hamel 43), namely, the Zaydis, the Ismailis, and the Ithna-Asharis, that is, the Fivers, the Seveners, and the Twelvers. As far as the enslaved are concerned, Shiism, which presents itself as "the religion of the oppressed" became "the religion of the oppressors." Its emancipatory abolitionist zeal only survived among the Mutazilites, the Qarmatians, and the Druze.

8.6 Imam Ja'far al-Sadiq:
Between Fact, Fiction, Fantasy, and Forgery

The compassionate sixth Imam starkly contrasts the rigid jurist depicted in Twelver Shiite sources who showed little care or concern for slaves. The canonical traditions of the Twelvers that were produced during 'Abbasid rule reflect the culture, laws, practices, and customs of the time. The Imam Ja'far al-Sadiq portrayed in Kulayni's *al-Kafi* comes across as a sex fiend. "The most enjoyable of things is sexual intercourse with women," said the sixth Imam (Kulayni, vol. 5: 290); "The best of women is … full of carnal desire" (Kulayni, vol. 5: 292), "The worst of women… refuses to yield … like a recalcitrant animal

82   Islam & Slavery

who refuses to allow riding" (Kulayni, vol. 5: 294). "Marry virgins," he told men (Kulayni, vol. 5: 302) while never stressing that men should remain virgins until marriage. Marry "women with large hips" (Kulayni, vol 5: 303), "brunettes with wide buttocks" (Kulayni, vol. 5: 303, 30), and women with blue eyes (Kulayni, vol. 5: 303).

The tastefully titled chapter on the "Anal of Women," or "Sodomizing the Women," which is attributed chiefly to Ja'far al-Sadiq, is stimulating (Kulayni, vol. 5: 471). When asked about sodomizing women, the sixth Imam responded: "She is a doll; you must not disappoint her" (Kulayni, vol. 5: 471). The translation on the Hubeali website has "She is your plaything" (vol. 5, chapter 178: 49). This is truly the epitome of good taste. The same can be said of the traditions stipulating that men can have intercourse -- namely, vaginal, and anal -- with nine-year-old girls (Kulayni, vol. 7: chapter 61). Muhammad Sarwar conveniently left these traditions untranslated (Kulayni, vol. 7: 363). However, they are found in the honest translation published by the Akhbari Shia website Hubeali which also includes the original Arabic.

Since women are so overwhelmingly attracted to men, they must be confined to their homes to protect them from their lust (Kulayni, vol. 5: 305). "The ambition of beasts is to fill their stomachs, and the ambition of women is to find men" (Kulayni, vol. 5: 305, 306). What is more, women have the sex drive of ten men (Kulayni, vol. 5: 307). Apparently, Ja'far al-Sadiq spoke out of experience, boasting that "I have put to the test white and dark-colored slave girls" (Kulayni, vol. 5: 303). What sort of a saint brags about his sexual conquests with enslaved girls? Questions need to be asked. Take, for example, the following traditions which trouble any conscience.

Ja'far al-Sadiq, it is reported, allowed masters to share their slave girls with other men: "If a person grants his slave girl to his brother [in faith for sexual purposes], the slave girl is permissible for him" (Kadivar, Kulayni [Arabic], vol. 5: 468; Tusi's *Tahdhib* vol. 7: 244, 'Amili, vol 21: 125). Virtually all Twelver jurists rejected this tradition and prohibited "loaning vaginas." The same applies to the Ismailis. As the sixth Imam is cited as saying, "the lending of private parts is fornication" (Nu'man, vol. 2: 234). However, he did insist that sexual intercourse was permitted through proprietary rights (Nu'man, vol. 2: 234). Women as property: the most perverse form of patriarchy and misogyny.

For some Muslim jurists, consensual wife-swapping or swinging is a mortal sin, punishable by death; however, there is no sin in sharing one's slave girl with other men with no regard for her consent, health, risk of sexually transmitted diseases, pregnancy, spiritual harm, and psychological and emotional damage. Although many Twelver Shiite jurists prohibit the loaning or lending of vaginas, as they put it, citing traditions that prohibit it (Nu'man, vol. 2: 234), some accept the tradition mentioned above as authentic and permit such practices. In the words of 'Abdul Karim Haeri, the director of the Shiite seminary in Karbala,

Allah willing, the Mahdi will arrive soon, and if there are people or nations that oppose the imam and fight him, when captured, they will be subject to the laws regarding slaves and slave girls. If someone buys five or ten of these slave girls and keeps them in his home, and then, say, he has friends over, he doesn't give his guest a slave girl with whom he had sex. He has several of them, and he can keep the surplus girls as reserve...

He can allow his guest to have sex with the slave girl. Instead of the friend having to marry the slave girl and get into problems with his family and so on, he resolves the problem. He goes to his friend's place for half an hour or so at night. He spends an hour there with [the slave girls], and when it's over, he goes back home, and if his wife asks him where he was, he has no problem [telling her he was with his friend]. This is because they are slave girls, and their owner can render them permissible to a third party. He doesn't need a marriage contract. (MEMRI)

Not only did the jurists refer to women as *'awrat* or vulvas, but they also described them as *furuj* or genitals. They were not women, or human beings, that were being loaned, borrowed, and shared between men, but they were vaginas. Instead of being people, they were reduced, in pornographic fashion, to private parts.

According to a tradition attributed to the sixth Imam, even if a slave girl is married and her husband is owned by the same master, the master has the right to have sex with her (Kulayni, Tusi, 'Amili, Ayyashi, Kadivar). He even allowed men to have sex with slave girls who were insane, and thereby incapable of consent (Kulayni, vol. 5, chapter 30: 322). This misogynistic, pro-slavery, Ja'far al-Sadiq, who argues that "women are the most effective soldiers of Iblis" (Harrani 429), and that they can be taken as sex slaves, cannot be the same one who condemned the institution of slavery and who is depicted as a saint and spiritual authority.

Who is the real Ja'far al-Sadiq? The herbalist? The master of occult sciences? The alchemist? The scientist? The traditionist? The Sunni jurist? The Sufi mystic? The god of the Ghulat? Or the infallible Shiite Imam and proof of God on Earth? Even Shiite sources present conflicting and mutually incompatible portraits of the man. Fortunately, the sixth Imam repeatedly stressed that Muslims should only accept traditions attributed to the Imams and the Prophet Muhammad if they agree with the Qur'an. As he said, "Whatever tradition does not agree with God's Book is rejected" (Tabarsi 378). Hence, following this standard, we can reject all traditions that contradict the Qur'an or are immoral, unethical, and irrational.

That would include the tradition in which Musa al-Kazim states that purchasing Slavic people enslaved by the Romans is permissible as it is a means of bringing them into Islam. This tradition, which Diakho wrongly attributes to 'Ali due to the agnomen Abu al-Hasan, the Father of Hassan, which, in this case, refers not to 'Ali ibn Abi Talib but to Musa al-Kazim, was used by Twelver Shiite jurists to justify enslaving the wrongfully enslaved. As Diakho notes, however,

84   Islam & Slavery

Muhammad Husayn Fadlullah (1935-2010), the Twelver Shiite religious authority, stressed that it was historically impossible to prove that the Prophet Muhammad held the view placed in the mouth of Musa al-Kazim (227-228).

For people of reason, as opposed to blind followers, it is apparent that the personas of the Prophet and the Imams were puppets for puppeteers. Their voices are lost among the cacophony of voices impersonating them. The *hadith* literature was like the social media of the time. It was a free for all. By and large, the Prophet, the companions, and the Imams are fictional characters and figures whose scripts and lines were written by traditionists and jurists. As the contradictory nature of the traditions demonstrates, the latter were putting words in the mouth of the former.

While it is acceptable to treat the positive traditions attributed to the Imams as authentic, it is unacceptable to do so with the negative ones. Attributing something good to people they never said could be treated as a compliment. However, attributing something evil to someone, which is false, is slander, libel, and defamation. If these terrible traditions are true, their authors were not infallible. *Bona fide* believers in the Imams refuse to insult them. It is, therefore, imperative to distinguish between the teachings of the twelve Imams, whatever they were, and those attributed to them.

While many opposing parties claimed them for prestige and authority, including Sunnis, Zaydis, Seveners, Twelvers, Ghulat groups, and Sufis, their teachings were misrepresented or falsified. Since they were viewed as a threat by ruling powers, they were kept under watch. Agents were assigned to spy on them, posing as students and followers, and acquiring the status of companions. These disinformation agents were tasked with corrupting the teachings of the Imams.

The Qarmatians, who believed in seven Imams, 'Ali, Hasan, Husayn, Zayn al-'Abidin, Muhammad al-Baqir, Ja'far al-Sadiq, and Muhammad ibn Isma'il, prohibited slavery, concubinage, polygyny, veiling, gender segregation, the seclusion of wives, and child marriages. They rebelled against the imposition of these practices on the part of the 'Abbasids. They created their egalitarian state according to the teachings they had received from the first half dozen Imams from *ahl al-bayt*. Their beliefs and practices were based on the teachings that had been transmitted to them. They certainly had collections of sayings from Ja'far al-Sadiq and the previous Imams of the Shiites. Unfortunately, none of their books have survived. According to the accounts of outsiders, the following can be gathered:

> The social principles of the Qarmatians were firstly social equality, modeled after Islamic teachings and philosophical principles. Secondly, the Qarmatians spread their notions of communal goodwill, regardless of race, social class, or religion. Thirdly, Qarmatians expropriated and redistributed land ownership to those in need, at no cost. Furthermore, they instituted gender equality in rights and obligations...
>
> With their state declared, the Qarmatians attempted to establish a system of social justice. They undertook experiments of communal

ownership of property and pooling resources. They promoted a utopian society, with equality between sexes, races, ethnicities, and classes of the "believers." Qarmatians abolished individual property, aimed to unite the working classes, and strove to establish absolute socialism. They put an end to feudalism, provided financial incentives to farmers to encourage them to exploit the land, and encouraged industry. Moreover, Qarmatians took control of foreign trade and targeted self-sufficiency...

In the early days, Hamdan Qarmat imposed various types of taxes on their supporters. In addition to various taxes on persons, men and women voluntarily contributed *khums*, (20%) of what they earned out of agricultural produce and trade profits. The money went into a common fund known as *al-Ilfa* (affinity coffer), whereby all the collected taxes belonged to the entire community. That money was redistributed in the community based on need. They also used this money to attract more followers, giving them a taste of the new age of salvation and prosperity... In effect, no Qarmatian owned more than his or her sword...

Since there was no compulsory method to enforce *khums*, the highest tax on earnings and savings, it is closer to being a voluntary payment. It is evident from various sources that discuss the Qarmatian socialist tax and proprietorship scheme that the communal social spirit surpassed the individuals' outlook to proprietorship and personal wealth. Everything belonged to the community, and it was the individual's obligation to defend that society's wealth, welfare, and sustainability... (Fahes 38-39)

Demonized as the Qarmatians were, their state's concern for the "welfare of the community and the resulting social order in Bahrain evoked the admiration of the non-Qarmatian observers who visited eastern Arabia before the downfall of the Qarmatian state" (Daftary, "Carmatians" 13). In the entirety of Islamic history, with the exception of the Qarmatian state and the short-lived Islamic statehood in Madinah (assuming the Qur'an served as a socio-religious anthology), there were no other attempts to establish a utopian society... (Fahes 41). The religious duty to Qarmatian individuals involved the creation of a happier and fairer earthly society... (Fahes 45)

The Qarmatian experiment was *avant-garde* in the sense that it came as a response to contemporary challenges and grievances. It evolved out of the schools of thought of the time and had a clear target of achieving a utopian society. That movement brought into the world what no other school of thought had been able to do since the tenth century: an adaptive revision of Islamic *mode de vie*, a resort to the core of the religious call, and last but not least, adaptation of the divine and the worldly. That movement, at least as far as its followers and citizens were concerned, arose out of the desire to attain happiness, justice, and welfare. They did not use religion to subdue the masses, nor did they use it to confer legitimacy to the ruling class. (Fahes 47-48)

If one thing is sure, the Qarmatian version of Shiite Islam radically differed from that of other Shia groups like the Zaydis, Musta'alis, Nizaris, and Ithna-Asharis. If there was an abolitionist Ja'far al-Sadiq, virtually no traces remain of him in Sevener and Twelver sources. On the contrary, he has been replaced by a sexist and misogynistic sixth Imam who fervently supported slavery, sex with slave girls, polygyny, veiling, maintaining women illiterate, and locking them away. Far from an abolitionist, a conscientious objector, or even a passive witness to slavery and concubinage, he is depicted as an active participant, one who promoted slavery and the sexual trafficking of women even if they were captured illegitimately in unjust wars. He is reported as having told his followers to buy and sell such slaves. And, like the other Imams, he is said to have purchased enslaved women and used them as sex slaves. When he died, he had sixty slave girls but only emancipated a third of them in his will (Barqi 20). These Imams, more mythological than historical, were not the same as those of the Qarmatians and other minority Shiite sects. The Imams were lost to history. All that remains is a sacred history, some of which is far from sacred.

8.7 The Schizophrenic *Sunnah*

In light of the above, the traditions regarding slavery should be viewed skeptically by any thinking person endued with a critical thinking capacity as they show the same schizophrenic nature as those related to women, in general, some which are sweet and heart-warming while others are viciously misogynistic. One cannot love and hate women at the same time. The traditions attributed to the Imams, like those attributed to the Prophet Muhammad, sound like Dr. Jekyll and Mr. Hyde. The same persons cannot have possibly stated them. The possibilities are three. The positive ones are true, and the negative ones are false, whereby Islam is vindicated. The negative ones are true, and the positive ones are false, in which case Islam is destroyed. Or both the positive and negative ones are all false, in which Islam the Good, and Islam the Bad, are equally annihilated or, as the Qur'anists would have it, leaving us with Qur'an as the sole source of Islam along with any traditions that agree with it.

Unlike Sunni jurists, who place the *hadith* before the Qur'an, claiming that the Qur'an needs the *sunnah* more than the *sunnah* needs the Qur'an, Usuli Twelver Shiites have always insisted, in theory, on placing the Qur'an before the *hadith*. According to their standards, a *hadith* must agree with the Qur'an to be accepted as authentic. They do not treat their collections of traditions as entirely authentic: each tradition must be assessed based on its merits. While this is a more rational approach to the material, their jurisprudential process still produced immoral and unethical edicts that contradicted Qur'anic values.

If the Qur'an rejects racism, how could Shiite jurists accept racist traditions attributed to the Prophet and the Imams and pass rulings based upon them? If the Qur'an rejects extramarital sex, how could Shiite jurists accept traditions that allowed it under the guise of slavery, concubinage, and temporary pleasure marriages, and issue edicts permitting it? Their methodology was different from that of the Sunnis; however, on matters relating to women and slavery, they came to the same conclusions. The common denominator between both groups is that they were men from the same cultural backgrounds.

Had the Qur'an been given to the Lakota, the Cree, the Kogi people, or the Polynesians, the outcome would have been radically different in terms of interpretation and application. Must the Qur'an be interpreted through Arab lenses? Or Persian and Pakistani ones, for that matter? If the Qur'an was intended for all humanity, then the rest of humanity has a right to interpret it and perhaps do greater justice to its text.

If we believe what has reached us, mostly myth and legend, devoid of historical accuracy and certainty, many Imams had slaves; however, they were generally given to them as *khums*. They reportedly treated them kindly and humanely (see Amrohi). The question must be asked: can one kindly and humanely have sex with a captive woman? If she submits, it is because she has no choice. She seeks to please her master to obtain better treatment and avoid being battered. And how would she feel about carrying the child of her rapist, even if giving birth to his offspring might result in her emancipation after her master's death? In any event, the Imams are said to have purchased many slaves to free them. In fact, many of their mothers were supposedly of noble lineage. At the same time, many Imams of the Shiites were purportedly poisoned. By whom, one may ask? By their slave girls. "With the new ethos of the Abbasid world," notes Leila Ahmed (b. 1940), the Egyptian American scholar of Islam, "women were reduced to resorting to manipulation, poison, and falsehood -- the means of the powerless" (83).

If Twelver Shiite sources are correct, which certainly does not seem to be the case, with traditionists themselves admitting that fifty, eighty, and even one hundred percent of them are weak or forged, then the Imams from the Household of the Prophet freed tens of thousands of slaves. Such claims might be hyperbolic, namely, attempts to present them as particularly pious. It could be argued that they tried to make the best of a bad situation. In other words, they could not change the socio-economic and political system. It has been claimed by some Shiite apologists that, had they had the power to do so, the Imams would have freed all enslaved people and abolished the institution. Such a position, however, is hard to defend after reading the chapters on slavery in Sevener and Twelver books of traditions and the rulings of their jurists over the ages. In fact, it comes across as entirely deceptive and disingenuous, a clear product of pious dissimulation or public relations. The Fivers, at least, have a history of categorizing slavery and concubinage as *makruh* or detestable. In Zaydi jurisprudence, moving from *makruh* to *haram* is a simple matter of degree. However, going from *halal* to *haram* is quite a leap for Sunnis, Twelvers, and Seveners.

Although they feature some emancipatory traditions, which encourage freeing enslaved Muslims, as opposed to non-Muslim slaves, Shiite sources, like Sunni ones, also contain many traditions condemning and cursing rebellious or runaway slaves, threatening them with punishment in this world and the hereafter. "God curses… the slave who does not obey his master," stated the Prophet Muhammad in one of them (Majlisi, vol. 22: 132). Whoever uttered these statements was no Harriet Tubman (1822-1918). There was no Underground Railroad in the Muslim world. Shiite sources also contain many pro-slavery traditions that are racist and sexist and denigrate human dignity.

According to Shiite traditions, the Imams had sex with slave girls without marrying them temporarily or permanently. These traditions claim that Ja'far al-Sadiq placed slaves in the same commercial category as animals, and encouraged his followers to buy slave girls and have sex with them (Kulayni, vol. 5: 187). "Buy and sell them," he said regarding Romans (vol. 5, chapter 92: 187). Despite the Prophet Muhammad's prohibition of beating slaves, the sixth Imam authorized it. When asked what his view was regarding beating slaves with a stick, he asserted that there was no problem with it. When a slave master asked him how many times he could beat his slave with stick, he said: "three, four, five" (Barqi 21). In fact, his father, Muhammad al-Baqir used to beat slave girls if they covered their hair like free women (Ibn Shaybah, Nu'man, vol. 1: 221).

When a man told the sixth Imam that he had purchased some slave girls and wanted to "prevail over them," the sixth Imam prescribed an aphrodisiac concoction. He told him to fry white onion in olive oil. When it was caramelized, he told him to fry an egg in it, sprinkle it with salt, and eat it. Not only was the sixth Imam a chef, but he was an herbalist and a spiritual counselor. The culinary Viagra he prescribed was also accompanied by a prayer: "O God, make lasting in them my pleasure, increase in them my desire, and make my weakness strong over them, by Your Majesty, my Master." Apparently, the recipe and supplication were a sexual success (Newman 172). If the purpose of marriage is sex, and the purported purpose of sex with slaves girls is to prevent fornication and adultery, why would a man buy slave girls if he did not have the physical prowess to have sex with them? Why was he not reproached by the Imam? Why was he not told to free the girls or marry them? Why did he fail to condemn slavery as he did in other traditions?

The tradition in question, which is only one of many, demonstrates that it is permissible to buy groups of kidnapped girls placed on sale in sex markets and, if one does not have the strength to rape them all, a sexual stimulant is in order. This is exactly what the psychopaths from ISIS did in Syria and Iraq. They believed that it was their duty to rape every single female captive that they abducted. All women were fair prey: Yezidis, Christians, Shiites, Sunnis, and even Salafi women who belonged to other militias. Even for these morally depraved degenerates, raping thousands upon thousands of females was beyond their physical capacity. Hence, they forced doctors and pharmacists to give them all the erectile disfunction medicine that was available in the region so that they could fulfil their divine duty to rape (Chesler 394). Of course, as people like Brown insist, there is no such thing as rape in Islamic law. Even when you rape a perfect stranger, it is not called *ightisab* or rape but *zinah bi al-jabr*, "fornication by force." What is more, according to Islamic law, the consent of wives and slaves is not required when it comes to sex. Their husbands and masters have the right to have sex with them. In their minds, just like one cannot rape one's wife, one cannot rape one's slave. The fact of the matter is one can rape one's wife and one can rape one's slave.

According to Twelver traditions, Ja'far al-Sadiq stated that masturbation was the same as fornication and adultery, that it was like fornicating with oneself, and that it was better to have sex with a slave than to pleasure oneself (Kulayni, vol. 5: 471-472; vol. 5). This is the supposed solution to masturbation and fornication? Raping slaves as a remedy to auto-erotic stimulation or premarital sex? This is a paradoxical form of chastity. Ethically speaking, is touching one's private parts worse than war, conquest, mass murder, enslavement, trafficking, and sexual bondage? As people of understanding ask: should one take lessons in ethics from such fabricated sayings and fictitious teachers?

For its proponents, be they Jewish, Christian, or Muslim, there is nothing inherently evil or sinful in slavery. According to them, religious guides were simply obeying the will and command of God. If that is the case, ask critics, should we believe in such a God? No, but this does not mean we should not believe in God. There is a difference between believing in God and believing what people say about God. The same applies to the Prophet Muhammad and the Imams. There is a difference between what people said they taught and what they actually taught. As for the twelve Imams, early Imami jurists like Ibn Junayd al-Iskafi, viewed them as fallible human beings who offered their personal opinions based on available evidence. Their views did not have legislative weight nor were they binding. The fact that they did not share the same views on many subjects shows that they engaged in independent legal reasoning.

Just like concubines were falsely attributed to the Prophet, it is possible that they were deceitfully imputed to the Imams. In the same fashion that propagandists lied about Imam Hasan's sexual insatiability and promiscuity, presenting him as a man who married and divorced women in groups of four, and had sex with hundreds of concubines, it is conceivable that they lied about the other Imams. Among the most common complaints made by Shiites against the Sunni caliphs is the fact that they had harems full of concubines. However, so did the Shiite Imams.

It is possible that the Imams purchased enslaved women, liberated, married them, and educated them. Some have suggested that the "concubines" of the Imams were the product of *taqiyyah* or pious dissimulation. If the heir of an Imam were known, his life would have been endangered. If an Imam had but one wife, the designated successor could have been easily identified and eliminated by the authorities. Hence, some of the Imams pretended to not have wives at all, and surrounded themselves with slave girls who were really just servants. The goal was to deceive and delude the repressive rulers.

It could also be claimed that the Imams were exactly the way they are depicted in Twelver Shiite literature, namely, men who had large harems of sex slaves as was common in the culture of the time. Considering the irreconcilable differences found in Sunni, Zaydi, Ismaili, Qarmatian, Alevi, Bektashi, Nusayri, Sufi, and Twelver accounts of the lives and teachings of the twelve Imams, it could be argued that this last scenario seems unlikely. Be that as it may, some Twelver Shiite traditions, false or authentic, do not paint a pretty picture of the Imams. Let the blame fall on the narrators and compilers of these traditions, the traditionists who treat them as genuine, and the jurists who rely upon them to issue legal rulings. I categorically reject their authenticity on grounds that they contradict the Qur'an, reason, and ethics. I cite them solely to expose the foundational sources of slavery and concubinage in Shiite jurisprudence and not to slander an entire faith tradition which has much to offer in terms of spirituality and the struggle for social justice. Self-respecting Shiite scholars reject these traditions as well.

8.8 Perpetuating Sexual Debauchery

Not only could Muslim men have four permanent wives, according to some Shiite traditions attributed to the Imams, but they could have hundreds, even thousands of temporary pleasure-wives and sex slaves (Kulayni, vol. 5: 413-414; 422). After all, temporary wives are like slave girls (Kulayni, vol. 5: 422, 413). "You can marry a thousand of them," proclaimed the sixth Imam since "they are on hire" (Kulayni, vol. 5: 413-413). Yes, indeed, they are open for business. Give them a handful of food, a coin, or a toothbrush, and they are good to go (Kulayni, vol. 5: 419). The contract can be as short as the act of copulation. As the sixth Imam said, the marriage contract can commence upon penetration and finish upon withdrawal, so long as one does not look at the woman afterward. How chivalrous! Even promiscuous women are hurt when men use them, leave them, and do not spend the night. A one-minute marriage for a one-minute man! How economical if he pays by the minute instead of by the act, the hour, or even the night. Sites of Shiite pilgrimage are just teaming with men seeking one-night or one-minute stands through *mut'ah* marriage (Nategh, The Guardian).

Regarding polygyny, the Qur'an warns that "it will not be within your powers to treat your wives with equal fairness, however much you may desire it" (4:129). As El Hamel notes, "this verse enlightens the previous verse [4:3] and unequivocally instructs a man on the impossibility of exercising fairness if he chooses to marry more than one woman; it preaches monogamy" (28). As Cyrille Moreno al-'Ajami notes, the Arabic term *zawj*, which is used in the Qur'an, means "half" or "pair" (2020: 43). *Zawaj* or marriage is the union of a man and a woman. It is inherently monogamistic. Many Muslim scholars, including Leila Ahmed (b.

1940), Fatima Mernessi (1940-2015), and Amina Wadud (b. 1952), have come to this inescapable conclusion (28). As Alexander Russell Webb wrote,

> Considering the character of the people, one can readily comprehend how utterly impossible it was for Mohammed to establish the monogamous system of marriage, even if he had been disposed to do so. His apparent purpose was to modify the existing evil and bring the system within the limits of justice and common decency. Some of the Mohammedan doctors hold that he plainly taught his followers that it was better to marry but one wife; others hold that he positively prohibited polygamy. The most rational conclusion, however, in view of the historical evidence, is that he dealt with the existing conditions so as to produce the best results and did not lay down a rule for future generations, leaving them instead, to formulate laws for their social government, in accordance with the moral doctrines of Islam, and adapted to more fully developed conditions. (43)

Despite the Qur'anic opposition to concubinage, corruption, dissipation, degeneracy, vice, turpitude, depravity, immodesty, and indecency, the sixth Imam allowed Muslim men to sleep between several free wives or slave girls at the same time because, after all, women are nothing but sex toys, or, as he put it, "women are like dolls" (Kulayni, vol. 5: 490, 470). When he learned that Shiites were practicing monogamy, he took refuge in God and His Messenger from such a practice and insisted that they abide by what God has made permissible and what God has made prohibited (*Tasfir Hub-e-Ali*: 4:22-41, Kulayni, al-Saffar).

So strongly did Ja'far al-Sadiq oppose monogamy and promote polygyny that he encouraged women to engage in as many temporary pleasure marriages as possible. After doing *mut'ah* with a man and waiting for forty-five days, "she can enjoy [*mut'ah*] with someone else" as "this is permissible for them both up to the Day of Judgment." As he explained, "she can do it with seven [different] men, and if she likes, she can do it with twenty [different] men as long as they remain in the world" (*Tasfir Hub-e-Ali*: 4:22-41, Kulayni, al-Saffar).

According to Muhammad al-Baqir: "There is no harm if a man sleeps between two wives or concubines; but he should not have intercourse with one of them while the other is looking on" (Nu'man, vol. 2: 196). The prohibition only applied to free wives. In fact, he explicitly permitted it in the presence of a slave girl (Nu'man, vol. 2: 196). Such rulings gave the green light to veritable orgies. "Do not have intercourse with one free-born woman in front of another," cautioned the sixth Imam. "As for [intercourse] with one bondmaid in front of another, there is no objection [to that]" (Newman). And this is not only a Shiite problem.

Sunni authorities, like Malik, reported that it was permissible to have sex with two slave girls at once. In fact, one companion of the Prophet, 'Abd Allah ibn 'Umar, the son of the second caliph, used to line up three concubines, side by side, on all fours, and break his Ramadan fast by mounting them, going from one to the other, as the call to prayer echoed at sunset. Ghazali presents this matter-of-factly in his chapter on the ethics of marriage and describes the person in question as an ascetic. In his slave code, Ibn al-Nujaym also decreed that gathering several concubines in a single room was permissible, even against their will (Diakho 119). Obviously, there were dissident voices on both the Sunni and the Shiite sides. Apparently, some people still had scruples.

When we read these accounts, we must ask ourselves: Is this the Islamic idea of purity, virtue, modesty, and righteousness? These traditions convey the hedonistic imagery of the *Thousand and One Arabian Nights* and contemporary adult entertainment. However, this was reality. As Janet Afary notes, "A master could sleep with several *kanizes* [sex slaves] at the same time, an action that would have been reprehensible with regard to his wife (though it did occur commonly in the royal harem)" (81). Prior to purchasing slaves in the market, it is reported that 'Abd Allah ibn 'Umar, like other men, used to fondle their buttocks and breasts (Bayhaqi, 'Abd al-Razzaq, Ibn Abi Shaybah). It was also normal to examine their teeth, like animals, as well as their private parts, to see if they were virgins or had any diseases, and to ensure they would be good breeders.

In fact, according to *al-Fatawa al-'Alamgiriyya* or *al-Fatawa al-Hindiyya*, a seventeenth-century socio-economic, political, military, ethical, and legal code of the Mughal Empire during the reign of Muhammad Muhiuddin Aurangzeb Alamgir (c. 1618-1707) the purchaser of a slave girl had the right to return her, for a full refund, if he found that her breasts were too big and saggy and if her vagina was too wide and loose as this would prevent the buyer from obtaining a maximum of pleasure from her which, after all, was her purpose. What is more, the purchaser could also return a slave girl if he found that she was not a virgin and had been sold as one as this would constitute false advertising (Lal 309). Indubitably, women were objects in "Islamic" law that could be bought and sold like animals or vehicles. After all, buyers had the right to take them for a "test drive" and return them for a full refund if they were unsatisfied with how they performed.

Even if a slave girl protested that she was a free woman, who had been unjustly enslaved in a war that was not Islamically justified, Ja'far al-Sadiq stated that men still had the right to buy her unless she could prove her claims (Kulayni, vol. 5, chapter 92: 188). How could an enslaved woman prove she was free? Show her passport? However, when it came to taking a woman as a temporary wife, the sixth Imam told his followers to take her word that she was not married (Kulayni, vol. 5, chapter 106: 423). In other words, if she claims that she is single but is married, it is on her, and you can still have sex with her. Likewise, if a slave girl claims she is a free woman, you can still buy her and copulate with her.

When asked whether Muslim men could purchase slaves, who were taken in unjust wars, including children who were stolen, including slave girls, as well as slave boys who had been castrated, Ja'far al-Sadiq stated that it was not unlawful because they were bringing them from paganism to Islam (Kulayni, vol. 5, chapter 92: 188). The tradition reads:

Chapter Eight

I once asked Abu al-Hasan [Musa al-Kazim] about Romans who invade *al-Saqabilah* [a people who lived between Bulgaria and Constantinople (Istanbul)], steal their children, slave girls, and slave boys, castrate the slave boys, and send them to Baghdad for the merchants. What do you say about them? We know they are stolen, and they were invaded wrongfully without declaring war among them. He [the Imam] said: "It is not unlawful to buy them because they have only taken them from paganism to Islam." (Kulayni [English], vol. 5, chapter 92: 188; Kulayni [Arabic] vol. 5: 210; 'Amili vol. 15: 131; vol. 18: 244; Tusi, *Tahdhib* vol. 6: 162)

Consequently, purchasing people kidnapped and enslaved outside of so-called legitimate warfare is perfectly permissible according to this line of thinking. If Shiites could only purchase slaves from legitimate wars authorized by the infallible Imams, argued Twelver jurists like Tusi, no Imami would ever have owned a slave. Hence, the permission to enslave the so-called "people of misguidance," namely the Sunnis and infidels captured by infidels. Some Twelver jurists go so far as permitting Muslims to purchase daughters sold by their fathers based on the authority of the sixth Imam ('Amili vol. 18: 246; Tusi's *Tahdhib* vol. 7: 77; Saduq, vol. 3: 83).

In light of these illuminated edicts, nothing would prevent Muslim men, pimps, and pedophiles, from buying girls and boys, for that matter, from Muslim and non-Muslim sexual trafficking networks. The "Muslim" grooming gangs in Europe have a green light. Self-professed Islamic sex traffickers are emboldened. The buyers of human beings, and the purchasers of sex slaves, are freed from the shame of sin. And while we are at it, why free the sex slaves of ISIS and other Islamist terrorists? Even though they were captured unlawfully, according to this line of reasoning, nothing would prevent Muslims from purchasing them. Regarding the trade in human flesh, Shiism was no different than Sunnism. After all, according to Islamic law there were three primary sources of slaves: capture in *jihad*, birth to slave parents, and purchase (Azumah 125). Consequently, "raiding... and kidnapping by Muslim individuals and communities became a popular sources of slaves" (125).

Twenty-first century Twelver Shiite jurists of the magnitude of Abu al-Qasim al-Khu'i (1899-1992) have ruled that it is permissible to enslave people outside of war based on the tradition of Musa al-Kazim. For Mostafa Moghaghegh Damad (b. 1945), such a ruling leaves him speechless. His outrage and indignation are evident and utterly justified:

First of all, where did this ruling come from?! What is the consequence of this? Where did Khoi's followers live? And how is this not explicit support for human trafficking? Any disbeliever, lady, or child, it does not matter; you can abduct them, take them out of polytheism, and send them to *dar al-Islam*! If the world knew about this ruling, they would not dare give us visas! We mentioned at the beginning we are living in a time of global communication, and global advancement; we cannot take slaves, period! Even if we accept the idea of spoils of war, they are to be treated as prisoners of war and not to be taken as slaves -- there is a big difference between these two notions.

What is even more interesting is when I discussed this with Ayatullah Shubayr Zanjani, he mentioned to me that almost everything this narrator talks about is slavery! It seems like he was a slave-seller himself and understood what the Imam said in a way that benefited him, or what we would say in today's terminology, it seems like there was a conflict of interest at play. This is just one of the conclusions we are facing due to the acceptance of solitary transmitted traditions on the mere basis of *fisq* and *'adl* [namely, whether or not the narrator was a bad Muslim, who was known to violate Islamic law, or whether he was a good, just, and practicing Muslim]

More than misrepresenting the statement of the seventh Imam, it could be argued that slave trader in question, or someone else cited in the chain, entirely fabricated this saying, and falsely attributed it to Musa al-Kazim. These slave traders could also be the source of the claim that the seventh Imam had a huge harem of sex slaves. Critics could as easily claim that the pro-slavery statements of Musa al-Kazim are exactly what one would expect from a slave master who bought and sold women, exploited their labor and sexuality, and used them for reproduction.

Although there are traditions that allow Muslims to enslave free people in and outside of war, there are others which state that they can only buy enslaved People of the Book if they acknowledge their slavery (Kulayni, vol. 5: 188) and others that prohibit the purchase of free people who were enslaved. On one occasion, 'Ali al-Rida was supposedly asked about buying captives. He explained that "if they are open enemies, you can buy [them], but if they are exiled and treated unjustly, then do not buy their captives" (Kulayni, vol. 5: 187). When asked about the People of the Book who, facing famine, offered to sell their children so that they may be fed, he responded that "You must not sell free people. It is now lawful for you as well as for the taxpayers" (Kulayni, vol. 5: 187). Rather than follow this tradition, which prohibited the enslavement of free people, and limited slavery to captives from just wars, many jurists relied upon the opposite rule that allowed Muslims to purchase those who were unlawfully enslaved. Finally, unlike the Qur'an, which encourages men to marry righteous slave girls, Ja'far al-Sadiq stated that it was not proper for a married man, with a free wife, to marry a slave girl, nor a single man unless it was an emergency (Kulayni, vol. 5: 326-327; Nu'man vol. 2: 231).

If the situation was terrible for sex slaves, it was not much better for free women who engaged in *mut'ah* marriages. In fact, in Twelver Shiite Traditions, the status of the temporary wife is equated to that of the sex-slave. This fact, however, should not cast a shadow on all of Shiism, which includes Zaydism,

Ismailism, and various so-called Ghulat groups, much less on all of Islam which is predominantly Sunni. For Sunnis, Fiver Shiites, Sevener Shiites, and Qur'anists, the Twelver practice of *mut'ah* or temporary marriage is nothing short of prostitution.

According to Sunni, Fiver, Sevener, and even Twelver traditions, Ja'far al-Sadiq strictly prohibited temporary pleasure marriages. In fact, he described it as *zina*,' namely, fornication or unlawful intercourse, and stated that only an immoral person would act thus (Nu'man, vol. 2: 214-216). He insisted that the validity of marriage depended on two witnesses, a dowry, and the intention of marrying for life. He prohibited marriage for a specific length of time. There are even traditions in Twelver sources that are opposed to temporary marriage; however, they were not acted upon. In one tradition, the sixth Imam told one of his followers not to insist upon *mut'ah* (Kulayni, vol. 5: 414). And in yet another one, he warned Muslims to "Stay away from it," asking, "Do you not feel ashamed of being in a place for which your virtuous brothers in belief and friends feel embarrassed?" (Kulayni, vol. 5: 415). Jurisprudentially, this last tradition provides sufficient grounds to prohibit the disgraceful practice.

Traditions of questionable moral content were concocted by predators so that they could profit from their prey, and some jurists were all the more willing to codify them into law. This hedonistic harem Islam may be heaven for men; however, it is hell for women. Rather than reject pro-slavery traditions as false, Twelver Shiite jurists employed them to create a jurisprudential architecture of slavery that is not substantially different from that of the 'Abbasids and other Sunnis. As Bernard K. Freamon notes,

> There is a fair amount of scholarly literature asserting that Shiism is more liberal and more tolerant of anti-slavery ideas and that emancipation of a slave is easier to achieve under the Shi'a jurisprudence... Close examination of the Safavid and Qajar histories does not support the assertion that Shiism, in practice, was more liberal and emancipatory than Sunni regimes... slavery as practiced under the Shi'a looked very much like slavery under the Sunnis. (2019: 380, note 30)

As Zahra Azhar and Masoud Noori have shown, Shiite scholars in Iran believed that slavery was "a means for non-believers to convert to obtain their eternal freedom as a reward for becoming Muslim." For them, abolishing slavery was the equivalent of abolishing a means towards human freedom.

8.9 Support for Slavery from Shiite Religious Authorities

If the twelve Imams were so anti-slavery, why did Twelver Shiite jurisprudence not reflect this reality? Why is it that Shiite Islam maintained slavery? The traditions attributed to the Imams helped consolidate, entrench, and legitimize the practice giving it the stamp of approval of God, the Prophet, and his Progeny. The jurists who did so did not fight the power or oppose oppression. They were not freedom fighters. On the contrary, they reinforced the slave laws of the time. They were happy and willing servants of the *status quo*.

Shiite scholars like Ibn Sina (980-1137) believed that light and dark-skinned people were determined by nature and climate to be slaves (Rehbari). Nasir al-Din al-Tusi (1201-1274), a Shiite scholar who specialized in ethics, argued that slaves were a gift from God (Rehbari). As Rehbari notes, "he admitted that some slaves were free 'by nature,' yet he recommended that they be well treated rather than liberated."

Shiite scholars like Mohammad Saleh Khatunabadi (1648-1714) wrote a work delineating who could be legitimately enslaved (Rahbari). When asked whether castrating male slaves warranted their automatic emancipation, Mirza Abdollah Isfahani (1656-1718) rejected the idea, thereby legitimizing the sexual dismemberment of enslaved men, and providing people with a "religious" justification to buy, own, and sell eunuchs (Rahbari). Far from fighting for freedom, Twelver Shiite scholars impeded abolition, and emancipation. As Freamon explains,

> After the British came to the realization that interpretations of Islamic law might have some impact on the negotiations, they embarked on a policy that sought to get an anti-slavery *fatwa*, or religious opinion, from the '*ulama*'.... The Iranian prime minister actually queried the *mujtahids*, both in Tehran and in the newly established pilgrimage cities of Karbala and Najaf, in Iraq, but the answers he received refused to declare the slave trade to be illegal under Shi'ah interpretations of the Islamic laws. The answers indicated that the buying and selling of enslaved persons, while abominable, was lawful under the *shari'ah* and for the government to prohibit it would in itself be a violation of Islamic laws. The answers were also disingenuous for ... the slave trade could not, under any rational application of Islamic law principles, be justified in the absence of war. It would be a fair inquiry for a contemporary observer to ask: Why did the '*ulama*' evade the facts? (2019: 385)

Referring to the research conducted by Behnaz Mirzai, a historian of modern Iran, Freamon notes,

> the '*ulama*' of Iran, the Shiite clerics of Najaf, Karbala, and Qum, were firmly of the opinion that the ownership of slaves and the buying and selling of slaves in a commercial slave trading enterprise, while perhaps abominable behaviors, were activities that were expressly allowed by the *shari'ah* and to prohibit such activities would clearly violate Islamic laws. (2019: 330)

Since the British could not find support from Twelver Shiite jurists in their attempt to abolish slavery, they tried using moral arguments with the leader of Persia and the well-known prophetic *hadith*, which asserted that "the worst of men is the seller of free men" (384). Ultimately, "it was fear of incurring the condemnation of the Shi'a *'ulama'* that prevented the Shah from abolishing slavery" (Freamon 385). To this day, most of the major Twelver Shiite jurists treat slavery and sexual bondage as normative and include rulings regarding them in their jurisprudential manuals. Speaking of slavery, Mohammad-Taqi Mesbah Yazdi (1935-2021), the notorious paleoconservative cleric, asserted that:

> If there's a war between us and the infidels, we'll take slaves. The ruling on slavery hasn't expired and is eternal. We'll take slaves and we'll bring them to the world of Islam and have them stay with Muslims. We'll guide them, make them Muslims, and then return them to their countries. (Soroush, Rajaee 178)

When 'Ali al-Sistani (b. 1930), the religious authority, was asked whether it was permissible to enslave women belonging to the infidels who make war against Muslims without the permission of the legitimate ruler, and whether the Muslims could take their women as concubines and have sex with them, he answered that "it is not allowed." However, the question hinged on "permission of the legitimate ruler." In other words, if the religious authority, supreme leader, or just Imam allowed slavery and concubinage, the answer would have been in the affirmative. If he prohibited such actions, it was because, as a traditionalist Shiite, who opposes Iran's concept of *wilayat al-faqih* or the rule of the jurist, he believes in the separation of Mosque and State.

That being said, there is no shortage of modern and contemporary Twelver Shiite scholars who support sexual slavery. The top aide of Muqtada al-Sadr (b. 1974), the Iraqi cleric, militia leader, and politician, told his supporters that if anyone captured a female British soldier, he could keep her as a slave (NBC News). Muhammad Ghazidadeh, among other Shiite scholars, also holds that the law can never change (Bauer 260). This applied to the right of husbands to hit their wives as much as it applied to slavery. Such attitudes may explain why some Muslim men are violent, controlling, and exceptionally oppressive to women. Regarding slavery, Ghazidadeh remarked that "this is a rule for all time. In one period of time we may use the rule, and in other periods we don't use it, but the rule is fixed" (Bauer 261). This was also the opinion of the late Sa'id al-Hakim (1936-2021), the Iraqi Twelver Shiite religious authority.

When asked about slavery, whether the Prophet Muhammad intended to abolish it gradually, and whether it was permissible or prohibited to own slaves in our day and age, Sa'id al-Hakim ruled that "the religious laws that concern slavery that Allah Almighty has legislated did not change and was not altered, but its subjects no longer exist in our times which made such laws unpractical" (Hakim).

In other words, Hakim viewed slavery as divinely sanctioned, rejected the claim that the Prophet Muhammad aimed at abolishing it incrementally, and insisted that Islamic laws regarding it remained valid and binding. If they were not implemented today, it was merely due to the absence of slaves to whom they apply. Were such slaves to become available, the Islamic rules would apply to them.

In *82 Questions*, 'Abd al-Husayn Dastghayb Shirazi (1913-1981), the Twelver Shiite jurist, exegete, and specialist in ethics, professed that "the story of slavery in Islam... constitutes one of the brightest pages of human history." He claims that,

> Islam never approved of slavery in principle as it strove hard with all the different means at its disposal to eliminate slavery once for all. It tolerated its existence for the time being just because it had no other alternative for it concerned not only Muslims but those people as well who were not under its direct control. They held the Muslims in servitude making them suffer the worst possible forms of humiliation and miseries which drove the Muslims to adopt with respect to these people a course of like treatment, at least in treating their prisoners of war as slaves though not in their actual transactions with these slaves afterwards.
>
> Islam could not affect the abolition of slavery so long as the world did not agree to put an end to the only source of slavery: enslavement of prisoners of war. So when that concord was achieved, Islam welcomed it as it formed the unalterable fundamental principle of its polity: liberty for all, equality for all.

Dastghayb Shirazi comes across as quite the abolitionist. However, when asked, "Is the buying and selling of slaves lawful in this age also?" and "Is it allowed to apprehend people from Africa etc. and sell them in other places?" the Twelver Shiite jurist, who was appointed the Friday prayer leader of Shiraz by Khomeini, ruled:

> Yes, it is permissible for a Muslim to apprehend an original disbeliever in any way and from anywhere and enslave him provided he is not under treaty or responsibility of any Muslim (*dhimmi*). After that his buying and selling is allowed.

'Abd al-Husayn Dastghayb Shirazi was described as a "highly religious" "nobleman" with "a lofty character and loving nature" who was "an excellent model of spirituality." He specialized in "Islamic ethics." In a clear-cut case of cognitive dissonance, Dastghayb Shirazi held a series of contradictory cognitions or thoughts. He praised and exalted "Islamic" slavery. He praised abolition and emancipation. He stressed that slavery violated the Islamic principle of liberty. He also insisted that slavery was permissible in all times and places and that Muslims were permitted to enslave any and all *kuffar*, infidels, disbelievers, or non-Muslims, unless they were protected by a covenant or the property of another Muslim. Dastghayb Shirazi's despicable, abhorrent, and abominable edict gives *carte blanche* to ancient and modern forms of slavery.

Even Yousef Saanei (1937-2020), the reformist religious authority, believed in slavery. When asked about scholars who hold that certain Qur'anic injections were time-bound, and limited to the period of the Prophet, he responded:

> They are wrong. They cannot say so since Qur'anic verses are eternal: "We have not sent thee but as a universal (Messenger) to men, giving them glad tidings, and warning them (against sins), but most men understand not." It might be true about a few specific cases but cannot be true about the general rules. For instance, the verses discussing slaves and slavery were applicable to that time but they are pointless today. However, if someday slavery becomes customary in the world again, the verses will be applicable again. But it would definitely be wrong to say that these verses belonged to that time and would never be applicable ever after.

Clearly, even some Twelver Shiite "reformists" are open to the reintroduction and revival of slavery.

The views of Hakim and Saanei differ notably from that of Nasr Makarem Shirazi (b. 1927), the Iranian religious authority, who argues that "Islam devised certain strategies to extensively and slowly fight slavery until it was totally eliminated." Indisputably, from the dawn of Islam until its dusk, we contend only with the interpretations of human beings, none of whom are infallible. When evaluating them, we must rely on reason and logic, morals and ethics, and the call of our human conscience. And since when do slaves no longer exist? There are more slaves now than at any other time in human history.

8.10 Conclusions

The problem of slavery is a universal one. It troubles the human spirit. "Our better angels seem to focus upon the triumph of abolitionism," notes Junius P. Rodriguez, an American historian, "rather than concentrating upon the dark past of human subjugation" (xvii). "Despite such efforts," he notes, "the fact remains that abolitionism would have been unnecessary had peoples not been enslaved in the first place" (xvii). "We want people to take a hard look at the fact that for most of their history, Jews, Christians, and Muslims tolerated slavery," says Bernadette Brooten, an American religious scholar. "It's codified in the writings." "When you take a deep look into ancient history," she notes, "slavery and chastity rarely co-exist." On the contrary, "Sexuality and slavery are intertwined from the beginning" (Howard).

Of all the world's people, the only ones still defending slavery in principle, and the only ones trying to revive it in practice, are Muslims. Omar Suleiman's claim that, besides ISIS, "no other Islamic movement… has called for a return to slavery" is patently untrue. Algerian and Nigerian Islamists have also reintroduced sexual slavery. He is correct, however, that certain groups, like Hizb al-Tahrir, call for a return of the caliphate but not a return to slavery. And he is correct that "there is a consensus among scholars against the perpetuation of slavery and against its reappearance in the present day," if he includes only abolitionist ones. There is indeed a worldwide legal and moral consensus against slavery on the part of humanity. It is high time for Muslims to join it. Rather than act as the torchbearers of freedom, some Muslim scholars wish to drag us back to the past, carrying balls and chains and slave collars with spikes. We resoundingly refuse.

Chapter Nine

Religious and Racial Reckoning

9.1 Introduction

Many Western Muslims, most of whom are of African ancestry and the descendants of enslaved people, were directly or indirectly inspired by the teachings of Master W.D. Fard, Elijah Muhammad, and Malcolm X. For them, Islam, as it was presented to them, was an anti-racist, anti-sexist, abolitionist religion. Christianity was synonymous with slavery, and Islam was equated with freedom. Islam, to them, was a protest movement intimately linked to the struggle for civil and human rights. What followed, the realization that comes from research and life experience, hit them hard and fast and left their heads spinning. Such was the case with Malcolm X when he gradually came to admit that the teachings of the Nation of Islam did not coincide with the reality of Islam as a world religion.

9.2 Facing Reality

Like the disillusioned Malcolm X, most members of the Nation of Islam eventually moved into Sunni Islam in search of a more "authentic" form of the faith that embraced the brotherhood and sisterhood of humanity. To their dismay, many of these Western Muslim converts and their families came to realize that people who profess the unity of God do not necessarily embrace the notion of human unity and universal human equality (see Freamon 2019: 91). They realized that Muslims did not historically put *tawhid* into social practice. Rather than slaughter and enslave one another, as the Arabs did during pre-Islamic times, Islamized Arabs redirected their rage and greed toward non-Arabs. Moreover, when non-Arabs became Islamic powerhouses, like the Persians and the Turks, they also massacred and subjugated non-Muslims. Once again, these Western Muslims were shell-shocked when faced with incontrovertible historical facts and textual evidence.

9.3 Between a Rock and a Hard Place: From Sunnism to Shiism and Beyond

Some Western Muslims were so dismayed at Sunni Islam's history of racism, sexism, and slavery, that they were lured into Shiite Islam, which was presented to them as a revolutionary religion, the faith of the oppressed, which was committed to fighting injustice and overthrowing oppressors. However, this "revolutionary Shiism" was a late-twentieth-century creation. Until the rise of Khomeini and ideologues of his ilk, Twelver Shiites showed little concern for the oppressed and the enslaved. They may have cared about the followers of their sect; however, that was the extent of their empathy. In North Africa and West Africa, some Sunni and Sufi movements struggled to free enslaved black Muslims. There was no similar phenomenon in the Shiite world. They showed no care or concern for black or white suffering.

After embracing an ideology that unabashedly defends the Qur'anicity and Islamicity of slavery and sexual bondage, some Western Shiites felt like fools who had been bamboozled. They found that Zaydism viewed slavery as *makruh* or detestable. However, they also learned that one of the Zaydi Imams from the seventh century used enslaved people as agricultural workers (Clarence-Smith 60). These Western converts realized that Shiism, like Sunnism, is not a religion that frees slaves, but has historically enslaved human beings and perpetuated a system of human exploitation and denigration. The Fatimids and the Safavids were just as imperialistic as their Sunni counterparts (Rahbari). In fact,

> The establishment of an Islamic empire did little to diminish the numbers and uses of slaves in Iranian society and economies. Indeed, slaves and the peddling trade in slaving greatly expanded during and after the Safavid rulers assumed power... Between 1840 and 1880, Iran's participation in the Indian Ocean trade surpassed all previous slave-trading practices including the pre-Safavid era. (Ricks)

In comic irony, some Western Muslims turned to 'Ibadi Islam, under the impression that it was more egalitarian. Where will they turn when they realize that the 'Ibadis were among the leading slave traders in the Muslim world? "As early as the eighth century," notes Azumah, "the Berber 'Ibadi community of North Africa virtually controlled the trade routes, and thus the traffic in black slaves" (144). In the vast global expanse of Islam, there was nowhere to flee from the shackles of slavery in practice, if not in theory. While traditional "Islamic" slavery and concubinage may have decreased, with only sporadic attempts to revive them, their ideological foundations continue to be taught, defended, disseminated, justified, and propagated to the following generations. For critics, abolitionists, and human rights activists, Jonathan A.C. Brown's *Slavery & Islam* is another link in that chain that gives legitimacy to abominations.

As Muhammad Diakho denounces, volumes of works detailing the Islamic laws of slavery continue to be published and taught in religious seminaries and universities. It is as if the religious scholars are awaiting the opportunity to put them back into practice. Not only must we remove slavery from manuals of Islamic jurisprudence, asserts Diakho, but Muslims must stop teaching it as if it were a legal practice (60).

9.4 Convert Clowns, Muslim Pimps, Players, and Hojabis

For the sake of honesty, it must be acknowledged that some Muslim converts and cultural Muslims enthusiastically embrace the concepts of polygyny, temporary pleasure marriages, and sexual slavery. They stress that these practices are particularly well suited to men, particularly African Americans. Some take many women in permanent marriages; however, they never provide for them or their children. Others opt for temporary marriages. Some Muslims, of conversion and culture, hook up with an endless stream of mostly non-Muslim women and some stary-eyed converts.

The Twelver Shiites, in particular, use temporary pleasure marriages as a tool of proselytization. Some men are attracted to Islam; however, the prohibition of fornication and adultery, and the prospect of chastity and monogamy, are obstacles to conversion. Some Shiite missionaries present Musa al-Kazim as a role model for African American men. Why? Because he was in and out of prison much of his life and spent his final years serving a twenty-year term. Why? Because he had three to five dozen children with different women while never getting married in his life. Such comparisons insult both black men and the seventh Imam.

For the record, these Twelver Shiite accounts, traditions, and biographies are in complete disagreement with the Sunni and Sufi ones. They also conflict with those transmitted by minority Shiite sects that are monogamist. It should also be stressed that some Twelver Shiite scholars call into question these controversial accounts of the concubines of the seventh Imam. The sources all stress that the mothers of his children were *umm walads*. Did they become free after they bore him children? Did he emancipate them upon marriage?

In any event, if some Muslim converts were prolific fornicators before Islam, they continue the same life of debauchery after embracing it: only now they can do so with a clear conscience and the promise of divine blessings. These men, like others of their kind, love temporary marriages. They provide them with sexual access to women, without any responsibility to provide for them. *Dios los cría y solitos se juntan*. For some Muslim converts, Islam is like a tag on a fake Gucci bag.

The problem in question is not limited to Western converts to Islam. It is also prevalent among Muslims of many different ethnic groups worldwide: Arab and Asian men who hook up with non-Muslim women in so-called *mut'ah* or *'urfi* marriages. Some Imams and shaykhs, most of them married, also abuse their power and influence to seduce young Muslim girls, and women under the guise of "secret marriages." Men will be men, and women will be women. It is not only Christian clergy who cause sexual scandals. It applies to Muslim clerics as well. Moreover, some of these unions include same-sex trysts between Sufi shaykhs and their male disciples and students. Some Muslim converts, who fled the lifestyle of the infidels, are shocked to find the same behavior among the believers.

Some of these pious players do not even bother to contract temporary marriages with white girls. No, they enslave them, simultaneously keeping three or four of them in their beds. After all, they are following the *sunnah*. "They are my slave girls," they claim, "white enemy booty." There are Arab and Pakistani men who own strip joints and cohabit with strippers on their staff. Once again, the same excuse is heard over and over again: they are my concubines. Black, non-Muslim pimps are not in the practice of invoking God, the Bible, or Christianity to justify their actions. In reality, the Muslim, so-called alpha males, who exploit women sexually, under the guise of polygyny, *mut'ah*, or concubinage, do not suffer from an excess of masculinity and virility, but rather, a shortage of self-control and morality.

If one studies the "Muslim" grooming gangs in the United Kingdom, France, the United States, and other nations, one finds that these pimps, pedophiles, kidnappers, human traffickers, and rapists rationalize their crimes on the basis of the Qur'an, the *sunnah*, and the *shari'ah* (Morrow 2020:120-129; see McLaughlin). 63% of rapes in Paris and 32% of rapes in the rest of France are committed by foreign nationals, virtually all of whom are Muslims. 87% of the victims of sexual assault in Paris are French citizens. Outside of Paris, 95% of the victims are French people (Valeurs Actuelles). Although they are only 12% of the population, Muslims make up forty to seventy percent of prisoners (Morrow 2020: 126).

In the United Kingdom, Muslims are also disproportionately represented in rape statistics. In fact, "from 1997 to 2019, out of the 377 men convicted of sex trafficking in the United Kingdom, 326 were Muslims (Morrow 2020: 122). Although Muslims are only 4% of the population, they represent 12% of convicted rapists (Morrow 2020: 126). They "commit sexual assault at a rate that is four times higher than their percentage of the population" (Morrow 2020: 126). Although Muslims are only 8.1% of the Swedish population, they are responsible for more than half of sexual assaults (Morrow: 2020: 125). The same phenomenon is found throughout Europe.

Many of the men in question, some of whom are also drug dealers, wear beards, dress "Islamically," attend mosques, pray, and fast. To celebrate 'Eid, some of them go out and gang-rape white Christian girls. Criminals they may be, in the eyes of Muslims and non-Muslims alike, however, they view themselves as good, God-fearing, committed Muslims. They are Islamist gangsters. Their worldview is a mutant, toxic, and perverse combination of radical religion, patriarchy, and misogyny. God, Muhammad, the Qur'an, and Islam are free of them. Even if they were not self-professed Muslims, they would still be animals. They are a disgrace to their religions, races, and cultures of origin. They deserve to be disowned.

The predators and domestic terrorists in question target predominantly non-Muslim women or females from their communities that they treat as hypocrites, apostates, and harlots. Some specialize in child pornography and the prostitution of children. They invoke the Prophet's marriage to a six-year-old girl, and his sex with her at the age of nine, as a justification. They cite works of Islamic jurisprudence that permit the marriage of minors. They stress that slavery and concubinage are perfectly Islamic. They believe that it is their Islamic right and duty to enslave, rape, traffic, and sell non-Muslim women.

Brown has the right to write. Critics have the right to respond and ask questions. Do works like those of Brown help or harm black people? For objectors, authoring a book about *Islam and Blackness* does not undo the damage that has been done. Do works like those of Brown help or harm women and Muslims? On the contrary, it could be argued that they harm women and empower and embolden extremists and misogynists. For critics, they fuel the fire of hatred and fanaticism rather than try to extinguish it. I must admit that some critics will claim that my work does more harm than good. How? By making Islam and Muslims look bad? That is not my intention. My goal is to denounce views that do so. How does justifying slavery and concubinage defend Islam? According to some views, it damages it beyond imagination.

As Freamon observed in his review of Brown's *Slavery & Islam*, "sections of the book… unabashedly seek to explain away and perhaps excuse the ubiquitous role that slavery and slave trading have played in Islamic political, economic, and legal history" (2021: 344). For Brown, slavery was not always "a gross, intrinsic moral evil at all points in history" (269). What is more, notes Freamon, his translation of "the Qur'anic phrase *ma malakat aymanukum* as meaning 'those whom you possess rightfully'… is not consistent with the great majority of renderings of the phrase (and its literal meaning) and it may subtly distort the Qur'anic message on slavery" (2021: 346). The Arabic language has several specific words that refers to concubines. If the Qur'an was speaking about concubines and sex slaves, why were they not used? Why employ this circumlocution over half a dozen times? The Qur'anic expression appears to introduce an entirely different notion; a relationship of a distinct nature.

For Brown, the fact that slavery is illegal in most majority-Muslim countries "does not mean that 'slavery is *haram*' is a legitimate interpretation of the Qur'an, Sunna, and Islam's legal tradition, let alone the sole valid one" (2020: 253). Come again? Slavery is *haram* is not a legitimate interpretation of the Qur'an, the *sunnah*, and the *shari'ah*? And even if it were legitimate, it would not be the only valid interpretation?

The Islamic legal tradition consists of a vast spectrum of opinion. Many scholars have been attempting to recover these long lost and forgotten views and showcase their diversity. In some cases, all the recorded views are valid. They deal with inconsequential matters like whether shellfish are *halal*, *haram* or *makruh*, how to perform *wudhu*, and how to position one's arms in prayer. In others, they include rulings that are entirely unacceptable according to any reasonable standard, including destroying synagogues and churches, expelling Jews, slaughtering non-Muslims, sharing slave girls for sex, having sexual relations with pre-pubescent girls, including babies, enslaving Muslims, permitting the traffic in eunuchs, and a host of other monstrosities. There are literally volumes of unacceptable legal opinions in Islam, including, as one can readily imagine based on this book, the permissibility of slavery and concubinage.

Is Brown an Islamic abolitionist? As far critics are concerned, he comes across as a proud apologist for slavery and sexual bondage, albeit in past times, and not in the present. When Muslims were denouncing ISIS for sexually assaulting captives, Brown focused on the fact that it was not rape according to Islamic law. In his words, "there is no such thing as non-consensual sex with a concubine" (Asharis Assemble, Spencer). What is more, "slave women do not have agency over their sexual access, so their owner can have sex with them." In other words, it is not rape: it is a right. Do such comments condemn radical Islamist rapists or give legitimacy to their crimes?

Brown may appraise "the two main contemporary Islamic arguments supporting abolition," namely, public interest, and consensus; however, "he rejects both arguments," asserting "the public interest argument is only a temporary fix" and "is skeptical about the sincerity of claims of *ijma*'" (Freamon 2021: 345-346). In fact, Brown doubts that it holds water (2020: 154). Rather than question the *ijma*' regarding the prohibition of slavery, why not call into question the so-called consensus regarding its permissibility? It was devoid of scriptural support and challenged from the seventh to the twenty-first century. In the words of Ware,

> Slavery's standing in Islamic law was contested. Some '*ulama*' challenged every aspect of the production and sale of human beings from the seventh century through the nineteenth. Some argued that no legal precedent existed for the forms of enslavement practiced during the expansion of the caliphate. Others sought inspiration in the Prophet's example and noted that … the Qur'an calls for pious manumission… Others noted that the Prophet himself freed anyone he had ever owned before he died. If the *sunnah* was so important, they suggest, Muslims should have done likewise. Still others challenged the weak legal basis for aggressive *jihad*, hoping to curb enslavement by curbing war. (112-113).

Tragically, traditional "Islamic" slavery and concubinage are alive and well in Mauritania. Hereditary slavery of blacks, all of whom are Muslims, continues to thrive in a society that has not evolved morally and ethically since Islam arrived there in the late seventh century. If being "traditional" is the litmus test, then Mauritania is a prime example of an "Islamic" society. Arab and Amazigh slave masters insist on their purportedly God-given, Prophet-given, and *shari'ah*-granted right to have sex with their slaves, an act viewed by these black Muslim girls and women for what it really is: sexual assault, rape, and violation.

Appallingly, some Western Muslim converts are proud to study "Islam" in Mauritania and boast of the "traditional" education they received. By whom? By the very men who pose the greatest obstacle to the emancipation of the enslaved black Muslims in the nation. Muhammad Hasan Dadaw (b. 1963) insists that *shari'ah* sanctioned slavery is not morally wrong (Brown 2020: 261). Hasan Wald

Binyamin (d. 2017) has even called his country's ban on slavery illegal (Brown 2020: 262). If these pro-slavery "scholars" knew anything about Islam, there would be no slaves in Mauritania. As Boubacar Ould Messaoud (b. 1945), the leader of *SOS Esclaves*, explains,

> Slavery was instrumentalized by the clerics of this country, who have a psychological and moral stranglehold on the majority of the illiterate country. For a large majority of slaves, it is a sacred duty to obey one's master. It is a *sine qua non* condition, according to their spirits deceived by religious sycophants, to reach the Paradise. Of course, Islam has nothing to do with that! These are individuals who distort divine words for their personal and tribal interests. This means that all of Mauritanian society is unaware of this social fact. We don't talk about it. (CRIDEM)

When enslaved black Mauritanian Muslims burn books of Maliki jurisprudence, such as the *Mukhtasar* of Khalil ibn Ishaq (d. 1365), which are used to justify slavery, does Brown cheer them on or accuse them of blasphemy and apostasy for doing so? The Arab and Berber slave masters in Mauritania follow "Islamic" law *to the letter*. They follow the rules of the classical Muslim jurists that Brown appears all so eager to excuse. Ironically, some Muslim converts of color, African Americans in particular, embrace Sunnism or neo-Sufism and promote the Maliki school of jurisprudence as one that is appealing to black people.

For Muslims with self-critical faith, and rational minds, there are many forms of Islam in the world, including the Islam of God and the Islam of Satan. Which one do slave masters follow? Do they belong to *ahl Allah*, *ahl al-sunnah*, *ahl al-bayt*, or *ahl al-Shaytan*? Do they belong to the People of God, the People of Tradition, the People of the House, or the People of Satan? Are they *ahl al-jinnah* or *ahl-jahannam*? Are they the People of Heaven or the People of Hell? The questions are harsh. The answers are harsher. However, what can be harsher than slavery itself?

As far as many faithful and conscientious Muslims are concerned, every enslaved man is a Bilal, and the Prophet freed Bilal. Every enslaved man is a Zayd ibn Harithah, a Yasir ibn Amir, an 'Ammar ibn Yasir, a Salman al-Farsi, a Suhayb al-Rumi, and a Shuqran and every enslaved woman is a Summayyah bint Khabbat. In their hearts and minds, every enslaved woman, who is used and abused by vicious and lascivious men, is a Zunayrah al-Rummiyah, the companion of the Prophet and the scribe of revelation.

Surprise, surprise. Most Muslims have never heard of Zunayrah. There is a reason. As far as spiritual, rational, and socially committed believers are concerned, the fraudulent religion that some Muslims have been taught is Slave Master Islam. It is the imperial Islam of the oppressors, created and concocted to serve their political, ideological, financial, and sexual interests. They have turned the Religion of Liberation into the Religion of Subjugation. They have transformed the Religion of Spiritual Ascension into the Religion of Oppression.

108   Islam & Slavery

True religious values lie in ruin. No more! As Mohammad Ali Amir-Moezzi (b. 1956), the Iranian Islamologist based in France, notes,

> Caliphal power set up a complex system of propaganda, censorship, and historical falsification... It forged an entire body of traditions falsely ascribed to the Prophet, drawing great scholars, judges, jurists, preachers, and historians into its service -- all this was within a policy of repression that was as savage as it was methodical. (qtd. Shoemaker 37)

While we must denounce Orientalist efforts to portray slavery as an inherent and immutable part of Islam, to present Western thought as the sole source of emancipation, and to accuse blacks of being the cause of their own enslavement to alleviate white guilt, it is hypocritical for Muslims, and the historical victims of Christian slavery, to ignore, minimize, or deny the magnitude of the "Islamic" slave trade. Both were equal in their evil and iniquity.

We must defend divine truth from demonic distortion and human hypocrisy. An immoral Islam is no Islam at all. For opponents of slavery and concubinage, the Islam that is propagated by slave masters, human traffickers, pimps, pedophiles, rapists and their apologists in academia and behind the minbar is a gutter religion. We must reject any interpretation of Islam that opposes its emancipatory and egalitarian principles. Yes to the Islam of freedom and justice and a resounding and emphatic no to the Islam of slavery and concubinage.

9.5 Conclusions

These reflections on the reality of sexual slavery and its horrors lead us to ask some fundamental soul-searching questions: Is imperialism Islamic? Is racism Islamic? Is sexism Islamic? Is exploitation Islamic? Is oppression Islamic? Was Muhammad an imperialist, a racist, a sexist, an exploiter, and an oppressor? The answers matters, as imperialism, racism, sexism, exploitation, and oppression are interwoven. If imperialism, racism, sexism, exploitation, and oppression are un-Islamic, then so is slavery, its concomitant, and the Prophet Muhammad is redeemed from the allegations that have been made against him and free of the sins that were enshrined as Islamic law by those who professed to follow in his footsteps.

To defend slavery and concubinage is not to defend Islam. It is to soil and offend it. Justifying and apologizing for so-called "Islamic" slavery and concubinage pushes people from Islam. Opposing such iniquities draws people in and retains them. This debate concerns Islam's heart and soul, its foundations, legacy, and future. It is an issue on which one cannot remain indifferent. It is a watershed issue if there ever was one, and a galvanizing and polarizing one. "Stand with the truthful" (9:119), counsels the Qur'an, and "stand up firmly for justice even if it is against yourselves, your parents, or close relatives" (4:135). As the Messenger of God asked: "O people, have I faithfully delivered unto you my message?" If so, then "deliver me, O my God, from the hand of the wicked, from the grasp of evil and cruel men" (Psalm 71).

Chapter Ten

No Means Yes, No Means Tie Her UP, NO Means Smack Her Up

10.1 Introduction

Although the notion that wives and slaves needed to consent to sex with their husbands is a relatively recent one in much of the world, it is objectively right, and did exist in some pre-modern cultures. Forcing one's wife to have sex was not acceptable in many of the indigenous cultures of North America. Such action is inconceivable in cultures that respect and revere women. As far as patriarchal Islamic law was concerned, Jonathan A.C. Brown notes, "consent for sexual relations was assumed or irrelevant" (96) whether a woman had a husband or a master. He quotes several scholars who admit that "there was no requirement for consent for sex from slave women in books of Islamic law" (96; see also 281).

10.2 Speak of the Devil

Brown may claim to have backtracked, and even deactivated his Facebook page, after his arguably scandalous speech, but fortunately, or unfortunately, depending on one's perspective, those posts have been preserved. As he wrote on Facebook, "there is no such thing as non-consensual sex with a concubine" (Asharis Assemble, Spencer). What is more, "slave women do not have agency over their sexual access, so their owner can have sex with them" (Asharis Assemble, Spencer). This elicited the following response from the author of Asharis Assemble,

> I don't know if I am weird or something but I thought sex without a choice = rape. But of course, that is why he is playing politics -- he has an idiosyncratic definition of rape. Or more likely, like others lately, he just wants to keep his Salafi/Deobandi etc. fan base happy. Never mind the abhorrence or disgust felt by non-Muslims or others...
>
> Basically, this is precisely their idea, found in many scholars' *fatwas* (and from the *hadith* literature which takes the Prophet himself attempting a rape as "canonical" -- in "Sahih al Bukhari" no less), that:
>
> 1) You take over a place, the soldiers wives and or perhaps even the civilian girls are now automatically "divorced" and can be made into slaves.

2) Your slaves are like your wives (except they aren't really as they had no choice. Not that Salafis give free women a choice either).

3) There is no such thing as marital rape.

4) Therefore you "can't" rape your slave as she is your property.

5) ENJOY!

Basically, ISIS can prove all of this from *hadith* and the opinions of the same scholars that Salafis and many others hold dear...

How does Brown's contribution help at all? He's basically admitting that the classical "authorities" allowed you to rape your slaves. At least he should say "but Muslims think these guys messed up, don't worry." But his Facebook comments appear to be compound dumbness.

Muslim speakers often say you are not allowed to hit a slave and thus you wouldn't rape her (standard Salafi argument to prove that slaves are not to be raped). They bring some narrations to show that this is a case, basically *hadith* which show that people who hit their slaves were compelled to set them free. But this is contradicted by the fact that these same people say that you can beat your wife according to the Qur'an and that, according to Brown, "slave women do not have agency over their sexual access, so their owner can have sex with them."

Isn't this just confusing, politician style jabberwocky gobbledygook double talk crap-ism? Also, since they are spamming us with the opinions of "classical jurists," from which classical jurist did they get this opinion that hitting precludes forced sex/rape of slaves? Or did they just make it up? It's also funny how the "jurists" and *hadiths* talk about not hitting your slave but this is extended to rape -- well, it's just like the thing about fornication and adultery, including rape!

You see, rape is such a minor thing that there is no need to address it specifically! I guess it is the same with murder and mutilation -- there's just no need to address it as it comes under "hitting!" I wonder what else comes under "hitting" if rape does. War? Manslaughter? Drone strikes? Nuclear Holocaust? Why, who knew that Sharia was so simple -- everything comes under "hitting!"

But then, strangely, when it came to non-Muslims, there WAS, all of a sudden, a death penalty for rape...curious!

This is why such "defenses" by people like Brown are frankly a bit rubbish and make no sense at all.

I mean come on, their way of making Islam "look good" is to say that you can take women as slaves and rape them, but don't leave a mark or it will come under hitting. And then you might get told off. Or get a small fine. Or nothing.

I get what they are trying to do. But it is dumb. And does not help at all. What would be more useful is if Brown used his history skills to say that "well, you know the Qur'an never says the majority is right, quite the opposite. Even if most or all Muslim scholars said this, it does not mean that Muslims or the Qur'an agree with this anymore than a Christian or a Hindu today would be beholden to the politicized and contextual *fatwas* of their scholars from the past which show a similar degree of indifference to coercive sex and slavery..."

Don't you think that it is TOTALLY MENTAL that the same group of people who argue that "free mixing" and a woman showing her face to men is HARAAM (forbidden) think it is fine to RAPE RANDOM WOMEN YOU JUST MET and not only look at them but actually have sex with them (but it's actually rape).

Could it be that these people studied *Fiqh* (jurisprudence or legal theory) while HIGH ON CRACK?

Yes boys, according to some Salafis, you can rape girls. But not look at them. Because rape isn't really rape. But looking REALLY is looking!

The proof of the banality of Brown's response and its unhelpfulness is obvious: Let's say that all Islamic scholars, ever from the most famous to your local imam said that raping slaves was fine and was not in fact rape. So there was a super *ijma'* on it. Would you agree with it? No (unless you are mental).

So in the end, you decided whether it made (moral) sense to YOU or not -- exactly as the Qur'an told you to. You are willing to ignore the opinions of every single scholar on this matter.

You know the funny thing? Even if (God forbid) the Qur'an itself told you rape was fine you still wouldn't follow it and would decide that Islam was not the religion for you. You would probably then proceed to kill the crap out of those who did follow such a book before they raped you or your family.

It's precisely because the Qur'an does NOT say dumb stuff like that that diverse people have accepted and followed Islam for as long and as widely as they have. The Qur'an tells you to contemplate and think and reason over matters of faith and morality and to resist oppression, blind following, and argument from authority.

When the angels questioned God about how come he was putting something on Earth which would result bloodshed (and the angels were right, mankind did indeed shed blood, even in God's name) He didn't give them a narration or a quote or a *fatwa* or say: "shut up, I'm God, how dare you test me?!"

Instead he said okay, let's talk about this, I'll show you -- I'll show you a rational proof that this creature is better than you. Let's check him out..

The logical consequence of demanding a *hadith* or a *fatwa* to tell you everything that is right or wrong is that Muslims are worse than non-Muslims, since they managed to work out that stuff like rape is wrong without a narration. So Islam doesn't work like that. Not real Islam anyway.

Islam is not really for people who refuse to use their brain. The Qur'an is quite explicit about that. If anyone bothered to read it instead of crap posts from Brown etc.

Also, don't you think that the Qur'an seems to assume that people are not TOTAL AMORAL PLONKERS and have a brain and some moral sense? Since the Qur'an tries to appeal to peoples' existing morality and intellect, perhaps the fact that some Muslims need a narration or a *fatwa* to tell them that rape is wrong or that you don't need four witnesses for rape tells us more about these people than Islam?

TRANSLATION: If you need someone to give you a narration or a *fatwa* explaining that raping people is wrong then providing this will probably not help you as you are WRONG IN THE HEAD and should probably be sent to PRISON (which you would presumably enjoy due to all of the rape that goes on there).

What's also funny is that if non-Muslims started practicing this *fatwa* in all the Muslim countries they are messing up i.e. saying that the women were deprived of sexual rights as they are slaves and started having sex with everyone's mum, sister, wife, and neighbor by force, do you think Brown or Muslims would be saying; "Hmm, curious, this reminds me of the *fatwa* of the classical scholars that says this is fine…" Poppycock!

Muslims subjected to such vile treatment by non-Muslims would be the first to say that this was a grave injustice. They sure as hell would not be posting dumb stuff about how slave women don't have agency over their vagina and other hogwash like that…

And while I am on the subject, as far as I am concerned, the actions of ISIS do not come under rape law and they most certainly don't come under fornication or adultery. These guys are not dirty old men hiding in parks but are systematically and "scientifically" raping captives. Rather this kind of behavior comes under *fasad fil 'ard* or "spreading corruption in the land…"

Funny how Salafists, who demand the death penalty for apostasy, adultery, and a whole heap of other things such as homosexuality (and anathematize anyone who disagrees), NONE of which are mentioned in the Qur'an AT ALL, then curiously forget to mandate the death penalty for the one thing for which it is mentioned in the Qur'an, namely *fasad*.

So the opinion of "classical scholars" on rape is hardly pertinent to the actions of ISIS since rape fans would already receive the death penalty for spreading *fasad* through coercive sex and the other dumb stuff they do.

Of course, stupid people will nevertheless choose their (Salafi) sources and claim that rape on an industrial scale as practiced by ISIS doesn't come under *fasad*, but we know otherwise don't we? Or do you still need a narration to tell you?

I get that Muslims are groping in the dark and desperate. They feel under siege, they are disempowered and with their scholarly institutions largely destroyed in the post-colonial period, they need someone who they think can help them. So they fall for people like Brown. It's understandable. But my question: ask yourself honestly -- did his post really help?

Brown even posted an article on "Rape in Islamic Law" on his Facebook page. The author from Asharis Assemble provides the following critical summary:

1) There is no specific punishment for rape in Islam (according to these people), it just comes under *zina* (= extramarital sex, whether adultery or fornication). So the punishment for rape in Islam is the same as fornication or adultery. And this helps our image how…?

2) You can get punished for rape by the death penalty though…but only if you are a non-Muslim raping a Muslim woman. [LAME EXCUSE TRIGGER WARNING]. It's because it's treason. Like apostasy. And all the other reasons we want to kill people for, which also come under treason. BTW, Muslims can't commit treason by raping someone though 'cos…ummmmm…uhhhh… Oh joy! Islamophobes debunked!

3) Raping slave girls is fine according to the "classical" sources (as edited by Salafis like Brown and Co. of course), but you have to pay a fine…to their owner. This makes Muslim look SOOOOOOOOO good!

4) If you are the person who got raped, rest assured, you won't be punished for fornication or adultery. Wow! Such a merciful religion! OR AN EVEN MORE SIMPLIFIED SUMMARY OF THIS POST: "There is no such thing as rape in Islamic law, it comes under fornication and adultery." You know since there is absolutely no difference between rape and fornication. And then Muslims wonder why people hate them. With friends like these…

I don't know to which allegations, or as he calls it "misinformation and ignorance being batted around over the issue of rape in Islamic Law" he was responding to. I don't really know what Brown thinks he is doing here -- if he is trying to "help" Muslims or just state the positions of previous jurists for academic purposes without commenting on them or giving his own opinion (and thereby providing more ammunition for Islamophobes in all of these scenarios).

If this is how the new generation of "white Salafis" such as Jonathan AC Brown er… "addresses" misinformation and "ignorance" then God help us.

All these people seem to have done is to confirm the worst accusations of Islamophobes and punish us additionally with an exercise in excessive verbiage.

10.3 Idyllic "Islamic" Slavery: A Muslim Man's Utopia?

Brown paints an idyllic picture of slaves as sexual partners that ignores its brutality, barbarity, and depravity (120-134). It reminds one of the idealized and romantic depictions of slavery in the southern United States found in some literature and films. Strange, but the last time I checked, Muhammad insisted that there was no *nikah*, marriage, or sex, as both are inseparable in Arabic, without the woman's consent (Bukhari, Muslim, Tirmidhi, Abu Dawud, Nasa'i). The Messenger of God was asked: "Should women be asked for their consent before marriage?" The Prophet responded: "Yes." And a weighty yes it was in a culture where women had few rights.

Thanks to culturally contaminated scholars for dollars, pre-Islamic mores prevailed in the so-called Muslim world. While there were some improvements in women's rights, there were also significant setbacks. In some cases, such as the innovation of large-scale, systematic slavery and concubinage, the situation for women deteriorated. Women, in this regard, were better off under the Jewish and Christian laws of the time. Neither the Jews nor the Christians of the time were involved in large-scale cross-continental slavery in the seventh and eighth century. What is more, their laws did not allow masters to have sex with their slaves. As for the Prophet Muhammad, he never initiated a planetary-wide slave trade targeting predominantly whites and blacks. He would have been appalled at such injustice and immorality.

10.4 Sex and Violence

As demonstrated in *The Most Controversial Qur'anic Verse,* based on empirical evidence, the Qur'an and the Prophet Muhammad prohibited domestic violence. Although there are traditions that permit it, there are others that prohibit it in no uncertain terms. Both Sunni and Shiite collections of traditions include sayings of the Prophet Muhammad where he orders men not to hit, beat, or slap their wives: *la tadribuhunna* (Abu Dawud and Majlisi). Those who developed Islamic law,

Chapter Ten

however, came to the opposite conclusion. As summarized in *The Most Controversial Qur'anic Verse*,

> Most Muslim jurists, throughout Islamic history, have ruled that wives are required to submit sexually to their husbands, that wives do not have the right to refuse sex, and that if they do so, their husbands have the right to force them. Some stress the right of men to beat, tie up, and rape their recalcitrant wives. These jurists relied, not on the Qur'an, but on traditions in which the Prophet Muhammad commands wives to worship their husbands, serve their every sexual whim, even having sex on the back of a quadruped. (2020: 286; see also 114-118, 136-137).

In the words of 'Abd al-Rahman al-Jaziri (1882-1941), "The followers of Abu Hanifah said: 'The right of sexual pleasure belongs to the man, not the woman, by that it is meant that the man has the right to force the woman to gratify himself sexually'" (113). Numerous authorities, including Abu Bakr ibn Mas'ud al-Kasani and Zayn al-Din ibn Ibrahim Ibn Nujaym, argued that husbands could have sex with their wives without their consent (Morrow 2020: 117). As Ayesha S. Chaudhry, a Canadian religious scholar of South Asian descent, notes, scholars like Hawwari, Ibn Abi Hatim, Ibn 'Atiyyah, Ibn al-Jawzi, al-Mawardi, Mujahid, Suyuti, and Tabari "explicitly stated that husbands could hit their wives until they were willing to have sex with them" (Morrow 2020: 117).

"Even if a man fractures [his wife's skull] or wounds her," argued Tabari, "there is no retaliation on him" (Morrow 2020: 118). For 'Ali al-Jassas, short of killing her, a husband could beat his wife to the point of wounding her without legal liability (Morrow 2020: 118). For 'Abd Allah ibn Ahmad al-Nasafi, unless the husband hits his wife more than one hundred times, he is not responsible if she dies due to the beating (Morrow 2020: 118). He went so far as to claim that a husband could kill his wife through copulation (Morrow 2020: 117). Despite claims that Muslim husbands could only hit, slap, or beat their wives "lightly," and symbolically, the fact remains that, under Islamic law, men were only held accountable and legally liable if they caused "severe injuries such as broken bones, loss of limbs, disfigurement, or death" (Chaudhry 97).

Intellectual and spiritual children should not accept the candy of adulterated Islam from human traffickers, sexual predators, and pedophiles, as the sugar-filled sweet is laced with poison. The Prophet Muhammad is free of these perverts. "Do not cause harm or return harm," he warned, "Whoever harms others, God will harm him" (Nasa'i). Moreover, "do not torture the creation of God" (Abu Dawud). Speaking of *la darar wa la dirar*, Diakho explains:

> This principle is well known to specialists in the sources of Islamic law... From the standpoint of Islamic ethics to harm another, regardless of the reason, is a wrong. To respond to a wrong with another wrong (equal treatment), only quantitatively increases the initial wrong, an attitude contrary to *'amr bi al-ma'ruf* or encouraging good. To reduce someone

to the status of servitude is, after physical death, the greatest evil that one could commit against all of humanity. (149)

These despicable traditions, in which the Prophet and the Imams allow husbands to take their wives and slave girls by force, and which stress that the right of pleasure is reserved to the man, contradict a body of sources that are kind, loving, caring, and compassionate. The Qur'an, for example, describes husbands and wives as "garments" for one another (2:187).

The Prophet Muhammad promoted foreplay. "When one wants to have sexual intercourse with one's wife," he advised, "one must not rush her, for women, too, have their needs [which must be fulfilled]" ('Amili). "When anyone of you has sex with his wife," he counseled, "then he should not go to them like birds; instead he should be slow and delaying" ('Amili). He stated that "No one among you should have sex with his wife like animals; rather there should be a messenger between them." When asked about the messenger, he said: "It means kissing and talking" (Kashani). When it came to sexual relations, the Messenger of God emphasized the importance of pleasure for both men and women.

Ja'far al-Sadiq said, "There should be mutual foreplay between them because it is better for sex" ('Amili). In another tradition, he warned men against climaxing before their wives as this could leave them in a state of sexual frustration that could lead them to sin. Hence, he stressed the importance of foreplay and the right of the woman to reach orgasm (Ibn Abi Dunya). Ja'far al-Sadiq and 'Ali al-Rida both said: "Woman is a source of pleasure, therefore do not harm her" ('Amili). This final tradition establishes a preeminent legal principle: "Do not harm women."

It is not as if Muslim scholars did not have choices. Either they relied on the wrong sources for their rulings, and failed to exercise due diligence, or they fabricated them outright. For Edip Yüksel, "the practice of slavery was justified and resurrected to a certain extent via the influence of Jewish and Christian scholars, as well as fabricated *hadith* and *shari'ah* laws, decades after Muhammad's departure" (101-102). Either way, they served the *status quo* seeking to please wicked rulers. They legitimized sexual slavery but wholly ignored the agricultural, military, and construction slavery surrounding them (Urban 8). As Chebel has noted, Arabs and Muslims actively participated in the slave trade, relying on deviant interpretations of the Qur'an to surround themselves with servants and concubines (289). The fact is that the Mosque did not remain neutral in the face of slavery. Rather than attempt to reform, and abolish it, Muslim jurists regulated it, producing slave codes which, as Chebel has noted, reflect "the highest degree of moral perversion" (106), "Verily, evil is their judgment" (Qur'an 16:59).

10.5 Facing the Music

Far from uncommon and limited to the upper echelons of society, slaves, and concubines were so common that, in certain times and place, they were found in every Muslim home, however humble (Clarence-Smith 2006: 10; Lal 43-44).

Wherever Islam was spread by the sword, hundreds of thousands of girls and women were enslaved. If we count the numbers cited in Islamic sources, millions upon millions of females were captured as concubines in Spain, North Africa, black Africa, the Middle East, and India. If the ratio of African slaves transported to the Americas consisted of one female for every two males, the opposite was true for those who were transported to the Muslim world.

If twenty-eight million black Africans were enslaved from the early days of Islam until the twentieth century, that would represent over eighteen million female slaves. If the total was eighteen million, we would be looking at twelve million. However, this figure do not include the millions of Amazigh, European, and Asian women who were also enslaved and forced into concubinage. Whenever it was involved in wars of conquest, the "Islamic" world was inundated with sex slaves.

Ever the optimist and a champion of feminism and freedom, Brown contends that "becoming a concubine was not necessarily a bad development for a female slave" (132-132); however, as Bernard K. Freamon understates, "it may be difficult to support" the "general statement… that elite slavery was always good for women" (346). In fact, "this is a species of the 'happy slave' argument, reminiscent of Aristotelian justifications for the practice" (2021: 346).

Some adult entertainers become rich and famous. Does that make pornography pure and good? Just because some women benefited from their status as slave wives to powerful and influential men, some even coming to rule over the empires that enslaved them and continued to enslave their people, does not make slavery good. As Kathryn A. Hain notes, "rape, nakedness, long-distance travel, and multiple exchanges erased the identity of… captives" (329). We cannot ignore the trauma caused by the slave raids, the slaughter of their menfolk, the suffering on the march, violent punishments, extreme insecurity, forced sexual relations, the unpredictable changing of ownership, and the scope of abuse, including that of children (Fisher 179). It was an act of physical, cultural, and spiritual genocide.

Early Muslim women knew exactly that it meant to be a concubine. The female companions of the Prophet proclaimed that they preferred to be martyred in battle than to be taken as sex slaves. Take the Battle of Yarmuk, for example, that took place in August of 636. Each time the outnumbered Muslim warriors would retreat, the ferocious Arab women, led by Hind bint 'Utbah, the wife of Abu Sufyan, would charge into battle to fight with tent poles. Each time their men ran away, the women would shame them into fighting on, singing: "O you who run from a constant woman / Who has both beauty and virtue; / And leave her to the infidel, The hated and evil infidel, / To possess, disgrace, and ruin" (Nicolle 71).

More than one thousand companions of the Prophet participated in the Battle of Yarmuk, including, Zubayr ibn al-'Awwam, Abu Sufyan, Sa'id ibn Zayd, Fadl ibn 'Abbas, 'Abd al-Rahman ibn Abi Bakr, 'Abd Allah ibn 'Umar, Aban ibn

'Uthman, 'Abd al-Rahman ibn Khalid, 'Abd Allah ibn Ja'far, 'Ammar ibn Yasir, Miqdad ibn Aswad, Abu Dharr al-Ghifari, Malik al-Ashtar, Abu Ayud al-Ansari, Qays ibn Sa'd, Hudhayfah ibn al-Yaman, 'Ubadah ibn Samit, Hisham ibn al-'As, Abu Hurayrah, and Ikrimah. How can concubinage be presented positively when the very womenfolk of the Prophet's companions preferred death before dishonor? Being a sex slave was just as degrading and demeaning to non-Muslim women as it was to Muslim women.

Truth be told, the "symphony of women's rights in Islam" that we were sold turns out to be a cacophony, a harsh, discordant mixture of ear-splitting sounds that damage the ear drum. The smooth-talking Muslim scholars and religious authorities who pretended to be pious turned out to be nothing but con artists, pimps, pedophiles, human traffickers, wife-beaters, and sexual predators. They were ravenous wolves in sheep's clothing, seeking prey. However, "not all of them are alike" (3:113).

10.6 The Worst of People

As the Prophet Muhammad said, "Terror and dismay will appear in my *ummah*. The people will turn to their scholars while they will be like monkeys and pigs" (Hakim); "The worst of people are corrupt scholars" (Abu Nu'aym and Darimi); "Soon nothing will remain of Islam except its name, and nothing will remain of the Qur'an but its script... In that day, your mosques will be well furnished, but your hearts and bodies will have no guidance. At that time, the worst people under the sky will be your scholars. Strife will originate with them and return to them" (Bayhaqi, Daylami, Kulayni, vol. 8: 262-263).

Although some Muslim scholars treat these traditions as dubious, they cannot deny the universal message of the Qur'an when it compares scholars who fail in their obligations to a "donkey laden with books" (62:5). Mind you, women-hating Islamists and terrorists also use all these citations to condemn scholars who are not radical and extreme enough. Be that as it may, neither God nor the Prophet Muhammad can be blamed for the corrupt interpretations of Islam that followed the revelation of the Qur'an. It is the men who made them that must be held accountable. "God, the Lord of the Throne, is far above the things they say" (21:22).

10.7 The Duty to Think

Many Muslims, particularly women, refuse to address issues like slavery, concubinage, domestic violence, marital rape, and female genital mutilation, as it threatens their Islamic identity. Any criticism of practices and interpretations, however legitimate, are viewed invariably as attacks against Islam when, in reality, they are directed towards the mortal and fallible men who made them. They are the subject of scholarly ire, not God and His Messenger, to whom misogynistic merchants of religion falsely attributed abominations and iniquities of all kinds, only to be swallowed, hook, line, and sinker by gullible followers, incapable of critical thinking and moral reasoning, who accepted their teachings based on blind faith alone.

Nobody escapes accountability. Being a *muqallid* or follower of a jurist does not save one from culpability in major sins. Each Muslim is responsible for engaging with the Qur'anic text (Barazangi 2006: 88). Since the Qur'an is timeless and universal, notes Cyrille Moreno al-'Ajami, it opposes traditionalism and following the herd (2020: 217). *Taqlid*, which derives from the Arabic word *qallada* or "to place a collar (*qiladah*) around the neck," turns Muslims into dogs on leashes, resigned to following the lead of a handful of male Muslim jurists. Many are those who prefer to maul their masters, flee to the woods, and run with the wolves, freely, as slaves of the Creator alone, and not dictatorial, totalitarian men who claim to speak for God, the Prophet, and even the conveniently Hidden Imam.

10.8 Conclusions

If Islam is a worldview that is all-encompassing and involves all spheres of life, and sexual relations are governed by religion, we can come to a simple and sane solution: if there is no compulsion in religion, then there is no compulsion in sexual intercourse. Women are not soulless sex dolls that cannot say no. When it comes to treating women, the Qur'an advises men to "live with them honorably" (4:19). It warns against harming and oppressing them (65:6). It calls upon husbands and wives to be soulmates (4:1). It states that "your spouses are a garment [of comfort, chastity, and protection] for you as you are for them" (2:187). It treats marriage as a sign of God: "And among His Signs is this that He created for you mates from among yourselves that ye may dwell in tranquility with them and He has put love and mercy between your (hearts); verily in that are Signs for those who reflect" (30:21). Such is the standard that is set. This is true Islam. Love it or leave it.

Chapter Eleven

No Real Abolitionist Movement Emerged in Islamic Civilization

11.1 Introduction

According to Bernard Lewis (1916-2018), the British American historian who specialized in Oriental studies, "Islamic abolitionism" is a contradiction in terms. (Clarence-Smith 2008: 1). Jonathan A.C. Brown appears to agree. After all, he claims that "no real indigenous abolitionist movement emerged in Islamic civilization" (2020: 264). For him, this is explained by the fact that "the majority of slaves... were women" (264). So much for the claim that Islam treats women with honor and dignity. On the contrary, such claims support the opposite, at least when it comes to dominant interpretations and applications of the Muslim faith. As Clarence-Smith confirms, "the consensus is that slaves consisted mainly of female domestics and concubines." The ugly ones were used for domestic labor, while the more attractive ones were used for sexual pleasure. A woman's value was based on her beauty. In fact, at the time and place that Islamic laws were being developed, "woman," "slave," and "object for sexual use" were essentially synonymous. Since women were property, why would men wish to relinquish their wealth willingly?

11.2 Sexual Slavery as Misogyny

The fact that most slaves in the Muslim world were women is misogyny made manifest. The Romans, the Europeans, and others, were more egalitarian, enslaving human beings of all genders. The Muslims, however, were concerned mainly with women. Enslaved men were generally prevented from breeding. Not only were they forced to satisfy the sexual needs of their masters, but some of the girls and women were shared with family members and friends. In contrast, others were forced into prostitution, which was prohibited in legal theory but not in practice. Yes, there were laws governing slavery; however, "the extreme privacy of the Muslim harem made it difficult to enforce legal constraints on owners" (Clarence-Smith).

While prohibiting sex was slave girls was difficult for Christians to enforce, permitting sex with slave girls was equally difficult for Muslims to manage.

Although they had rights in legal books, slaves had little to no legal recourse in the court system. Some enslaved women may have made it before judges to complain of ill-treatment; however, such instances were few and far between. Women chained to beds or locked in homes or estates can scarcely make it before a judge to file a complaint. Fear and violence kept them in a state of terrified submission. Despair and hopelessness kept them in check. Most females were trapped without hope of escape, freedom, or human dignity. At the most, they could hope for some social mobility for themselves and the children of their rapists.

What hope did a Slavic or Berber woman have of returning to her family when confined to a harem in Yemen? What hope did an Ethiopian girl have to return to Africa as a slave in the Indian Subcontinent? Many resigned themselves. They tried to make the best out of a bad situation. As El Hamel notes, "they were forced to navigate within the sexual desire of their masters to secure a better position within a society where gender was hierarchical: patrilineal and patriarchal" (11).

Enslaved women rebelled and revolted in myriad ways. There was no escape for female slaves of Muslim men in this life or the hereafter. When they died, claims a saying of the Prophet Muhammad, non-Muslim women would be sent to hell, after which God would remove them from the flames, only to make them the eternal sex slaves of Muslim men in heaven (Morrow 2020: 287). They were trapped in an eternal cycle of torture and torment. Whores in this life and the hereafter.

As for the children of the *mushrikin*, polytheists or unbelievers, who presumably were innocent of their parents' infidelity, they could only aspire to be slaves in the hereafter. As the Prophet Muhammad stated, "The children of the *mushrikin* are servants of the people of Paradise" (Ibn Mandah, Abu Nu'aym, Abu Ya'la, Albani). To be fair, however, we must acknowledge that some Muslim scholars, including the infamous Ibn Taymiyyah (1263-1328), rejected this tradition. Once again, Muslim scholars had choices. Rather than reject women-hating, pro-slavery traditions, many traditionists classified them as authentic, and jurists used them as evidence to pass laws. "Ah! What an evil (choice)!" (16:59).

11.3 Collective Culpability

"Slavery," notes Freamon, "was an integral part of the daily life of the 'Abbasids" (2019: 198). Whether they were rich or poor, most Muslim men, in certain times and places, owned slaves, many of whom were concubines. As a result of Islamic imperialism, "there was certainly no shortage of concubines in the early days of the 'Abbasid Empire" (Freamon 2019: 199). In fact, "it was common practice for marauding and victorious soldiers of the caliphate, after vanquishing their enemies, to kill the men and 'treat the women as their wives without marrying them'" (Freamon 2019: 199). As a result, a staggering number of girls and women were condemned to lives of sexual bondage. Under the Safavids, as it was under

Chapter Eleven   123

other dynasties, male and female slaves were forced to provide sexual services by prostitution at private parties (Sherley). In fact,

> There is ample and continuous evidence of "Habashi," "Zangi," "Indian," and "Caucasian" sex slaves, military slaves, and slave servants in brothels, teahouses, harems, and in the middle and upper-class Iranian families and among pastoral clans from the early 1500s to the beginning of the twentieth century. (Rahbari)

As Freamon reports, "the harem of 'Abd al-Rahman III of Cordoba (912-961) contained six thousand concubines" (2019: 296; Clarence-Smith 2006: 89; Chebel 88). The harem of the Fatimid caliphs in Cairo "had twice as many" (Segal 39; Chebel 88). Akbar the [not so] Great (1542-1605) reportedly owned five thousand female captives as concubines (Banno 354). Al-Mutawakkil's (822-861) had four thousand (Clarence-Smith 2006: 89). Sultan Ghiath-Ud-Din of Malwa (1469-1500) had fifteen thousand female slaves (Chebel 63-64).

Akbar's harem was surpassed by his son, Jehangir, who had six thousand (Chebel 63). Shah Safi's (r. 1629-1642) harem featured three hundred female sex slaves (Rahbari). Moreover, as El Hamel points out, Moulay Ismail's (r. 1672-1727) harem contained hundreds to thousands of women of all nationalities (196). He reportedly sired over one thousand two hundred children through his wives and thousands of sex slaves (Milton 120).

Ibn Saud, the king of Saudi Arabia, who died in 1953, owned more than three thousand slave girls, some of whom he would gift to his colleagues so that they could satisfy their lust with them (Chebel 407-408). In any event, that still leaves an enormous contingent of sexually frustrated women.

The question must be asked: does sexual slavery and the harem culture embody piety or degeneracy? The Byzantine Emperor, Leo III, the Isaurian (717-741), was correct to condemn the debauchery of Muslims with their concubines, men who would use them sexually and then sell them as if they were "dumb cattle" (Robinson 96-97). After all, is sexual slavery a pillar of Islam? It is virtuous? Is it good? Or is it inherently evil? If so, it was consonant with the Qur'an's call for justice to eradicate it. The only shame is that Muslims did not do so sooner, and that Christians acted first.

The failure to abolish slavery cannot be blamed on Islam as if it were some sentient being and not the projection of Muslim men. In response to the question: "Why didn't Islam abolish slavery?" Muhammad Diakho provided the proper response. "Since Islam never instituted slavery, one cannot expect it to abolish it" (39). In other words, the problem of slavery was inherited. It was one that was almost universal. If Islam did not abolish it with immediate effect, neither did Christianity, Judaism, or other world religions. Although some Muslims opposed it, and tried to undermine and abolish it, many others, the wealthy and the powerful, expanded, and institutionalized it. The problem was so vast and deeply entrenched that it could not be grasped, much less contained. It was like trying to gather water with one's hands.

If the Qur'an did not institute slavery, how did it enter Islamic law? As Muhammad Diakho demonstrates, slavery in Islamic law is based on custom (*al-'urf*) and the *status quo* (*al-istishab*) whose sole function is to embrace anything compatible with the principles of Islam from customs and traditions (10). If slavery was integrated into Islamic law, it was through secondary sources of law (10). However, these secondary sources of law cannot take priority over primary sources. In the case of slavery, they most certainly did. "Far is Islam… from participating by its principles and general rules -- the genuine ones -- from such a humanely shameful and religiously condemnable enterprise" (Diakho 60). As Diakho rightly argues, slavery is an "inhumane system" (10), an "infamy" (215), and "a barbaric violation of fundamental Islamic rights" (170-171).

11.4 Conclusions

Brown's claim that abolitionism in the Islamic world was not indigenous and was the product of Western influence and pressure is entirely untrue. The same goes for Mustafa Akyol's claim that "we Muslims abolished slavery only thanks to the encouragement, even pressure, from Western governments" (2021: 9). As William Gervase Clarence-Smith had demonstrated in due detail, "the Islamic [abolitionist] debate was clearly rooted in arguments that stretched back to the origins of the faith" (2006: 19). Muslim abolitionists were not merely mimicking the West, as Brown implies in his book. They were not imitating the infidels. They realized that "the foundations of slavery in the original texts were weak, exacerbating a permanent tension between religious belief and social reality" (Clarence-Smith 2006:19).

Islamic abolitionists appealed to their conscience. In their hearts and minds, slavery, in both theory and social reality, could not be reconciled with morality and human dignity. It was an assault on their faith and an offense to their humanity. They courageously stood against the *status quo*, opposing secular and religious leaders. Their works and activism are prime examples of applied Islamic ethics. They are people who put their faith into practice. "Despite repeated and insisting calls," points out Diakho, "slavery, the most abhorrent form of injustice and inequity, continued to be transmitted from generation to generation" (57). While human beings cannot determine outcomes, they can control efforts. They will be judged based on what they did. Those who opposed slavery will get their rich rewards, as will those who sanctioned it and continue to do so. And "God is never unjust in even the least degree" (4:40).

Chapter Twelve

I Own You:
Your Ass is Literally Mine

12.1 Introduction

In a lecture delivered on February 7, 2017, Jonathan A.C. Brown asserted that it was "not morally wrong to own somebody," that "human beings have not thought of consent as the essential feature of morally correct sexual activity," and that "we fetishize the idea of [sexual] autonomy" (Strauss, see also Lee and Crookston). He even argues that age is arbitrary when it comes to sexual consent (2020: 278). These talking points, which he elaborates upon in *Slavery & Islam*, are scandalous. While some Muslims praised him for supposedly speaking the "truth" without fear, many were ashamed, embarrassed, and enraged. Is it morally right to own people? Is it correct that consent is not required for sexual relations in Islam? And is it true, as Brown suggests, that the age of majority is meaningless?

12.2 Old Enough to Bleed

Not only does Brown note that sexual slavery was a central part of Arab and Ottoman slavery, which is factual and historical, but he also appears to trivialize age of consent (2020: 278-281). In his words, "the capacity to consent... is... totally arbitrary" (2020: 278). Since "individuals mature at different times... only a case-by-case evaluation would reflect accurately when a person was able to make good decisions" (2020: 278). Would that be sixteen years of age? Thirteen years of age? Nine years of age? For Brown, age "is, in and of itself, meaningless" (2020: 279).

"Like an alchemical spell," writes Brown, "age-based consent transmutes sex from immoral to illegal into something legal and morally passable" (2020: 279). "Yet this capacity," he continues, "just appears in a person, one day, on a certain birthday" (2020: 279). "Its absence prior to that," he notes, "makes someone a sex offender" (2020: 279). "Its presence a day later makes sex unobjectionable" (2020: 279). Brown views age of consent as "a fiction" (2020: 280). Should we therefore remove age of consent laws and deal with each case individually? That would be a *shariʿah*-spreader's dream come true; thereby allowing Muslim men to marry thirteen-year-old girls, nine-year-old girls, and even nursing babies. How perfect for men: girls of any age whose consent is not required for marriage or intimate relations.

According to Islamic law, we are lectured, "the consent of the wife was assumed by virtue of the marriage contract itself" (2020: 281). "In the case of the slave-concubine," he continues, "consent was irrelevant because of the master's ownership of the woman in question" (2020: 281). If this is not trivializing the age of consent, what is? Societies need to set limits. The bar should not be too high, but nor should it be too low. For consistency, enforcement, and protection of vulnerable minors, a number is needed, with exceptions in some instances. Unlike Islamic law, the *Catechism of the Roman Catholic Church* is clear when it comes to consent.

> The Church holds the exchange of consent between the spouses to be the indispensable element that "makes the marriage." If consent is lacking, there is no marriage.
>
> 1627 The consent consists in a "human act by which the partners mutually give themselves to each other:" "take you to be my wife" -- "I take you to be my husband." This consent that binds the spouses to each other finds its fulfillment in the two "becoming one flesh."
>
> 1628 The consent must be an act of the will of each of the contracting parties, free of coercion or grave external fear. No human power can substitute for this consent. If this freedom is lacking the marriage is invalid.

In much of the Muslim world, however, arranged or forced marriages remain the order of the day. Sexual pleasure is viewed as the husband's right and not the wife's. According to some scholars, a wife has the right to receive sexual intercourse once every four months. According to others, it is just once in her life. The man, however, must be serviced by his wife upon demand.

12.3 Islam: A Pimp's Paradise?

While his language is more elevated than that of pimps and slave masters, critics could claim that Jonathan A.C. Brown voices the very same view they hold, namely, that it is not wrong to own someone, and that consent is not necessary when it comes to sexual conduct. Decidedly, the women they exploit do not feel the same way whether they live in the twenty-first or the tenth century. They know that forced prostitution and sexual servitude are wrong. Some Muslims may have thought that slavery was not wrong: the slaves and the families they were torn from certainly did not feel the same way. The husband, children, and father of the woman who was dragged away by Muslim raiders and invaders and taken to a distant land to be sold as a sex slave certainly did not think that slavery and concubinage were moral and ethical. Call it what you want: they called it inherently and absolutely evil.

Chapter Twelve

12.4 Thou Shalt Emasculate Boys

What was the fate of those who were attacked, invaded, and conquered by Muslim forces? Men not killed in battle were forced into physical labor or military service. Girls and women were compelled to become domestic servants, nannies, cooks, singers, dancers, exotic entertainers, and sex slaves. The case of the boys was heartbreaking. Christian children were "harvested" by the Turks (Clarence-Smith 2006: 36-37). Many were destined to be sexually exploited by pederasts.

12.5 Booty Boys

The boys that were enslaved by Muslim invaders, raiders, and slave traders were incorporated into the Janissary infantry corps, where a culture of homosexuality was encouraged (Clarence-Smith 2006: 37). And many castrated boys also served as sex slaves for Muslim men, as a foretaste of the boys that were purportedly promised to them in Paradise (24:32). Those that survived, at least, as ninety percent of the victims of emasculation died from the process in certain regions (Pavlu). In others, the death rate was around fifteen percent (Clarence-Smith 47). Either way, this disregard for human life was blasphemous. The blame, however, does not fall solely on Islamic civilization. As Bernard K. Freamon explains,

> The practice of employing a eunuch, a male slave whose testicles have been ablated by one of several methods or whose sexual organs have been completely removed, is ancient. Annals attesting to the employment of eunuchs, generally in a governmental, imperial, or military capacity, can be found in historical records of the Chou Dynasty in China, and imperial entities in Mesopotamia, Syria, India, Africa, Asia Minor, and Europe. (2019: 303)

This practice of emasculation, it should be stressed, was prohibited by the Prophet Muhammad (Clarence-Smith 2006: 46m 82-83). As Freamon explains,

> the Prophet Muhammad condemned the practice, and the Islamic law, in no uncertain terms, prohibits the mutilation of the human body, whether the victim be enslaved or free. Nonetheless, the practice flourished in the earliest imperial enterprises after the death of the Prophet and grew to be an important aspect of the Muslim political conceptions of slavery. (2019: 304)

For most of Islamic history, the castration of boys and men was not exceptional: it was frequent as eunuchs fetched a higher price (Levy 77). Since it was "a high-risk procedure, with heavy losses," their production "contributed significantly to the fatality statistics" (Fisher 293). Is a religion what it teaches or what is practices? Is it a matter of theory or application? What matters most is how a religion is understood and how it is lived. In the reality of this world, Islam is what Muslims do. While Muslims cannot be blamed for commencing this condemnable practice, they are responsible for continuing, reinvigorating, and institutionalizing it.

12.6 And Boys will be Toys: The Eunuch as an Essential Component of Islamic Civilization

Under Muslim rule, which spanned over a thousand years, the treatment of captive boys was brutal, sadistic, traumatizing, desexualizing, and dehumanizing. "When the 'Abbasids took over imperial centers formerly administered by the Byzantines," notes Freamon, "the practice of using eunuchs to perform tasks for the state (caliphate) was robustly revived" (2019: 68). As Freamon explains, "many of the slaves working in the palaces and caliphal residences were eunuchs -- enslaved castrated males imported primarily from Africa, India, and the Caucasus Mountains" (2019: 198-199).

Al-Muqtadir, the 'Abbasid caliph who ruled from 908 to 932 CE, "employed 11,000 eunuchs, 7,000 of whom were black, and 4,000 were white" (Freamon 2019: 304). Ironically, although radical Islamists oppose homosexuality and transsexuality, the Islamic Empire they admire, and the caliphate they wish to recreate, had a long history of turning boys into eunuchs. Sultan Hossein (r. 1694-1722), the Safavid Shah, had five thousand slaves, both men and women, including one hundred black eunuchs (Ricks). Under the Safavids, "the practice of non-heterosexual relationships was accepted and prevalent" (Rahbari). The brothels in Persia were filled with male sex slaves (Rahbari). As for Moulay Ismail from Morocco, (r. 1672-1727), he had hundreds to thousands of eunuchs at his service (El Hamel 198). As late as 1908, Islam's last sultan and caliph, Abdul Hamid, "still had a harem of 370 women and 127 eunuchs" (Bink).

Although it should be remembered that "Islam borrowed the practice of eunuchism from the pre-Islamic societies that presaged it" (Freamon 2019: 303), and did not introduce it, the practice eventually became synonymous with it. Consequently, some scholars view slavery and the existence of the eunuch as the very essence of Muslim society (Freamon 2019: 306). Without them, no society could claim to be Muslim (Freamon 2019: 306). While eunuchs played many societal roles, they were also used as male concubines (Freamon 2019: 242). Since the use of castrated boys was central to slavery in the Muslim world, how can anyone, and any man for that matter, support and defend such an institution? "That was wrong," they will argue, but "slavery is right if it's done the right way." No, it is not.

12.7 Castrated Cold-Blooded Killers and Concubine Hunters

While many young male slaves were destined to be concubines and prostitutes in the Muslim world, a considerable contingent of them was created to become castrated, cold-blooded killers, concubine hunters, and harem enforcers. As Azumah describes,

> The operation, done on boys aged between eight and ten, though prohibited under Islam, was carried out with an exceedingly high death rate. Gustav Nachtigal was told that on the whole about 30 per cent survived the operation… while other estimates put the mortality rate at up to 80 per cent. This barbaric act was made particularly cruel for black victims in that, in contrast to their white counterparts whose operation did not deny them the ability to perform coitus, the castration of blacks involved what was popularly referred to as "level with the abdomen," i.e. a complete amputation of the genitalia…

It should be stressed that white slaves, or Mamluks, suffered the loss of their testicles (Segal 52). Blacks, however, suffered the loss of their penises as well (Segal 52). Speak of fear of black sexuality. Imagine the psychological devastation of being entirely emasculated, with one's testicles, scrotum, and penis amputated, and to watch, powerlessly, as beautiful black girls and women are sexually abused by Arab, Berber, and Turkish slave masters. To compound their trauma, these black eunuchs were used as harem guards. They were also used as military slaves, tasked with capturing men, women, and children, of their race, and other races, so that they could be subjected to the same fate.

In 2017 I performed a pilgrimage to Iraq for Arba'in, the commemoration of the martyrdom of Imam Husayn. I was in the company of a band of black Muslims from the Nation of Islam. One of them carried old photographs of gut-wrenching lynchings, and would show them to Iraqis at every opportunity, shouting: "See what they do to black people in America!" "See what some people did, long ago," I thought. Imagine how this black American Muslim would react at seeing artistic depictions of black African boys and teenagers being castrated by Muslims, Arab and otherwise, and having their private parts entirely excised. This crime against God and humanity was committed against millions of black Africans. Up to ninety percent of the victims died in the process. These emasculation facilities produced mass graves of dead boys who passed away as a result of an operation that can only be described as torture.

Millions of bodies, corpses, and skeletons of black African human beings littered the deserts of Arabia as a result of the so-called "Islamic" slave trade. Millions of blacks died during the Atlantic crossing. The current calculations speak of at least two million. That does not even include those who died during slave raids and the long march to the ships. Likewise, millions of blacks died during the trans-Saharan crossing and the forced voyages across the Red Sea and Indian Ocean. That does not even include those who were slaughtered during the slave raids. For white Christians as well as Arab, Berber, and Turkish Muslims, blacks, and other people, were entirely disposable and dispensable. They treated livestock better than their fellow human beings. According to some Muslim jurists, it was prohibited to castrate animals and to beat them. These same scholars sat still and did nothing about the castration and beating of black slaves.

If castration was prohibited under Islamic law, why was it allowed to flourish and prosper? Why did it become the norm? After all, these were Muslim lands, under Muslim laws. If Afro-descendants in the Americas continue to suffer from the generational trauma of slavery, consider the case of slaves in the Muslim world who were condemned to being concubines or castrated thugs, killers, and kidnappers. In the words of John Owen Hunwick,

> It is a curious irony that while the female slave's best chance of a life of ease and respect was through the exploitation of her female sexuality as a concubine and ultimately as a mother, the male slave's surest road to prosperity and power lay in having his own sexuality sacrificed through a transformation whose physical and emotional pain can better be imagined than described. (Azumah 159)

Nevertheless, perhaps we should describe the extremely painful and risky process involved. According to most accounts, the procedure was primarily performed by Jewish specialists. The child or young man would be tied while men would pin him down on a table. Most often, the procedure was performed on boys between the ages of ten and fifteen (Chebel 82). The genitals would be washed in pepper or a hot chili sauce. In some parts, it was henna that was used. The penis and testicles would be amputated with one swift slice. A tube was then inserted into the urethra to allow urination during healing, and hot oil was poured over the wound to cauterize it. Bandages were applied. The patient or victim of torture to be precise was buried in sand until he hopefully healed. He would not be allowed to drink water for three days.

In most cases, the victim of castration and emasculation would die. The pain alone was enough to cause a stroke or cardiac arrest. According to Chebel, ninety boys would die so that ten eunuchs could be produced (82). After all, no anesthesia was used in the process and no antibiotics were available. Lack of hygiene resulted in infection, and infection led to death. For the fortunate or unfortunate few who survived, the healing process would last one hundred days, during which they could not wear clothing. Those who endured the unimaginable and excruciating ordeal suffered severe permanent psychological, emotional, and physical trauma (see Chebel 75-82). Their suicide rate must have been disproportionately high.

The eunuchs who survived the inhuman ordeal fetched the highest prices as they could serve as harem guards. They were even used as security guards at the Kaabah in Mecca into modern times. Some rose to high administrative ranks. The perversity of the process was not lost on Malek Chebel. A society was created in which men had more women than they could please, and which other men, had they not been castrated, could have done in their place (79).

While castration might have been illegal, in theory, according to some jurists, it was unequivocally permitted in practice. It is called a precedent, a past principle, rule, edict, or decision considered authoritative and binding in future cases. In the case of Islamic law, the rule lasted for nearly a millennia and a half, until Muslim governments were pressured into prohibiting slavery. As Ronald Segal notes, "the history of Islam, like that of other great religions, is replete with contradictions between precept and practice" (13). Muslims must therefore strive to realign their religious rules with higher moral objectives and restore Islam's balance and equilibrium. The Qur'an had warned men against hoarding wealth and the love of lust:

> Fair in the eyes of men is the love of things they covet: Women and sons; Heaped-up hoards of gold and silver; horses branded (for blood and excellence); and (wealth of) cattle and well-tilled land. Such are the possessions of this world's life; but in nearness to God is the best of the goals (to return to). (3:14)

The Qur'an described the desire of men to acquire more than one woman as an act of greed (4:128). Many companions of the Prophet, their followers, and their successors, got caught up in the frenzy of the early conquests. Motivated by materialism, ambition, envy, hedonism, racism, and lust, they engaged in an orgy of bloodshed, colonialism, and imperialism, treating their victims worse than the Arab idolaters had ever treated the Prophet Muhammad and his early followers. The persecuted became the persecutors. The oppressed became the oppressors. And the enslaved became enslavers. Ah, but "beware of the supplication of the oppressed," warned the Prophet Muhammad, "for even if he is an unbeliever, there is no barrier between it and God" (Ahmad).

12.8 Conclusions

Neither slavery, concubinage, pedophilia, pederasty, nor eunuchism were the products of Islam. They were borrowed from the pre-Islamic societies and cultures that predated it. While slavery, concubinage, and pedophilia were avidly embraced by many Muslim rulers and jurists, and were enshrined in Islamic jurisprudence as permissible, pederasty and eunuchism were prohibited in theory yet tolerated in practice.

Muslims who engaged in such despicable behavior sought justification in the Qur'an's depiction of paradise which promised "youths (handsome) as pearls well-guarded" (52:24) and "immortal boys" (56:17-18) like "scattered pearls" (76:19) who would be "boys of their own" (52:24). Since the female virgins of Paradise were also described as "hidden pearls" (56:22-23), some Muslims dreamed of an eternity of pederasty. While most Qur'anic commentators concluded that the boys of heaven were simply servants, for Muhammad Jalal Kishk (1929-1993), the Islamist author of *A Muslim's Thoughts about the Sexual Question*, not only was sexual attraction to boys normal, but the boys of Paradise that were described in the Qur'an were created for sexual pleasure (Massad 204). In fact, this is conveyed in some dubious traditions attributed to the Prophet.

In one tradition, the Prophet Muhammad warns men to "Beware of handsome boys because their mischief is more than that of girls" (Majlisi, *Haqqul Yaqeen*: 848). In another, he warns that "One who kisses a boy with lust, on the Day of Judgement, the Almighty will put a bridle of fire in his mouth" (Majlisi, *Haqqul*

Yaqeen: 848). Such traditions date from a time and place when sexual attraction to boys on the part of men was viewed as even more tempting than that of women. Some Sufi orders were centered around the homo-erotic contemplation of pre-pubescent boys.

According to al-Ghazzali, 'Umar (c. 582/583-644) ran inside his home and locked the door after he saw a young boy he described as a *fitnah*, trial, or temptation. He then stated that the Prophet Muhammad had forbidden men to look at, speak with, or sit with, such boys. Many Muslim scholars and jurists also insisted that boys could be nineteen times more seductive than women. They claimed that there were two devils with every woman but eighteen with every boy. According to Ibn 'Abidin, if a boy reached puberty, but had no facial hair, he had to be treated like a woman; namely, his entire body, from head to toe, was '*awrah*. Some jurists even treated boys' voices like those of women: forbidden to be heard as it was a source of sexual arousal. The fanatics, who had suppressed female beauty from the public sphere, turned their pedophilic gaze toward little boys. In light of the alternative, and what it implies, Christoph Luxenberg's rendering of virgins (*hur*) and boys (*wildan*) of Paradise into grapes and wine must be welcomed (247-291). Otherwise, one would be best embracing the view of Cyrille Moreno al-'Ajami for whom *hur* is an adjective meaning "pure" in a saintly sense.

The Prophet Muhammad unequivocally prohibited the castration of human beings. "Whoever kills his slave," he said, "we will kill him" (Tirmidhi). "Whoever cuts off his nose," he said, "we will cut off his nose (Tirmidhi 106). And "Whoever castrates his slave, we will castrate him," (Hakim, see Diakho 106). Rather than accept these traditions at face value, Muslim jurists, in Machiavellian manner, ruled that it was only the creation of eunuchs that was prohibited and that their purchase was permitted. Had they had the moral and intellectual sense to prohibit the purchase of eunuchs, production would have decreased or even ceased. On the contrary, "the demand for slaves, including talented and literate non-Muslim eunuchs, was enormous across the Islamic world at the time of the early 'Abbasid caliphate (mid-eighth to late tenth century)" (Valante 174).

Rather than acting as scholars for hire, who produced edicts upon demand to suit the needs of the oppressive religious, political, and economic elite, the '*ulama*' should have taken a stand against slavery and concubinage rather than try to regulate it. Moreover, ordinary Muslims should have made the moral choice to not partake in imperialistic wars and slave raids, not to traffic human beings, castrate boys and men, and purchase and exploit slaves. Slavery, in the Christian West was mostly confined to the upper classes. According to the Census Bureau, 1.4% of free people owned slaves in the United States in 1860. Until the practice was abolished, however, slavery was pervasive in many parts of the Muslim world, so much so that many households owned slaves. Although the Prophet Muhammad had prohibited the castration of slaves, it was only in 1908 that a majority of scholars who gathered at a congress decreed that it was prohibited, not only to make eunuchs, but to own them as well (Clarence-Smith 2008: 18). And even so, their edict was contested.

Chapter Thirteen

The Moral Conundrum of Slavery

13.1 Introduction

When confronting the moral conundrum of slavery, Jonathan A.C. Brown claims that Muslims can adopt three approaches: 1) "totally overhaul the manner in which the Qur'an and the Prophet's life are read and understood" (2020: 196); 2) "follow the secular path… and deny that Islam's scripture represents a direct and untouched revelation from God, professing instead that it is a text produced by humans in history" (2020: 198); or 3) "affirm the standard understanding of the Prophet's life and the Qur'an's overall content on slavery but simply concede that these two sources were wrong on the moral problem of slavery" (2020: 198). For Brown, "the first is utterly unconvincing" while "the second and third entail denial of fundamental pillars of the Islamic creed" (2020: 196). In fact, he insists, in the excommunicatory language of Islamist extremists, that they take one "out of the fold of Islam" and into the realm of "disbelief" (2020: 198). These are not the only available options.

For critics, such conclusions can only come from someone who separates a text from its context and does not consider the socio-political and economic impulses that produced unethical edicts. Historicizing the Qur'an is not a denial of its divine origin. A classic stands the test of time. Although it is informed by the history of ideas, is the product of a particular time and place, and reflects those realities, it has universal appeal. It connects the past and the present and is relevant to multiple generations. The universality of the Qur'an is not to be found in its letter but in its spirit. Except for myopic jurists, who care only about deriving archaic rules and regulations, Muslims, past and present, have not turned to the Qur'an to see how many lashes they should give an adulterer or which limb to cut off a thief but in search of spiritual inspiration and moral guidance. Some Muslims have missed the big picture. Rather than contemplate the vast horizon in all its beauty, they stare down at their stinky feet. God did not bring the universe into existence for people to enslave their neighbors and rape their wives and daughters.

13.2 Reforming, Dismantling and Eradicating Slavery

Is it not possible that God and the Prophet intended to ban slavery or, at the very least, institute a system that would reform and phase it out? Although God is

Patient, waiting for more than a millennium is a little exaggerated as a transition period. For those with understanding, God and His Prophet were not endorsing evil. They set about dismantling it. It may have been evil; however, it was lesser than some of its alternatives, namely, the wholesale slaughter of captives, men, women, and children, as practiced by other peoples and cultures. It was not a matter of passing a law that could not be enforced. It was a question of changing people, cultures, and societies. Before saving bodies, souls had to be saved. It would take pure souls to abolish slavery and concubinage. People were a work in progress.

"Because the Qur'an does not state explicitly that slavery is abolished," writes Riffat Hassan (b. 1943), the Pakistani American theologian and leading feminist scholar of the Qur'an, "it does not follow that it is to be continued, particularly in view of the numerous ways in which the Qur'an seeks to eliminate this absolute evil" (244). Conditions needed to be created to ensure a permanent end to the practice. After all, God does not change the conditions of a people until they change what is in themselves (Qur'an 13:11). As Chebel notes, slaves were the mirror reflections of the despotic and iniquitous feudal societies in which they were exploited (95). The issue was not religious, argues Chebel, it was social and jurisprudential (95). Corrupt people create corrupt societies.

Azumah, like Brown, believes that "the Qur'an accepts and endorses the basic inequality between master and slave as part of the divinely established order" (124) and cites the following verse to support his claims:

> God coineth a similitude: (on the one hand) a (mere) chattel slave, who hath control of nothing, and (on the other hand) one on whom We have bestowed a fair provision from Us, and he spendeth thereof secretly and openly. Are they equal? Praise be to God! But most of them know not. (16:75)

This verse does not justify slavery. It is a parable that condemns those who compare God to His creation. It compares the disbeliever and the believer; the idolater, who loves other than God, and the monotheist, who worships and obeys Him. It is the example of the idol and the True God. According to 'Ali ibn Ahmad al-Wahidi (d. 1075), the Qur'an commentator, the verse was revealed regarding two men, Hisham ibn 'Amr, who used to spend his wealth openly and in secret, and his client Abu al-Jawza,' who used to bid him to stop doing so. To claim, as Azuma does, that the Qur'an divinely ordains slavery in 16:75 is like claiming that Jesus did the same in his parable of the worthless slaves (Luke 17:10). Both Jesus and Muhammad encouraged people to become slaves of God.

Although many Orientalists and Western writers argued that slavery was inherent to Islam, others dissented. Gottlieb Wilhelm Leitner (1840-1899), a British Orientalist, countered claims that slavery was "the inevitable consequence of Mohammedan government" (Ware 112). In his words,

This is a great libel on that religion as the assertion would be on

> Christianity, that it was in favor of slavery because Christ, although confronted by one of its cruelest forms in the Roman Empire, did not attempt to legislate, as Muhammad did, for its eventual abolition in this world, but merely promised spiritual freedom to the repentant servants of sin, whether bond or free. (Ware 112)

Cardinal Charles Lavigerie (1825-1892) declared in 1888 that "The Qur'an does not enjoin slavery… The Qur'an… places the liberty of captives at the top of a list of merciful deeds through which believers may be worthy of heaven. Strictly speaking, nothing would prick the consciences of Muslims in the abolition of slavery" (Clarence-Smith 2006: 17). Samuel Marinus Zwemer (1867-1952), nicknamed the Apostle to Islam, conceded in 1907 that "some Moslem apologists of the present day contend that Mohammed looked upon the custom as temporary in nature" (Clarence-Smith 2006: 18). Sir Henry Bartle Edward Frere (1815-1884) also wrote in 1873 that "the gradual extinction of slavery involves nothing repugnant to the law of the Koran, as interpreted by the most learned of men in the best times, and under the most orthodox and best Mahommedan rulers" (Clarence-Smith 2006: 18).

The Dutch Islamicist, Christiaan Snouck Hurgronje (1857-1936) remarked in 1886 that "slavery would disappear, if ever Islam could draw near to its own ideals" (Clarence-Smith 2006: 18). He later noted that "according to Mohammedan principles, slavery is an institution destined to disappear … [and is not] indispensable to the integrity of Islam" (Clarence-Smith 2006: 18). For Eldon Rutter, a British explorer who completed the pilgrimage to Mecca in 1925-1926, "The Koran rightly practiced would soon bring about the complete cessation of slavery" (Freamon 2019: 139). In the 1930s, Bertram Thomas (1892-1950) went so far as to claim that Muslims, by failing to abolish slavery, had betrayed the Prophet (Clarence-Smith 2006: 18). "In the unabatement of slavery," he wrote, "Arabia has been false to her Prophet" (Freamon 2019: 139).

At its onset, Islam appeared to be liberating. As Bernard K. Freamon notes, "the 'pietistic egalitarianism' … found in the verses and in the example of the Prophet Muhammad … constituted a significant substantive change in the approach to slavery in the new world created by Islam" (2019: 147). The early Muslims endeavored to free enslaved people. The most notable emancipated slaves from Mecca included Bilal al-Habashi and Zunayrah or Zinnirah al-Rumiyyah, both of whom were freed by Abu Bakr. Both had been tortured for their faith in Islam. The case of the latter was especially tragic. A Greek Christian woman, owned by 'Umar ibn al-Khattab before his conversion, Zunayrah was a public concubine collectively owned by the Banu Makhzum tribe.

As Mansour Fahmy (1886-1959), the Egyptian sociologist and pioneer of Islamic feminism, noted in his 1913 thesis, in seventh-century Arabia, there were cases in which slave girls were not distributed among individual owners. In places like Mecca and Medina, some were owned by the tribe, and treated as "public women," who were forced to satisfy the needs of any man who propositioned them (Chebel 65). This inhumanity may have triggered the revelation requiring women who went out at night to distinguish themselves as free women to prevent them from being perceived as tribally owned sex slaves (33:59).

Neither Bilal nor Zinnirah were freed solely because they were among the first Muslims and companions of the Prophet. They were liberated because of the inhumanity of their condition. Zinnirah "became one of Muhammad's first scribes, formally recording his revelations" (Jebara 136). If there was nothing wrong with being a concubine, why did Abu Bakr free her with the encouragement of the Prophet? Because she was owned collectively and forced into prostitution? In that case, Muhammad could have insisted that only her primary owner, 'Umar ibn al-Khattab, could legally have sex with her. Was she freed only because she was a Muslim? That would be quite the hypocritical double standard.

The early Muslims, it seems, recognized that the institution of slavery and concubinage was evil and dehumanizing. For Fred Donner (b. 1945), the American scholar of Islam, there is no evidence to suggest that the Prophet Muhammad had any intention of conquest beyond Arabia: survival was his strategy (Akyol 2022: 281, note 56). For Chebel, the Qur'an wanted to put an end to slavery through a concrete plan of emancipation which was followed by Abu Bakr (d. 634), who spent his fortune on freeing slaves, but which was thwarted by 'Umar (d. 644), the second caliph (15). Be that as it may, emancipatory Islam was short-lived and soon devolved into *jahiliyyah*-infused imperialism. A movement opposed to oppression became the tool of oppressors. As Freamon points out,

> this "pietistic egalitarianism" was swallowed up and ignored by later Muslim imperial leaders, and the legions of jurists who gave them jurisprudential advice and guidance over the centuries. In fact, it was slavery, and slave trading, sometimes in its most brutal and inegalitarian manifestations, that enabled the Muslim imperial entities to achieve spectacular economic and political success in their conquest of other societies. (2019: 147)

"Slavery and slave trading," notes Freamon, "became the primary engine that fueled the development and success of Muslim empires even when there was clearly no warrant for a lawful *jihad*" (2019: 145, see also 2019: 205). Muslims manifestly strayed from the moral message of the Qur'an. As Freamon points out, "the Qur'an actually predicts that its own egalitarian message will get lost as a result of the human love of hierarchy and inequality (28:76-88)" (2019: 145). As he explains,

> the Qur'anic message requiring implementation of a pietistic egalitarianism was lost until very recently and, among the Muslims, an impoverished view of human equality firmly took hold in Islamic societies and lasted for much of the time up to and including the present. Slavery and slave trading, on the other hand, became the primary engine

Chapter Thirteen

that fueled the development and success of Muslim empires even when there was clearly no warrant for a lawful *jihad*. (Freamon 2019: 145)

While Brown amply documents attempts to regulate slavery in Islam and grant slaves limited rights, he claims that Muslims did nothing to abolish its practice, and that those who called for abolition were only concerned about emancipating enslaved Muslims (2020: 201-213). Since it served their interests, "there was never any suggestion that the institution ought to be abolished" by court clerics and the servants of the *status quo* (Freamon 2019: 158). For Muhammad al-Maghili (d. 1505), the North African Berber scholar from Tlemcen, in what is now modern Algeria, the purification of Islamic practices involved "unlimited license for *jihad*, enslavement, political arrests, confiscation of goods, morality police, strict dress codes for women, and the expulsion of Jews" (Ware 206). For extremists and terrorists of all times, this is Islam.

To the disbelief of many Muslims, who believe that Islam's early success under the Prophet Muhammad was due to its liberating impulse, Brown even wonders whether slavery is in the DNA of Islam or whether it is an emancipatory force (2020: 204). Even Amina Wadud, an African American Muslim scholar, "is skeptical that the Islamic tradition would ever have contributed significantly to the moral or theological impetus behind what was ultimately the European-led project of abolition" (Brown 204). Mustafa Akyol (b. 1972), the progressive Turkish writer and journalist, feels the same way:

An interesting test case was the Muslim reaction to the greatest moral progress in modern history, the abolition of slavery. When the idea, and the pressure, came to the Muslim world from Britain in the mid-19th century, Islamic liberals embraced it and even found inspiration in the Qur'an's moral call for "freeing a neck." But Islamic traditionalists strongly objected. First, because no moral wisdom could ever come from the infidels. Second, because the Sharia, which had mitigated but also justified slavery, could never change. No wonder slavery legally continued in Saudi Arabia until 1962 and in Mauritania until 1981.

Brown also quotes Abdullahi an-Na'im (b. 1946), a Sudanese Muslim reformist, who observes that Islamic law is devoid of any "internal mechanism" that could have ended slavery (204). In other words, were it not for the West, Christian or secular, slavery would still be the order of the day if the power of Islam dominated the world. If this is true, this should serve as food for thought for the millions of blacks who have embraced Islam, believing that it was an anti-racist emancipatory force. If we believe in scholars like Brown, it most certainly is not. Perhaps they should become secularists, humanists, leftists, socialists, or communists. At least, those people do not believe in slavery. Perhaps they should embrace Christianity or Judaism as the followers of these faiths have rejected slavery for centuries.

Why remain in the ranks of Muslims, the last-standing supporters of slavery in the world? When Jamil al-Amin (b. 1943) was at the University of Toronto for a lecture, an infuriated black woman asked him how he could be a Muslim in light of the historical crimes and atrocities that Arabs had committed against Africans. His response, which many thought was on point at the time, was that "not all Muslims are Arabs, and not all Arabs are Muslims." Yeah, right, as if non-Muslims and non-Arabs were center stage in the "Islamic" slave trade that cost millions of black African lives. As Muslims, we have a duty to tell the truth.

On that much needed note, the Nation of Islam's racist and antisemitic attempt to scapegoat the Jews for slavery is a historical travesty. Louis Farrakhan's *Secret Relationship between Blacks and Jews*, which claims that Jews dominated the Atlantic slave trade is a work of pseudo-scholarship. Any Muslim, with a degree of self-critical faith, should acknowledge the role played by Muslims in the Atlantic, Sub-Saharan, and Indian ocean slave trade. Jews played a minimal role in slavery. Christians and Muslims played a major one.

The fact remains that "while the early nineteenth-century abolition of the slave trade significantly affected the trans-Atlantic slave trade, the trans-Saharan slave trade continued to flourish throughout the nineteenth century as demand for slaves increased" (El Hamel 241). While Europeans and Americans were abolishing slavery and emancipating slaves, the Muslims were not doing the same. On the contrary, they were increasing the production of slaves to meet the market's demands. Slavery was supported by Muslim leaders and scholars (El Hamel 244). As the Moroccan sultan, Moulay 'Abd al-Rahman (1778-1859) stated,

> the making of slaves and trading therewith… is confirmed by our book, as also by the *sunnah* of our Prophet… furthermore there is not any controversy between the Oolamma on that subject, and no one can allow what is prohibited or prohibit that which is made lawful. (El Hamel 244)

Islam did not fail Muslims. Muslims failed Islam. God did not fail human beings. Human beings failed God. As Fatima Mernissi (1940-2015), the Moroccan sociologist and feminist, noted,

> Muslims, beginning in the seventh century, could have started elaborating laws that would have realized the Prophet's dream of an egalitarian society. But it was not until the twentieth century that with much anguish -- and under pressure from the "immoral infidels," otherwise known as the colonizers -- they renounced slavery. (153)

13.3 Conclusions

Muslims can try to defend their religion until they are blue in the face and claim that Islam opposes slavery. However, the facts speak for themselves. Muslim majority nations were the last to abolish slavery, as recently as the mid to late twentieth century, and only did so as a result of external pressure from Western nations and internal pressure from the Islamic abolitionists that Jonathan A.C. Brown criticizes (Akyol 2021: 39, see also Clarence-Smith 2006: 11). If Brown should be given credit for anything, argues Mustafa Akyol in a tweet from September 7, 2020, it is for correcting the apologetical and denialist Muslim views on slavery. However, from Brown's findings, Akyol comes to the opposite conclusion. Unlike Brown, who questions if abolition was moral, Akyol argues that it was a tremendous moral progress and a huge lesson that moral truths are universal. Moral Muslims would agree wholeheartedly.

The facts are the facts. The Iranians formally banned slavery in 1929; the Ottomans in 1933; the Saudis in 1962; the Omanis and Yemenis in 1970; the Mauritanians in 1981, and the Pakistanis in 1992. In contrast, the State of Vermont abolished slavery in 1777, Britain banned it in 1807, the United States in 1808, Spain in 1811, Sweden in 1813, the Netherlands in 1814, France in 1817, and Portugal in 1819. Some European nations took longer to outlaw slavery in their colonies; however, they did so: Denmark in 1846, France in 1848, Portugal in 1858, and the Netherlands in 1861.

The United States emancipated its slaves in 1863 and prohibited the practice of slavery in the Thirteenth Amendment to the *Constitution* in 1865. Slavery was abolished in Cuba in 1886, and Brazil did the same in 1888. The League of Nations adopted the *Slavery Convention* in 1926, banning the enslavement of human beings, while in 1948, the United Nations adopted the *Universal Declaration of Human Rights*, which includes the article "No one shall be held in slavery or servitude; slavery and the slave trade shall be prohibited in all their forms." And yet many Muslim scholars continue to insist that God ordains slavery and concubinage, and that nobody has the right to abolish them. Talk about a race to the bottom. Talk about crabs dragging crabs down into the bucket. These are bottom feeders, scavengers, and carrion eaters living in the darkness of the abyss.

Chapter Fourteen

The Illusion of Abolition in the Muslim World

14.1 Introduction

Despite its prohibition, slavery continued to flourish in many parts of the Muslim world. Although it was prohibited in practice by secular laws, it was never prohibited religiously in the minds of many Muslims. It was secular Muslim leaders who banned slavery, not at the encouragement of Muslim clerics, and not with their support, but despite their objections. As Bernard K. Freamon notes, "Muslim secular leaders early on came to see that abolition was in the best interest of their societies and their governments" (2019: 365). They rose against the retrograde, literalist, and obscurantist Muslim clerics who were weighing their societies down under a crushing burden of ignorance, intolerance, extremism, and fanaticism. They aspired to a better world. They wanted Islam to blossom and they understood that it needed the oxygen of freedom to do so.

14.2 Slavery is Alive and Well in the Muslim World

Despite the positive changes that were taking place throughout the world and within Islam itself, the court clerics, the hand kissers of kings, the status-quo scholars for hire, the Pharisees of Islam, and the Imams who lead to the fire, as one can only expect, held fast to the weight of their scholarly tradition regarding slavery and concubinage as it dragged them into the dark depths of the ocean of perdition. As a result, slavery was banned in secular practice, but not in religious theory. "There was no great 'sea change' in attitudes on the morality of slavery in the Muslim world," writes Freamon, and "there was … no internal moral introspection among Muslims on the issue" (2019: 479). As Matthew C. Gordon notes,

> No moral opprobrium has clung to slavery… The decision of Arab states to abolish slavery during this century was taken for reasons that had little to do with the moral aspects of the issue… That slavery and the slave trade were inherently evil and therefore merited abolition were thoughts alien to Arab heads of state and their followers. (Azumah 154)

Consequently, they "missed the opportunity to confront… the profound moral dilemmas" posed by slavery (2019: 479). In light of these facts, it is not surprising that many Muslim-majority nations have some of the highest rates of slavery in the world, including forced labor, forced marriage, and sex trafficking. As Freamon relates,

> Gulf workplace conditions are horrific for such construction workers, generally from Sub-Saharan Africa, India, Pakistan, and several other South Asian and Southeast countries. They are routinely denied access to water and shade in 122-degree … heat, and shelter provided for them at the end of the workday is unsanitary and dehumanizing. It is estimated that 4,000 workers will die by 2022 as Qatar completes the building of its projects for the FIFA World Cup tournament… Death rates in other Persian Gulf … [countries] are similarly very high, compared to death rates in construction projects in other parts of the world. The Nation and the organization Foreign Policy in Focus recently described the situation as a "Kingdom of slaves in the Persian Gulf." (2019: 462)

According to the United Nations International Labor Organization, some six hundred thousand people have been tricked and trapped into forced labor in the Middle East (UN). In Dubai alone, it is estimated that "45,000 women are trapped in prostitution networks," not to mention teenage boys (Rosenblum). For Amalia Rosenblum, "visiting Dubai is like standing on the sidelines of a gang rape." I have been there, and I would agree. I have never seen such a materialistic and hedonistic culture in my travels around the world. It is a supremely unspiritual place where hearts are more arid than the desert sands. The fact, however, is that slavery, both traditional and modern, continues to be practiced throughout much of the Muslim world as the harrowing account of Malek Chebel documents, namely, his work on slavery in the lands of Islam.

Unlike Malcolm X, who was hosted by Saudi Arab despotism, and whose emotions overwhelmed him, other converts never saw the Muslim world with rosy colored shades when they traveled there. Neither faith nor culture shock fogged their critical reasoning capacity. They remained sober and lucid. They saw the good, yes indeed, but they also saw the bad. Unlike Malcolm X, whose sense of critical thinking was stumped, due perhaps to culture shock, rendering him as short-sighted as Stevie Wonder, their moral compasses remained operative.

As Bernard K. Freamon has noted, far from abolishing the trade in human flesh, "slavery, in its modern manifestations, remains alive and well in the Muslim world today" (2021: 346-347). What is more, "attitudes toward 'those whom your right hands possess' in the Muslim world have not improved and perhaps have even gotten worse" (Freamon 2019, 462-463). Consequently, "the abolition of slavery in the Muslim world has largely been an illusion" (Freamon 2019: 6). And if they do not enslave people in wars, and use and abuse conquered women sexually, Freamon fears that it is not because Muslims believe that it is wrong, merely that slavery's "history of illegality, and the world's condemnation of it"

Chapter Fourteen 145

make them hesitant to do so (Freamon 2019: 146). According to this somber analysis, if power dynamics were to change in the world, it is conceivable that some Muslims might get emboldened, resulting in a resurgence of overt, old-fashioned, slavery, which is a staggering thought indeed. Whether it is Boko Haram in Nigeria, the Armed Islamic Group in Algeria, or ISIS in the Levant and Iraq, where Islamists attempt to impose their "Islam," slavery resurfaces in all its terrifying dimensions.

Aside from being sexist, slavery is profoundly racist. As El Hamel has shown, "racialist ideas and positions became not only an ideology of enslavement but also a structure based on patterns of colors and cultural prejudice" (10-11). Blacks were marginalized and subject to racist treatment (El Hamel 90-91). Slavery was racialized and, in the case of Morocco under Moulay Ismail (r. 1672-1727), free black African Muslims were explicitly targeted (El Hamel 155-184). Shaykh Jasus condemned such actions and was executed for doing so (El Hamel 167-168). Other scholars, like al-'Arabi Burdulla (d. 1721) objected to the Sultan's project (El Hamel 168-169). Ahmad b. 'Ajiba at-Titwani (1747-1809) was equally opposed to the enslavement of black Muslims (El Hamel 169). Virtually all other Muslim scholars and jurists supported it. Just as there were pro-slavery and anti-slavery scholars in the past, the same applies to the twenty-first century. So, whose side are you on?

Despite claims that there is no racism in Islam, racism is very much alive in the Muslim world, and much of it is the heritage of slavery. As Haider Hamoudi notes,

> Much of the Muslim world contains not only structures and institutions that perpetuate racial hierarchies and subjugate those of African descent, but a great deal of outright and rather shameless racism as well. Nowhere is this truer than in the Arab world. Perhaps the best example of this is the deplorable colloquialism throughout the Arab world describing blacks, including and perhaps especially those whose forebearers were brought to the region as slaves from the *Zanj*, by the term *'abd*, which is Arabic for "slave." These individuals are not slaves, even under an expanded definition that encompasses guest workers exploited in the Gulf.
>
> And yet, in ways that might seem disturbingly resonant to American audiences, they do not hold high places in government, are not represented in significant numbers in professional classes, are clustered in neighborhoods characterized by extreme poverty and neglect, and those that do reach levels of prominence tend to do so in fields such as sports and entertainment. Intermarriage is unthinkable and a black person appearing at a social club is either a waiter or a driver. These are not merely products of structural inequalities and marginalization. Arab fathers admit quite openly that they would never give their consent to

their daughter marrying an (in their words) *'abd*, and any suggestion that a black person be admitted as a member to an exclusive social club is more often met with derision and ridicule…

From Morocco to the Middle East, and far into the Arab diaspora in Europe and the Americas, many Arabs continue to refer to a black human being as an *'abd* or slave, a racial slur that is the equivalent of the English term "nigger," when the Qur'an itself deliberately avoids describing enslaved persons as such, much less free people. The n-word and the a-word are the same (Abdul-Samad). As Ware notes,

> Many Senegalese Muslims consider Arab racism more virulent than its European cousin, claiming that "white" Mauritians (*baydan*) are more likely to use *'abd* (slave) to refer to a black person than a French person is to use the word *nègre*. (24).

Fortunately, in the past few years, the issue of anti-black racism in the Arab world and in Arab communities abroad has attracted some attention (Arabiyya, Farhat, and others). As Mona Eltahawy (b. 1967), the Egyptian-American journalist, admits, "We are a racist people." Muslims must stop denying the reality of racism in their communities. The same goes with sexual slavery in Islam. As Peter Gray puts it, it is "the elephant in the room." Far from being color-blind,

> Light-skinned Muslims are as color-conscious as European societies and harbor racial prejudice against blacks. Blacks are stereotyped and demonized in Muslim sources as sub-human, at best, and non-human, at worst. Light-skin Muslim racial prejudice against Africans is reflected most in the institution of marriage. Since medieval times, Arabs, Berbers, Moors, Asians, Persians, Turks, etc. have regarded any relationship between their female folk and African males as a socio-religious anathema. (233)

These light-skinned Muslims engaged in the systematic and mass enslavement of black Africans, reducing them to a class of deprived and despised people (233). By embracing Islam, some Afro-descendants have done nothing but move from Islamabad to Islamaworse. In fact, many black Africans are active participants in the oppression and exploitation of their people. As Muhammad Diakho, a black African Muslim jurist exposes, many Islamized blacks continue to practice slavery in many parts of the African continent, including Senegal, Mali, Mauritania, Gambia, Sudan, and elsewhere (57-61). Numerous black African ethnic groups are notorious for their practice of slavery, including the Soninke, the Peul, the Wolof, the Bambara, the Mandinka, the Mossi, the Khassonké, and the Mallinké (57-59). Far from apologetic, they insist that the perpetuation of slavery is part and parcel of the Islamic religion (57-61). Millions of black African Muslims insist that obeying Islamic laws regarding slavery is obeying God! (57)

14.3 God Does Not Change the Condition of a People Until they Change Themselves

Rather than strengthen Islamic arguments against slavery, Jonathan A.C. Brown focuses on rebuking or delegitimizing them as falling outside the mainstream Muslim tradition. Why is it that Egyptian Muslims collectively concluded that slavery was unacceptable? Was this view imposed on them by infidels? Or were they responding to their religious conscience? As Freamon explains,

> Abolition, in the strict juridical sense, never really happened in Egypt, The Egyptian government never enacted a domestic law abolishing slavery. Yet slavery effectively "vanished" from Egypt in the late nineteenth and early twentieth centuries. The disappearance of slavery and slave trading in Egypt happened very rapidly, perhaps within twenty years. It appears that, in one generation, Egyptians determined that slavery should be no more… The consensus was so powerful that there was actually no need for a written law. The practice just stopped. (2019: 417, 419; see also 1998: 59)

Why this happened in Egypt and not elsewhere is anybody's wonder. Freamon proposes three possibilities: 1) "revived and reinterpreted conceptions of human equality and piety under the classical or perhaps a modernist version of Islamic law;" 2) the emergence of a nationalist view of relationships; and/or 3) the need to join the modern world (2019: 419).

Brown rejects the claim that there is a consensus on abolition of slavery on the part of Muslim scholars (2020: 252-255). Freamon disagrees and cites the *Letter to al-Baghdadi* as "evidence of a consensus that needs to be implemented" (2019: 505). While it is filled with flaws, questionable content, weak arguments, and even feeble evidence, as Sultan Shahin has shown, its section on slavery was mostly sound. It reads:

> No scholar of Islam disputes that one of Islam's aims is to abolish slavery. God says: "And what will show you what the obstacle is?, the freeing of a slave, or to give food on a day of hunger" (90: 12-14); and: "then [the penalty for them is] the setting free of a slave before they touch one another" (58:3). The Prophet Muhammad's *sunnah* is that he freed all male and female slaves who were in his possession or who had been given to him. For over a century, Muslims, and indeed the entire world, have been united in the prohibition and criminalization of slavery, which was a milestone in human history when it was finally achieved.
>
> The Prophet said regarding the pre-Islamic "League of the Virtuous" (*hilf al-fudul*) during the time of *jahiliyyah*: "Had I been asked to fulfil it in Islam, I would oblige." After a century of Muslim consensus on the prohibition of slavery, you have violated this; you have taken women as concubines and thus revived strife and sedition (*fitnah*), and corruption

and lewdness on the earth. You have resuscitated something that the *shari'ah* has worked tirelessly to undo and has been considered forbidden by consensus for over a century. Indeed all the Muslim countries in the world are signatories of anti-slavery conventions. God says: "And fulfil the covenant. Indeed the covenant will be enquired into" (Al-Isra', 17:34) You bear the responsibility of this great crime and all the reactions which this may lead to against all Muslims.

Regrettably, it is false that "no scholar of Islam disputes that one of Islam's aims it to abolish slavery." As Fajri Matahati Muhammadin (b. 1987), an Indonesian jurist, points out,

The majority opinion in medieval scholarship says that when a Muslim army conquers an army from the "People of the Book," it is up to the Muslim leader to decide the fate of the war captives: execution, release, or enslavement, based on what the leader considers to be in the best interest of the Muslims (Ibn Rushd 2000: 456). This does seem to be the only way that a person can be enslaved; therefore, Islamic law, according to the medieval scholars, eliminates other but not all means to enslave people.

The *Open Letter* also claims that there has been a Muslim consensus against slavery for the past century. This is not the case at all. As Muhammadin recognizes,

The *Open Letter* seems to refer to the world movement in abolishing slavery, and the Slavery Conventions may indeed be among the landmark events. It is true that a majority of Muslim nations are parties to the Slavery Conventions in 1926 and 1956. The problem is that the slavery abolition voice from the Muslim world was not necessarily through the consensus of scholars, but rather the leader of nations as parties to the Slavery Conventions instead of scholars. This is not to mention that much of the Islamic world at the time was colonialized (e.g., Saudi Arabia, Jordan, Indonesia, etc.) and the Ottoman Empire has just collapsed.

The scholars, on the other hand, are not really unanimous. The Saudi Arabia Committee of Fatwa issued a *fatwa* reaffirming the position of the medieval majority (Al-Lajnah: Ftw. 1977). They also issued another *fatwa* that emphasized that all Imams (great scholars) agree that this law is still applicable today (Al-Lajnah: Ftw. 515). This is apart from Saudi Arabia being party to the Slavery Conventions. Even Az-Zuhayli, one of the most prominent contemporary Shafi'i scholars -- despite the Al-Azhar *fatwa* (Dar Al-Ifta) -- reaffirms this position (Az-Zuhayli 2011: 84-86) while also emphasizing the need to gradually eliminate slavery (Az-Zuhayli 1998: 5916).

It is possible, however, that by "scholars," the authors of the *Letter to Baghdadi* were excluding and perhaps ex-communicating the radical, pro-slavery party, whether they were Salafis, Sunnis, or Shiites, and only considering so-called moderates as *bona fide* scholars. This poses problems as the *Letter to Baghdadi* is filled with extremist ideas that modern Muslim scholars and intellectuals reject.

When the authors of the *Letter to Baghdadi* speak of "consensus," they do not appear to refer solely to scholars but the Muslim community. It should also be remembered that consensus means general agreement and not uniformity. Undoubtedly, most medieval Muslim scholars supported slavery as divinely ordained. There was a consensus in favor of slavery. In fact, when Muslim jurists speak of consensus, they speak of "the consensus of the scholars we follow," namely, like-minded people who live in the same echo chamber. Over the past century and a half, however, Muslim scholars have been divided over the subject.

The extremists and the conservatives support slavery. The same goes for some reformists. For the Salafist, Saleh al-Fawzan (b. 1933), a member of the Senior Council of Clerics of Saudi Arabia, a member of the Council of Religious Edicts and Research, Imam of the Prince Mitaeb Mosque in Riyadh, and professor at Mohammad Bin Saud Islamic University, "Slavery is a part of Islam. Slavery is part of *jihad*, and *jihad* will remain as long there is Islam" (Pipes). He rejects the idea that slavery has been abolished. He claims that those who espouse such views are "ignorant, not scholars" and that "whoever says such things is an infidel." If he wishes to see an infidel, it could be countered, all he has to do is look in the mirror.

Not only do they defend the Islamicity of slavery, but the extremists also wish to resurrect it. For Abu Ishaq al-Huwayni (b. 1956), the Egyptian Salafist, "when I want a sex-slave, I go to the market and pick whichever female I desire and buy her" (Ibrahim). Salwa al-Mutairi, a Kuwaiti socio-political activist, who is widely viewed as complete and total quack, expressly seeks to "revive the institution of sex-slavery." She claims that,

> According to Islam, sex slaves are not at all forbidden. Quite the contrary, the rules regulating sex slaves differ from those for free women [i.e., Muslim women]: the latter's body must be covered entirely, except for her face and hands, whereas the sex-slave is kept naked from the bellybutton on up -- she is different from the free woman; the free woman has to be married properly to her husband, but the sex-slave -- he just buys her and that's that... For example, in the Chechnyan war, surely there are female Russian captives. So go and buy those and sell them here in Kuwait; better that than have our men engage in forbidden sexual relations. I don't see any problem in this, no problem at all... And the greatest example we have is Harun al-Rashid: when he died, he had 2,000 sex slaves -- so it's okay, nothing wrong with it. (Ibrahim)

The perverse and sadistic fantasies of the radical Islamists have come true. Terrorists like the *Groupe Armé Islamique*, Boko Haram, and Daesh, among many others, have revived it with horrific and traumatic consequences. It should be stressed, however, that the views and actions of the pro-slavery savages are not representative of Islam as understood by most modern-day Muslims. As Kecia Ali notes, without producing any statistical evidence from surveys, "the vast majority of Muslims do not consider slavery, especially slave concubinage, to be acceptable practices in the modern world" (2017: 63).

The question begs to be asked: how many Muslims consider slavery permissible in an Islamic state, past, present, or future? Principles are perennial. Right and wrong are retroactive. Female genital mutilation was only criminalized in many nations in the late twentieth and early twenty-first century. Was it morally right before that? Morals do not have an expiration date. When it comes to slavery and concubinage, the matter is black and white. There is no room for nuance. Abolitionists could not care less about the shades of gray. They take no prisoners. The lesson to learn from the mistakes of the past is not to repeat them.

As far as al-Azhar, the so-called voice of Sunni orthodoxy, is concerned, the gradual elimination of slavery was one of the goals of Islam. This process culminated in an international treaty abolishing slavery in 1860, prohibiting it according to Islamic law. As the edict explains,

> Islam came to find slavery existing in every part of the world. At that time, slavery was practiced through different means; people were enslaved through kidnapping and abduction, wars, and debts. Islam abolished all of these means with the exclusion of the enslavement of war prisoners. In its characteristic manner of introducing rulings, Islam did not abruptly abolish slavery but banned it by degrees to maintain social stability. The phenomenon of slavery existed in all the communities around the world, and slaves were considered an important resource in the social and economic life of ancient times.

Enslavement

Enslavement [in general] and the enslavement of prisoners of wars was legally institutionalized worldwide. Islam limited the sources of slavery to abolish it; Islam prohibited enslaving anyone except those captured in battles when Muslims fought and defended themselves against tyrant enemies. This prohibition included the offspring of previously taken slaves. Islam allowed the enslavement of those who fought against Muslims in non-Muslim countries including women and children. However, only the Muslim ruler was entitled to decide this according to what he sees as being in the best interest of Muslims. It was categorically forbidden to enslave anyone who did not fight Muslims. Enslaving a warrior is less evil than killing him. Islam prohibited the killing of female captives of war and substituted this with enslavement. In spite of this, Islam set certain ethics for the good treatment of slaves. It urged Muslims to treat them kindly, not harm them, and prohibited aggression against them.

Out of its eagerness to free all people, Islam expanded the means for emancipating slaves by making the manumission of a slave an [atonement] of sins. These include breaking the fast in Ramadan, *zihar* (wherein a husband deems his wife as unlawful to him as his mother), involuntary manslaughter, breaking oaths, and the like. At the outset, Islam urged its followers to emancipate slaves and then limited the sources of slavery to help in its abolishment.

Islam commanded Muslims to treat slaves kindly until they obtained their freedom. This was stated in multiple texts of the *shari'ah* in which slaves were described as brothers to their masters since they shared with them the brotherhood of humanity, which necessitated being merciful towards them and respecting their dignity. Mercy towards slaves was expanded, and their emancipation was prescribed as an expiation for beating or abusing them. As a result of such great mercy towards slaves, people entered Islam in multitudes.

Islam's Stance on Slavery

Islam observed a noble stance towards the institution of slavery; it limited its sources, increased the means towards their freedom, and exhorted Muslims to treat them kindly and emancipate them. This differed from what prevailed worldwide at that time and [the evil practices] of slave traders in later centuries after the discovery of the New World. Slavery ended worldwide after the international treaty for the abolishment of slavery was signed in Berlin in 1860 AD. This has become a binding system that disallows anyone to enslave another.

Ruling

Based on the above, slavery is impermissible in the *shari'ah*. By virtue of the above-mentioned treaty, all humans are deemed free and cannot be bought or sold. Muslims signed international treaties to end slavery which came in accordance with Islam's desire to limit its sources and expand the means towards freedom. Thus, all people are free as God the Almighty created them.

The anti-slavery edict from al-Azhar is authoritative to Sunni Muslims. However, it perpetuates the false and debunked notion that "Islamic" slavery "differed from what prevailed at that time and … in later centuries after the discovery of the New World." This is what happens when introverted religious scholars who study Islam, and nothing else, including history and other fields, issue *fatwas*. They live in isolation chambers. They know everything about nothing but nothing about everything. They know texts but nothing about contexts.

While this was not always the case, Freamon believes that "there is now a firm Islamic jurisprudential and legal basis for declaring that slavery in Islam can and should be abolished, even under a government bound by the *shari'ah*" (2019: 465). In his view,

> It is arguable that an *ijma'* or juristic consensus on the abolition of slavery now exists among Islamic jurists... no self-respecting *mujtahid* would disagree with the conclusion that it is impossible to legally purchase a slave in any open market in the world today and that slavery and slave trading should remain illegal. (Freamon 2019: 502)

Brown presents the arguments of those who wish to revive slavery and sexual servitude as "a morally acceptable and valid tool of statecraft" (2020: 252-255). For critics, this sounds exactly like what Serbian chetniks, the gang-rapists of Bosnian Muslim women, would say. This sound exactly like what the Janjaweed, the Arab Sudanese rapists, torturers, and murderers of black women, would say. However, as Clarence-Smith points out,

> the seeming Sunni consensus on slavery was full of fissures, from the time of the Prophet himself. An elaborate law of slavery was incrementally erected on foundations which were so flimsy as to pose a constant threat to the viability of the whole tottering edifice. (2006: 47)

Opposition to slavery is as old as Islam itself. The Islamic Empire, however, overthrew the Islamic Republic. "The initial message of the Qur'an," notes El Hamel, "was gradually eroded by the elitist regime's political and power aspirations" (46). The Islamic law that they developed codified "male-dominated and male-sanctioned interpretations of the Qur'an and the *Hadith*" to create "a patriarchal idol-model legal discourse" (46). Although the Qur'an "emphasized that *jihad* must be a just legal war in self-defense only," the interpreters of Islamic law decided to make non-Muslims "the enslavable other" (El Hamel 82).

Rather than "a defense against unjust acts or foreign encroachment," slave master scholars turned *jihad* into "a state-sponsored ... holy war for the expansion of the religion of Islam" (El Hamel 82). As Azumah notes, "the main justification for slavery in classical Muslim thought, borne out in practice by generations of Muslims, is non-belief in Islam, *kufr*" (117). The spread of Islam, like of Christianity during the conquest of the Americas, was a pretext. For many Muslims, soldiers, and leaders, the real motivation was power and greed. It was religion at the service of the Empire. The essence of the Islamic faith was not the problem, but its interpretation and application. While most Muslim scholars set out to serve an Islam of imperialism and slavery, there were dissenters. As Mustafa Akyol points out, Ata ibn Abi Rahah (c. 646-732), an early Medinan scholar, "argued that the verses about fighting non-Muslims 'were prescribed only during the time of the Prophet and his companions,' while universally, it is 'never permissible to fight those who do not fight'" (2022: 177). While it might be necessary to take prisoners of war during a defensive war, and hold them for ransom, there is no basis in the Qur'an for engaging in aggressive wars to hunt, enslave, and sell women into sexual servitude.

The early Islamic governor of Egypt (d. 656-658) made a treaty with Nubia, which required them to provide three hundred and sixty slaves per year to the Muslim Arabs (El Hamel 114, Azumah 122, 141). 'Uqba b. Nafi' (d. 683), the nephew of 'Amr ibn al-'As (d. 664), who invaded the Maghreb, was overtly racist toward Imazighen, and sought to subdue and humiliate them (El Hamel 114). Musa ibn Nusayr (c. 640-c. 716), the governor of Tunisia in 705, captured three hundred thousand Imazighen during his campaigns (El Hamel 115). The Middle East was so flooded with slaves that human beings became devalued to the point where "a man, his wife, and his children, were sold for a mere fifty dirhams" (El Hamel 115). Tariq b. Ziyad (c. 670-720), a Berber Umayyad commander, was explicitly clear that the conquest of Morocco was motivated by a desire to acquire sex slaves (El Hamel 116). Sultan Mahmoud captured half a million slaves during his campaign in 1001-1002. When he attacked the Punjab, he took so many slaves that they became devalued (Lal 20). When the Almoravids invaded Ghana in 1054-1055, they "violated its women" (El Hamel 121).

In later legal theory, developed centuries after the Prophet's passing, Muslim men were supposed to give captive women a waiting period of one menstrual cycle prior to having sexual intercourse with them, to ensure that they were not pregnant. In practice, however, Muslim warriors, like non-Muslims, to be fair, raped women during and after battles. And while this was technically viewed as fornication, and not rape as it most certainly was, Muslim jurists waived its punishment. Shaybani (749-805) was asked about the case of a warrior who had sexual intercourse with a slave girl prior to the distribution of the booty, resulting in the pregnancy of the girl, who then claims parentage of the child. The jurist ruled that "punishment [for *zina*, or fornication] would be waived, but [the warrior] would have to pay the nuptial gift, and the slave girl and her child remain as part of the spoil until it is divided among the warriors" (Khadduri 115). In his view, "the parentage of the child would not be established" (115).

Clearly, the crime committed was *zinah bi al-jabr*, as the warrior was not entitled to have sex with the slave girl prior to becoming his personal property. Consent matters not: only ownership and property rights. Since he committed fornication by force with the girl, the fighter has to pay her dowry. Considering that the combatant did not wait for the girl to have her period, parentage of the child can not be established. If born nine months exactly after the sexual assault, the child almost certainly belonged to the Muslim. However, the jurist ruled that the child belonged to the mother and, since the children of slaves are slaves, it would be treated as part of the booty nine months down the road. The mother and child could thus be separated.

If this is how Islamic law operated, the offspring of Muslim rapists were born into slavery. If the Prophet claimed that *al-walad li al-firash* or "the offspring belongs to the owner of the bed," it could be argued that men are responsible for the children they bring into the world through a wife, a sex partner, or slave. However, Muslim jurists went in the opposite direction, ruling that illegitimate

154   Islam & Slavery

children had no rights to financial support or inheritance. It comes as no surprise that many Muslim men, who have children out of wedlock, refuse to pay child support on grounds that it is un-Islamic. They find support from their shaykhs and imams.

As one can imagine, and as history witnesses, many warriors did not have the patience to wait until the booty was distributed to sexually assault captive women. In many cases, they helped themselves, knowing that no punishment would be inflicted upon them. If a man was within his right to force himself upon his wife, as marriage was viewed as consent to sex, so was a man within his right to force himself upon captive or enslaved women. The honesty of Rudolph T. Ware III is refreshing. "After a defeat," he recognizes, "there was no respect for women, free or slave. They were almost certain to be raped… and then sold or distributed as booty, forced to live the rest of their lives as purchased women, concubines, with no standing, honor, or dignity" (154).

In light of the above, it is no surprise that there were no abolitionists among the imperialists. Since when are slave traders and slave masters opposed to slavery? Opposition to slavery, concubinage, and polygyny was found among those who opposed the Empire, including the Qarmatians (El Hamel 26), and the Druze (Clarence-Smith 2006: 59, Obeid 77), both Ismaili Shiite off-shoots. According to Leila Ahmed, the early Kharijites rejected concubinage (Ahmed 71). The more moderate 'Ibadis, however, became notorious slave-raiders and traders, veritable pirates, and pillagers of the desert. Other sources suggest that the Kharijites only banned concubinage without the wife's consent.

While the Druze, who refer to themselves as *muwwahidun*, Unitarians or Monotheists, once followed the Fatimid jurisprudence as codified in the *Da'a'im* of al-Qadi al-Nu'man (d. 974 CE), they believe that the legal *shari'ah* was a steppingstone to the spiritual *shari'ah*, the *shari'ah al-ruhaniyyah*. Hence, in 1019, the Druze asked the chief judge of the Fatimid state to adjudicate their cases according to the standards of the spiritual law (122). As Nejla M. Abu-Izzeddin points out,

> *Al-sharia'h al-ruhaniyyah*, however, differs in two fundamental provisions from the *Da'a'im:* The abolition of slavery and of polygamy. The Covenant (*Mithaq*) by which the convert binds himself to the faith stipulates that the adherent should be in full possession of his liberty, that he is not held in bondage to anyone and therefore has the power to determine his conduct, and that his adherence should be his own free choice, not influenced by coercion. The Covenant, Baha' al-Din says, abolished slavery. *Al-shari'ah al-ruhaniyyah* confirmed the abolition by forbidding "the sale of human beings."

> The revolutionary significance of this law is more fully realized when it is seen in its historical setting against a background where the institution of slavery was common among societies of various cultures. Not until eight centuries later was slavery abolished by law in countries

Chapter Fourteen

of Western civilization. Similarly, the abolition of polygamy within a community living in a society where polygamy was widely practiced was a revolutionary measure. The institution of monogamy is prominent among the factors contributing to raising the status of Druze women. (122)

As Anis Obeid explains in *The Druze: Their Faith in Tawhid*,

> Monogamy was clearly affirmed and is strictly enforced. The Druze were not the first to advocate strict monogamy, being preceded in that by the Mutazilites and the Qarmatians, but the Druze were the first sect in Islam to institutionalize monogamy in their civil codes. In fact, the Druze refer to several passages in the Qur'an that place major constraints on the practice of polygamy.

> For example, the Qur'an insists on absolute equality among all the wives in case of polygamy. In the eyes of the Druze, this condition is impossible to satisfy, and so polygamy should be prohibited. In a public declaration, al-Mu'izz, the grandfather of al-Hakim, instructed his subjects: "Be faithful to the one woman who is your partner. Refrain from excessive lust, and relations with multiple women... as this will lead to your exhaustion physically and mentally. One man is for one woman." By the time of al-Hakim this admonition had become an inviolable rule and remains so to this day.

> Likewise, the legal age of marriage for girls was raised to fifteen years, and commitment to marriage had to be with the full consent of the woman as an adult... Extending the principle of safeguarding the brethren to women also meant abolition of slavery... The sanctity of the human body was upheld for both men and women, and no form of white slavery could be condoned. Sex is an act of procreation and intimacy in the sanctity of monogamous marriage, and not an untamed instinct in search of indiscriminate satisfaction.... (183)

In accordance with the ruling of al-Hakim (r. 996-1021), the highest authority of the Fatimid state, the Druze outlawed slavery. Perhaps he was inspired by one of his predecessors, al-Mu'izz li-Din Allah (r. 953-975), who had offered to free any slave who converted to Shiism (Chebel 52). As Baha' al-Din (d. after 1042 CE) explained,

> [al-Hakim] ordered the freedom of all the slaves and those who were otherwise owned, in a special decree that was absolute, forceful, and irrevocable, such that no one could return to a state of being owned or enslaved or being subject to summary punishment. That [decree] was meant for all races and groups [such that] no one could object to it or deny the [civil] rights of these people in any way. Whosoever does not comply with this order would be damned as an oppressor... This

156   Islam & Slavery

[measure] cuts the road on those who claim to be what they are not and who would like to return to the practice of slavery… This decree was issued for no purpose except to please God. (Obeid 186)

In later times, it was the Ahmadiyyah, a revivalist movement, viewed by most Muslims as being outside the fold of mainstream Islam, that opposed aggressive *jihad* and slavery. For Abdullah Dibba, an Ahmadi scholar, "It is severe intellectual dishonesty to say Prophet Muhammad… promoted slavery -- he was the one man who effectively abolished slavery." Another Ahmadi scholar, Nasiruddin Hamid, argues that "Islam created a social structure, which closed the doors of enslavement and opened many ways through which slaves could be freed and justly integrated into society." If the social vice of slavery persisted and expanded exponentially it was not due to pristine Islam, but in spite of it. It was the result of disregarding and desecrating Qur'anic teachings.

Besides enslaved African Muslims in the United States, who railed against racism and slavery and eventually obtained their freedom, Alexander Russell Webb (1846-1916), one of the first prominent white Muslim converts, was outspoken in his opposition to slavery and concubinage. As he wrote in his *magnum opus, Islam in America,*

> Slavery and concubinage are not allowed by the Koran, and the spirit of the Islamic religious and civil laws are diametrically opposed to it. The Koran says: "Have naught to do with adultery, for it is a foul thing and an evil way." "Speak unto the believers that they restrain their eyes and observe continence. Thus will they be more pure…" Sir W. Muir, in his *Life of Mahomet,* could neither quote any verse of the Koran sanctioning the enslavement of the captives of war or servile concubinage nor relate any instances of them during the several battles described therein.
>
> Slaves are mentioned in the Koran *de facto* but not *de jure.* The Koran took several measures to abolish future slavery. The steps for its abolition were taken in every moral, legal, religious, and political department. The liberation of slaves was morally declared to be a work of piety and righteousness. Legally, the slaves were to be emancipated on their agreeing to pay a ransom. They were to be set at liberty as a penalty for culpable homicide or in expiation for the use of an objectionable form of divorce, and they were also to be manumitted from the public funds out of the poor taxes. They were religiously to be freed in expiation of a false oath taken by mistake. These were the measures for the abolition of existing slavery; the future slavery was abolished by the Koran by putting the axe deep into its root and by annihilating its real source. (51-52)

The Nation of Islam, founded by Master W.D. Fard, on July 4, 1930, was inherently anti-slavery. This manifests that moral evolution is not always found in the mainstream of a religious tradition. In Islam, freedom fighters were found on the fringes. How ironic it was that Master Fard claimed to have come from

Mecca when, in fact, it became the center of the slave trade in the world well into the twentieth century (Azumah 146). If Master Fard was so anti-slavery, how, where, and when did he develop this conviction? Certainly not from the Sunni or Shiite Arabs, Afghans, or Indians. Unless he acquired this belief from Noble Drew 'Ali or other African Americans, the only abolitionists in the Muslim world at the time were the Druze, the Ahmadiyyah, and a handful of Muslim modernists. If he originated from the region of Afghanistan, Iran, Baluchistan, and what is now Pakistan, where there are no Druze, he could only have learned about their abolitionism at their religious centers in the United States. Otherwise, he adopted the arguments of the Ahmadiyyah or modernist Sunnis. Either way, if W.D. Fard was not God, he was a godsend.

Brown does touch briefly and superficially upon the anti-slavery arguments advanced by modernist and progressive Muslim scholars; however, he fails to give them the coverage they deserve (2020: 196-199, 205, 218-221). By labeling them as such, however, it seems he wishes to deny their Islamic legitimacy. Moreover, he barely gives any attention to Twelver Shiite arguments against slavery. One of the exceptions is the seminal *hadith* in which the Prophet Muhammad declared that slave traders were the worst of human beings (2020: 237). In 1847, six Persian jurists ruled that, based on this saying, slavery was an abomination (Clarence-Smith 2006: 130). This was a legal decree below prohibition; however, it was a step forward unless it was issued under pious dissimulation. In a "deft piece of casuistry," a senior jurist argued that only the selling of slaves was censured and not their purchase (Clarence-Smith 2006: 130). Others, however, showed greater textual and moral integrity.

As Clarence-Smith describes, "a pamphlet, published in Calcutta in 1871, argued that holy war had been suspended since the occultation of the twelfth Imam and that the making of new slaves in war was thus illegitimate" (2006: 130). In 1912, 'Ali Nur 'Ali Shah "issued an uncompromising *fatwa*" in which he stated that "the purchase and sale of human beings is contrary to the dictates of religion and the practice of civilization; and therefore in our eyes any persons, men or women alike, who are claimed as slaves, are in legal fact completely free, and the equals of all other Muslims in their community" (Clarence-Smith 2006: 130-131). Clarence-Smith identifies him as Wafa 'Ali Shah (1847-1918), "both *mujtahid* and head of the Nimatullahi Sufi order" who was a lover of freedom (2006: 131). If this is the case, this was the edict of a Sufi shaykh and not one that had the support of the Shiite seminary, headed by the sources of emulation, an institution that, at times, has been hostile towards Sufism. Finally, Agha Khan III (r. 1885-1957), the leader of the Nizari Ismailis, supported the abolition of slavery (Clarence-Smith 2006: 132).

While, admittedly, most Twelver Shiite jurists continue to believe that the Islamic laws regarding slavery are binding, including sex with enslaved women (Hamoudi 2015: 27, 2016: 371-376), although they are currently inapplicable, some have had the moral courage to oppose this abominable practice. That would include Muhammad Husayn Fadlullah (1935-2010) (Brown 399, note 73) and Mostafa Mohaghegh-Damad (Takim 2021). Fadlullah argued that the Qur'an mentioned slavery but did not mandate it. On the contrary, it aimed to eliminate it. In his words,

> the Qur'an has talked about slavery and slaves, and we note that Islam, in its experiments in dealing with the issue of slavery, was able in a peaceful way to end the issue of slavery in the entire Islamic world, and if there are some Islamic countries that deal with slavery realistically, Islamic *ijtihad* when it examines these phenomena, which exist, for example, in Sudan or in Mauritania, considers that this slavery that exists in reality has no legitimacy.

While Fadlullah should be applauded for asserting that the slavery practiced in the Sudan and Mauritania is un-Islamic, his claim that Islam abolished slavery in the entire Islamic world is farcical. It was Western Christians, secularists, and liberals, who put an end to slavery in the world. He did, however, issue an important edict on the subject. It reads,

> Slavery no longer has any reality, and no one can enslave the other, but it was in an earlier time when non-Muslims were enslaved in wars, so Islam used to enslave infidel combatants out of reciprocity; however, it freed slaves with the aim of eradicating this institution. (2023)

Mostafa Mohaghegh-Damad's approached the issue in a more sophisticated manner. He argued that,

> In the engagements which took place at the time of the rise of Islam, slavery was considered permissible. This was because of the necessity of retaliation or, in the terminology of international law, balance of power. Each side would take slaves. If a Muslim were taken prisoner, the enemy would enslave him and he could be bought and sold. Islam was not able at that time to abolish slavery; had it done so unilaterally, it would have made itself weaker in relation to those who sought to destroy it. (One should also take note of the fact that even when slavery was a common feature of warfare it was only permissible [*ja'iz*] to enslave others; it was not a religious duty [*wajib*] or ruling principle of Islam.) The times have now changed. Society has evolved and the international community has agreed to abolish slavery; the institution of slavery has disappeared. It is now necessary to conclude that slavery is also forbidden by Islamic law, for the basis of application of the law of slavery has changed. The jurist cannot claim that since in the past prisoners of war were enslaved, they must be enslaved today. Islamic countries have readily signed the international conventions on slavery, and the abolition of slavery is not in any way inconsistent with Islamic law. (219)

As far as Saeed Akhtar Rizvi (1927-2002), a Twelver Shiite jurist, was concerned, "Islam's objective was in time to create a society free from this pernicious institution." This is a far cry from Abul al-A'la al-Mawdudi (1903-1979), who proclaimed that the harem was "the last place of refuge where Islam guards its civilization and culture" (Clarence-Smith 2006: 188). Compare this to the views of Liyakat Takim, a Twelver Shiite academic, who has taken a clear stance on the subject. In his view,

> The selling and purchase of humans is unethical and an affront to human values. However, in a world where slavery was rampant and Muslims were often enslaved, Muslims could not be prohibited from capturing slaves who could be used to ransom Muslim ones. The Qur'anic endorsement of slavery cannot be extended to modern times when the institution has been abolished. Texts that argue for the acceptance of slavery today should be rejected, since the permission to enslave was temporary. This is especially so because the Qur'an encourages and even requires manumission of slaves in many verses. Hence, although contemporary judicial manuals still discuss the topic, slavery-related edicts should not be seen as part of normative Islam. Rather than merely omitting the discussion of slavery in their texts, jurists should unreservedly prohibit the institution. (211)

As for Brown's book, it is supposedly aimed at readers "who want to understand how Muslims conceptualized, practiced, and eventually abolished slavery in Islam" (3). Fair enough. Its tone, however, is hardly constructive, nor did he need to act as the Devil's Advocate. He goes out of his way to discredit the denunciations of slavery and its prohibition by Muhammad Yaqoubi (b. 1963), as well as the scholars who signed the *Open Letter to Baghdadi* (Brown 2020: 257). Brown alleges that their arguments "depend... on a regnant international legal and moral consensus," as opposed to the Qur'an and the Prophet (2020: 258).

As Brown writes, "the end of slavery is the natal miracle of European civilization" (2020: 215). However, for Islamists, "Christian," "European," and "Western" are code words for "un-Islamic." Hence, for them, to defend slavery is to defend Islam. They have no appreciation for the dignity of the human person. While the abolition of slavery on the part of the Western world was a feat of historical proportions which was motivated, in part, by a faith-based humanitarian movement, the real reason it was prohibited was economic (Rizvi).

As a result of increased industrialization, slaves were replaced with indentured laborers and factory workers, who were less expensive than slaves and whose condition in life was equally miserable, if not worse. The capitalists no longer needed to feed, house, and clothe slaves. Unlike slavery, labor forces could be increased and decreased with immediate effect. If it was in the interest of masters and plantation owners to keep their slaves healthy, to protect their investment, factory owners could exploit workers as much as they wanted, in horrific and unhealthy conditions, only to discard them and replace them with others when they got ill or died. This reality does not make slavery better than freedom. It simply shows that both systems were deleterious. The transition from slavery to freedom was mismanaged. The consequences are seen to this day. In much of the Western world, the descendants of enslaved Africans have not made a full recovery socio-economically.

Brown treats Qur'anic verses that are descriptive as if they were prescriptive. Like the medieval Muslim jurists he cites, his Qur'anic analysis is atomistic, and his methodology is myopic. It ignores the moral and ethical message of the Qur'an and the teachings of the Prophet Muhammad. It fails to distinguish between the eternal and the temporal, the universal and the historical, the mutable and the immutable, and the inessential from the essential. It ignores the gradualist approach espoused by God and His Prophet, namely, that of incremental change over time. This was the position of Rashid Rida (1865-1935), as influenced by Muhammad 'Abduh (1849-1905) (Freamon 2019: 158: note 226), the latter having attacked concubinage in an edict found in his papers after his death (Clarence-Smith 2008: 14). This was the perspective of Fazlur Rahman (1919-1988) (Mir-Hosseini 37). This gradualist view is also shared by Naser Makarem Shirazi (b. 1927), the Twelver Shiite religious authority. As far as Amina Wadud is concerned,

> Some prevailing practices were so bad they had to be prohibited explicitly and immediately: infanticide, sexual abuse of slave girls, denial of inheritance to women… to name a few. Other practices had to be modified: polygamy, unconstrained divorce, conjugal violence, and concubinage, for example. (9)

If Muslims could not take non-Muslim prisoners and exchange them for Muslim ones held by the enemy, they would have been placed at a disadvantage (Azumah 125). Muslims were abiding more or less by the international norms of the age. Islam did not start from scratch. There was no year zero. There was no complete break from the past. The early Muslims operated within existing legal and cultural frameworks, adapting, and modifying them as required.

Brown mentions that scholars debate the extent to which Islamic law inherited Near Eastern laws and practices (2020: 76-82). There is no doubt that "Arab customary law recognized and condoned the institution of slavery as did Greek law, Roman law, Hebrew law, ancient Persian law, Byzantine Christian law, African customary law, Hindu law, and most of the other legal systems in the larger Middle Eastern region" (Freamon 2019: 86-87). When Islam exploded on the scene in the seventh century, it inherited slavery and concubinage from pre-Islamic societies (Freamon 2019: 294). They were not practices unique to Islam (Freamon 2019: 294). As Leila Ahmed notes, "by Sassanian times, when concubines numbered in the thousands, a harem of 365 concubines would have come to seem modest" (18).

When it came to legitimizing slavery and concubinage, Muslim jurists from all schools "incorporated existing pre-Islamic cultural practices rather than adopting and adhering to what the Qur'an expresses with respect to new ethical tenets for social relations" (El Hamel 22-23). Some scholars, like Yousef Eshkevari (b. 1950), insist that ninety-nine percent of Islamic laws were borrowed from pre-existing legal systems and customs. They were adopted and endorsed (Takim 2022: 133, note 72). If that is the case, then they are not written in stone. They are not the product of God. They are the product of fallible men. They were conjectural (Takim 2022: 77). They are, therefore, malleable, and mutable. To criticize and condemn slavery and sexual servitude is not to attack the Creator or even the Prophet, but to attack all oppressive man-made systems and interpretations. It is *tawhid* in practice: the attempt to unify and make one.

However, the fact is that the mass, systematic, and unrestricted concubinage that arose after the passing of the Prophet Muhammad was not modeled on a pre-Islamic model. As Robinson notes,

> Concubinage of this form was not an extension of the *Hijazi* practice. Part of this has been established ... with the quantitative analysis of the *Nasab Quraysh* showing that no *Qurayshi* before the generation of Muhammad's grandfather... is recorded as having had a concubine as a mother... With the taking of concubines, and the full acceptance of their offspring, the Muslims did something that contrasted with the prevailing norms of every major Near-Eastern religious practice of the conquest era, including that of the pre-Islamic *Hijaz*. By allowing unlimited concubinage, they were overturning the Roman understanding of it being a monogamous institution, and by allowing it at all, they were in conflict with Jewish and Christian law.

As surprising as it may be to some, this "unprecedented sea-change in seventh-century Arab social behavior" was not related to the revelation of Islam "as neither in the Prophet's practice nor in the Qur'an do we find the normative framework for the *umm walad* and the *hajin*" (Robinson). The Qur'an does speak of *ma malakat aymanakum* or "that which your right hands possess." However, as Robinson remarks,

> this does not mean she is a slave, and a free Arab woman taken in battle from a local tribe is a very different category of person to a non-Arab concubine far removed from her family. The Qur'an also makes no mention of the status of her children... As Brockopp notes, *ma malakat aymanakum* could refer to a lesser type of marriage; indeed, it does bring to mind the Roman institution of *in manus* marriage, which was a lower class of marriage in comparison to the full variety.

In fact, the term *umm walad*, which is so central to the concept of Islamic concubinage, cannot be found in the sources concerned with Muhammad's time (Robinson). Far from being a *sunnah* of the Prophet Muhammad, "concubinage was not a common occurrence in the prophetic era" (Robinson). It was only after the conquests began that Arabs started to take concubines in large numbers

(Robinson). As Elizabeth Urban perceives, "the Umayyad caliphs came to rely increasingly on concubinage as a reproductive practice in order to consolidate political power in the Umayyad family alone" (5-6).

Since Arab Muslims were a small minority that ruled over a vast non-Muslim majority, and many of the men were genealogically precarious, they needed to increase their numbers to consolidate their power. Tribal loyalties, rivalry, dowries, and issues of inheritance complicated matters. The appeal of concubinage was that it could provide large numbers of sons and increase the most important social relationships: father-son, brother-brother, and cousin-uncle. The greater the connections, the greater the success (Robinson). Hence, "the Islamic message was tailored to appeal to men in a similar situation" (Robinson). The more egalitarian vision of the *ummah*, which the Prophet Muhammad had tried to create by brothering Muslims in Medina after the Hijrah, was lost and replaced with the old tribal loyalties (Robinson).

While "the need to produce sons was partly satisfied through polygamy... marriage was costly and could be problematic given the split loyalties of wives." "By allowing sexual intercourse with the newly acquired foreign slave women," notes Robinson," and recognizing the children of these unions as legitimate from birth, Islamic society offered an attractive supplement to standard marriage" (Robinson). Most importantly and most consequentially:

> By the time the legal schools were establishing themselves in the 'Abbasid period, the concubine was an established element of the Islamic court. The lawyers were unlikely to develop or maintain a legal position of prohibition as it would have brought them into conflict with their political superiors, and so concubinage became an unremarkable part of normative Islam... Unlike some other aspects of sexual ethics practiced by the first Muslims, concubinage did not veer towards the norms of the first societies conquered by Arabs because it was too useful to too many elites over too long a period of time.

As Robinson's genealogical study of the Quraysh, the tribe of Muhammad, reveals, "the normalization of concubinage cannot ... be characterized as an Islamization of *Hijazi* or Near Eastern cultural/legal practices." Rather, it was "the result of human innovation" (Robinson). Since the early Islamic elites needed sons, they resorted to purchasing concubines (Robinson). "Eventually," he notes, "legal cover was provided for this by a creative interpretation of the *hadith* and the Qur'an ... predominantly... the Qur'anic expression *ma malakat aymanakum* (Robinson). These findings are earth-shattering in importance.

Neither God nor the Prophet Muhammad instituted so-called Islamic concubinage. It was an innovation introduced by the Umayyads, who appear to have been determined to devastate Christian views of slavery and sexuality. Concubinage became entrenched and institutionalized under the 'Abbasids and was codified into law by jurists centuries after the passing of the Prophet, based on pragmatic, self-serving, manufactured, and imaginary interpretations of the

Qur'an. On concubinage, Sunni and Shiite jurists came to the same conclusions because they were the products of the same societies and, quite often, the sons of such unions. As much as the Twelver Shiites wish to present themselves as a persecuted minority that was oppressed by and opposed to the 'Abbasids, leading Imami Shiite families and scholars became deeply embedded in their administration filling essential functions at court.

The occultation of the twelfth Imam was a dream come true for the 'Abbasids as it reduced or neutralized the threat of Shiite revolts. It was in their interest to promote Twelver Shiism as a quietist sect that patiently awaited the return of a Hidden Imam. The canonical books of Shiite traditions, and the jurisprudence derived from them, are not substantially different from the Sunni ones. They all reflect the norms, values, and views that dominated when they were concocted. Sunnism and Twelver Shiism reflect the mores of 'Abbasid times. The chasm between them and the Prophet Muhammad spans centuries. The gap was filled in with material that justified forced conversion, imperialism, and slavery, not to mention, polygyny, pedophilia, and slave-concubinage, the most degrading and dehumanizing form of prostitution. However, the example of the Prophet Muhammad prevails. After he reconquered Mecca, not a single woman, infidel or otherwise, was enslaved and made a concubine. Such is the prophetic precedent.

To claim that "questioning humanly inferred juristic proclamations or scholarly consensus is... challenging God's legislation … is almost tantamount to claiming that the Divine speaks to or through the jurists" (Takim 2022: 28). As Takim puts it plainly, the issuance of immoral edicts is produced by the sacralization of religious laws (2022: 185). As for the Qur'an, it is finite, not infinite. It contains some of the Word of God but not its totality. It is not the sole source of law in Islam. In fact, as Brown admits, "the Qur'an is not first and foremost a book of law" (70). The Qur'an may be the Word of God in Muslim theology; however, its interpretation is the Word of Man. Consequently, we have the right and obligation to reinterpret Islamic *shari'ah* law. As Cyrille Moreno al-'Ajami, the specialist in exegesis, notes, "the Qur'an is not necessarily the reflection of Islam and vice versa." In fact, he denounces the hypocrisy of the exegetes who "fully legalized the sexual abuse of female slaves" while the Qur'an prohibited the practice and called upon Muslims to marry them (2020: 103-104). As he expresses, "what form of violence against human beings is worst than rape!" (2020: 104).

As Muslims, we are not bound to repeat past mistakes. We are perfectly entitled; in fact, we are obliged to develop laws based on the moral and ethical principles espoused by the Qur'an, the Prophet, and other sources. The Messenger of God encouraged Muslims to acquire the attributes of God, namely, to manifest His qualities so that we could serve as His Reflection. Consequently, we must align our laws with the Most Beautiful Names of God. If God is Just, we must strive to ensure that our laws are just. If God is Merciful, we should insist that laws be merciful. If God is Loving, then our laws should be loving. There is nothing sacred in slavery, sexual bondage, sex with children, and violence against women. An Omnipotent and Omniscient deity is above legislating moral abominations. There is such a thing as moral absolutes. We must uphold perennial principles.

The Prophet Muhammad was not all-powerful. He did not have a magic wand. He started a process of moral, social, economic, and political reform with lofty goals, aims, and higher objectives. How much can any man, even a Messenger of God, accomplish in a mere twenty-three years? He was persecuted and powerless for the first thirteen years. He only had power and influence over a limited area for ten years. If early Muslims had followed the Freedom Verses (47: 4-5), which were binding and could not be abrogated, Sayyid Ahmad Khan (1817-1898) believed that slavery would have been abolished within a generation (Clarence-Smith 2008: 6). Fadel Abdullah also claimed that "only deviation from Islam prevented [the] elimination of slavery within the first few decades of Islam" (Azumah 153).

As Muhammad Diakho explains, Muhammad received his revelation at a time when slaves were oppressed, not only in Arabia, but throughout the world (131). Specific laws could not have eradicated slavery (131). What needed to be disseminated were universal principles upon which abolitionism could be founded (131). For Azumah, however, such views "compromise facts and truth in order to 'defend Islam'" (153-154). Be that as it may, moral, social, and political evolution takes time. In some areas, it can take generations, centuries, and millennia. The moral and ethical trajectory of Islam was shot off course. For some, who wish to freeze dry Islam and follow a fossilized fragment of the faith, its development ceased in the fourteenth century, in fact, or the seventh century, in myth.

Had the early Muslims faithfully followed the Qur'anic ethos, and the precedent of the Prophet, asserted Rashid Rida (1865-1935), slavery would have disappeared in the Islamic world within a century (Brown 207). Although Brown quotes this view, he brushes it aside coldly: "the simple fact is that Islam did not bring slavery to an end" (207). "If anything," he admits, "Islamic civilization fashioned the institution... into a social and political model" (Brown 207). Yes, indeed, they perfected the slave state. It is a source of shame, not of pride. An apology is in order, and reparations must be made through investment, development, infrastructure, education, and healthcare. The Arabs and the Turks owe a debt to black Africa and African descendants in the Muslim world. It must be repaid. Even Brown considers this crucial question:

> Regarding slavery in the Americas, as a person who has benefitted from the expropriated land, lives and labor of millions of Native Americans and Africans (many of whom were Muslims), it is the responsibility of me and others like me to pay reparations to their descendants (does this mean Muslims must pay reparations?) (11)

Not only did the Qur'an institute measures for the progressive emancipation of enslaved human beings, but it also facilitated their access to civil and economic society by calling former slave masters to provide them with restitution, a move that was met with hostility:

> And God has made some of you excel others in the means of subsistence, so those who are made to excel do not give away their sustenance to those whom their right hands possess so that they should be equal therein; is it then the favor of God which they deny? (16:71)

As al-'Ajami notes, "the idea was so revolutionary and egalitarian that a majority of exegetes strove to modify its meaning" (2020: 100).

While Brown acknowledges that the Qur'an and the *hadith* encourage the emancipation of slaves, he does not believe that they form the basis for a theology and jurisprudence of abolition. A just jurist, however, has ample Qur'anic evidence to prohibit slavery, not the least of which is verse 2:177 which asserts that "It is not righteousness that ye turn your faces to the East and the West; but righteous is he who ... set slaves free," and verse 47:4 which calls upon Muslims to let the captives go free. As Freamon notes, Sayyid Qutb (1906-1966) "disagreed with the conclusion that verse 47:4 permits the enslavement of prisoners of war" (2019: 498). In fact, "he argued that the plain text of the verse only contemplates the setting of prisoners free, gratis, or for ransom" (2019: 498). As Rashid Rida (1865-1935) asserts,

> Nowhere in the Qur'an is enslavement prescribed for captives of *jihad*. No verse calls for such enslavement. Moreover, it does not allow it. It is inconceivable that the Qur'an would call for the enslavement of free men, even if they were captives (before their captivity), while calling for the emancipation of slaves in more than one of its verses. (Diakho 146-147)

When it comes to enslaving prisoners, the Qur'an and the *sunnah* are clear. "Neither implicitly nor explicitly does the Qur'an recognize the right to reduce war prisoners to slavery; the Prophet never did such a thing" (Diakho 137). Early Muslim jurists recognized this fact. As Abu 'Ubayd (c. 770-838) noted in his *Kitab al-amwal*, the Prophet provided leaders with three options regarding the captives of a just *jihad*: pardon, ransom, or death (Diakho 137). The Prophet used all these methods (Diakho 138). He never condemned captives and their future offspring to slavery.

"If neither the Qur'an nor the Prophet instituted the practice of reducing war captives to slavery," asks Muhammad Diakho, "where does this new institution come from?" (Diakho 139). All fingers point to the second caliph, 'Umar ibn al-Khattab, who decreed that non-Arabs could be enslaved (139-140). "It was during this period, namely, right after the death of the Prophet Muhammad," notes Diakho, "that the founding principles that we have already evoked, under the pressure of great dignitaries, were set aside to turn back to pre-Islamic customs and practices" (142).

For Ghulam Ahmed Parwez (1903-1985), the references to slaves in the Qur'an applied only to people enslaved during the time of the Prophet Muhammad's revelations (Clarence-Smith 2008: 9; Parwez 82). He interpreted 47:4 as closing the door of future slavery forever: "whatever happened in the subsequent history was the responsibility of Muslims, and not of the Qur'an" (9).

As Mohsen Kadivar notes, Islamic law stipulates seven cause of enslavement: 1) getting captured in war; 2) slavery through overpowering; 3) slavery through purchase made from a guardian; 4) transfer of slavery from parents to their children; 5) enslavement through confession; 6) slavery of a parentless child from the land of disbelief; 7) and purchasing someone from the marketplace of non-Muslims. As he points out, "none of the seven causes of slavery have a Qur'anic origin." In fact, "the Qur'an has not even discussed slavery through captivity in war, let alone approved of it." Regarding 4:74, Kadivar observes that,

> In this verse, two solutions have been presented regarding captives of war: freedom without ransom, and freedom with ransom, such as exchanging them for Muslim captives, taking reparations, etc. However, a third solution by the name of slavery has neither come in the content of this verse, nor is it deducible from it, rather, taking captives as slaves is not provable through the Holy Qur'an. Yes, this ruling is derived from the *sunnah* and the traditions...

After studying the sayings used to support slavery, Kadivar concludes that "in none of the traditions is there an indication that slavery was a permanently immutable law." According to Kadivar, notes Llyod Ridgeon,

> The way of reasonable people (which of necessity is just and rational) abrogates practices that are considered irrational and unjust, and promote corruption, and which are based on specific commands that endorse outdated customs such as wife-beating, polygamy, slavery, etc. which "traditional Islam" holds to be eternal And unchanging. (223)

For Abdul Malik Mujahid, the call to "release them by grace or by ransom" "was ordered in a context when there were no prison systems or prisoner-of-war camps." "Army commanders," he explains, "were either to free prisoners without financial compensation or to hold them for ransom." This is also the view of 'Ali Mohammad Dastghaib Shirazi (b. 1935), the Iranian Twelver Shiite source of emulation. Commenting on 47:4, he noted that,

> It does not mention the enslaving of prisoners, which would have enforced it as a permanent rule of war, what it explicitly laid down is rather the ransoming or setting them free as a favor, for it is these two that the Qur'an prescribed as a permanent law of war.

The Qur'an also encourages and even requires Muslims to emancipate their slaves and provide them with a means of sustenance (24:33). In Twelver Shiite jurisprudence, slaves could be freed by contract, will, ownership of blood relatives, partial freedom, giving birth to a master's child, accepting Islam before the master, physical harm, physical ailment, death of a master without inheritors, as expiation, as a tax, and after seven years of service (Peiravi). As is noted in *The Study Qur'an*, "some consider it obligatory to contract emancipation with slaves if one knows *any good in them*... while others read this as a recommendation, a kind of guidance, so that an owner cannot be compelled by the request of a slave for freedom" (Nasr 877). Commentaries have consequences. In many cases, they do not reflect God's will but the commentator's intention.

For the Zahiri school of jurisprudence, manumission contracts were mandatory. The Shafi'i, Maliki, and Hanbali schools treat them as recommended and praiseworthy. The right to an emancipation clause or contract has been emphasized by Khaled Abou El Fadl. In his words,

> The right to *mukatabah* is commanded by the Qur'an in *surat al-Nur* 33. Per the *mukatabah* procedure, a slave buys his/her own freedom from his/her master. It is clear that the Qur'an makes such a right mandatory, but Muslim jurists debated whether the slave owner has the power to refuse the *mukatabah* option. Numerous Muslim jurists held that the public treasury is obligated to assist slaves in buying their freedom from their owners. This money can come from the *zakat* collected by the state. Many jurists held that judges can and should order slave owners to enter into *mukatabah* contracts where a fair price is set, and the slave purchases his freedom through his labor or through public funds. The abduction of people for the purpose of enslaving them was considered a major sin (*kabirah min al-kaba'ir*). Moreover, buying or selling slaves is considered *haram*. The only legal venue for obtaining slaves was prisoners of war. So if the state made the moral decision not to enslave prisoners of war, there would be no slavery. Jonathan Brown seems incapable of understanding this point. (2023)

If the Qur'an can be used to abolish slavery, so can the *hadith* and the *sunnah*. A just jurist could also embrace the anti-slavery sayings of the Prophet as authentic while rejecting the pro-slavery ones as forgeries. It is a matter of choice. Even if we treat them all as authentic, the fact remains that there is no indication in any of them that "slavery was a permanently immutable law" (Kadivar). Finally, rather than rely only on a hundred-some-odd verses of the Qur'an, along with legally oriented prophetic traditions, jurists must expand their repertoire and draw from the ethical instructions found in the *hadith*, particularly the *hadith qudsi*, as well as the fields of *mantiq*, logic, and *akhlaq*, ethics. As Diakho rightly asks,

> Why have the principles of equality of men never worked in favor of the slave? What about the principle of the inviolability of one's rights? What about the principle of the non-superiority of races as of classes? What about the principles that protect the dignity of man, his property, and his family... Can't these same *hadith* serve as legislative texts? (11)

The Qur'an and the *sunnah*, as well as the general rules of Muslim law, are all in agreement when it comes to such an inhuman phenomenon such as slavery, that lowers the status of a man, who is equal in rights, to that of an object, and children to the level of lunatics, idiots, and the comatose. (38)

As Muhammad Diakho has noted, it is difficult for Muslim jurists to free themselves from the shackles of the shaykhs, ideological terror, and a largely decadent jurisprudence, especially when any deviation from their rulings is viewed, not only as heresy, but as active participation in a "conspiracy against Islam" (14-15). This very notion of "enemies" and "plotters" has become a fatal fixation for some Muslims, one that blinds them from the internal causes of their decadence (15). For Diakho,

It is grotesque and unacceptable for any theologian who respects himself and his religion to believe that Islam, its revelation, and prophetic tradition, would have maintained, until the present, a large part of the "non-Arab" *ummah*, in a permanent state of slavery. Such an affirmation is false and unjustified. The Qur'an never stops reminding people of their natural equality and liberty from the moment of their birth. (56)

14.4 Conclusions

While eradicating the evil of slavery is no easy task, one that has tremendous economic consequences, and must involve a considerable amount of social engineering to remove resentment, racism, sexism, and classism, and ensure that those who are free have the means to earn an equitable livelihood, the Qur'an establishes emancipation as a higher objective of Islam. "What will make you know what the steep path is?" asks God in the Qur'an, "It is the freeing of a slave" (90:12-13). As Clarence-Smith points out, Muslim "jurists found reasons to nullify God's seemingly clear instructions to free prisoners after wars" (2006: 25). They appealed to "public interest" and invoked the principle of "abrogation" to neutralize the Qur'anic call for emancipation (Clarence-Smith 2006: 25). In many cases, however, exegetes conveniently ignored commenting upon these verses and jurists refused to use them to derive rulings. They refused to ban slavery for economic reasons. This begs the question: are people made to serve the economy, or is the economy made to serve people? Humanity comes first, not the economic and sexual interests of mass murderers, plunderers, enslavers, exploiters, oppressors, and rapists.

Chapter Fifteen

The Horrors of "Islamic" Slavery

15.1 Introduction

The laws of slavery that Jonathan A.C. Brown so adamantly defends as Qur'anically and prophetically based and divinely decreed were developed and instituted centuries after the passing of Muhammad, the Messenger of God. He fails to distinguish between slavery during the rule of the Prophet Muhammad in Medina and slavery as it was developed after his passing, particularly under the Umayyads, but mainly under the 'Abbasids and their successors, including the Fatimids, Safavids, Ottomans, and others.

Under the Prophet Muhammad's rule, slavery was temporary. Slaves could work their way to freedom or wait to be ransomed. They were to be treated as brothers and sisters. They were treated as part of the family. They were not to be mistreated. The Prophet warned that anyone who hit a slave would be hit, and anyone who castrated a slave would be castrated as punishment. These slaves, primarily prisoners of war, were more like servants. They engaged in housework, labor, agriculture, or trades. The families to whom they were entrusted were encouraged to emancipate and marry them.

If anything, the type of slavery under the Prophet Muhammad's rule resembled the one practiced among some North American Natives. Captives were assigned to a family. They became part of the family and part of the tribe. Female war captives were placed under the custody and protection of older couples to prevent them from being taken advantage of or seduced by younger warriors. In many cases, when the time came for captives to be liberated, they refused to return to their tribe of origin. They had fully integrated into their new family, clan, tribe, and nation. Consequently, this practice can scarcely be called "slavery."

If prisoners of war were given the option of being placed in prisons or internment camps, or placed in the custody of a family or an employer, where they could be paroled to serve the war effort or to await a prisoner exchange, most would prefer to work on a farm, a factory, a bakery, or to practice a trade than to live in cramped and confined conditions. The right to an emancipation contract, and a maximum of seven years of service to provide reparations through physical labor, not sexual services, were reasonable. Regrettably, they were rarely applied, implemented, and respected.

The type of temporary bondage that occurred in Medina, under the *ummah* of Islam, did not remotely resemble the type that was practiced by the ancient Romans or by European Christians from the fifteenth century to the nineteenth century, much less the slavery and concubinage that started after the early Muslim conquests into the Levant, the Middle East, North Africa, and Europe. This type of mass-scale slavery, involving the genocide of millions of human beings, the emasculation of millions of boys, and the reduction of millions of women to sexual slavery, was an innovation, not only in Islam but in slavery itself. If anything, it inspired the trans-Atlantic Slave Trade.

15.2 The Blind Following the Blind

Jonathan A.C. Brown appears to reject the possibility that the companions, their followers, and the generations that succeeded them failed to live up to the standards of the Qur'an and the Prophet and fell short in meeting their higher objectives. The dogma of the "inherent goodness" of the companions of the Prophet has long been rejected by Shiism. Sunnism should seriously reconsider this notion without falling into the Twelver Shiite trap that presents their Imams as infallible. Only God is infallible. Nobody should be followed blindly, uncritically, and unquestionably. As for the early Muslims, history speaks for itself, and actions speak louder than words.

Children of concubines were rare during the time of Muhammad's father and grandfather (Majeid 16-17). However, their numbers grew exponentially with the early Muslim conquests (Majeid 11-12, 20-21). Eager for booty, both literally and metaphorically, Muslim imperialists engaged in endless conquests (Dashti 181-191, Shoemaker 215). As Brown admits, "the number of concubines taken by Muslims jumped dramatically with the early Islamic conquests" (114). The horrors committed by these "pious predecessors," as Brown describes them, were atrocious, and later Muslims were no better in theory or practice. Yes, there were good Muslims, but also some very bad ones. The same applies to all populations.

As William Gervase Clarence-Smith details, the slave raids of the Muslims were brutal, the forced marches were traumatic, and the slave markets were demeaning and dehumanizing (2006: 5). Enslaved men were branded, on their feet or their faces, and were regularly beaten and brutalized (2006: 4). They died of exposure. Some froze to death (5). Others were worked to death.

Foreign women, black, Berber, and European, among others, were condemned to a life of domestic labor and/or sexual servitude, objects of entertainment for predominantly Arab, Persian, and Turkish men. Some were subjected to female genital mutilation, including circumcision and infibulation (Clarence-Smith 2006: 81, 158). They were chattel to be bought, traded, and sold like animals. How many Western women would embrace Islam if presented with these facts? They can claim that these are pre-Islamic cultural practices. That does not change the fact that female circumcision is based on traditions attributed to the Prophet Muhammad and Ja'far al-Sadiq.

Chapter Fifteen 171

In both Sunni and Shiite traditions, the Prophet Muhammad is portrayed as approving and overseeing female circumcision and instructing women on how to perform the procedure (Abu Dawud, Kulayni, vol. 6, chapter 24: 33, vol. 5, chapter 35: 103-104). He said, "Circumcision is a law for men and a preservation of honor for women" (Ahmad and Abu Dawud). As for the sixth Imam, he stated that "Circumcision is a *sunnah* for men and an honor for women" (Tabataba'i 148). He also said, "Circumcision for girls is a noble trait, but it is not of the *sunnah* or obligatory; however, a noble trait is a very preferred matter" (Kulayni, vol. 6, chapter 24: 33).

Most jurists of all schools treated these traditions as authentic. The Shafi'i school ruled that female genital mutilation was obligatory. Most Maliki scholars viewed it as obligatory, while some treated it as recommended. The Hanafi school considered it a *sunnah*, while the Hanbali school held two views: that it was either obligatory or optional. Historically, virtually all Ja'fari scholars viewed it as recommended, whereas the Ismailis considered it obligatory. Even the rationalist Mutazilites supported the practice. Female genital mutilation is common practice among the Musta'ali Ismailis. The Druze, however, who are a Fatimid Ismaili offshoot, prohibited the practice in the eleventh century (Obeid 150, 185).

Women, in the view of many Muslims, were supposed to be sources of pleasure for men as opposed to recipients of pleasure. When a female's clitoris is cut off, and even her labia, going so far in some cases as sewing the vagina shut, she is condemned to a life of sexual frustration, as fundamental structures of orgasm have been excised. Whether it involves clitoridectomy, "the partial or total removal of the clitoris;" excision, "the partial or total removal of the clitoris and the inner labia;" infibulation, "the narrowing of the vaginal opening by creating a covering or seal;" or other harmful procedures, including "pricking, piercing, incising, scraping, and cauterizing the genital area," female genital mutilation is a human rights violation and a crime against humanity (National FGM Center).

Although some classical and modern scholars have objected to female genital mutilation and have pointed out that the traditions in question are weak, uncorroborated, and unsubstantiated (Rashid 290-291), many modern Muslim scholars continue to support and promote it, referring to it deceptively as "lowering" or "sunnah," claiming that it is not the same as FGM, and that it increases the pleasure of the woman.

Not only did non-Muslim women have to fear captivity, but they also had to fear female genital mutilation and a life of sexual slavery. The Imazighen, even if they embraced Islam, were compelled to pay the *jizyah* by offering their daughters as sex slaves to Arab Muslim invaders (Morrow 2021: 90). Iberian Muslims were treated as second-class citizens by Arab Muslims. Black Africans, among others, converted to Islam to reduce the risk of being enslaved by Arabs. As J.S. Trimingham observed,

Most people join... Islam ... from what we call secondary motives...

> Freedom of choice is rarely involved in a change of religion. Conversions, in general, take place, not because of a new insight into reality, but are determined by factors over which most people have no control. (Azumah 55)

Sincere or not, these conversions were often futile. As Freamon recognizes, "African Muslims could not always count on their adherence to the Islamic faith as protection against enslavement" (1998: 55). On the contrary, they were enslaved by the millions. As Rudolph T. Ware has observed, these enslaved black African Muslims included *huffaz*, people who had memorized the entirety of the Qur'an and had thus internalized it. If burning ink-and-paper copies of the Qur'an scandalizes Muslims so much, where was the outrage when Walking Qur'ans were placed in chains?

Despite cries to the contrary, "Islamic" slavery was inherently racist and religiously bigoted. After all, Arab Muslim scholars and jurists insisted that it was prohibited to enslave Arabs (Brown 364, note 86, Freamon 2019: 167-168). That is racism manifest. It was a sexual conquest that targeted women of other races and ethnicities. It was very much the same "sex *jihad*" that inspires some foreign Muslims from North Africa, black Africa, the Middle East, and Asia, to rape white Christian women in Europe and the Western world in general (Morrow 2020: 120-127).

While Muslims targeted non-Muslims of all races and believed that all infidels could and should be conquered and enslaved, "the classical Muslim ideology of enslavement is that blacks became legitimate slaves by virtue of the color of their skin" (Azumah 128). Tabari, for example, cited six prophetic traditions to support the claim that Ham, the son of Noah, was cursed by his father, turning him and his descendants dark and with curly hair (Azumah 129). "Just as *kufr* is a synonym for servitude in classical Muslim thought," notes Azumah, "the color black became the most obvious sign of servitude… to be black is to be a slave" (129). "Although slave-raiding and even slave-trading was patently illegal under the *shari'ah*," acknowledges Freamon,

> Islamic legal institutions did little to stem the time of slaves entering Islamic ports until well into the 19th century. In addition… Arab slave-raiders continued to plunder Sub-Saharan Africa long after slave-raiding had ceased to be profitable or acceptable in Europe and India and on the Asian steppes. John Ralph Willis has persuasively argued that the history and culture of the Arab polity supported a racism based on skin color, which allowed the extensive slave-raiding and trading activities to continue after the advent of Islam. (1998: 55)

As evidence that "Islamic" slavery was inherently racist, Muslims created a hierarchy of slaves in which their race determined their destiny. Black men were destined to hard labor. When gelded, they made good guards. Berber and Turkish men were enlisted in the army. Abyssinian women were viewed as beautiful. They

Chapter Fifteen 173

made good concubines but bad workers. Sudanese women were for hard work, but not for sex. Circassian women were not suitable for labor. They were valued for their beauty, their service as sex slaves, and their abilities to sing and dance (Powell). Eve Troutt Powell's claim that "if you were Circassian in the Ottoman Empire, it was a wonderful thing in some ways to be a slave, because when you were freed, you could often reach the uppermost levels of power, short of being the Sultan himself" is reprehensible. Her romantic notions of "Islamic" slavery are disturbing. Her claim that the Islamic trade in blacks did not come close to the numbers in the West is equally devoid of foundation.

"If Muslims enslaved so many blacks, where are their descendants?" asked one African American and Canadian shaykh. The answer is that they had none as they were castrated. Hence, they left little diaspora. As George La Rue notes, "high mortality rates and low rates of reproduction among enslaved populations" resulted in a "scarcity of second-generation slaves." In other words, they were expendable, disposable, and replaceable with freshly arrived slaves. The few blacks that reproduced were African female sex slaves, mostly the lighter-skinned ones. Since the fathers of their children, grandchildren, and great-grand-children were typically light-skinned Arabs, Turks, or Imazighen, their African genes were diluted and, in some cases, bred out of existence.

While the number of blacks, who descend from slaves, in the Arab and Asian world does not compare to the number found in the Americas, there are still African descendants in many Arab and Asian nations. In the Americas, there was much less miscegenation between European masters and African slaves. What is more, many descendants of African slaves in the Muslim world do not identify as black and insist that they are Imazighen, Arabs, Persians, Pakistanis, or otherwise. Since slavery ended relatively recently, as compared to the Western world, and there was no civil rights movement, many Afro-descendants in the Muslim world are ashamed of their ancestry. It is a skeleton best kept in the closet. Timidly, some so-called Arabs or Afro-Arabs, have started to reaffirm their black, African, identity, in the face of white Arab and Berber racism. When asked if he identified as an Arab, Boubacar Ould Messaoud (b. 1945), the Mauritanian anti-slavery activist, responded,

Whether the Moors or the Haratins consider themselves Arabs, these are stories! I am not an Arab. It is not because my parents or I were slaves to Hassaniya-speaking individuals that I became Arab. I shout it to all Mauritanian intellectuals who equate language with identity: are black Americans Anglo-Saxons? Are Brazilian blacks Portuguese? Are the black Angolans Portuguese? We must stop with this intellectual dishonesty that stems from a deep unresolved identity complex. They want to make me an Arab, to continue to give the majority to a community group. So I don't consider myself an Arab. (CRIDEM)

In a predatory fashion, the Prophet Muhammad is falsely made to say that it is good for non-Muslims to be enslaved as it brings them into Islam by force. In a tradition, albeit weak, that was used to justify such an attitude, he laughed with joy at "the non-Arab people whom the warriors of the Holy War have captured and made to enter Islam" (Azumah 128). Muslim apologists pretend that slavery in Islamic lands was more humane than slavery in Christian ones. Even Muhammad Hamidullah (1908-2002) comes across as a dishonest used car salesman when he describes the institution of slavery in Islam as a "house of humanitarian correction" (Azumah 161). It was more like a hell-hole of corruption.

Unlike slavery in the southern United States, where, at the most, a male slave could rise from being a field Negro to a house Negro or a plantation supervisor, and a female could rise from being a cotton picker to a household servant, cook, or concubine, there were more options for upward mobility and emancipation in the Muslim world. Among the Mamluks, for example, "the corps of eunuchs" was one of the few ways a black could attain higher office (Azumah 161). Blacks could serve in the infantry; however, the cavalry mainly consisted of men of Turkish origin (Azumah 1258). The situation reminds one of the United States, where many blacks can only advance in life by committing crimes for their imperialist masters through military service. Many of them end up as casualties of war. They were like the black buffalo soldiers in the United States. The only way they could humanize themselves in the eyes of the whites was by killing indigenous people.

The fact that enslaved people in the Muslim world had some avenues for advancement does not change the fact that slavery was sickening, degrading, dehumanizing, savage, and cruel. While there were exceptions, they did not make the rule. Enslaved people were treated harshly and discriminated against. Moreover, the black soldiers in question, virtually all of whom were made into eunuchs, were used to conquer, massacre, and enslave others worldwide. While one can empathize with the black Muslim slaves who revolted to attain freedom, and gain political power, one can hardly empathize with those who harvested millions of slaves for the Islamic Empire. In the words of Azumah,

> Contrary to theories of a humane Muslim slavery, the institution and practice of slavery in Muslim societies was as cruel and harsh as any other slave system… slaves constituted a class of deprived people with the chains of servitude and caste inferiority riveted on their offspring. They were totally denied civil status, and their exclusion from responsible office was reinforced by the entire weight of Islamic law, Muslim social practice, and traditional stigma. Numerous slave revolts… high death and low birth rates amongst slaves in Muslim lands, desertions, and countless attempts at desertion, all belie the theory of idyllic Muslim slavery. (169)

If blacks were used to draw people into Islam in the past, they continue to be used to do so in the present. Although now they do so as freemen, most do not do it for free. They spread Islam among blacks, and others, because it benefits them. Some receive free higher education in Saudi Arabia, Iran, and elsewhere. Some secure jobs and salaries. They are rarely, ever, free, and independent actors. They are on the payroll of the pale skins, predominantly Arabs and Persians. As critics ask: how broken and brainwashed does a black man have to be to defend and justify slavery, insist that it is divinely ordained, and, in some cases, support its reintroduction? No more than black slaves who embraced the Christian religion of their slave masters. Those, at least, opposed slavery, fought against it in the Civil War, and struggled for civil and human rights in the sixties. You do not see any trying to crawl back onto the plantation like some black Muslims do. Perhaps, some of these black Muslims dream of becoming slave masters themselves and pimp-daddies to enslaved girls and women. Islam can be liberation and salvation; however, it can also be damnation.

Whether they serve the Saudis, the Iranians, or transnational terrorist groups, black radical Islamists are fifth columnists serving Islamic imperialism. Since they operate within the Western world, recruit within our borders, and struggle to overthrow the institutions that freed them in the first place and ensured the international abolition of slavery, the enemy has breached the gates. The spread of moderate, tolerant, loving, socially conscious, and compassionate spiritual Islam is not a problem. The problem, better yet, the grave existential threat, is the dissemination of radical political Islam, jihadism, and Islamic imperialism. The spread of *shari'ah* law, which, according to dominant interpretations, legalizes, and even commands the conquest of non-Muslims, their forced conversion or slaughter, their submission, subjugation, and humiliation, their bondage and enslavement, and the reduction of their women and girls to sexual slavery, poses a threat to human civilization.

If Islam becomes a dominant world power and culture in the future, we must be wary of the type of Islam that it will be. Will it be an Islam of moderation and tolerance or an Islam of extremism and intolerance? It might be a mixture of both. After all, socialism and communism had many faces. The same ideology produced social democrats, liberation theologians, and despots, dictators, and genocidal totalitarian demagogues. The left may include figures like Che Guevara; however, it also include the likes of Mao (1893-1976), Stalin (1878-1953), and Pol Pot (1925-1998). While the Islamic movement includes the likes of 'Ali Shariati (1933-1977), it also includes people like Abu Bakr al-Baghdadi (1971-2019), the infamous leader of Daesh or ISIS. The universe of Islam is vast, as are its interpretations.

While emancipatory and abolitionist Islam is welcomed, positive, and uplifting, there is no place for slave master Islam in the land of the free. We must do away with the deeply authoritarian and intolerant interpretations that dominate certain strands of Islam. As Halim Rane suggests, we must re-examine the Qur'an, the Covenants of the Prophet, and other original texts to realign Islam with its ethical vision (Nestby). It is not merely a matter of reforming these immoral and archaic rules but removing and replacing them entirely. Muslims need a new Islamic legal code based on the Qur'an alone.

176   Islam & Slavery

As Giancarlo Anello notes in his study on the *Charter of Medina*, the only apostates are those who deny basic and fundamental communal values, namely, constitutional rights and civil law. They are the ones who should be considered enemies of society, sanctioned, and even excluded from any possibility of inclusion (21). The world, as a whole, has rejected and outlawed slavery and concubinage. Those who oppose this world consensus deprive themselves of world citizenship.

15.3 The "Islamic" Slave Trade

The so-called "Islamic" slave trade that Muslims initiated was as abominable as the trans-Atlantic one commenced by European Christians in which Arab, Berber, and African Muslims were equally complicit. "The history of slavery in Morocco," writes Chouki El Hamel, or better yet, the history of slavery in the Muslim world, "cannot be considered separately from the racial terror of the global slave trade" (4).

As a result of the "Islamic" slave trade, "tens of millions of people were placed under the Muslim yoke over the centuries, and yet servitude remains marginal to general accounts of Islamic history" (Clarence-Smith n. date). Millions of boys were castrated, many of whom died in the process. Millions of girls and women were torn from their families, raped, and subjected to a life of sexual slavery. Millions of human beings were murdered. This is not hyperbole. Male slaves, in the Muslim world, worked in inhumane, brutally hot conditions, with little to eat or drink (Freamon 2019: 204). As Tabari observes, they were "literally pinned down there, hopeless, and homeless," receiving only "a few handfuls of meal" (Azumah 162). In the marshes of Iraq, these horrific conditions led to a series of slave revolts in 689-690, 694, and 869 (Freamon 2019: 204, 300, Azumah 162, Chebel 129-131).

Between 1530 to 1780, "up to 1,250,000 Christian captives entered the Maghrib" (Clarence-Smith 2006: 12). Between 1453 to 1700, the Ottomans alone imported around 2.5 million human beings from the Black Sea region into Istanbul (Eltis and Engerman, Clarence-Smith 2006: 13). It is also calculated that they imported more than 1.3 million enslaved human beings into the Ottoman Middle East and India, the Red Sea, and the Gulf of Aden, Ottoman Egypt, and Ottoman North Africa (Encyclopedia.com). "During the Ottoman Empire," writes Mustafa Akyol, "slave traders were hunting people, often women, with raids among non-Muslim peoples in Africa, Circassia, and Georgia, to sell them in the slave markets of Istanbul, Basra, or Mecca" (2022: 61-62). As for the Crimean Tatars, they "seized about 1,750,000 Ukrainians, Poles, and Russians from 1468 to 1694" (Clarence-Smith 2006: 13).

According to the calculations of historian Robert C. Davis (b. 1948), Muslim pirates from North Africa abducted and enslaved more than one million Europeans between 1530 and 1780 (8, 23). Entire villages and coastal areas in Italy, Spain, Portugal, and France were depopulated, including some as far as

Chapter Fifteen 177

Britain, Ireland, and Iceland (8, 17, 60-61, 191, 238, note 60). The victims were not targeted solely because of their race but because of their religion. During the sixteenth and seventeenth centuries, these Muslim pirates from the Barbary Coast were outproducing the trans-Atlantic slave trade (Davis xxvi). Furthermore, that does not even consider the slaving activities in the Levant and Eastern Europe (Davis xxvi).

Muslim apologists might argue that Islam encourages the humane treatment of slaves. This may be true under the rule of the Prophet Muhammad. However, the history of the nearly thousand and a half years that followed speaks for itself. European Christian slaves were beaten with sticks, abused, starved, deprived of water, called faithless dogs, locked up in filthy, overcrowded barracks and pens, and worked to death (Davis 16-17, 79, 127, 128, 129, 130, 131; Khan 291-299). Not only were many of the enslaved males forcibly circumcised, but many of the young males and females were forced to serve as sex slaves and prostitutes (Davis 125-127, 184). Where was the outcry on the part of Muslim leaders and clerics?

The death rate of enslaved Europeans in North Africa was dismal. Of nine hundred and eighty-nine French seamen captured by Muslim corsairs between 1628 and 1634, twelve percent died (Davis 16). Of the two thousand four hundred and fifty Christian slaves brought to Tripoli between 1668-1678, an average of twenty percent died each year (Davis 16). Of the four hundred and fifty villagers taken from the Venetian outpost of Perasto in 1624, roughly a third had died within a year (Davis 17). Of the nearly four hundred Islanders captured by Algerians in 1627, only seven were still alive eight years later (Davis 17). When the plague hit Tripoli in 1675, the mortality rate of enslaved Christian Europeans rose from twenty percent yearly to forty percent (Davis 17).

If the Mediterranean slave trade was horrific, so was the Sub-Saharan one. If Muslims from the Barbary Coast enslaved over a million European Christians, "historians estimate that between 650 and 1900, 10 to 18 million people were enslaved by Arab slave traders and taken from Africa across the Red Sea, Indian Ocean, and Sahara Desert" (Segal 56, Lumen, see Pavlu, see also Clarence-Smith 2006: 11-12). As John Dewar Gleissner notes in *Prisons and Slavery*,

> The Arabs' treatment of black Africans can aptly be termed an African Holocaust. Arabs killed more Africans in transit, especially when crossing the Sahara Desert, than Europeans and Americans, and over more centuries, both before and after the years of the Atlantic slave trade. Arab Muslims began extracting millions of black African slaves centuries before Christian nations did. Arab slave traders removed slaves from Africa for about 13 centuries, compared to three centuries of the Atlantic slave trade. African slaves transported by Arabs across the Sahara Desert died more often than slaves making the Middle Passage to the New World by ship. Slaves invariably died within five years if they worked in the Ottoman Empire's Sahara salt mines. (106)

In an interview addressing his book, *The Legacy of Arab-Islam in Africa*, John Allembillah Azumah, shared some traumatizing statistics:

> While two out of every three slaves shipped across the Atlantic were men, the proportions were reversed in the Islamic slave trade. Two women for every man were enslaved by the Muslims. While the mortality rate of the slaves being transported across the Atlantic was as high as 10%, the percentage of the slaves dying in transit in the Tran-Saharan and East African slave market was a staggering 80 to 90%.
>
> While almost all the slaves shipped across the Atlantic were for agricultural work, most of the slaves destined for the Muslim Middle East were for sexual exploitation as concubines in harems and for military service. While many children were born to the slaves in the Americas, the millions of their descendants are citizens in Brazil and the United States today. Very few descendants of the slaves who ended up in the Middle East survived. While most slaves who went to the Americas could marry and have families, most of the male slaves destined for the Middle East were castrated, and most of the children born to the women were killed at birth.
>
> A minimum of 28 million Africans were enslaved in the Muslim Middle East. Since at least 80% of those captured by the Muslim slave traders were calculated to have died before reaching the slave markets, it is believed that the death toll from 1,400 years of Arab and Muslim slave raids into Africa could have been as high as 112 million. (Elder)

This is hardly a full survey of the statistics. As Bernard K. Freamon summarizes, the nearly millennium and a half of Muslim slave trading,

> produced widespread death, great and prolonged suffering, the wholesale destruction of many communities, and the uprooting of families and social relationships in societies stretching from East to West Africa to India and Southeast Asia. This event might be described as a "holocaust," in the same way that the transatlantic slave trade and the extermination of the Jews and other minorities in Nazi Germany have similarly been described. (2019: 510)

The horrors described by Azumah show a complete and total contempt for the lives of black people (142-145). Men were hacked and clubbed to death during slave raids, the old were left to starve, and women and children were carried away (Azumah 150). In some cases, "two thirds of the victims of slave raids were normally murdered" (Azumah 150). Major Denham, an eyewitness to the "Islamic" slave trade, notes that the Arabs laughed heartily at his expression of horror when he saw the countless skeletons of black men, women, and children strewn throughout the desert (Azumah 145). "They are only blacks," the Arabs told him (Azumah 145).

Muslims, particularly black Western Muslims may relish in bashing the trans-

Atlantic slave trade. The fact remains, however, that during the sixteenth and into the seventeenth century, the "Islamic" slave trade in the Mediterranean outproduced the trans-Atlantic slave (Davis xxvi). In the Arab, Persian, and Pakistani worlds, the descendants of black African slaves continue to be treated as second-class citizens. As the World Directory of Minorities and Indigenous Peoples relate,

> Black Iraqis continue to face systematic discrimination and marginalization. They are continually referred to as '*abd* (slave) and their communities suffer from disproportionately high illiteracy and unemployment rates. The community has not developed a professional class and not a single black Iraqi holds a high-level position in government. Many cannot find employment other than as laborers or domestic workers. Those who make a living through music and dance have had their livelihoods threatened by hardline Islamist groups who rose to prominence after 2003 and disapprove of such activities. (Minority Rights, see also Flintoff and International Republican Institute)

Although all African slaves in Iraq were legally emancipated in the 1950s, the Arab tribes continued to consider their descendants to be slaves like their ancestors (Chebel 131). During the pilgrimage to Najaf and Karbala in 2017, some of the Black Muslims from the Nation of asked Iraqi and Iranian officials: "Where are you hiding all the black people?"

While it varies in severity, anti-black racism is also prevalent in Mauritania, Sudan, Egypt, and the Maghreb. In Mauritania, where slavery still survives, and the number of enslaved people reaches one hundred thousand to half a million, they are subject to undeclared apartheid (Bouknight and Hucks). In the Sudan, they have been subject to ethnic, racial, and cultural extermination. In Egypt, racial slurs prevail against black men, while black women tend to be sexually harassed like most other women. In the Maghreb, Afro-Arabs are victims of stigma and prejudice; however, black African refugees have been brutalized and enslaved in places like Libya.

15.4 Comparing and Contrasting

It is morally abhorrent to try to minimize the magnitude of the atrocities committed by Muslims, in the name of Islam, against fellow Muslims, both black and Berber, as well as non-Muslims from all walks of life, and blasphemous claim they had the blessing of God and His Prophet. We have a duty to tell the truth. As Freamon notes,

> Muslims and scholars of Islam around the world have a special Qur'anic responsibility to educate Muslims about the history of slavery and slave trading in their communities and to engage the partisans, jurists, and ideologues supporting the reestablishment of slavery and slave trading

in fierce dialogue on this point, questioning both their view of the historical facts supporting their claims and their understanding of the role of Islamic law in contemporary Muslim societies. (2019: 465)

Compare, as Mohsen Kadivar, has done, the rules regarding slavery found in contemporary Islamic jurisprudence with modern human rights and decide which one is more morally and ethically elevated.

Contemporary Islam	Human Rights
If the parents are slaves, the child is also born a slave.	Every single person is born free.
Slaves and free people differ in a number of areas relating to laws, identity, and rights.	All people are equal to one another in terms of rights and identity.
In seven different ways a free man can be taken as a slave.	A person is not allowed to be taken as a slave in any form.
Until one of the forms of freedom occur, the person shall continue to be a slave.	It is not allowed to keep anyone as a slave.
Trading slaves is permissible within the guidelines of Islamic law.	Trading slaves is absolutely impermissible.
All the residents in a country at war with an Islamic army, irrespective of being civilian or not, man, women, or child, can be taken as slaves and can be distributed amongst the Islamic government, military leaders, and soldiers.	Prisoners of war are in no circumstances to be taken as slaves and are granted specific rights as protection.
Only with the permission of the owner can a slave possess something, and any money earned automatically belongs to the owner.	The hard work of a person is included within his right of possession, and all money earned belongs completely to them.

It is not necessary that the slave approves of his lifestyle, occupation, or house. The slave is compelled to obey the owner and accept his decision.	Every individual has the freedom to choose their own lifestyle, occupation, and house. Nobody has the right to force them in such decisions.
The owner has the right to take the child from his slave after 7 years and sell him as a slave. The owner has the right to split the marriage of his slave and declare it void. The marriage of someone who was a freeman becomes void after being taken as a slave.	No one has the right to split up another family unit and split a child from his parents or split a wife from her husband.
The marriage of the slave is completely at the discretion of the owner. The owner can marry the slave to whomsoever he wishes, and he can prevent the slave from marrying someone he/she intends to. The owner can also prevent the slave from marrying completely.	Nobody can compel another person to marry someone against their will. Marriage without the consent of both parties is not valid.
An owner has the right to sexual relations with his slave girl regardless of whether she provides consent or not. The owner can provide his slave girl for sexual relations to someone else.	Sexual relations with females without their consent is completely prohibited. No one has the right to put a female at the sexual services of another man.
The owner, (even if he not a jurist nor someone who is just), has the right to punish the slave within the parameters of Islamic law.	Nobody has the right to take the role of a judge or court and punish someone.
The punishment of a slave is	All men are equal in front of the

technically half that of a free man. If a free man kills a slave, there is to be retribution; however, if a slave kills a free man the slave shall have retribution.	law, and all punishments are to be extracted equally.
Without the permission of the owner, a slave does not have the right to leisure, relaxation, education, a private life, or training.	Every person has the right to leisure, relaxation, education, a private life and training.
Without the permission of the owner, it is not permissible to partake in communal or social affairs.	Every person has the right to participate in their communal and social affairs.

(Kadivar)

Which legal system would one prefer to live under if given a choice? Under so-called Islamic law or a liberal, secular, Western democracy that strives to uphold civil and human rights?

15.5 Conclusions

As Fazlur Rahman (1919-1988) exclaimed, "no intelligent and morally sensitive Muslim" can argue in favor of slavery today as "surely the whole tenor of the teaching of the Qur'an is that there should be no slavery at all" (Clarence-Smith 2006: 217). As Khaled Abou El-Fadl has concluded in *Speaking in God's Name: Islamic Law, Authority, and Women*, "Muslims of previous generations reached the awareness that slavery is immoral and unlawful, as a matter of conscience" (269). What is more, Qadi 'Abd al-Jabbar, the Mutazilite author of *al-Mughni*, a multi-volume work, concluded that slavery is inherently immoral, even in reciprocal retaliation.

'Abd al-Jabbar asserted that slavery was *qubhun li dhatihi wa laysat min makarim al-akhlaq* which can be translated as "immoral in essence and not from noble virtues" or "inherently immoral and unbefitting of the loftiness of moral values." The word *qubh* is the opposite of *hasan* or good. If *husn* means moral, *qubh* means immoral. It means bad, evil, abominable, foul, shameful, unseemly, unsightly, ugly, or hideous. 'Abd al-Jabbar states that slavery is not from *makarim al-akhlaq*, namely, it is not from the noble, good, gracious, decent virtues, morals, manners, and character in Islam.

Finally, as Abou El-Fadl notes, it was "the rationalists, such as ... [Ahmad] Bek Shafiq, who were able to go beyond investigating legalistic rules of manumission, or issuing general exhortations against owning slaves, and in many ways to go beyond the literal words of the religious text in condemning the very institution of slavery as inherently immoral, and therefore, un-Islamic." He stated that slavery was *tunafi makarim al-akhlaq wa hiya ithm wa fasad fa laysat min al-Islam*, namely, that slavery was "incompatible with good morals, was a sin and a crime, was corrupt, depraved, and wicked, and was not Islamic." To quote from the Qur'an, "Truth has come, and falsehood has vanished" (17:81).

Chapter Sixteen

The Islamic Basis
for the Abolition of Slavery

16.1 Introduction

As far as critics are concerned, not only does Jonathan A.C. Brown defend an outdated, obsolete, and retrograde interpretation of Islam, which he views as traditional, but he appears to be oblivious or entirely dismissive of the jurisprudential tools that can be deployed to prohibit slavery, including: *akhlaq* (ethics), *'aql* (reason), *'adl* (justice), *'urf* (local practice) of people of sound mind (*'uqala'*), *maqasid* (higher objectives), *maslahah* (common good), and *zaman wa makan* (time and place), as well as *la haraj* (no difficulty) and *la darar* (no harm) (see Takim 2022: 4, 194).

The ideals upon which Islam should be interpreted also include freedom, mercy, chivalry, tolerance, empathy, human dignity, spirituality, peace, rule of law, human rights, morality and values (Hosseini Nasab). The eternal and universal values of Islam include decency and fairness (Kadivar qtd. Mir-Hosseini 197).

For a law to be Islamic, it must be compatible with human nature and rationality (Hosseini Nasab). In fact, Najm al-Din al-Tufi (1276-1316), the philosopher and jurist, went so far as to argue that "human interest" "could override even the Qur'an and the *sunnah* (Akyol 2022: 81-82). Ibn Rush (1126-1198), the jurist, theologian, and philosopher, also believed that "unwritten laws" or universal values could contradict written laws, such as the *shari'ah* (Akyol 2022: 118).

16.2 Islamic Abolitionism

Jonathan A.C. Brown does note that the Islamic tradition is filled with scriptural and prophetic exhortations to free slaves; however, he claims that they reached absurd proportions (86). He acknowledges the well-known Shiite *hadith*, recorded by Kulayni, in which the Prophet asserts that "The worst of people is the one who sells people" (*Sharr al-nas man ba'a al-nas*), recognizing that "the unrestricted wording of this *hadith* made it ideal for providing a prophetic mandate for prohibiting slavery;" however, Brown casts it aside by stating that it is non-existent in Sunni sources (237). As Ware notes,

> Muslim jurists codified slavery, a matter of pre-Islamic law in the lands that became the caliphate, as if it enjoyed the unambiguous approval of God and Prophet. These medieval jurists were functionaries in expansionist slaving states, so it is not surprising that they protected property rights and condoned slaving and slave trafficking. Nowhere in the history of Islamic legal thought is the worldly imprint of the caliphate as clear as in the sophistry used to make perpetual aggressive *jihad* (and its corollary, slavery) appear as divinely ordained. (113)

"Such exegetical exercises," notes Clarence-Smith, which included disregarding the *hadith* in question, "had the paradoxical outcome of seeming to mock the Qur'an" (Ware 113). This tradition, which can be translated as "Slave traders are the worst of people" could easily form the basis for a complete prohibition of slavery in Islam. It is cited by Kulayni's *al-Kafi* (vol. 5: 114), Tusi's *Tahdhib al-ahkam* (vol. 6: 362), 'Amili's *Wasa'il al-shi'ah* (vol. 17: 136), and Saduq's *'Illal al-shara'i* (vol. 2: 530). It was included by G.W. Leitner in *Muhammadanism* (17; Ware 113). Links to the primary Arabic sources are found in the bibliography and "The Issue of Slavery in Contemporary Islam" by Mohsen Kadivar.

The tradition in question is transmitted by Muhammad ibn al-Hassan al-Saffar al-Qummi (d. 903), the author of *Basa'ir al-darajat*, one of the earliest books of Shiite traditions, which is considered as important as the Four Books of Kulayni, Saduq, and Tusi. He transmits the saying on the authority of his teacher, Ahmad ibn Muhammad al-Barqi (c. 818/816-887/888 or 893/894). Ja'far ibn Yahya used to transmit traditions from his father, Yahya ibn Abi al-'Ala,' who was reportedly a companion of Ja'far al-Sadiq and, according to some sources, Muhammad al-Baqir as well.

Yahya ibn Abi al-'Ala' was regarded as weak according to Sunni traditionists like Daraqutni (c. 918-995), al-Nasa'i (829-915), and Ibn Abi Hatim al-Razi (854-938). Ahmad ibn al-Hanbal (780-855) said that "Yahya ibn al-'Ala' al-Razi is a liar [and] a *rafidi* who fabricates *hadith*." Ibn Hibban (884-965) stated that he was untrustworthy. Yahya ibn Abi al-'Ala' is treated as *matruk* or "abandoned" according to Najm 'Abd al-Rahman Khalaf (1989). This term refers to narrators accused of forgery.

However, Ishaq ibn 'Ammar, a companion of Ja'far al-Sadiq and Imam Musa al-Kazim, is viewed as reliable and trustworthy by Twelver Shiite scholars. As can be expected, forgers of traditions used to attribute the sayings they transmitted on the authority of trustworthy narrators. The fact that the saying of Ja'far al-Sadiq was narrated on the authority of Ishaq ibn 'Ammar does not mean that it is authentic. On the contrary, the fact that it was attributed to him by Yahya ibn Abi al-'Ala' would make it untrustworthy according to Sunni standards. As easy as it is to weaken a tradition, it is just as easy to strengthen one.

Muslims have been subjected to a bait and switch and sleight of hand. Some of them have been peddled a false Prophet of Doom in place of a Prophet of Mercy, Compassion, and Justice. Is the real Jesus the Jesus of the Christian crusaders and slave masters? Is the real Jesus the Jesus of white supremacists like the Ku Klux Klan? Or is the real Jesus the Jesus of love of faithful, devout, and pious Christians, men, women, and saints? The same goes for the Prophet Muhammad.

Is the real Muhammad the racist, sexist, warrior, and enslaver that he is portrayed to be in some Muslim sources? Or is the real Muhammad the praiseworthy prophet and the best of humanity? Let us face reality and stop the insanity. Those who love Muhammad do not drag his name through the mud and accuse him of endorsing slavery and concubinage. They view him as humane as opposed to inhumane. His name means "praiseworthy" not "blameworthy."

The Prophet Muhammad was the product of his time. He was bound to socio-political and economic strictures. He did not have the power to abolish slavery nationally and internationally. That does not mean that he condoned it. On the contrary, he condemned it. He said that the most wicked of people are slave traders (Kulayni), those who buy and sell human beings, and those who traffic in human flesh. He said that "God will forgive every sin except... selling a free person" (Majlisi, vol. 68: 331).

In a similar tradition of seminal importance, found in Shaykh Saduq's *Khisal*, a man asks the Prophet Muhammad what work he should do. The Messenger of God warned him against four professions, including "selling slaves" (Saduq [English]). He explained: *wa ama al-nikhas fa-innahu qad atani Jibra'il, 'alayhi al-salam, fa-qala: ya Muhammad inna shirara ummatika al-ladhna yabi'una al-nas.* This is translated by Ali Peiravi, and Talat June Peiravi, as "Selling slaves is a bad job since Gabriel descended to me and said: 'Those who sell slaves are the worst people among your followers'" (Saduq [English]). K.A. Mirza translates the tradition as "Once Jibrail came to Prophet Muhammad and said: "Prophet of God, the meanest and most mischievous persons in your *ummah* are those who sell human beings" (94). A better translation, in my mind, would be: "Regarding the slave trade, Gabriel, peace be upon him, told me: 'O Muhammad! Verily, the worst of your *ummah* are those who sell human beings." This tradition, if genuine, would provide strong support for Islamic abolitionism. If Muhammad opposed slavery, and Gabriel opposed slavery, then it goes without saying that God opposes slavery.

The tradition in question is related by Muhammad ibn al-Hasan ibn Ahmad ibn al-Walid from Muhammad ibn al-Hassan al-Saffar who quoted Ahmad ibn Abu 'Abd Allah al-Barqi on the authority of Muhammad ibn 'Isa, on the authority of 'Ubaydullah al-Dihqan, on the authority of Durust, on the authority of Ibrahim ibn 'Abd al-Hamid, on the authority of Abu al-Hasan Musa ibn Ja'far al-Kazim.

Muhammad ibn al-Hasan ibn Ahmad ibn al-Walid (883/884-954/955) was a famous Twelver Shiite traditionist from Qum. He was the teacher of Shaykh Saduq. Muhammad ibn al-Hassan al-Saffar (d. 903) was an Imami Shiite traditionist from Qum, a companion of Hasan al-'Askari (c. 844- 874), and the author of *Basa'ir al-darajat*, an early Shiite *hadith* collection on the Imamate.

Ahmad ibn Muhammad al-Barqi (d. 887/888 or 893/894) was a renowned Shiite *hadith* scholar and historian and the author of *al-Mahasin*, one of the most important Shiite book of traditions. He is treated as trustworthy by Twelver Shiite traditionists, although some acknowledge that he quoted sayings from unreliable narrators. He is respected as a narrator by some Sunnis.

Muhammad ibn 'Isa (796/797-after 868 CE), was a companion of 'Ali al-Rida, Muhammad al-Taqi, 'Ali al-Naqi, and Hasan al-'Askari. Twelver Shiite scholars trust his traditions. 'Ubaydullah ibn Ahmad al-Dihqan, however, is treated as a weak narrator who narrated the *Book of Durust ibn 'Abi Mansur* (Modarressi 1: 83). This is one of the sixteen surviving *usul* or sources compiled by the companions of Ja'far al-Sadiq, out of an alleged four hundred. As for Ibrahim ibn 'Abd al-Hamid, he quoted traditions on Musa al-Kazim's authority (c. 745-799).

This tradition is said to trace back to Musa al-Kazim, the seventh infallible Imam of the Twelver Shiites. While their traditionists accept any tradition quoted from their Imams, Sunni traditionists only accept them if the chain continues back to the Prophet Muhammad. Like most Twelver Shiite traditions, this one is *mu'allaq* or "hanging." It fails to provide the complete *isnad* or chain of narration. It is also *munqati'* or "broken" as it does not include links between Musa al-Kazim and the successor or companion of the Prophet Muhammad who narrated it. The Twelvers claim that any tradition of the Imams traces back to the Prophet Muhammad through their predecessors, in this case, the sixth, fifth, fourth, third, second, and first Imam.

It is improbable that hundreds of thousands of prophetic traditions were transmitted through Zayn al-'Abidin, who was only twenty-two years of age at the time his father Husayn ibn 'Ali was martyred. When confronted with this inconvenient fact, Twelver traditionists claim that the Imams acquired their knowledge directly from God, a claim that non-Shiites refuse to accept, and academics and historians cannot consider, as it is not verifiable.

Even if, for the sake of argument, we accept the claim that Musa al-Kazim quoted this tradition, and that it traces back to the Prophet Muhammad, its content is problematic. Why are slave traders treated as part of the *ummah* of Muhammad, and who were these slave traders who were supposedly part of his community of believers? Slavery was a marginal phenomenon during the period of the revelations of the Prophet Muhammad and his rule in Medina. There was no large-scale, systematic, intercontinental slave trade during this time. The claim that Gabriel was talking about the Prophet's future *ummah* seems untenable.

In summary, this abolitionist tradition is weak according to traditional Twelver Shiite and Sunni standards. However, the same could be said of the traditions quoted by Twelver Shiites and Sunnis to support slavery. After all, the sixth Imam supposedly said:

> Act according to any traditions that are brought to you if they agree with the Qur'an irrespective of whether an honest man or a wicked man brings

it. On the other hand, do not act according to any traditions brought to you that disagree with the Qur'an. (Tabarsi 380)

If we follow this principle, then the tradition of Musa al-Kazim, in which the angel Gabriel tells the Prophet Muhammad "the worst of your *ummah* are those who sell human beings," and the tradition in which Ja'far al-Sadiq asserts "the worst of people is the one who sells people," can be treated as trustworthy, authentic, and genuine. As 'Ali said, "Look at what is being said, not who is saying it." Ideally, of course, one should consider both. If these traditions are genuine, the accounts that these two Imams supported and encouraged slavery, permitted the beating of slaves, and had scores of sex slaves, are scandalous and salacious fabrications.

If we operate on the basis of the inherent inauthenticity of all traditions, thus leveling the playing field, we can rely on content as opposed to chains of narration when it comes to identifying traditions that agree, or disagree, with the Qur'an. The math is quite basic, really.

A *hadith* is considered to be authentic if a chain of narrations can be traced reliably back to the Prophet. Theoretically, this approach is suggestive of accuracy, and by extension, reliability. In practice, proven by way of statistical analysis, such an approach is absurd. A conversation between two individuals is never conveyed and understood to full accuracy. Subconscious biases of understanding are encoded into language. Linguistic abilities of language are extremely limited... In furtherance, verbal communication is contextualized through tone and body language.

The number of words in any language are finite; to explain any word, there are a limited number of words, expressions and phrases within that very language that are available, none of which offer absolute justice. Moreover, colloquialism, dialect, understanding of words and sentence structure further adds to the subjectivity. On the unrealistic assumption that the second party fully shares such linguistic qualities, only then will the message be conveyed with full accuracy. Realistically, this is never the case. Conversation allows for dialogue; every spoken sentence adds an additional dynamic which further-contextualizes the use of words, facilitating understanding. Such dynamics do not apply to textual narrations.

55% of a conversation is body language, 38% is tone of voice and 7% are words. This suggests that 93% of understanding is lost textually, assuming the negation of any additional dynamics which offer clarification. *Hadiths* are often isolated conversations or monologues without any wider context. Acceptance of authenticity assumes language is 100% efficient as a means of communication. The above-mentioned biases further dilute the effectiveness of such communication and further

190 Islam & Slavery

undermines the accuracy of textual narrations.

For the sake of prudence, instead of 5%, let us magnify this figure by a factor of 10 and assume the reliability of such communication is 50%. We are all familiar with Chinese Whispers. How long does it take for the original message to get lost in transmission? Let us apply the following mathematical model: $[(0.5)^n-1]*100$, where n is the number of participants in a chain of narration. With three participants, accuracy is 25%; with five participants, accuracy is 6.25%; with ten participants, accuracy falls to 0.20%, and 0.006% with 15 participants. There are six collections of *hadith*. Let us ignore 5 of those 6 for the sake of prudence. Sahih al-Bukhari is considered to be the most accurate collection, which contains 9,505 narrations. Assuming there are 10 members in each chain as a ballpark proxy measurement, bearing in mind the above-applied prudence adjustment, and mitigation of 5 of 6 books, the likeliness of all being accurate is 0 -- statistical impossibility.

Let us add some additional variables which further mitigates the accuracy; namely, colloquialism, cognitive recognition, memory, understanding, perception, subconscious biases, language, effectiveness of translation, geography, cultural norms, and innate human dispositions. All the variables assume sincerity. In furtherance, let us consider a malicious participant in the chain who willfully corrupts the transmission. Imagine playing Chinese whispers with a single member who willfully distorts the message for whatever motive.

As mentioned earlier, an additional dynamic of accuracy is dialogue. A methodology of verifying *hadith* is to analyze multiple chains of the same narration. Again, the accuracy of such chains depends on how close to the original source the chain forked. Earlier forks suggest increased accuracy; conversely, later forks distort accuracy. Furthermore, how can we reconcile contradictory or inconsistent narrations? Assuming both contradictions are accurate, without transmitted context, the wisdom behind the narration is lost.

The above-mentioned variables amplify the subjectivity of understanding through transmission, which is why we have so many sects and groups within the religion. (Bhatti)

Not only has the historical-critical approach to the *hadith* demonstrated their inherent unreliability, but memory science has closed the case (Shoemaker 148-170). The *hadith* sciences are an exercise in futility. Why dabble in the dubious? Why swim in a fetid ocean of falsehood when one can stand on firm ground with the Qur'an? Surely, we should not be slaves of the *sunnah*, the Word of Men; stick to the Word of God and strive to be slaves of God and servants of goodness.

Rather than reflect the words of the historical Prophet Muhammad, Ja'far al-Sadiq, or Musa al-Kazim, the two anti-slavery traditions in question might have been circulated by one of the narrators in the chain who was opposed to the

Chapter Sixteen 191

practice. This is not an indictment since the traditions used to support the practice are forgeries concocted by slave traders and slave masters. When faced with traditions used to promote slavery, and traditions used to oppose slavery, one should treat the latter as authentic as they coincide with Qur'anic values.

Considering that the wholesale rejection of the *hadith* literature is not palatable or acceptable to most Sunnis and Shiites, another approach could be considered. It could be claimed that the anti-slavery traditions of the Prophet Muhammad, Ja'far al-Sadiq, and Musa al-Kazim are authentic and that their chains of narrations were deliberately weakened by scholars who upheld slavery and had a vested interest in the human flesh trade. Rather than weakened, their chains can be fortified, and their narrators treated as trustworthy. One even wonders how many abolitionist traditions were extirpated by the partisans of pro-slavery Islam.

As Ware notes, "The Qur'an discusses slavery as a fact of human society" (113). This much is true. Not so his claim that it neither condoned nor condemned it (113). The Qur'an denounces Pharoah as an unjust, arrogant, and corrupt tyrant, sinner, liar, wrongdoer, despot, oppressor, and transgressor for having enslaved the Children of Israel (2:49; 26:2; 7:103; 7:104; 7:127; 8:54; 10:83; 20:24; 23:47; 28:8; 40:28; 44:31). It describes slavery as a "terrible torment" in which sons were slaughtered and daughters were kept alive, namely, to keep as concubines (2:49; 7:127; 7:141; 14:6; 28:4). As such, Pharoah and his people deserved a severe penalty (2:50; 3:11; 7:103: 7:130; 8:52: 8:54; 10:88; 11:97; 17:102; 20:79; 73:16). They were an insolent, criminal and disobedient people (10:75; 28:32; 38:12; 66:11). The Qur'an establishes that God was on the side of the enslaved, not the enslavers and oppressors (7:137). It describes Pharoah, the enslaver, and those who support slavery, as being evil (40:37; 40:45).

Enslaving free people, as Muslims did in most cases throughout history, in unjust slave raids and wars of aggression and conquest, is prohibited in the Qur'an. Although it is clearly a major, greater, or mortal sin, it does not appear as such on most of the lists of *kaba'ir* prepared by Muslim authorities over the ages. Incredibly, most of the theologians and jurists in question could not differentiate between mortal and venial sins.

Mortal sins, for people like 'Abd al-Husayn Dastghaib Shirazi (d. 1913-1981) include such things like singing, music, and masturbation or, for Dhahabi, making images, arguing, collecting taxes, a wife disobeying her husband, and a slave running away from his master. This last one should not come as a surprise. After all, he was an intransigent supporter of slavery. Unlike the Sunni lists of major sins, the Twelver Shiite ones that I consulted include supporting oppressors as a major sin, which it most certainly is. In fact, a huge body of traditions, attributed to the Prophet and the Imams, condemns associating with oppressors and cooperating with them. These traditions command Muslims to side with the oppressed against their oppressors. How Shiite scholars failed to extend this principle to slavery is ethically and logically incomprehensible.

192   Islam & Slavery

Many Muslim scholars treated minor sins as major ones and yet excluded the enslavement of free people. Based on Qur'anic evidence alone, enslaving free people is prohibited. What is more, it could be argued that the punishment for doing so is death. Although Ware's claim that "the Qur'an discusses slavery as a fact of human society, neither condoning nor condemning it" (113), is incorrect, the rest of Ware's remarks are right on the mark. As he stresses,

> Countless verses promote manumission. Countless sayings attributed to the Prophet echo the call. Nonetheless -- and without support in any foundation text -- many scholars came to see slavery as a legitimate punishment for unbelief. Slowly, a "fragile Sunni consensus" on slavery's permissibility gathered the strength of precedent and became an unquestioned part of Islamic legal practice. But even this consensus was disputed, especially in the African West, where successive generations of jurists in Timbuktu pulled at the loose threads of this consensus. (113)

Unlike Brown, who contends in his book that the consensus of scholars is in favor of slavery, Clarence-Smith points out that opposition to slavery has a long history in Islam. These abolitionists included revolutionary millenarians who claimed the right to abolish laws, reshape them, and oppose slavery; peaceful mystics who wished to integrate formerly enslaved people into Islam; literalists who questioned the legitimacy of servitude of concubines, slave soldiers, eunuchs, and slave officials; rationalists who advocated returning to the spirit of the Qur'an; radicals who asserted that "God had abolished slavery through his revelations to the Prophet, and that Muslims had willfully refused to obey the divine command," and gradualists who espoused incremental steps toward emancipation (Clarence-Smith 2006: 21, 216-217, see also Clarence-Smith, Freamon 2019: 368). As Clarence-Smith elaborates,

> Opposition to slavery did not begin as a result of Western influence, as is so often assumed, for the Druze abolished slavery in the eleventh century... In the case of Akbar, Mughal emperor of India from 1556-1605, there was a possibility that slavery might have withered away, if his reforms had been continued...
>
> The emergence of fully-fledged Islamic abolitionism from the 1870s was no mere response to Western pressure. Reformers of various kinds returned to the original texts of the faith, especially the Qur'an, as part of a broader movement of revival and renewal. Rather to their surprise, they discovered that the foundations for slavery in holy writ were extremely shaky, not to say non-existent. The Qur'an nowhere explicitly allowed the making of any new slaves by anybody save the Prophet himself and called repeatedly for the manumission of existing slaves. The *hadith* literature was scarcely more supportive of slavery, and many reformers queried the authenticity of some of these traditions. The entire edifice of slavery, accounting for a third of the compendium of holy law most used in Inner and South Asia, was found to be built on a cumulative

Chapter Sixteen

set of dubious exegetical exercises.

The reformers split into four broad groups. In more rural and remote areas, some '*ulama*,' usually with a Sufi background, evolved a quasi-abolitionist stance. In its most extreme form, as enunciated by Ahmad b. Khalid al-Nasiri of Salé in Morocco, no wars since the times of the companions of the Prophet could be dignified with the epithet of holy, and thus no slaves had been taken legitimately after those early years. As unbroken servile descent from the slaves of that time could not be proven, all slaves should be freed. Musa Kamara later spread such notions in West Africa.

An even more radical version of liberation emerged from millenarian Mahdist movements. One, based in what are today Nigeria and Niger in the 1900s, called for the root and branch abolition of slavery. This was part of the process of filling the earth with justice prior to the imminent last judgment. Other millenarian movements were rarely so explicit, but often contained an emancipatory potential.

Gradualist modernists were often more urban and middle class, and less likely to be drawn from the ranks of the '*ulama*.' They became more numerous and influential as the twentieth century progressed. They were particularly inspired by Sayyid Amir 'Ali, a Shi'i lay reformer from Bengal, and Muhammad 'Abduh, grand mufti of Egypt. They argued that the Prophet personally opposed slavery. However, he risked losing his following had he explicitly banned the institution. Since the infidel had adopted abolition, the time was now ripe for the command of God and the desire of His messenger to be fulfilled.

Radical modernists, in contrast, held that the Prophet had openly prohibited the making of new slaves, and ordered the freeing of existing ones. Subsequent generations of Muslims had therefore sinned grievously by failing to heed his commands. Indeed, this might have been one of the reasons for which the infidel had become so powerful relative to the believers. The early torchbearers of this strand of abolitionism were Sayyid Ahmad Khan and Maulvi Chiragh Ali, in India, and Musa Jarulla Bigi, in Russian Tatarstan. The Lahori branch of the Ahmadiyya took a similar position, but its "heretical" status limited its influence. (n. date)

Bernard K. Freamon mentions other Islamic abolitionists, including Sayyid Qutb (1906-1966). The Qur'anic commentator believed that Qur'an 3:64, which prohibits people from taking others as lords and masters, was an emancipation proclamation (Freamon 2019: 139). In Qutb's interpretation, Islam was "total liberation of man from enslavement by others" (Freamon 2019: 497). Freamon also mentions Muhammad Baqir al-Sadr (1935-1980), an Iraqi Twelver Shiite jurist, who wrote, "man's submission to God in Islam… is the toll whereby man breaks all other chains of submission or slavery... Therefore no power on earth has the right to fare with his destiny" (2019: 495). "According to Baqir al-Sadr," notes Freamon, "any legal or moral regime permitting slavery is inconsistent with true monotheism" (2019: 495). Morteza Muttahari (1919-1979), an Iranian Twelver Shiite scholar, also opposed slavery. He argued that, according to Qur'an 3:64, social freedom is sacred and that if there is true social freedom, in the Islamic sense, there could be no slavery (Freamon 2019: 495-496).

Unlike Brown, who adheres to the view that slavery and concubinage are divinely ordained, Clarence-Smith rejects the claim that there is only one genuinely Islamic point of view in any period. "From the time of the Prophet himself," he explains, "believers held different views about social and political organization" (2006: 19). "Slavery, even mitigated by ameliorationist tendencies," he explains, "was the clearest negation of a socially egalitarian vision of the faith" (2006: 19). Although "a libertarian whiff accompanied the birth of Islam" (Clarence-Smith 6: 2006), it was snuffed out after the passing of the Prophet Muhammad.

Unlike Brown, Freamon acknowledges, in the very title of his book, that slavery is a problem. Rather than defend the dominant interpretation of Islam, and the slave master *status quo* it upholds, he seeks to defend human freedom as something fundamentally sacred. Freamon admits that the rules mandating the taking of slaves as "war booty" are "troubling" (Freamon 2019: 139) and that the institution of slavery poses "profound moral dilemmas" (Freamon 2019: 479).

Brown, however, seeks to "reconcile modern moral certainties with the infallibility of God's message" (back cover). So, in his mind, the man-made interpretation of the Qur'an and the *hadith*, as found in the *shari'ah*, is infallible, and we must conform to it regardless of the objections of our intellects and our souls. Freamon, however, has enough conscience to realize that "slavery and slave trading were and still remain vexing problems in the Muslim world that have never been solved" (2019: 7). Unlike Brown, who seems to set out to justify "Islamic" slavery, as opposed to simply describe its history, making outrageous rationalizations, Freamon fully explores the profound moral, ethical, and legal problems that it poses. Brown comes across as dogmatic and unapologetic. Freamon, however, is pragmatic and solution focused.

Unlike Brown, Freamon expresses a fervent desire to "inform and educate... readers... Muslim and non-Muslim and motivate them to continue to struggle against slavery in all its forms" (2019: 19). He does not defend the indefensible. He does not engage in apologetics. He tackles the "jurisprudential problems" raised by the history and legacy of an Islamic "slavery-condoning-religio-legal culture" (Freamon 2019: 8). As he notes, the failure to resolve these issues "explains why slavery and slave trading have reemerged in the Muslim world in contemporary times" (Freamon 2019: 8). Consequently, he sets to resolve them using an Islamic jurisprudential methodology (2019: 8)

Professor Freamon, who happens to be an African American Muslim jurist, commences his book with a seminal citation, the final words of Muhammad, the Messenger of God, in which he warned his followers to "fear God about those whom your right hands possess" (2019: 1, see also Azumah 161). As Freamon rightly notes, "this statement," which was cited by Abu Dawud, on the authority of 'Ali, "shows that the enslaved, their condition, and their treatment were of the greatest concern to the Prophet as he lay dying" (2019: 2). It was a "weighty and important admonition to those that surrounded him" (Freamon 2019: 2).

For the sake of academic honesty, it must be admitted that there are many conflicting accounts regarding the last words of the Messenger of God. The Shiites, for example, claim that the Prophet wanted to appoint 'Ali as his successor in writing, but was prevented by 'Umar. If the tradition attributed to 'Ali himself is indeed authentic, then it is possible that the Prophet intended to emancipate enslaved human beings as his final act in this worldly life.

Moving from the end of the Prophet's mission, Freamon examines the emancipatory origins of Islam as manifested in the early Qur'anic verses that were revealed in Mecca. As the author notes, "Muhammad and his early followers interpreted this worldview to emphatically reject the domination of any person by other persons or by any class or group of oppressors" (Freamon 2019: 91). "The text of the Qur'an," he explains,

> argued vigorously that worldly distinctions between human beings based on tribe, ethnicity, language, class, caste, wealth, lineage, or national origin should be abolished.... the new Islamic message attacking hierarchy and privilege immediately attracted slaves, former slaves, women, the poor, and disenfranchised members of weak and discredited clans among the Meccan tribes. What emerges from this history is an ideal stressing that an egalitarian emancipatory piety is an important behavioral criterion in the Islamic worldview. (Freamon 2019: 97)

Although Islamic scripture touches upon slavery, all the Qur'anic verses that deal with it "are situated in a context that overwhelmingly encourages emancipation" (Freamon 2019: 494). "It must be said then," writes Freamon, "that the Qur'an seeks to establish an emancipatory ethic on the issue of slavery" (2019: 494).

After examining the Qur'an's references to slavery, Freamon surveys the Prophet Muhammad's emancipatory traditions and those used to construct a jurisprudence of slavery (2019: 147-158). The fact remains, however, that the traditions attributed to the Prophet Muhammad are almost entirely false. As Freamon acknowledges,

> Professor Schacht persuasively argued that the constructions of almost all the *ahadith*, including those that had been previously considered to be "sound" or "valid," were, in fact, the product of a terribly inaccurate backward-looking methodology and were fraught with error, exaggeration, and outright fabrication as a result of the political,

economic, social, and personal influences on the transmitters of the *ahadith*. (2019: 149)

When they can plausibly trace back to the Prophet and agree with the ethical and moral message of the Qur'an, traditions can be treated as authentic and acted upon. That would include the Prophet's condemnation against the man "who sells a free man as a slave and devours his price" (Bukhari) (Freamon 2019: 494-495). However, they must be decisively dismissed and discarded when they endorse abominations. The traditions attributed to the Messenger of God must be purged based on whether or not they accord with perennial moral and ethical principles.

"Many Muslims," writes Freamon, "are now shocked at the realization that a substantial body of their religious law, law that on its face appears to condone slavery, might actually be... plainly condemnable and wrong-headed on the issue" (2019: 486). In his view, they are ready for reform, in the English sense of change or improvement. They are ready for *islah*, in the Arabic sense of improving, correcting, emending, repairing, restoring, rectifying, and reconciling. They recognize that,

> the right to be free from slavery, like the right to be free from genocide, torture, racial discrimination, and piracy, is a jurisprudential universal, with no competent legal system or government able to deny its existence or permit derogation from its tenets. (Freamon 2019: 464)

As Freamon writes, "there is a worldwide consensus ... holding that slavery is illegal under international law and a violation of *jus cogens* principles" (2019: 515). Consequently, "it is in the Muslim public interest to join that consensus" (2019: 515). Abdulaziz Bayindir, however, has made a pertinent point in his seminal, grammatically grounded, study on "Captivity, Slavery and Concubinage According to the Qur'an." As he notes, the *Letter to Baghdadi* claims that,

> For over a hundred years, Muslims, and even the whole world, have reached a consensus ... on forbidding the enslavement and considering it as a crime. This is of great importance in the history of Islam. It is ...forbidden to have a slave after enslavement is abolished by consensus.

Bayindir questions how the hundred and twenty-six signatories can consider themselves scholars when they ignore the fact that slavery and concubinage were abolished by the fourth verse of Surah Muhammad, which commands Muslims to ransom captives or "set them free" (47:4). As he has shown in his study,

> It is against the rulings of the Qur'an to enslave male or female war captives and to have sexual relations with them without marriage. Although the verses about this subject are clear, by distorting the meanings of words, a false perception was created, and it has been turned into the common view of all sects including Sunni and Shia that captives can be enslaved, and female captives can also be used as concubines...

Scholars of all sects, including both Sunni and Shia... only know the fictions about the Book, not the Book itself. They only make assumptions about it. In their opinion, the scholars of their sects do not make mistakes; they don't say anything that opposes the rulings of the Qur'an or the example of the Prophet. Especially if there is... consensus of Islamic scholars on a subject, then that opinion cannot be possibly wrong. Therefore, these people who obey the previous scholars without questioning think that they are experts in Islam. The books they write serve for nothing but reiterating and transferring the wrong assumptions to the next generations.

These scholars may be forgiven by God because they don't know it. But the ones who have written those books and attributed their own false decrees to the Qur'an by means of perception management ... will most probably not be saved.... I would like to call out to them with the following words of Jesus: "You have a fine way of setting aside the commands of God in order to observe your own traditions!" (Mark 7:9)

Although Qur'anists like Abdulaziz Bayindir only resurfaced in the twentieth and twenty-first centuries in any meaningful fashion, they have forcefully denounced slavery and concubinage. In *Slavery: A Fundamental Historical Overview*, Ahmed Subhy Mansour (b. 1949) describes how slavery is the product of a perverse understanding of *jihad* as aggressive as opposed to defensive. As he explains,

After Muhammad's death, the Quraysh tribe committed the crime of Arab conquests in Egypt, Iraq, the Levant, etc., and such aggressive fights were for the sake of the devils as Arabs scrambled for loot and invasions to settle elsewhere away from Arabian deserts, as they coveted riches of other neighboring countries. Thus, the Quraysh tribesmen established a vast empire that they called "caliphate." Such terrible error led most Arabs to reject the Qur'an (the only and true celestial source of Islam) and its legislations, to eventually establish the earthly, man-made, fabricated religions to replace Islam. Such man-made creeds had ample room to express and realize whims and desires of people inside the so-called caliphate. Such devilish, aggressive Arab conquests included many features of grave injustice, including enslavement. This led to the fact that Arabs at the time and in later eras overlooked the Qur'anic legislations to alleviate, remedy, and solve the problem of slavery, as these Qur'anic legislations were replaced by the Sunnite legislations that endorse and allow enslavement by virtue of fabricated oral *hadiths* traditions ascribed wrongly and falsely to Muhammad decades after his death and written down later on in the Abbasid era, more than one century after his decease. Among such falsehoods ascribed to Muhammad, there is a biography of lies that portrays and sketches his character in a corrupt, distorted way that contradicts his character

198   Islam & Slavery

features mentioned in the Qur'an. Consequently, enslavement is a legacy, imposed on Islam that has been confiscated and distorted by Arab conquerors, bequeathed to us within conquests and the caliphate ruling system. Such legacy of enslavement derived from Sunnite religion has been revived recently in our modern age by the Wahabi-Sunnite terrorists of ISIS.

Mansour examines slavery in the Qur'an. He finds that the Qur'an never mentions "slaves" or "enslavement" and that scholars imposed false meanings upon Qur'anic terminology, misapplying the term *'abd* to denote a slave when is signifies a servant of God. As Mansour notes, the Qur'an uses the term *'abid* to denote all of humanity. In other words, the "slaves" in the Qur'an are slaves of God, not human property.

For Mansour, the Islamic jurisprudence of slavery is not grounded in the Qur'an. It is imposed upon it. As he explains, the primary objective of the Qur'an is to establish justice. Hence, "enslavement is prohibited in the first place and is to be nipped in the bud from the very beginning because it is a grave injustice." Consequently, "enslavement is ... prohibited in Islam." This explains why God required Muslims to emancipate slaves to atone for sins, promising great rewards in return, and encouraged Muslims to marry and free them.

As far as Mansour is concerned, Islam is the Qur'an only. If Muhammad Diakho blamed 'Umar for reintroducing slavery in a return to *jahiliyyah*, Mansour blames Abu Bakr, 'Umar, 'Uthman, and 'Ali, as well as their successors, for failing to follow the Qur'an and instituting religious terror by means of conquest, massacres, enslavement, and other heinous crimes. Mansour provides an overview of slavery in Muslim history, painting a sordid portrait. He is adamant that the crimes committed by Muslims contradicted the teachings of Islam as contained in the Qur'an. Mansour examines the subject of slavery in Sunni Islam, demolishing the *hadith* literature that was fabricated to support it. He surveys the types of slavery that prevailed in the Muslim world, denouncing the debauchery and degeneracy of the promiscuous caliphs and the culture they fostered. Among his many conclusions, he finds that,

> [An] Islamic country is a peaceful one that never commits aggression and never begins to transgress against anyone, and thus, there is no room for it to enslave anyone or even to capture POWs... Hence, the source of enslavement is prohibited in such Islamic country. Moreover, freeing slaves coming from outside a given an Islamic country into it by buying them is available as an Islamic duty by the pious, righteous rich persons.

Edip Yüksel's stance on slavery and concubinage is coherent, courageous, and commendable. In his view,

> The widely practiced slavery was abolished by the Qur'an (3:79, 4:3,25,92, 5:89, 8:67, 24:32-33, 58:3-4, 90:13, 2:286, 12:39-42, 79:24). The Qur'an rejects slavery not as one of the big sins, but as the greatest

Chapter Sixteen 199

sin and crime, equivalent of setting up partners to God, which is an unforgivable sin if maintained until death. The Qur'an unequivocally rejects accepting other than God as lord/master (*rabb*). Claiming to be the lord/master of someone is tantamount to claiming to be God (12:39-40, 3:64, 9:31).

Verse 16:75-76 compares a slave with a free person and emphasizes the importance of being a free person. No wonder the Qur'an condemns Pharaoh for his claim of being the lord and master of other people (79:15-26). God saved the Jews from slavery and reminded them that their freedom was more important than the variety of foods they were missing (2:57-61). The Qur'an warns Muhammad not to capture and imprison his enemies during peacetime and gives him permission for such only as a measure against those who participate in war (8:67). The Qur'an acknowledges the fact that those who set up partners with God had slaves (24:32, 16:75) and freeing them is considered an activity and a quality of Muslims (90:13).

16.3 Conclusions

Although there will always be opposition in the ranks of the extremists, fanatics, fundamentalists, radicals, conservatives, and some self-identified traditionalists, who will insist that the Qur'an, the *sunnah*, and the *shari'ah* continue to permit slavery, and that nobody can prohibit what God and His Prophet have permitted, Bernard K. Freamon believes that "Islamic jurisprudence might now be prepared to see slavery as an 'evil' that undermines the public interest" (2019: 480, 513). He believes there is now a sufficiently strong "jurisprudential basis for abolishing slavery in Islamic law" (Freamon 2019: 515). As he explains in his book, Freamon believes that a "competent understanding of the texts and the legal history of slavery and slave trading in the Muslim world will lead jurists to conclude that there *must* be a *de jure* abolition" (2019: 465). By opposing slavery and concubinage, Muslims are not following a consensus established by the West a century and a half ago. Rather, they are following the consensus, a standard, a goal, and objective set by the Qur'an in the seventh century. Islam was knocked off course by the Umayyads and the 'Abbasids, a path their friends and foes followed. It is high time that we corrected the course. And since God knows best, the Qur'an prohibited concubinage and instituted measures to ensure the elimination of slavery.

Conclusions

For so-called traditional, conservative, or radical Muslim, who wish to defend the Islamic *status quo* on slavery and concubinage, and turn faith into an instrument of permanent inequality and iniquity, Jonathan A.C. Brown's book will serve them well. As he puts it plainly, "We cannot pretend it is not part of our religion; it is present in the Qur'an we read every day in our prayers" (4). In fact, we can, and we must. It may be part of Brown's religion, but it most certainly is not part of the Islam of many other Muslims, many of whom are profoundly offended by the claim that it forms a fundamental, essential, and immutable part of their faith.

Why would any Jew or Christian, in our day and age, write a book insisting that the slave trade was Biblically based? Why would any Muslim, in our day and age, write a book insisting that the slavery practiced by Muslims for over a millennium was consonant with the teachings of the Qur'an and the Prophet Muhammad? It is one thing to provide a historical overview of slavery in Islam, and explain the basis for past views, with the caveat that Muslims no longer agree with such interpretations. It is another to justify slavery and concubinage religiously and accuse those who oppose them in principle of being outside the fold of the faith. Muslims have moved forward by leaps and bounds. As far as critics are concerned, Brown, a white Muslim academic, wants to drag them back to the slave age. His stance is emboldened by black Muslim scholars who, as Malcolm X put it, "are trying to crawl back on the plantation."

Is slavery a religious obligation in Islam? Is it an article of faith? It most certainly is not. It is ironic that the Salafi/Wahhabis, the so-called anti-innovation champions, are those who profess to believe in slavery. By elevating slavery to an article of belief, making it mandatory to believe, and insisting that those who oppose it are hypocrites, apostates, and infidels, they have essentially corrupted the Islamic creed. Deaf, dumb, and blind, they follow in the footsteps of falsehood. God does not put people in chains. God is the ultimate breaker of chains. Any "god" who does otherwise is no god at all but the concoction of evil human minds.

The inhumanity of humanity has no limits. 'Abd al-'Aziz ibn Ahmad al-Bukhari (d. 1330), for example, went so far as to state that "slaves are in the category of the dead" (Azumah 167). Like zombies, they were very much the living dead who were devoid of the rights of the living. As Azumah notes,

The very status of the slave is, therefore, cruel. It is legal, social, and psychological death! Notwithstanding the conviction of past Muslim (and Christian) slavers that slavery was a blessing in disguise to its victims... even slavers were under no illusion whatsoever that slavery was a dreadful condition. No stipulation or magnanimity of individual slavers could make this hideous institution one to be lauded, more so when it is sanctioned and perpetuated in the name of God. (167-168)

Although Muslims from various races and sects supported and engaged in slavery, they did so, not because of the Qur'an, but despite it. As Chouki El Hamel asserts, "The Qur'an legalized manumission and did not institutionalize slavery" (45). What is more, "The Qur'an, the primary and fundamental sources of Islam and Islamic law, does not authorize or formalize using slaves as concubines" (17). On the contrary, "the Qur'an places a high priority on manumitting slaves with the ultimate goal of abolishing slavery" (17). In fact, "No single verse of the Qur'an calls for the acceptance of slavery as a social practice. The Qur'an contains no word on the treatment of slaves to indicate that it condones slavery's existence and continuity" (El Hamel 42). As Abdul Malik Mujahid observes, "there is not a single verse in the Qur'an that encourages or commands people to take others as slaves. Also, there is nothing to suggest that it is the Divine Will for the practice of slavery to continue until the end of time."

As far as Fadel Abdullah is concerned, "everything in Islam in relation to slavery was intended to eliminate an existing, disagreeable, and deep-rooted institution" and if Muslims practiced slavery, it was due to their "deviation from Islam" (Azumah 118). If Islam is opposed to slavery, Azumah rightly asks, which Islam are we talking about? (118). It most certainly is not its dominant historical interpretation that Jonathan A.C. Brown callously defends. Azumah is also correct to point out that Muslims did not merely continue a deep-rooted tradition. They altered its meaning and intensified it (118). In fact, they transformed it "from a marginal social phenomena to a wide-scale institutionalized practice" (123).

"If Muslim slavery is a result of deviation or misuse of Islam," wonders Azumah, "it is amazing that Muslims, from the companions in Arabia to India, Turkey, and right across to West Africa, from the seventh century down to the twenty-first century, could have got it so badly wrong on this one single issue" (178). The same critique, however, could be directed toward Christianity. If Jesus never condoned slavery, why is it that Christians engaged in slavery? After all, Muhammad was but a man and a mortal (41:6). How could he be blamed for failing to eradicate slavery when Jesus, "God in Person," according to Christians, could not accomplish such a task? If you cannot count on God, how can you count on a man like Muhammad?

This reminds me of a famous story. During British colonial rule in India, a Christian missionary once asked why God did nothing about the murder of Husayn, the grandson of the Prophet. "He did something," responded the Muslim shaykh the Christian was debating. "What did he do?" he asked. "He cried," said the shaykh, leaving the audience of thousands of Muslims perplexed. "He cried:

'How can I save your grandson, O Muhammad, when I could not even save my own son?" The crowd erupted in laughter. After all, if God could not stop the crucifixion of His own son, how could he be expected to stop slavery.

Not only did Christians not prohibit slavery, but they also expanded it into a massive cross-continental enterprise. Azumah, as a Christian, and an ex-Muslim, should not throw stones. Both Christianity and Islam were used to justify and perpetuate an abhorrent institution. That being said, dismissing enslavement as a mere "deviation" of Islam is "infantile escapism" on the part of those who are unable or unwilling to face the Islamic past (Azumah 178). Muslims and Christians are accountable for their interpretations and actions. They did "get it all wrong" and "were so selfish as to misuse Islam to satisfy their selfish human needs" (178). The same applies to the pro-slavery Christians.

As far as abolitionists are concerned, the Qur'an's emancipatory ethos was established from the moment of its emergence. While weak, powerless, impoverished, and persecuted, God set the goal, the higher ethical objective, the path that is steep, namely, "freeing the slave" (90:12-13). For Freamon, the revelation of surah 90 is "the most compelling proof of the Qur'an philosophy of freedom and its insistence on the ultimate abolition of slavery" (1998: 38). The Qur'an described the righteous as those who "set slaves free" (2:174). It encouraged free men to marry and emancipate enslaved women (4:25). As Freamon notes, "this approach to slavery is a radical departure from that of the revealed texts that preceded the revelation of the Qur'an" (1998: 40).

Justice is a central theme in the Qur'an. It commands Muslims to "dispense justice" (7:181), "stand firmly for justice" (4:135), "judge with justice" (4:58), "fight them on until... there prevails justice" (2:193), "stand firm on justice" (3:18), and "be just; that is next to piety" (5:8). The question must be asked: is slavery just? If it is not just, it is an affront to divine justice. For Abdul Malik Mujahid, "supporting the anti-slavery movement is in line with a Muslim's duty to be just as emphasized in the Qur'an." The Qur'an also commands believers to "enjoin the good and forbid the wrong" (3:104, 3:110, 9:71, 9:112, 31:17). Is slavery good, or is it evil? Is it right, or is it wrong? If it is wrong, our duty as Muslims is to oppose it in all its manifestations.

As Abdul Malik Mujahid points out, the fact that the Qur'an mentions the existence of slavery in passing cannot be equated with approval and encouragement. Those vague descriptive verses cannot form the basis of binding legal injunctions while ignoring the clear and precise prescriptive verses that speak toward its abolition. Doing so is a clear violation of Islamic principles. As he explains,

> God has never ordered anyone to establish slavery, nor is there any verse
> in the Qur'an that commands the practice to be continued or reinstated.
> Likewise, God has instructed us to follow Him, the Prophet, and our
> Leaders: "Believers, obey God and the messenger and those among you

who have been entrusted with authority. If you have a dispute about anything, refer it to God and the Messenger, if you truly believe in God and the Last Day. This is best to do and in turn gives the best results" (4:59). They have all prohibited slavery through their commandments and treaties, and it is a sin to violate such treaties.

Not only is Asifa Quraishi-Landes "not convinced that sex with one's slaves is approved of the Qur'an in the first place" (178), but she also stresses that "the slavery framework and its resulting doctrine are not dictated by scripture, so we are not obligated to perpetuate them today" (174). For Khaled al-Mullah, a leading Iraqi Sunni scholar and head of the Iraqi Scholars Association, "The *shari'ah* does not allow us to capture women as [slave girls]. The times of taking captives, the times of slavery, are over." While he admitted that controversial texts existed in Islamic jurisprudential sources, he argued that "the biggest mistake of the religious institution is not being able to get rid of these texts" (MEMRI). To be blunt, "The religious institution does not have the courage to say, at the very least, that these texts are unsuitable for the world today" (MEMRI).

Women, Africans, Imazighen, Europeans, or people historically enslaved by Muslims should probably scrutinize their conscience. Otherwise, they show an astonishing lack of discernment. Brown's apology for "Islamic" slavery results from an approach that idolizes and deifies medieval interpretations and treats the men who made them as morally and spiritually superior to all others. The Qur'an, however, warns against taking "doctors of law" and "clerics" as "lords besides God" (9:31). It calls people to human conscience, to Natural Law, *al-fitrah*, an innate belief in God and a sense of good. Truth transcends religious texts and the interpretations of men.

To be fair, transparent, and balanced, Brown insists that his book is "not an apology for slavery" and that he is only "recognizing a reality" (9). He finds it unusual that "scholars writing on slavery are expected to pause at some point to reaffirm slavery's moral abhorrence" (8). As he notes, "Not to do so... or worst of all, to raise even the possibility of moral relativism in judging it, are all likely to be branded as an apology for slavery" (8). Such critics are correct. Writing a book that fails to criticize slavery is like writing one about pedophilia that does not condemn the practice. An author could counter that "I wanted to be descriptive as opposed to prescriptive." However, the failure to pass judgement is itself a judgment. According to the *Fiqh Encyclopedia*,

> Passive silence is not evidence by itself for consent or disagreement; it is for this reason that the *fiqh* rule necessitates the following: "No statement can be attributed to a person who remains silent, but silence when one should speak is a statement (i.e. consent and approval)." This is so if it is accompanied by indications and circumstances which prove that it is an approval.

In some cases, silence indicates consent. In others, silence is a sin and an act of

Conclusions 205

complicity. Is it proper to write a biography of Hitler or a book about the Nazis without mentioning the Holocaust? When we study the Aztecs and the Mayas, should we rationalize and relativize human sacrifice? Sure, we can try to understand how they viewed the world and try to see things from their point of view. However, we should never lose our moral footing. After all, Nezahualcoyotl (1402-1472), the ruler of Texcoco, opposed polytheism and human sacrifice. Some indigenous peoples of the America enslaved prisoners of war and debtors. However, there were First Nations that opposed slavery. Who speaks for Islam? Who speaks for the Qur'an? And who speaks for God? The supporters of slavery? Or its opponents?

Doubtlessly and unfortunately, Brown's book has been taken as a show of soft or tacit support for slavery by Islamists and Islamophobes. Muslims and non-Muslims who refuse to be bogged down by past mistakes and misinterpretations, and who believe in a living, evolving, Islam that is aligned with morals, ethics, liberty, justice, and equality, will be sorely disappointed by Brown's book. *Islam and the Abolition of Slavery* by William Gervase Clarence-Smith, cited by Brown but once, is far superior in every sense to his *Slavery & Islam*. The same can be said of *Possessed by the Right hand: The Problem of Slavery in Islamic Law and Muslim Cultures* by Bernard K. Freamon, a *magnum opus* with a mission: the prohibition of slavery in Islamic jurisprudence, for which he has launched a website: www.ijma-on-slavery.org.

Despite its potential, some critics suggest that this effort was hamstrung by Freamon himself by asserting that only "qualified jurists" who were "fluent in Arabic" were invited to participate in formulating Islamic arguments against slavery. What constitutes a "qualified jurist?" Some *fuqaha'* would argue that the Western-educated Freamon is unqualified unless he was traditionally trained in an Islamic seminary and reached the level of *ijtihad*.

Are Twelver Shiite *mujtahids* qualified? What about the jurists from the 'Ibadi school? Are the Mutazilites competent? If it is up to Muslim jurists to prohibit slavery, as Freamon contends, which school of law should they follow? Each school employs a particular methodology when it comes to deriving rulings. Individual jurists use different legal techniques, strategies, evidence, and arguments. How can these be reconciled? What is more, with rare exception, all of their approaches failed to result in rulings outlawing slavery and concubinage. The devil is in the details. For some scholars, the Islamic legal system is not the solution. It is very much the problem. Muslim jurists boxed themselves in. They created a hierarchical system in which free men were on top and enslaved women were on the bottom. The very foundations of their jurisprudential architecture must be dismantled. Hence, for Mohsen Kadivar, and other Shiite reformists, no rulings will be reformed until the structural principles of Islamic jurisprudence are reformed. The problem, however, is far more profound.

The Qur'an is not a lawbook. It is a code of ethics. Its principles are shared by all civilized societies: honesty, helping others, compassion, justice, equity,

206   Islam & Slavery

protection, and equality… ('Ajami 2020: 22). Laws, however, are temporal and can be changed. Ethics are universal and immutable. For Cyrille Moreno al-'Ajami,

> The Qur'an is not a legal or penal code… Its only objective is to guide human beings to salvation, to edify their hearts, and purify their souls. It does not support the thesis of a Divine Law or a *shari'ah* which is responsible for guiding human beings in every area. This totalitarian vision contradicts the spirit and letter of the Qur'an.
>
> The Qur'an does not legislate laws. Rather, it gives rights, notably to the most destitute: women, slaves, children, and minorities. A right, even if Qur'anic, is not a law. A law, by definition, is changeable, whereas a right is inalienable in essence.
>
> In most cases, these Qur'anic rights do not correspond with the jurisprudential developments of Islamic law which, on the contrary, had a tendency of distancing themselves from them… Qur'anic rights are, by their very revealed origin, inalienable. Islamic law, which is the product of human reasoning, is by nature fallible and variable. (40-41)

As al-'Ajami insists, "no logical argument supports the thesis of an immutable divine law that applies until the end of times" (2020: 40). If that were the case, "human beings would have to be intangible and time immobile; otherwise, we would have to return to an eternal Middle Age" (40). For al-'Ajami, Muslims should not study the Qur'an through the prism of Islam (2020: 307). Their understanding of the Qur'an should not be colored by the exegetes and the jurists who developed the historical religion of Islam (2020: 307). Admittedly, this approach forces us out our comfort zones and can be profoundly destabilizing (2020: 307). However, in so doing, it becomes clear that the laws of Islam sometimes contradict the Qur'anic message (2020: 307). In fact, "Islam has largely emancipated itself from the Qur'an" (2020: 19). How so?

1) By supplementing it with the *hadith*, sayings of the Prophet Muhammad which were concocted to fill a legal void (20). They were also a means to legitimize pre-Islamic beliefs and superstitions like demonic possession, magic, the evil eye, legends, and animistic myths (220). 2) By claiming that God revealed a Qur'anic legislation that represents Divine Law when, in reality, the *shari'ah* is a straight path, a moral and ethical way, and not an orthopraxic law (28, 34). 3) By developing an "Islamic" jurisprudence that pragmatically substituted the Qur'an (21) and absorbed local customs and laws from the Jews, Romans, and Persians (23, 29). By legitimizing their thirst for power in the name of God, Muslim authorities opened the gates of hell on earth (28).

A return to the Qur'an, pure and pristine, and unadulterated by extraneous influences is in order. As al-'Ajami explains, the aim of this approach is not to redefine, *ex nihilo*, a new Muslim identity, but to call Muslims to center themselves on the Qur'an and to rediscover its fundamental teachings that have

Conclusions 207

been buried under centuries of dust by customs and traditions, religious and otherwise (2020: 15). In his words, "Where Islam is the Law, the Qur'an is the Way. Where Islam is tradition, the Qur'an is innovation. Where Islam is closure, the Qur'an is an aperture. Where Islam is the past, the Qur'an is the future" (2020: 307). For jurists and attorneys, Islam is a set of rules, regulations, and laws. Law takes primacy over spirituality. As Sufi authorities long understood, the commanding God of the jurists cannot be loved. Only the God of creativity, love, mercy, and compassion can fill the hearts of the faithful.

Laws, however essential, are not made solely by jurists. Laws are made by governments. Laws are proposed by people and passed by their representatives. As such, people are their own rulers. Muslims should not be at the mercy of the jurists. They should not live under the dictatorship of the *fuquha*.' It is not the duty of the people to obey them blindly. They are accountable to the people; not the other way around. Since Islamic jurisprudence has proven itself incapable of evolving and responding to the changing needs of society, and the jurists themselves are only accustomed to giving orders, having zero tolerance for criticism of any kind, Muslims have found secular law far more amenable to influence and change. After all, "religion has always been central in the rationalization of historic slavery and of the slave trade" (Iddrisu).

Islam cannot be reduced to Islamic law as the jurists would have it. When they speak of studying Islam, what they mean is studying *fiqh* or jurisprudence. They barely study anything else. This reductionism is the primary cause of the plight of the Muslim world. All Muslims have a role to play in the development of Islamic law. Rulings require the consensus of the community for legitimacy. The Qur'an describes believers as those "who [conduct] their affairs by mutual consultation among themselves" (42:39). Even the Prophet Muhammad was told to "take counsel" with the people (3:159). It was his duty to do so. When creating the *Constitution of Medina,* the Messenger of God consulted with all parties: Jews, Muslims, Christians, and pagans. His continued leadership over the community in Medina depended on yearly approval by means of pledges of allegiance. Would he have continued to rule without popular legitimacy? Clearly, the formulation of laws should involve, not only jurists, but all the '*ulama*,' in the broadest sense of the term, namely, experts in all relevant domains. Islamic law must be a collective effort on the part of the educated members of the community.

As for the claim that only people who are proficient in Arabic can have a say in matters of Islamic law, it is devoid of basis. It merely entrenches Arab supremacy. If the Qur'an is universal it cannot be the sole property of the Arabs. It belongs to all of humanity. It is the message that matters; not its medium (14:4). The fact of the matter is that most Arabs are not fluent in Modern Standard Arabic, much less the classical Arabic of the seventh century. Khomeini studied in Persian, wrote in Persian, and taught in Persian. His Arabic language books were translated from Persian. Yaser Arafat (1929-2004) was renowned for his mastery of classical Arabic. Khomeini could not even converse with him. Does this

208   Islam & Slavery

suggest that Khomeini was not a qualified *mujtahid*? After all, he became *a marja' al-taqlid*, a source of emulation.

I met with Sa'id al-Hakim (1936-2021). I spoke to him in classical Arabic. However, as his top aides explained, "The sayyid only speaks 'ghetto' Arabic." While I spoke to him in *fushah*, he responded in *'amiyyah*, the Iraqi dialect spoken in the slums which, in turn, had to be translated to me by his aide into classical Arabic. If he was proficient in *fushah*, why did he not speak to me directly in that language? It was nonsensical. I did not doubt, however, that he was a qualified jurist.

The law is the law is the law. The language does not matter. Islamic studies are conducted in English in most of the world. Otherwise, people study in French, Spanish, German, or other languages. At Islamic seminaries in Iran, courses are primarily taught in Persian. In Pakistan, they are taught in Urdu. In Indonesia, they are taught in Indonesian. Traditionally, to be an *'alim*, a scholar, or a *faqih*, a jurist, one was required to have enough knowledge of Arabic to use a dictionary. Many Muslim scholars and jurists have what is known as "reading comprehension." They understand Arabic. They can read it. They can write it. They can translate it. They can conduct research in the language. They might not speak it fluently, due do a dearth in speakers of classical Arabic in the world; however, they are perfectly qualified and competent scholars. What is more, Arabic is no longer the dominant language of Islam and Islamic Studies. It has long been surpassed by English. There are more works on Islam in English than in the Arabic language.

As can be appreciated from this study, works like *Slavery & Islam* by Brown weaken faith in Islam. Works like *Islam and the Abolition of Slavery* by Clarence Smith, and *Possessed by the Right Hand*, by Freamon, strengthen it. When they read Brown, many Muslims think: "If this is Islam, then I am not a Muslim." When they read Clarence-Smith and Freamon, they assert: "This is my Islam. I am proud to be a Muslim." As Freamon has demonstrated, "the abolition of slavery is not and has never been an impossibility in Islamic jurisprudence" (1998: 6). On the contrary, it "can rather easily articulate the normative abolition of slavery and offer judicial support to those who continue to struggle against slavery and slave-trading in its modern-day forms" (1998: 6). In fact, "there now appears to be broad consensus among both lay Muslims and expert Muslim jurists that slavery is *haram* (legally forbidden) and that no true Islamic state can allow it to exist" (1998: 7). As he asserts, "the time has come for the formal recognition of the consensus that slavery is unacceptable to Muslims and that it has been juridically abolished" (1998: 8).

For some Islamic abolitionists and enslaved human beings, such an effort is emasculated and emasculating, demeaning and degrading. It is hurtful and humiliating. It is like a eunuch asking for his testicles back. For them, one does not ask for rights. One asserts them. From their perspective, it is undignified for slaves to plead to plantation owners for their freedom. One does not supplicate for freedom to slavers. One is not compelled to convince criminals of their crimes. One does not appeal for mercy from the very jurists who legalized and codified slavery. One burns their books of laws and hangs them from their turbans. Muslims are well within their rights to excommunicate those who enslave them and to declare *jihad* against them. They have placed themselves outside the fold of the faith.

The black slaves of Christian and Muslim masters were devoid of any duty to educate them about the evils of slavery and its illegality according to the doctrines of the Bible and the Qur'an. Regardless of their religion, God was on their side. Even if we removed the religious equation, they had every right to rebel and revolt and bring slave masters to justice. If the enslaved blacks in the Americas were entitled to fight their English, French, Spanish, Portuguese, and Dutch slave masters, who claimed to be Christians, then the enslaved blacks in North Africa, the Middle East, and Asia, had every right to rise against their Arab, Berber, and Turkish slave masters, who professed to be Muslims.

For Freamon, *ijma*' or consensus is the key to abolition and prohibition in Islam. If there was a *shari*'*ah*, a Divine Law, and God was the sole Legislator, explains Cyrille Moreno al-'Ajami, the exegete of the Qur'an, then all laws would be found in the Qur'an. There would be no need for the *sunnah*, analogy, and the consensus of jurists. It was these three supplementary sources of law that entrenched slavery in Islam. So why should consensus suddenly come to rescue and be some sort of saving grace?

Enslaved human beings are not required to wait for any "formal recognition that slavery is unacceptable." They are not in need of "juridical abolishment." Their freedom cannot wait. Slavery does not suddenly become *haram* due to the illusory and unattained consensus of twenty-first century scholars. Who cares if there is no unanimity of opinion among Islamic jurists? Slavery is intrinsically prohibited. It is de-facto *haram* presently and retroactively. What is more, if Christianity and Islam were impediments to freedom, the enslaved had every right to abandon them and embrace an emancipatory ideology.

The religion with God is not submission to slave masters. It is surrender to God and God alone. The religion with God is freedom. Hence, for Islamic abolitionists, liberty is Islam and Islam is liberty. As 'Ali expounded, reason is more important than religion for religion will not lead to reason but reason will always lead to religion. Hence, if presented with two options -- oppressive Islam or freedom -- the only choice is freedom. It is that freedom to think, and reason, that leads to faith and morality. Consequently, for Muslim abolitionists, the answer is Islam *and* freedom. However, this can only be so if Islam *is* freedom. When we invite people to Islam, we invite them, not to slavery, but to liberty.

Being faithful to Islam does not require us to remain fossilized and repeat the errors made in the past. It should, however, be centered on the Qur'an. There is a difference between what Islam, as a historical religion developed by human beings, says about a certain subject, and what the Qur'an says. The sacralization of the *shari'ah* has led many Muslims to believe that Islamic law is part and parcel of the Qur'anic revelation ('Ajami 2020: 24). Hence, they believe that it is fixed and cannot be modified in content or form (2020: 24).

Being devoted to Islamic jurisprudence does not mean we must perpetuate and defend mistaken and misguided medieval rulings. "Theoretically," notes al-'Ajami, "the great jurists from the classical period always recalled, without any ambiguity, that Islamic law was a human effort" (2020: 23). Consequently, "it was possible and even desirable to call into question its conclusions" (2020: 23). It is therefore possible and constructive to point out the discrepancies between the points of view of many Muslim and the ethical spirit of the Qur'an (2020: 24).

"Anybody who claims to know the absolute truth of the Qur'an," writes El Hamel, "and tries to impose it on others, is ultimately taking the place of God" (21). Hence, "the act and the continuous process of interpretation are logical, and its outcome is never fixed or closed" (21). As Leila Ahmed notes,

> the uniformity of interpretation and the generally minimal differences characterizing the versions of Islam that survived reflect not unanimity of understanding but rather the triumph of the religious and social vision of the 'Abbasid state at this formative moment in history. (99)

During its early centuries, Islam was interpreted in profoundly different ways. From the dawn of Islam and throughout most of its history, Muslims rebelled against patriarchy, misogyny, polygyny, marriage with pre-pubescent girls, imperialism, despotism, racism, sexism, slavery, concubinage, sexual segregation, and the veil. The opponents of misogynistic Islam put up a fierce fight. The revolted in a hundred and one ways. Signs of resistance are scattered throughout Islamic history. Simply because sexist slave master Islam prevailed does not mean it was the religion's true and divinely intended interpretation.

Being committed to Islam means adhering to the elevated moral and ethical message of the Qur'an and the moral teachings of the Prophet Muhammad, and striving to reach their ultimate objectives. This is particularly critical when Salafi-Wahhabi-Takfiri extremists and terrorists have not only "called for the reinstatement of slavery as an integral part of the *shari'ah* in an Islamic state" (Clarence-Smith n. date), but have reimplemented it with horrific, dehumanizing, consequences. Those who fail to do so, and defend so-called "Islamic" slavery, refusing to recognize that slavery and concubinage are objectively, intrinsically, and inherently wrong are the ones who are morally compromised.

Simply because the practice of slavery was legalized does not mean that it was right. Decriminalizing alcohol and drugs do not make their abuse right. Decriminalizing fornication, adultery, and prostitution does not make them moral. They remain among the most serious of sins. The same can be said of slavery and concubinage. Muslims should have the minds and morals to assert, as Nathaniel Matthew does, that "the traffic, past and present, of human beings in bondage was, and is unethical, immoral and illegal." And most do. In fact, "Western notions of abolitionist freedom have already fused with Islamic values, and ... it is dangerous

Conclusions 211

to try to extract one from the other." And it is the most natural of things. As 'Ali, Socrates, and Plato said, "Do not force your children to be raised the same way you have been raised, for they have been born for a different age from yours" (Hosni).

"To achieve the eradication of slavery throughout the world and to avoid the danger of its resurgence," warns Clarence-Smith, "people of all beliefs should begin by uniting in humble apology for the pain and sorrow inflicted on generations of coerced and humiliated human beings" (2006: 233). Muslim scholars should be spurning and prohibiting "Islamic" slavery, not justifying, promoting, and providing excuses for it. For Freamon, the solution to this problem is not anti-Islamic. It is profoundly Islamic and Qur'anic. It involves following the overarching ethical message of the Qur'an. "If human beings shaped their actions according to the Qur'an," he writes, "it would lead to a society that is slavery-free" (Freamon 2019: 140). For Freamon, "we will see an end to slavery in the Muslim world when … Islamic principles … begin to be implemented by Muslims in a robust and internally oriented fashion" (2019: 515). For critics, it must be conceded, those principles are the ones that produced the problem in the first place. If they are sincere in their faith and principles, the abolitionist followers of the Islamic faith will need to make themselves heard. As Abdul Malik Mujahid puts it,

> Muslims around the world must be at the forefront of speaking out against slavery and rape based on God's Commandments for emancipation, Islam's emphasis on establishing an egalitarian society, and the Prophet's movement for the liberation of slaves. Our voices must be louder than those of groups like Daesh and Boko Haram.

What is more, they need to be louder than Jonathan A.C. Brown, who wonders if slavery is in the DNA of Islam (204). It may be in the DNA of his Islam, and most forms of Islam for that matter, but it certainly is not in the DNA of the Islam followed by many other Muslims, past and present. For Chebel, slavery is not intrinsic to Islam. It is something that was grafted upon it. It is a parasite attached to a host. It is a blood-sucking, life-draining tape worm that must be expelled. It is an endoparasitoid extraterrestrial species, like the face-hugger creature from the film *Alien* (1979), which "impregnates" its host with an embryo, known as a "chest-buster." After a gestation period, it erupts violently from its host's chest, resulting in the latter's death.

Regarding slavery and concubinage, we should not seek guidance from classical Sunni, Shiite, or 'Ibadi authorities. We should stick to the Qur'an, which, on this matter, was honestly interpreted by some of the Mutazilites, the Qarmatians, the Druze, the Ahmadiyyah, and the early Nation of Islam, along with the modernists, reformists, and Qur'anists, not to mention many progressive Sunni and Twelver Shiite scholars who dared to break rank from the consensus of their previous scholars. Unlike Elijah Muhammad and W.D. Fard, however, Louis

Islam & Slavery

Farrakhan (b. 1933) has failed to stand against the enslavement, rape, and slaughter of non-Muslim blacks in the Sudan.

Pro-slavery and pro-concubinage Islam is a genetically altered mutant. Unfortunately, unlike most mutants, this one has been able to reproduce and spread by some diabolical twist of faith and genetics. For the sake of humanity, and out of respect and reverence for God and His Prophet, it must be emasculated or subjected to chemical, theological, and jurisprudential castration. Those who defend and justify slavery and concubinage will bear their sin. Their millions of victims will testify against them on the Day of Judgment if one believes in such things. Otherwise, if one believes in such things, they will be reincarnated as cockroaches in their next lives. At the very least, they will go down in history in ignonimity. In the words of the Qur'an,

> Whenever a group enters Hell, it will curse the preceding one until they are all gathered inside, the followers will say about their leaders, "Our Lord! They have misled us, so multiply their torment in the Fire." He will answer, "It has already been multiplied for all, but you do not know." (7:38)

As the Prophet Muhammad asserted, let those who would make eunuchs become eunuchs themselves (Abu Dawud, Nasa'i, Hakim). May those who enslave be enslaved in Hell in the hereafter. May they suffer as they made others suffer. May justice be done. May the misguided be guided. And may God forgive those who repent, atone, and make amends for, verily, "whosoever repents and does righteous good deeds, then verily, he repents towards God with true repentance" (25:71). "Exalted is God above whatever they associate with Him!" (23:92, 28:68, 37:159). "Truth stands clear from falsehood" (2:256).

Post Scriptum

After his controversial 2017 lecture on slavery in Islam, which Umar Lee described as "a 90-minute defense of slavery which included an explicit endorsement of non-consensual sex" (Loiaconi), Dr. Jonathan A.C. Brown was reportedly bombarded "with death threats and rape threats" towards his family (Brown 2017). Such despicable acts are immoral and criminal and should be prosecuted to the fullest extent of the law. Brown has academic freedom, as do his opponents. He has the right to express his views, and others have the right to challenge them. Nobody has the right to threaten others for exercising their right to freedom of expression. In Islam, the basic principle is as follows,

> Call people to the path of your Lord with wisdom and good advice and argue with them in the most courteous way, for your Lord knows best who strays from His path, and knows best who is rightly guided. Call thou to the way of thy Lord with wisdom and fairer admonishment. And dispute with them in a way that is fairer. (16:125)

Unfortunately, this tolerant approach is not one that is shared by radical Islamists and Muslim fundamentalists. In fact, in light of his published statements, critics could argue that Brown himself engages in threats of a religious nature when he intimates that, according to Islam, Muslims who oppose slavery and concubinage are hypocrites, unbelievers, and apostates who are outside the fold of the faith. The seriousness of such accusations is not always apparent to non-Muslims; however, Muslims, who have engaged with Salafis, Wahhabis, and Takfiris, radicals and extremists, are well-aware of their implications.

Although Brown only uses the first part of the equation, "you are a hypocrite / infidel / apostate / unbeliever," critics could argue that the second part is implied: "and your blood is *halal*," namely, "it is permissible to shed your blood and take your life." This is an accurate reflection of Islamist and Jihadist ideology and practice. While he does provide grounds for *takfir*, I do not believe that Brown calls for the killing of people. The fact, however, is that there is nothing new under the sun. When the Ottomans attempted to abolish slavery, they were accused of apostasy. The grand sharif of Mecca, 'Abd al-Muttalib ibn Ghalib, revolted against them for this very reason in 1856 (Akyol 2022: 63).

Despite their differences of opinion on slavery and concubinage in Islam, neither Brown, nor his opponents deserve to be subjected to bullying, harassment, intimidation, or threats. Such behavior cannot be countenanced. In Islam, and

214   Islam & Slavery

civilized and polite society for that matter, debates, however heated or passionate, should be evidence-based. As the Qur'an says, "produce your proof if ye are truthful" (2:111; 27:64). Arguments are countered with arguments.

Academic debate does not take place on Facebook, Twitter, or social media. It takes place through peer-reviewed articles and publications. It is not violent. It is not directed at people. It is intellectual jousting. It is a game of chess. It is a battle of books. The arguments are not personal. They are not slanderous or libelous. Scholars and academics can and should disagree with each other's ideas without threatening and excommunicating one another. Let us disagree without being disagreeable.

I do not take issue with Jonathan Brown as a person. I find some of the ideas that he shares to be morally objectionable and unconscionable. I feel compelled to call them out. In fact, I sincerely believe that it is my duty to do so. I will not waste my time debating with Islamist terrorists like ISIS, Boko Haram, and others. They lack all legitimacy. I will, however, engage with Western academics and professors like Brown who claim that "the permissibility of slavery and concubinage is undeniable in the Qur'an" (Brown 2020: 196). Since they educate students and train future scholars, they hold a great deal of sway. If an ignoramus psychopath says that "slavery and concubinage are permissible in Islam," it carries no weight. Killer clowns who read *Islam for Dummies* have no credibility. However, when an influential American Muslim professor and department chair says the same thing it is even more dangerous and insidious.

My philosophical objective is to provide people, in general, and Muslims in particular, with the full spectrum on opinions on the subject of slavery in Islamic thought. I wish to give them options. In so doing, they might come to realize that Islam is not monochromatic but polychromatic. It constitutes a rich and colorful tapestry. It can be a life-giving elixir as opposed to a toxic, corrosive, reactive, and explosive poison.

As can be appreciated, I do not see eye-to-eye with Jonathan Brown on the subject of slavery and concubinage. That being said, we do agree with one another on other matters and we have both altered our views throughout our lives. Others can do so, as well. My views on slavery and concubinage in Islam could be wrong. If so, that would place me at a fork in the road. However, they could also be right. If so, others will be forced to select which path to follow. These are questions posed by Brown himself,

> Why do our scriptures condone slavery and why did our prophets practice it? How can we venerate people and texts -- the Prophets, Founding Fathers, a scripture or founding document -- that considered slavery valid or normal? And, if we see clear and egregious moral wrongs that those people and texts so conspicuously missed, whey are we venerating or honoring them in the first place? (3) ... Can't we just conclude that the Bible, Qur'an, Aristotle, etc. were wrong on slavery but still have much else to offer us? We could certainly conclude that,

> but do we usually take moral, legal or spiritual advice from those who support slavery? (9)

Such "all or nothing" thinking is neither sound nor productive. One takes what is good from any and all sources and one rejects what is not. That is how knowledge, science, and societies advance and evolve.

For the sake of transparency and balance, it should be acknowledged that Brown recanted some of his views in "Apology without Apologetics," published in *Muslim Matters* on February 16, 2017. He claimed, for example, that his quotes were taken out of context, that "rape in Islam is *haram* (prohibited)," that "non-consensual sex is wrong and forbidden in Islam," that "the *shariʿah* saw freedom as the natural state (*asl*) of all humans" and that it "aimed towards freedom." He also admitted that slavery in Islam "could become racialized" despite prior claims to the contrary. This fact, however, was already well-established for, as Chouki El Hamel has shown, "late seventeenth century Morocco did, in fact, demonstrate the exploitation of blacks and the ideological foundation for a society divided by skin color" (10). The same can be said for other parts of the Muslim world. Under the Safavids, slavery was both racialized and gendered. White women who were enslaved were used as concubines, singers, dancers, and prostitutes (Floor). Black women were used as nannies, cooks, and domestic servants (Floor). White men were used for military service (Floor). Black ones, since they were viewed as unattractive, were castrated and used as harem guards. Most eunuchs were black Africans (Floor).

Undoubtedly, "Muslims across racial, sectarian, and geographical boundaries justified enslavement mainly on religious grounds" (Azumah 233). They specifically targeted non-Muslims for enslavement. Slave raids were often directed at Christians (Floor). The fact remains, however, that in addition to religion, "light-skinned Muslims placed black Africans under a mythological curse which fettered them to servitude" (233). As Malek Chebel notes, in the collective subconscious of the Arabs, the word "slave" need not be mentioned. The very word "black" is a synonym for "slave" (47).

Brown stated in his "Apology" that "Muslims began curtailing slavery early on" and claimed that "in the 1000s, the great Persian scholar Juwayni gave a *fatwa* that slave girls captured in Central Asia should not be sold as concubines" (2017). However, as Brown wrote in his 2019/2020 book, this was not because he viewed it as illegal or immoral but because the proper procedures for capturing and distributing them were regularly ignored (2020: 89). What is more, it was a question of caution: not an outright prohibition. In his "Apology," Brown purports that "in the 1780s, the scholar-king of Senegal 'Abd al-Qadir Kan abolished slavery in his realm" (2017). This is misleading. In fact, as Brown writes in his 2019/2020 book, Kan only "prohibited selling any slave to a Muslim trader the seller thought might sell them to Europeans" (2020: 208). According to Brown, he did not abolish slavery in his land. For Ware, however, 'Abd al-Qadir Kan's goal was more ambitious, namely, ending the Atlantic slave trade from his territory as well as emancipating the slaves with it, namely, "abolishing the institution of slavery" (114). He even notes that Thomas Clarkson (d. 1846), the Christian abolitionist, was "a great admirer of Senegambia's Muslim abolitionists" (244).

Brown asserts that Ahmed Bey (1784-1851) banned the slave trade in Tunis and emancipated all the slaves in his realm in 1846 (2017). Omar Suleiman may claim that "Tunisia abolished slavery in 1846, nineteen years before the thirteenth amendment was ratified in the United States" all he wants. However, in his 2019/2020 book, Brown explains that this was done under European pressure (228), that it was based on the notion that slavery is "permissible but not required" (229), and that it was prohibited in that particular case because it was violating the stipulations of the *shariʿah* (230-231). So, when Omar Suleiman suggests that the case of Tunisia is "a closer representation of the Islamic tradition," he is most certainly correct. However, it was not an absolute and unconditional prohibition of slavery. It came from a position that viewed slavery, if properly practiced, as sanctioned by the *shariʿah*. It leaves the door open to its reintroduction.

Finally, Brown concludes that "as a Muslim today, I can say emphatically that slavery is wrong, and that Islam prohibits it" and that "this has been the consensus of the *ʿulama*'" (2017). To clarify, he only states that slavery is currently wrong; not that "Islamic" slavery was wrong in the past. What was done by Muslims in the past to blacks, Imazighen, Europeans, and other populations that were enslaved and whose women were turned in sex toys and trollops, was perfectly permissible in his mind according to Islam. If Muslims could do it, then so could non-Muslims. And who cares if blacks, Imazighen, and others also practiced slavery in an attenuated form. Most cultures of the world practice pimping and prostitution. That does not justify it. For many believers and thinkers, slavery and concubinage belong in the same category of major and mortal sins such as murder, theft, fornication, and adultery.

If Brown is right, and "Islamic" slavery was not inherently wrong, then Muslims have no moral authority to condemn the slave trade of the Christians, Jews, and others. What? Muslims were not as bad at doing something bad? The claim that Muslims treated their slaves, who were domestic servants, better than Christian Americans, and even as part of their families, is hardly a consolation. Nannies, cooks, and maids did not have it as bad as sex slaves, military slaves, or plantation slaves. A house nigger was still a house nigger and they were referred precisely in the same derogatory way in Arabic and other languages. What about those engaged in forced labor? Those who were worked to death? Those who were forced to kill and conquer for their masters? Those who were forced to have sex? Those used as reproductive factories? And those who were shared with and sold to other men? Some pimps are less brutal than others. They are still pimps. Slavery is slavery and whores are whores. They are not sex workers. They are sex slaves. The righteous stand on the side of the victims; not the victimizers.

If Muslim men can take non-Muslim women as sex slaves, then non-Muslim men can do the same to Muslim women. Wicked is what wicked does. For this reason the Mujahidin of Afghanistan refused to enslave Russian women. As 'Abdullah Azzam (1941-1989), the founding father of the global *jihad* movement, and the godfather of Islamist terrorism, reasoned, "If we take one Russian woman, they will take a hundred Muslim women and violate them" (Yehoshua, Green, and Agron). Since it could not be regulated and could lead to abuses, senior al-Qaeda ideologue, 'Attiyat Allah al-Libi (1969-2011) also rejected sexual slavery. Moreover, some Jabhat al-Nusrah leaders vehemently oppose sexual slavery, viewing it as rape, a serious crime, and a major sin in Islam. This is incredible. When it comes to slavery and concubinage, some Islamist extremists and terrorists stand on a higher plateau that so-called traditional Muslim scholars and academics.

Brown may have claimed that "Islam prohibits slavery" in 2017; however, he argues the opposite in his 2019/2020 book. Its central thesis is that Islam does indeed permit slavery and concubinage. And while he described slavery as "a universal wrong across time and space" in 2017, he was seemingly referring to "our American slavery" that was "a manifestation of absolute domination of one human being by another" (Brown 2017). He does not appear to have been condemning "Islamic" slavery as a comparable evil which it most certainly was. It is like arguing whether the German genocide was better than the Cambodian genocide or if the Rwandan genocide was worse than the Bosnian genocide. Genocide is genocide.

The Qur'an and the Talmud are clear that taking an innocent life is as grievous a sin as killing all of humanity (5:32). If we cannot defend the death of one innocent person, how can we excuse the millions of deaths produced by the Muslim slave trade? What is most scandalous about slavery in the lands of Islam is not the quantity, notes Chebel, but its very principle (87). For Chebel, the slavery practiced by Muslims was monstrous and barbaric (87). The slaves of Muslims suffered as much as the slaves of Christians. Listening to Gnawa lyrics is like listening to Bob Marley or the Blues. The blacks of Morocco, descendants of slaves, continue to sing the songs of their ancestors in which they chronicled the hardship and privations of exile and slavery. "Our religion is not slavery," they sang, "we are the people of liberty!"

Brown may have claimed in 2017 that there was scholarly consensus among Muslims on the prohibition of slavery. However, his 2019/2020 book insists that no such agreement exists. He stresses that the "consensus on abolition" claim was novel and only appeared in the past two decades (Brown 2020: 252). He wonders whether it stands up and holds water (253-254). He concludes that "it does not seem likely" and that "a number of major, widely and well-regarded *'ulama'* would undermine it" (253-254). As Brown stresses, "leading contemporary scholars such as Buti, Qaradawi, and Usmani do not consider *riqq* [slavery] to be inherently wrong such that it would be branded *haram* [prohibited] under the Shariah" (2020: 254). "For them," writes Brown, slavery "is a legitimate component of the Islamic legal and institutional heritage that was legitimately employed in the past and could well be used in the future" (2020: 254). For Brown, the belief, shared by most of humanity, that all slavery is evil is the product of an "upstart consensus" (8). Not so. As Nathaniel Mathews notes,

> Formerly enslaved Muslims also helped to reshape community perceptions of slavery. In East Africa especially, the abolition of slavery coincided with the new popularity of Sufi brotherhoods as tools for the mass propagation of Islam. Sufism became the language by which formerly servile people appropriated the message of Islam to undermine the *ijma*' around the social status of slaves and ex-slaves.

> In Lamu, Kenya, the 'Alawi shaykh Habib Saleh angered the town's former slaveholding elite by teaching ex-slaves. In Bagamoyo, Tanzania, an ex-slave from the Congo rose to become a Sufi shaykh and one of the most knowledgeable scholars of the region; he faced strong opposition from former slave owners.

> The first five decades of the twentieth century in Africa revealed Muslims reshaping the consensus on slavery. This process of reshaping *ijma*' was not only an elite scholarly one; it included formerly enslaved Muslims, who contested their rights within the idioms of Islam, molding Islamic cultural repertoires to critique the exclusionary social practices of Muslim elites.

> Traditions, Islam included, are not closed caskets but open conversations and debates often characterized by shifting notions of what is permissible. Slavery is one such shifting notion. There is nothing in the Islamic tradition mandating slavery. Thus, the overwhelming majority of Muslims today find slavery distasteful and have no desire to practice it.

As far as his opponents are concerned, the ideology espoused by Brown -- one that legitimizes slavery and concubinage based on manifestly twisted interpretations of the Qur'an, falsehoods attributed to the Prophet Muhammad, and the self-serving rules of sexist and misogynistic medieval scholars -- is a carcinogenic Islam that should not be allowed to metastasize. It is an invasive weed that must be uprooted. It is a Sheriff John Brown Islam that must be shot down: by scholarly and spiritual means, of course. It is an Islam that believes that morality is determined by Islamic jurisprudence when, in fact, what we need is an Islamic jurisprudence determined by morality. As Mohsen Kadivar, the Iranian *mujtahid*, explains,

> Justice and reason are not religious values or subordinate to religion, rather they are prior to religion and fall in line of the causes of religious law. It is religion that must be just and reasonable, not that justice and reason be religious… Humans with their dependency on their own pure innate nature choose a religion which is just and reasonable.

The scholars at the service of Imperial Islam place texts above principles when, in reality, texts should be accepted or rejected based on whether they meet moral standards. Whether they defend "Islamic" slavery in theory or practice, universally or temporally, they should consider the Golden Rule: do not do unto others as you would not have them do unto you.

Defenders of "Islamic" slavery should ask themselves: "Would you like to be enslaved?" "Would you like to be castrated?" "Would you like your son to be turned into a eunuch?" "Would you like your wife or daughter to be taken captive by foreigners of another faith, dragged to another country, subjected to genital mutilation, paraded naked, poked, and prodded, auctioned off to the highest bidding pervert, and forced to work as a sex slave? If so, you should cry "all praise be to Satan" instead of "all praise be to God." If not, then take refuge in God from Satan the Rejected.

Slavery is not an essential and integral part of Islam. The laws that jurists developed were incidental. Abolishing slavery does not damage the Islamic religion. On the contrary, it strengthens and realigns it with Qur'anic ethical ideals and higher objectives. It helps it reach the goal to which it always aimed. After all, noted Diakho, "It is admitted by all jurists and specialists in the foundations of jurisprudence... that 'protecting the dignity and honor (*al-'ird*) of human beings is one of the five higher objectives of the *shari'ah*'" (27). The classical Islamic jurisprudence regarding slavery does not meet this goal.

The dominant and domineering versions of Islam have little to nothing in common with original Islam, the Islam initiated and disseminated by the Prophet Muhammad. Pre-Islamic and un-Islamic winds dragged dust, garbage, slag, and other elements alien to the Qur'anic essence into the Islamic religion. Our task is, God willing, to help bring Islam back to its origin and essence. And for that megaproject, the hundreds of tons of un-Islamic elements that turned it into a multiform mixture of tragicomic nonsense ranging from "simple" configurations and non-Islamic procedures to tremendous deformations, protrusions, eccentricities, and horrible elements that have nothing to do with the original message, must continue to be removed. The purification process relies on reason, justice, wisdom, and revelation. Muslims must emancipate themselves from mental slavery.

As for Brown's penchant for provoking Muslims to criticize the Prophet Muhammad, many of his critics would argue, without trepidation, that a man who does not own a slave is morally superior to a man that does in the same fashion that a man who does not have sex with children is morally superior to one who does. And they would ask, how is having four wives and a limitless number of sex slaves compatible with morality, chastity, equality, the dignity of the human person, respect for women, the sanctity of marriage, and the traditional nuclear family? It is religiously and institutionally sanctioned hedonism and debauchery that serves the interests of sexist, lust-crazed, women-hating men who view females as servants, sexual objects, property, chattel, and livestock. And no, Muslim critics of slavery and concubinage do not insult the Messenger of God.

220   Islam & Slavery

They refuse to believe the lies that have been attributed to a man of "moral excellence" (68:4; 33:21), a "mercy to the worlds" (21:107), a person who was "kind and merciful" (9:128), and a "lamp that dispels darkness" (33:46). Does the hat fit or does it not? If not, it is time to toss it in the trash and replace the knock-off, fake, and replica with the genuine article.

Moral Muslims with minds do not seek to replace the Muhammad of the *hadith* and history with the Muhammad of the Qur'an, an empty vessel, to fill it with their liberal, Western, post-enlightenment, secular, humanistic values. As far as they are concerned, Muhammad was the vessel of the Qur'an. The Qur'an is Muhammad and Muhammad is the Qur'an. In other words, he was the embodiment of the Word of God, the Qur'an walking, and the Qur'an talking. Any tradition that agrees with the Qur'an, they gladly accept. However, they reject anything and everything that opposes its moral and ethical message.

Even if we accept that the Prophet Muhammad did not explicitly prohibit slavery and planned to eradicate it in incremental steps over time, that does not suggest that he supported it. Temporarily tolerating something while ameliorating it is not the same as endorsing and condoning it. The purpose of regulating prostitution is not to promote it, and profit from it, but to protect prostitutes and reduce the spread of sexually transmitted infections. Women working in brothels or street corners are safer than those chained to beds in dark basements. It is easier to police. The purpose of regulating alcohol is to control its quality and avoid cases of poisoning. The purpose of regulating pornography is to provide some oversight, thereby preventing it from being produced underground, where women are at increased risk. The fact that social workers try to help sex workers does not mean they support human trafficking, prostitution, and pimping. Feeding the homeless does not mean that one endorses homelessness. Treating drug addicts does not mean that one defends the drug trade. Human beings try to help those in need directly. They also strive for social justice by advocating policy change and lobbying for legislation.

Slavery and concubinage were a world-scale problem. No single person or nation could have stopped such practices. It required the combined efforts of legions of actors, activists, and power brokers centuries to prohibit slavery according to international law. It took the might of entire empires to convince the world to abandon slavery using a combination of moral arguments, pressure, and coercion. However, such is diplomacy, both soft and hard. Study the *Chronology of World Slavery* and see how long it took us to reach where we are. It is preposterous to expect that the Prophet Muhammad could have single-handedly stopped slavery. As Ali Dashti (1897-1982), the Iranian writer, stated, "It is absurd ... to argue... that the Prophet Mohammed ought to have acted like Abraham Lincoln in regard to slavery" (182). It is only fair to ask: "why didn't Islam prohibit slavery?" if we ask it of everyone else. "Why didn't Judaism prohibit it?" Why didn't Christianity prohibit it? Why didn't Hinduism, Taoism, and Buddhism not prohibit it?

Muhammad did not have the means to abolish the slave trade. He did not have a standing, salaried, army. Most soldiers went to war in search of a share of the booty. Although he had some representatives here and there, Muhammad did not have a government with ministers and civil servants. Of course, he wanted to see an end to slavery and concubinage. However, there was not a glimmer of hope that such a thing could take place on the distant horizon on a worldwide scale. He did, however, do everything he could to gradually eradicate the practice in the areas under his direct rule. Regrettably, his policy was not followed by any of those who succeeded him due to various circumstances. Had Muslims followed the instructions of the Prophet Muhammad Tamim Ansary believes that "slavery might have ended in the Muslim world in the early days of the khalifate" (51). "Instead," he notes, "Muslim societies regressed in this matter" (51). "Since Islam condemned slavery," asks Fatima Mernissi, "how was it able to continue to exist?" (151). Her answer is succinct:

> Through linguistic and legal tricks, as always. There would be quibbles about the identity of a slave. Islam forbids that a Muslim be reduced to slavery? Never mind, we will look elsewhere. It will be non-Muslims who will be made slaves. The era of the great Muslim conquests was used to reduce conquered peoples to slavery. (151)

As can be appreciated, a comparison of what Brown said in his 2017 lecture, what he said in his "Apology," and what he wrote in his 2019/2020 book, suggests to critics that Brown engages in a dual discourse. For them, his 2017 "Apology" does not appear to be an apology but an effort at spin and damage control. It was a public relations exercise. Had he sincerely recanted some of his views that should have been reflected in his book in 2019 and 2020. He wrote, "slavery, *riqq* included, is illegal and should remain so" (282). However, on what Islamic basis does he make that determination? That "God wishes freedom" and that "Islam can give no reason this should not be done" (264). What a limp, impotent, and sterile argument. After all, he devotes over four hundred pages to defending "Islamic" slavery and concubinage and playing the role of the Devil's Advocate. He stressed that, unlike ISIS and other Islamists, he does not advocate a revival of *riqq*. However, his book serves as a legal and theological validation of "Islamic" slavery. As much as Islamic sources may encourage masters to treat their slaves kindly, can one truly be kind to those robbed of their first rights of humanity? (Azumah 167).

While Muslims readily claim that "God judges actions according to intentions" (Bukhari and Muslims), some even use this argument to justify suicide bombings directed at defenseless men, women, and children. Brown claims that he intended to provide a history of the Muslim view on slavery. In his view, "these people criticizing me don't know the difference between the past and the present tense" (Strauss). However, his 2017 lecture and 2019/2020 book indicate otherwise.

Presenting arguments pasts is one thing. Defending and justifying them is another as is trying to hamstring the arguments of Muslim abolitionists. More disturbing is asserting that those who do not share the classical Muslim view on slavery and concubinage are outside the fold of the Islamic faith. Intent aside, there is also the issue of impact. How was *Slavery & Islam* received and perceived? Was it viewed merely as descriptive or as prescriptive? Far too many Muslims have viewed it as the latter.

Some Muslim reviewers praised him for standing against Western ideas and influences and defending their belief in "Islamic" slavery. Others argued that it was only natural for slavery to resurface with the breakdown of society due to environmental degradation or worldwide war. One such reviewer expressed that,

> if slavery ever comes back, it will be in some kind of post-civilizational collapse scenario where... human society will naturally coalesce into a hierarchy, and a new slave class will appear to work the fields, do menial tasks, and for females, provide sexual pleasure for the men who are at the top. (Younus)

The fact of the matter is slavery is alive and well throughout the world. White slavery is at an all time high. Child sex trafficking rings are prospering more than ever. Traditional, "Islamic" slavery thrives in the Sudan, Mauritania, and wherever the Salafi Jihadists find a foothold. For critical thinkers and close readers, it is Brown who does not know the difference between the past and present.

The style of slavery that Brown defends as "Islamic" is the same that exists today. It features chattel slavery, in which humans are bought and sold like property. It includes hereditary slavery, namely, the children of enslaved women. It features the enslavement of captives in war zones. It also consists of children and women kidnapped in slave raids by human trafficking rings. It includes forced marriage and marriage by abduction. Finally, it involves women and children who are bought and sold on the black market.

Every "legal" avenue for acquiring slaves according to Islamic law is available today, not only on the dark web and black market, but on the open market in parts of the world. Apologists for slavery should meet and speak with victims of the modern-day slave trade, "Islamic" or otherwise. They should hear the cries, and wipe the tears, of black, Muslim girls, who are raped by their "white" Arab and Berber Muslim masters in Mauritania. They should speak with the victims of Muslim pimps, groomers, and rape gangs in the United Kingdom and France. They should show some empathy for the girls and women that were abducted, sexually trafficked, sold, bought, and raped by Islamists in Sudan, Syria, Iraq, Algeria, Nigeria, Somalia, the Philippines, and elsewhere. They should sign up for some sensitivity training.

Do apologists for "Islamic" slavery have any idea how triggering their posts, comments, speeches, and books can be to some men, women, and children? Are they devoid of compassion, mercy, morals, or common sense? As woke wackos would say, their apology for "Islamic" slavery, however theoretical, descriptive, and historical, inflicts violence upon enslaved and trafficked men, women, and children. For some critics, Muslim converts who support, defend, or justify "Islamic" slavery would have been better off remaining Christians. Jesus taught the faithful to love others, not attack, slaughter, conquer, capture, enslave, and rape them. Otherwise, they could have chosen to follow the Sufi path of love. They can also correct course, as may others have done, including myself.

Another reviewer, İbrahim Kılıçaslan, explains that in Brown's mind "a Muslim's framework of morality should not be guided by the morality produced by the post-Industrial Revolution Western values." Instead, "the pre-modern Islamic scriptural tradition must outweigh other sources of morality" (272). In other words, modern Muslims should learn their values from medieval Muslim misogynists, the sexist and racist jurists who supported slavery, human trafficking, and sexual bondage, instead of the Qur'an itself.

For the Islamist radicals at *Muslim Skeptic*, "slavery, conquest, patriarchal authority... are parts of Islam, as encapsulated in the Qur'an, Sunna, and the scholarly tradition." As for 'A'ishah, they insist that "there is no legitimate scholarly disagreement on her being six years of age when she married the Prophet." The extremists at the site assert that,

> What Brown should be commended for in this essay is resisting the temptation to condemn slavery as inherently evil. Brown seems to be aware of the fact that condemning slavery as inherently evil would be tantamount to condemning the Prophet and Islam as a whole. After all, the Prophet owned slaves. And Islam permitted owning slaves.

For some readers, Brown's *Slavery & Islam* is an instruction manual for slavery and concubinage that should be studied in every madrasah and Islamic Sunday school. By refusing to condemn the past for the sake of the future, Brown sets a dangerous precedent. If we do not learn from mistakes past, we are bound to repeat them. Brown's book, whether he likes it or not, inspires traffickers and slave masters. It gives them a sense of legitimacy. It assuages their consciences. It helps them sleep better at night.

Sadly, finding Muslim scholars who are willing to support the thesis that slavery and concubinage are *haram* is a challenging task. In contrast, Brown's book has received endorsements from people who could only be described as radical Islamists, jihadists, and terrorist apologists. Does Daesh, Boko Haram, al-Shabab, or other Salafi-Wahhabi-Takfiri insurgents and terrorists, support my stance? Do "Muslim" rape gangs back my position? Or do they agree with Brown that God, the Qur'an, the Prophet, the *sunnah*, and the *sharia'h* permit human bondage and sexual slavery? Whose book would these people back? Certainly not mine.

Rather than modify his views, or soften his tone, after his controversial 2017 lecture, Jonathan A.C. Brown seems to have strengthened his stance out of supposed respect for the Muslim tradition. While he admitted in *Slavery & Islam* that "Muslims can choose, and have chosen, to eliminate *riqq* as a legal phenomenon" and that "the Prophet would most likely be very pleased with that," he insisted that "*riqq* is not grossly and intrinsically wrong" (274). In his view, "slavery is morally wrong because it has become customary to consider it morally wrong" (274). As he stresses, he has "no qualms about condemning all forms of what is conventionally termed 'slavery' today" (275). Presumably that would include sex trafficking, child sex trafficking, forced labor, bonded labor or debt bondage, domestic servitude, forced child labor, and the unlawful recruitment and use of child soldiers. Traditional "Islamic" slavery included all of the above. However, in addition, it forced enslaved adults into military slavery. With all due respect, what is wrong now was wrong then.

Brown believes that it is "most likely" that the Prophet would support the legal abolition of slavery. If the Messenger of God was a man of "moral excellence" (68:4; 33:21), a "mercy to the worlds" (21:107), and a "lamp that dispels darkness" (33:46), who was "kind and merciful" (9:128), I have no doubt that he would be horrified by the crimes committed in the name of Islam. Not only would the Prophet Muhammad be pleased with abolition -- a plan he put into motion -- but he would be displeased that it took Muslims so long to do so. If God is indeed, the Most Compassionate, the Most Merciful, and the Most Loving, how could He condone the horrors of slavery? Does God not care about human suffering? For Shabbir Ally, the specialist in Qur'anic exegesis, the answer is self-evident: "Yes, God will be pleased that the world has abolished slavery and concubinage. Also, God will be pleased that Muslims had progressed their stance on slavery and concubinage currently."

Brown also stressed that slavery is "not grossly and intrinsically wrong" (274) If it is not wrong, why outlaw it? Wrong is wrong regardless of what laws say. Domestic violence was only outlawed in the Western world a few decades ago. That does not mean that it was not a sin to beat one's wife before it was criminalized. Adultery is wrong irrespective of whether it is criminalized. Merely because it is legal to marry and have intercourse with prepubescent girls in places like Yemen does not make it morally right. Slavery is not right merely because it is legal. At what point was it right to engage in slave raids and aggressive imperialistic wars, enslave human beings, and condemn them to a life of physical and sexual servitude?

Brown claims that it is only now perceived as morally wrong because "it has become customary to consider it morally wrong" (274). Sorry, but opposing slavery sounds like a good custom to me. Slavery apologists, "Islamic" and otherwise, contend that opponents of slavery are projecting modern values on pre-modern terms. They pretend that the "benign" and "beneficial" slavery in the Muslim world was entirely different from the type that prevailed in the Americas. They ignore the fact that plantation and agricultural slavery did exist in the Muslim world and that its conditions, in southern Iraq, were, by all accounts, even worse than those in the southern United States. What is more, black slaves in the Americas were not routinely castrated or victims of female genital mutilation. People have opposed slavery throughout history. Bartolomé de las Casas (1484-1566), a Spanish clergyman and historian, was simply sickened by the institution and petitioned the Spanish Crown to put it to an end in all of its forms. The victims of slavery, throughout the world, all denounced it. Were they imposing alien ideas from another era?

The enslavement of whites, blacks, and others -- men, women, and children -- in the name of Islam, by Muslim hypocrites, oppressors, sinners, and criminals, was morally wrong. "Islamic" slavery was as abominable as "Christian" slavery. "Islamic" slavery, it should be stressed, was no more "Islamic" than "Christian" slavery was Christian. Muhammad is no more to blame than Christ. Christian slavers and abolitionists read the same Bible. The same goes for Muslim slavers and abolitionists. They read the same Qur'an. However, they came to radically different conclusions. Pour water on a clean person, it comes out clean. Pour it on an unclean person, it comes out filthy. The interpretation depends on the interpreter. Meaning is mediated.

What was done to blacks was wrong, irrespective of whether it was done by Muslims or Christians. It is immaterial if it was done in the New World or the Old World. We cannot tell blacks that what was done to their ancestors by Christians was wrong but that what was done to them by Muslims was right. We cannot say that slavery only became wrong after it was abolished in the Muslim world but that the slavery that took place before the ban was right. It was wrong all along. Laws lag behind moral and ethics. In many cases, they are in open conflict. Legal evolution takes time. Nobody, Muslim or Christian, should be trying to defend and reimplement medieval laws. We can study and analyze them, but we should not try to emulate them. Let us be moral and modern Homo sapiens, not primitive cave-dwelling Neanderthals. The journey to God is vertical, not horizontal. We must move up, not down. Life is movement. Inertia is death. The spiritual path is a pilgrimage of self-perfection in which souls are supposed to acquire the names and attributes of God.

As Brown makes manifest, he is not prepared to denounce the mass-scale slavery that Muslims practiced from the seventh century until it was outlawed in the nineteenth and twentieth centuries. In fact, he is unapologetic. "I feel no inadequacy in my religion's late arrival to the abolitionist front" (275). No human being with a conscience or any moral compass can stand before the millions of victims of the "Islamic" slave trade on the Day of Judgment and tell them that they got what they deserved. "What was done to you, o souls of slaves -- the slaughter, the abduction, the beatings, the rapes, and the forced labor -- was not 'grossly and intrinsically wrong!'"

Malek Chebel, the Algerian philosopher and anthropologist of religions, showed a far greater sense of humanity when, speaking of slaves in the lands of Islam, acknowledged that "their shame is our shame" (492). Chebel admitted that his study of slavery in the Muslim world changed him. He was no longer the same person after he completed it. He was changed humanly and intellectually (291). He is not the only one who has been inexorably marked and altered for life.

Instead of defending slavery and claiming that "almost all moral authorities in human history thought it was right" (9), Barnaby Crowcroft suggests that Brown should have answered "some of the great outstanding questions in this field: for example, how far a philosophical system that... sanctions enslavement... can accept universalist conceptions, such as ... equality." After all, since "Jonathan Brown was attacked by pundits" after his 2017 lecture, "this was his chance to provide a scholar's reply." "Instead," complains Crowcroft, "he has given us three hundred pages of amateur epistemology and callow whataboutery." This leaves one question hanging: "Will a real Islamic scholar please stand up?" Many have.

Sadaf F. Jaffer (b. 1983), the South Asian American scholar of Islam and elected official, was "frankly appalled by Professor Brown's comments that minimized the severity of the institution of slavery, as well as the importance of consent in sexual relationships" (Strauss). "As scholars," she notes,

> it is important that we teach Islam as a human and historical phenomenon. It is not acceptable to simply relativize the concepts of slavery, human autonomy, and consent, to the point where they have no meaning. We have to think about the impact of our comments on our students and the university community. (Strauss)

In response to Brown's views on slavery, Edip Yüksel, the Qur'an commentator, denounced him as "a fraud" whose job is "to promote fabricated *hadith* against the Qur'an to keep the 'Muslim world' backward.'" Yüksel accused Brown of "promoting *hadith* books that teach as religion: slavery, stoning to death, sex slaves, pedophilia, killing heretics, forcing people to pray, in sum, every evil committed by ISIS!"

Although it is legitimate to present the classical view of mainstream Islam on slavery, Ayesha S. Chaudhry points out that "looking at the past is always a selective act" (Strauss). If we are to follow an example from the Prophet Muhammad, she stresses, it would be freeing Bilal, a black slave, and placing him in a position of prominence (Strauss). "The other alternative," she notes, "is to look at what living Muslims are doing. There are 1.6 or 1.7 billion Muslims living in the world today, and their practice also has an authoritative status." "Slavery is an institution," notes Chaudhry, "and Muslims as an overwhelming majority believe that slavery is illegal and immoral. So, Jack Brown arguing that it is not a moral evil stands in contrast with what the majority of Muslims believe" (Strauss).

Finally, although Mustafa Akyol found Jonathan A.C. Brown's work refreshing, in that it acknowledged Islam's role in slavery, and was not apologetic or denialist, the Turkish author came to opposite conclusions. For Akyol, the Qur'anic verses referencing slavery are strikingly contextual and reflected the reality of the time. For him, the crucial question is: "Does the Qur'an's reference to slaves mean that in an ideal Muslim society, there should be slaves?" (Akyol 2022: 161). It most certainly does not.

As Muhammad Diakho has demonstrated in *L'eslavage en Islam: entre les traditions arabes et les principes de l'Islam* [*Slavery in Islam: Between Arab Traditions and the Principles of Islam*], 1) slavery in Islam is rooted in the racial distinction between Arabs, who cannot be enslaved, and all other populations of the world, who can; 2) that the enslavement of prisoners of *jihad* is new ruling, and one that was added to the three options provided in the Qur'an and the *sunnah*; 3) that *jihad* was a pretext used to wage war against populations, Muslims included, with the specific purpose of reducing them to slavery; 3) that concubinage or *tassarri* is not rooted in the Qur'an; and that the Qur'anic and prophetic positions were against taking more than four women, fornicating, and forcing women into sexual corruption, simply skirted; 4) that a distinction needs to be made between slavery as a socio-cultural phenomenon and slavery as an ideology; 5) and that the respect for the pious predecessors cannot override the rules established by the Qur'an and the *sunnah* (17-21).

Rather than view their opinions as universally binding, notes Diakho, the companions of the Prophet viewed them as applying to particular situations (21). What is more, they were far from infallible. In fact, as Diakho has demonstrated, "certain companions of the Prophet were indeed responsible for reintegrating slavery -- which had been programmed to disappear -- into the system of Islamic law" (19-20). The main culprit was 'Umar ibn al-Khattab (d. 644) and his underlings like 'Amr ibn al-'As (d. 664). Rather than rely upon the Qur'an and continue the revolution initiated by the Prophet Muhammad, jurists recovered *jahiliyyah* practices and reintegrated them into a dying Islamic ideology (247). The message of the Prophet Muhammad was subverted. The counterrevolutionaries triumphed. Emancipatory Islam was emasculated. The ship of salvation was skuttled. The enemies of the Muhammad danced upon his grave as they hunted down his descendants to ensure that his true teachings never surfaced again.

All praise is due to God, the Good, to whom no evil can be attributed, and blessed be His Prophet, the pure, the merciful, and the just, who was above any of the blemishes attributed to him by the internal enemies of Islam. "Speak truth" (33:70), says God in the Qur'an, and "Speak justice" (4:135). Freedom and justice for all. As Master W.D. Fard taught, we believe in Justice, Freedom, Equality, and Islam, and we resoundingly reject the Islam of Innovation of the Umayyads, 'Abbasids, and their successors, as well as its modern manifestation in the West, Klansman Islam! Get your Kloran out of our Koran! The religion with God is Equality, and there is no equality in slavery. As Riffat Hassan observes,

> It is a profound irony and tragedy that the Qur'an, despite its strong affirmation of human equality and the need to do justice to all of Allah's creatures, has been interpreted by many Muslims, both ancient and

> modern, as sanctioning various forms of human inequality and even enslavement. (1990 n page)

Muslims must have the moral integrity and ethical fortitude to assert in absolute fashion that slavery and concubinage were wrong, are wrong, and will forever be wrong. What was done to black people, and other enslaved populations, by Muslims and non-Muslims, was unconscionable. What was done to women was insufferable. Was the taking of "comfort women" by the Japanese imperialists before and during World War II permissible? After all, it is "undeniable" that the Qur'an permits concubinage.

Not only should the door to slavery and concubinage be slammed and bolted shut once and for all, but it should be bricked up. No crack, crevasse, or aperture should be left open in Islamic jurisprudence that could potentially allow any remote possibility of its revival. Past rulings on these matters must be denounced and rejected. The laws governing "Islamic" slavery and concubinage should be permanently removed from manuals of jurisprudence. They should no longer be taught as universal and immutable laws, awaiting the moment for their reintroduction.

It is a shame, an abomination, and a disgrace, that virtually every Muslim scholar consulted, including blacks, believe in the permissibility of slavery and concubinage, and that only an infinitesimally small number of them are willing to assert, in no uncertain terms, that they are prohibited. Even some of those who publicly claim that Islam put an end to slavery admit the opposite in private. They speak with forked tongues. This can lead many to conclude that Islam is beyond redemption and cannot be reformed and redeemed. Islam, however, is not a person. Islam does not speak. Islam does not think. Islam is what Muslims do with it. The shaykhs, muftis, imams, and "ayatollahs" are not the representatives of God on earth. They are not the guardians and owners of Islam. Reason is the representative of God in each human being. Every single person is a viceregent of God on earth imbued with a pure, primordial, nature. If the so-called scholars of Islam are not fit to lead, then they can, will, and should be supplanted by the Muslim masses, the vast majority of whom oppose the evil and inequity of slavery and concubinage. We were made in the image of God. Human beings are the mirrors in which God sees Him/Herself. How, then, can we enslave and exploit one another?

Appendix 1

Grounds for the Prohibition
of Slavery and Concubinage

Select Ethical Evidence from the Qur'an

1. The Qur'an calls for justice. "Stand firmly for justice" (4:135); "Do not exceed the limits" (2:190); "Upon you is [responsibility] for yourselves" (5:105); "Do not incline to those who do injustice" (11:113). Slavery and concubinage are unjust. Opposing them is just.
2. The Qur'an condemns sin. "Do not cooperate in sin" (5:2). Slavery and concubinage are sins against God and crimes against humanity.
3. The Qur'an condemns aggression: "Do not cooperate in... aggression" (5:2). The slave trade was an act of global aggression. Sexual relations with enslaved girls and women is a form of sexual aggression.
4. The Qur'an condemns transgressors. "God loves not transgressors" (2:190; 7:55). Enslavers, slave traders, and slave owners are transgressors.
5. The Qur'an condemns oppression (2:217). It states that oppression is worse than slaughter (2:217). There is no question that slavery and concubinage are oppressive and murderous.
6. The Qur'an condemns excess. "God loves not those given to excess" (5:90). The harem culture is one of excess. The men involved in such practices hoard human beings; thereby depriving them from others or depriving such people of their inherent right to freedom.
7. The Qur'an condemns trespassers. "God loves not those who trespass bounds" (7:55). Enslaving human people, trafficking, and exploiting them is to trespass the bounds of human dignity.
8. The Qur'an condemns corruption. "God loves not corruption" (2:205; 5:67; 28:77). Slavery and concubinage are the pinnacles of personal and societal corruption.
9. The Qur'an condemns wrongdoers. "God loves not the wrongdoers" (3:57; 3:140; 42:40). Those who participate in the slave and sex trade are wrongdoers.
10. The Qur'an condemns waste. "God loves not the wasters" (6:141; 7:31). The slave trade cost millions of human lives. During slave raids, thousands would

be slaughtered, including men and elderly people, only to take hundreds of boys, girls, and women as captives. Eighty to ninety percent of enslaved black Africans died before reaching the slave markets in the Middle East. In addition, the production of eunuchs on an industrial scale resulted in death rates as high as ninety percent. Slave traders showed a callous contempt for human life.

11. The Qur'an condemns materialism. "God loves not those who exult in riches" (28:76). The slave economy and the harem culture, in which ownership of men and women are signs of wealth and power, is the peak of materialism.

12. The Qur'an condemns treachery. "God loves not the treacherous" (8:58). The slave trade is the peak of treachery. The same goes for the sex trade.

13. The Qur'an condemns perfidy and criminality. "God loves not one given to perfidy and crime" (4:107). All those involved in the slave trade and concubinage were thieves, robbers, and criminals, from the enslavers to the traders and purchasers.

14. The Qur'an condemns evil. "God loves not that evil be noised about in public" (4:148). For those of understanding, slavery is an inherent evil, and God loves not evil.

15. The Qur'an calls for equality. It states that "We created you from a single (pair) of a male and a female, and made you into nations and tribes, that ye may know other" (49:13). Enslaving one another and sexually conquering women of other races, religions, or sects is not a way to know one another. Nobody is superior based on color, language, race, and religion. The more pious one is, the better one is. As Fatima Mernissi (d. 2015) asserted, "The principle of equality ... was set forth by the Prophet and regulated by the Koran, which condemned slavery. Whether the Muslims obeyed the orders of God and his Prophet regarding slavery is another story" (148).

16. The Qur'an observes that "among His signs is... the diversity... of ... your colors" (30:22). Conquering other human beings, slaughtering their men and elderly women, and taking their girls and young women as concubines, is hardly a celebration of diversity. Despite dubious traditions to the contrary, the Qur'an, the Prophet, and Islam are opposed to racism and religious bigotry. Except for defensive battles, the wars, invasions, conquests, and slave raids conducted by Muslims throughout history targeted human beings due to their race, religion, or gender. The Qur'an, however, insists that human beings are "all one from another" (4:26). There was no imperialism in the Islam of the Prophet Muhammad.

17. The Qur'an calls for freedom (2:117; 2:178; 2:221: 4:3; 4:24; 4:25; 4:36; 4:92; 5:89; 9:60; 23:6; 24:31: 24:32: 24:33; 24:58: 24:58; 30:28; 33:50; 33:52; 33:55; 70:30). Muslims must stand on the side of freedom, defend freedom, and fight those who wish to deprive human beings of freedom.

18. The Qur'an calls on people to promote the good and forbid the wrong (3:104; 3:110; 9:71; 9:112; 31:17; 5:105). Freedom is good. Slavery and concubinage

Appendix 1 231

are wrong. Promoting abolition is good, while defending and justifying slavery and concubinage is wrong.

19. The Qur'an encourages Muslims to forgive others as they would like God to forgive them (24: 22).

20. The Qur'an opposes sexual immorality (24:19). Slavery and concubinage are immoral.

21. The Qur'an requires that punishment be just and proportionate (16:126). Condemning specific races and religions to slavery and concubinage is fundamentally unfair.

22. The Qur'an states that believers should not sit in the company of those who mock religion (4:140). Supporting slavery and concubinage insults the Prophet Muhammad, Islam, and God.

23. The Qur'an prohibits Muslims from entering homes without permission (24:27-28). What are we to make of entering people's nations and homes, without permission, to murder, rape, rob, kidnap, traffic, and exploit human beings?

24. The Qur'an says that Muslims should care for the less fortunate (24:22). Would that not include the welfare of the enslaved?

25. The Qur'an says that Muslims should verify information from dubious sources before acting upon it (49:6). They should never accept that slavery and concubinage are permissible when the human conscience, intellect, and primordial nature object to them in principle.

26. The Qur'an prohibits lying (22:30). It is a lie to claim that God and His Prophet gave slavery and concubinage their blessings. When they hear such rumors, they should say: "This is an obvious falsehood" (24:12).

27. The Qur'an prohibits deriding and insulting other human beings (49:11). To justify enslaving blacks and other populations, Muslims slandered and stereotyped them to dehumanize them and justify their enslavement. They were supposed to turn away from ill speech (23:3).

28. The Qur'an commands Muslims to be humble and to spread peace (25:63). To conquer and enslave others embodies arrogance and warmongering.

29. The Qur'an commands Muslims to respond to evil with good (41:34).

30. The Qur'an prohibits Muslims from deceiving people in trade (6:152). However, deceit was central to the sale of enslaved human beings.

31. The Qur'an commands Muslims to honor their treaties (9:4). They were supposed to keep their trusts and promises (23:8). The Prophet Muhammad concluded covenants of protection with the Christians of the World. Waging war against peaceful Christians, and enslaving them, was prohibited. He warned that a terrible punishment would befall Muslims if they violated the pledges he had given to Christians.

32. The Qur'an commands Muslims to be peacemakers (49:9), not warmongers and slavers.

33. The Qur'an states that Muslims are "compassionate amongst each other"

232 Islam & Slavery

(48:29). Slavery is not compassion. Hence, one cannot enslave Muslims and their progeny.

34. The Qur'an commands Muslims to restrain their anger (3:134). The rage and hatred against non-Arabs and non-Muslims that motivated wars of conquest and slavery were un-Islamic. The Qur'an warns Muslims against letting hatred lead them to injustice (6:108).

35. Slavery and concubinage are not consistent with the Qur'anic concept of ethics such as *khayr* (goodness), *maslahah* (public interest), *birr* (righteousness), *qist* (equity*), *'adl* (equilibrium and justice), *haqq* (truth and right), *ma'ruf* (known and approved), *nahi 'an al-munkar* (prohibiting wrong), and *taqwah* (piety).

Select Legal Evidence from the Qur'an

36. The Qur'an does not command slavery and concubinage.

37. The edicts that support slavery and concubinage rely upon Qur'anic passages that are implicit, as opposed to explicit, and descriptive as opposed to prescriptive.

38. Slavery and concubinage are not obligatory. One cannot permit what is prohibited nor prohibit what is obligatory.

39. The Qur'an presents slavery is a negative light. The Pharoah is presented as a sinful tyrant for having enslaved and subjugated the Israelites (26:2; 7:127; 23:47). It intimates that the Egyptians used Israelite women as concubines (7:127). The Qur'an criticizes later Israelites for doing to others what was done to them: "If they come to you as captives, you ransom them, although their eviction was forbidden to you" (2:85). As God asks in the Qur'an: "Do you believe in part of the scripture and disbelieve in part?" (2:85). This same critique could apply to Muslims who would purchase, and in some cases free, slaves they had no right to enslave in the first place, as was with the case with black African Muslims. Rather than "follow what God has revealed," they answer that "we will follow that which we found our fathers doing" (2:170). Instead of following the emancipatory passages of the Qur'an, the Arabs preferred to maintain the pre-Islamic slave culture of their forefathers.

40. The Qur'an does not present slavery as divinely ordained. It does not claim that slaves are getting their just dues. The Qur'an presents enslaved human beings as powerless and pitiful to evoke human compassion and mercy. As we read in the Qur'an,

God coineth a similitude: (on the one hand) a (mere) chattel slave, who hath control of nothing, and (on the other hand) one on whom We have bestowed a fair provision from Us, and he spendeth thereof secretly and openly. Are they equal? Praise be to God! But most of them know not. (16:75)

41. The Qur'an asserts that Muslims have duties and obligations toward "the

Appendix 1

captive" (76:8). That includes defending their rights, feeding, clothing, and emancipating them.

42. The Qur'an aims at emancipating those deprived of liberty (2:117; 4:25; 4:92; 5:89; 14:31; 24:33; 58:3; 90:1-20).

43. The Qur'an commands Muslims to "Write out a deed of manumission for such of your slaves that desire their freedom in lieu of payment -- if you see any good in them -- and give them out of the wealth that God has given you" (24:33). Most Sunni schools of jurisprudence viewed this as recommended, but not mandatory. Zahiri jurists believed that it was obligatory. Relying on a *hadith* from Ja'far al-Sadiq, Twelver Shiite jurists also placed a maximum seven-year limit to slavery; thereby providing a path to emancipation.

44. According to the Qur'an, prisoners of wars are to be held for ransom. Since there were no camps to detain prisoners, they were paroled and placed under the supervision of families, until they were freed, ransomed, or earned their freedom through work. "When ye have thoroughly subdued them," states the Qur'an, "thereafter (it is time for) either generosity or ransom" (47:4).

45. The Qur'an encourages Muslims to free enslaved people. "It is righteousness," states the Qur'an, "to... spend of your substance... for the ransom of slaves" (2:1777).

46. The Qur'an orders Muslims to "Marry women of your choice... or (a captive) that your right hands possess" (4:3). The Qur'an does not command men to capture or purchase enslaved women and exploit them sexually.

47. The Qur'an commands Muslims to "Marry those among you who are single, or the virtuous ones among your slaves, male or female" (24:32). If a man had the right to have sex with his female slave, then this verse would effectively be granting the same privilege to women. If women should not have sex with their male slaves, it goes without saying that men should not be entitled to have sex with their female ones.

48. Verse 4:24 should not read as "[Prohibited to you in marriage are] married women, except those whom your right hands possess" but "the chaste ones from among the women, but not your female slaves." The verse allowed men to contract a lower type of marriage with former slave girls, one in which both parties could terminate at any time, in which any child was legitimate and entitled to provision, and one in which there was no inheritance due to the wife.

In ancient Rome, there were two types of marriage, *cum manu* or "in hand" and *sine manu* or "out of hand." In this first marriage, the wife was released from her family's control and fell under that of her husband. All her property, including her dowry, was passed to her husband. In return, however, she could inherit from her husband. The "in hand" marriage was for life. The husband was the provider. The wife was the custodian of the home. The husband had the right to divorce in cases of serious moral infractions, such as adultery. He also had the right to punish her physically. It was a patriarchal autocratic marriage.

In the second type, the "out of hand" marriage, the wife remained under the legal control of her father. This was the most common type of marriage among the Romans. The property rights of the wife did not change. She remained a free woman who was not under the control of her husband. She did not inherit from her husband or her children. The man maintained his property, and the woman maintained hers. Both the husband and the woman had the right to file for divorce. No cause was required. Upon the death of her father, she became *sui iuris*, namely, "of one's own rights." It was a "free marriage" that was more egalitarian. It protected the property of women. Unlike the "in hand" marriage, which excluded women from the public sphere of males, the "out of hand" marriage granted women greater freedom and social power.

When the Qur'an states, "If any of you have not the means wherewith to wed free believing women, they may wed believing girls from among those whom your right hands possess" (4:25), it is not permitting sex outside of marriage with slave girls or concubinage. Rather, it is referring to the precursor of *mut'ah* marriage, namely, temporary, or fixed-term marriages which, in its origin, was simply the "out of hand" marriage of the ancient Romans. S.V. Mir Ahmed Ali appears to have perceived this distinction when he commented that the Qur'an called for Muslims take enslaved women as regular wives and not as concubines. As he explained,

Such women are drawn from the lowest levels of society whence their morals are also very low. However, to treat alike a woman from a respectable family of high moral degree of conduct, character, and dignity, and the one from the slums without any morals or modesty or any regard to self-respect, will never be justice. Justice will be to treat each kind with full regard to its personal standard. (365)

The Qur'anic verse distinguishes between women who are *muhsanat*, namely, free Muslim women who are virtuous and of noble birth, and *malakat aymanukum*, "possessed by the right hand," which is identical to the Latin expression *secundum manus sue potentiam*, and which refers to wives who came from military conquests (Hanne 274).

Due to the disruption that foreign women could cause in terms of inheritance, as well as family and tribal alliances and dynamics, the Qur'an, to accommodate this reality, distinguishes between free, Arab, women, who could inherit in return for restrictions on their rights and freedoms, and former female captives, who were given greater freedom, the right to divorce, and leniency in matters of sexual indiscretions, in return for lack of inheritance.

49. The Qur'an prohibits unlawful sexual intercourse. "Do not approach unlawful sexual intercourse. Indeed, it is ever an immorality and evil as a way" (17:32). While the Qur'an may speak of "those who guard their chastity, except with their wives/husbands and those whom their right hands possess" (70:29-30),

the ones possessed by the right hand must be married to them according to 4:25. It positively states: "marry them" (4:25). Having sex with slave girls, without emancipating and marrying them, is an act or fornication, adultery, and rape. As the Qur'anic Path explains, "this Qur'anic law is ignored by ... so-called Muslims when it is clearly there... In the name of God and Islam, they fornicate and commit adultery!" As the Qur'an describes,

When they commit an indecent act, they say "We found our fathers doing it and God commanded us to do it too." Say: "God does not command indecency, or do you say things about God you do not know." (7:28)

As the Qur'an warns,

There is a sort of person who pays for distracting *hadith* intending, without knowledge, to lead others away from God's way, and to make a mockery of it. These will have a humiliating punishment! And when Our Verses are recited to such a person, he turns away arrogantly, as if he had not heard them! as if there were heaviness in his ears! Give him good news of a painful punishment! (31:6-7)

Rather than follow the clear Qur'an, "when he learns something from our verses, he scorns them! Such people will have a humiliating punishment!" (45:9). As the Qur'anic Path describes,

To this day in the so-called "Muslim" world, men have sexual relations with many slaves or servants despite being married. As with many so-called "authentic" Islamic teachings, this is another innovation that violates Qur'anic teachings.

In the Qur'an, marriage is continuously stressed as the only way for men and women to come together and form a relationship and where sexual activity can take place. This concept is so important, that a worldly punishment for anyone having sex with any other than his or her married spouse is deserving of one-hundred lashes (24:2).

50. "Coerce not your [slave] maidens [*fatayat*] into whoredom," warns the Qur'an, "if they happen to be desirous of marriage" (24:33). The term *bigha'* refers not only to prostitution but to libertinism, sexual inhibition, lewdness, lasciviousness, sexual immorality, sexual intercourse, fornication, adultery, whoredom, harlotry, and concubinage. It prohibits the sexual use, abuse, and exploitation of slave girls.

51. The Qur'an asserts that "it is not lawful for you to become heirs to women against their will" (4:19). Consequently, one cannot purchase a woman, loan a woman, trade a woman, exchange a woman, or pass down a woman by inheritance. People are not property. They cannot be taken by force.

52. When it comes to treating women, the Qur'an advises men to "live with them honorably" (4:19).

53. The Qur'an warns against harming and oppressing women (65:6).
54. The Qur'an calls upon men and women, and husbands and wives, to be soulmates (4:1). Unless a woman suffers from Stockholm syndrome, she will not fall madly in love with her captor and rapist.
55. The Qur'an states that "your spouses are a garment [of comfort, chastity, and protection] for you as you are for them" (2:187).
56. The Qur'an treats marriage, not solely as a contract, but also as a sign of God: "And among His Signs is this that He created for you mates from among yourselves that ye may dwell in tranquility with them and He has put love and mercy between your (hearts); verily in that are Signs for those who reflect" (30:21).
57. God places the burden on human beings to eradicate slavery and concubinage. "God changes not what is in a people until they change what is in themselves" (13:11). People need to reform themselves, their laws, and even their religions.
58. The Qur'an calls upon people to think, reason, and reflect over seven hundred times (30:8, 2:170; 16:44; 13:3; 10:24; 6:50; 12:111; 3:190-191; 36:46; 16:79; 29:20…). "Surely the worst of living creatures in the sight of God are the deaf and dumb who do not use reason" (8:22); "He lays abomination upon those who do not reason" (10:100). It calls upon Muslims to be "people of understanding" (39:18) and to make decisions based on proof and evidence (2:111). People devoid of critical thinking are described as having eyes that do not see and ears that do not hear (7:179). They are more heedless and astray than livestock (7:179).
59. The Qur'an says: "He did create in pairs, male and female" (53:45). The Qur'anic ideal is the union of a male and a female; not a male, and four females, and a hundred and one sex slaves.
60. The Qur'an says: "Women impure for men impure, and men impure for women impure, and women of purity for men of purity, and men of purity for women of purity" (24:26). Sexually assaulting female captives, and having harems full of sex slaves, is not purity: it is impurity.

Select Evidence from Reason

61. Human beings own themselves. They have autonomy and agency.
62. Slavery is racist.
63. Concubinage is racist and sexist.
64. Slavery and concubinage are unjust.
65. Slavery is immoral.
66. Slavery is unethical.
67. Slavery is inhumane and cruel.
68. Slaves are not property. They are people.
69. Slaves were denied full rights.
70. Slaves were denied human dignity.

Appendix 1

71. Slaves were not provided for properly. Their food, clothing, and medical care were inadequate.
72. Slaves were routinely mistreated, abused, and brutalized.
73. Male slaves were routinely castrated.
74. Female slaves were sexually abused.
75. Slaves were worked to death.
76. Slaves were psychologically and emotionally traumatized.
77. Islamic laws regarding slavery were repressive.
78. Islamic laws aimed to moderate the abuses inherent to slavery were rarely applied.
79. Rather than phase slavery out, Islamic laws entrenched, institutionalized, and expanded it.
80. The descendants of slaves suffer from generational trauma.
81. The slave trade devastated families, political structures, and societies.
82. Slavery is against the will of God. No good God, who is worthy of worship, would condone slavery and concubinage.
83. If human beings are made in the image of God, no human being should enslave another.
84. Judaism, Christianity, and Islam teach that human beings are equal in the sight of God. Slavery entrenches inequality.
85. Slavery promotes hatred rather than love. It opposes the Golden Rule, shared by most world religions, to love their neighbor.
86. Societies in which slavery flourishes are sick. They concentrate wealth in the hands of elites while masses of slaves suffer and languish in poverty and misery.
87. Slavery fosters fear and insecurity in society.
88. Slave societies are socially restrictive.
89. The traditions in which the Prophet Muhammad and the twelve Imams supported slavery and concubinage are forgeries as they contradict the Qur'an.
90. The traditions in which the Prophet Muhammad and the twelve Imams opposed slavery and concubinage are authentic and, even if they are not, they still agree with the Qur'an.
91. The arguments used by Muslims who support slavery and concubinage are the same as those advanced by white Protestant Christian advocates of slavery. They lost the debate. Some Muslims, however, wish to keep it alive and revive obsolete and debunked arguments.

Select Evidence from the Example of the Prophet Muhammad

92. The Prophet Muhammad freed Zinnirah al-Rumiyyah from sexual slavery. She was a concubine who was owned collectively by a clan from the tribe of

Quraysh. The Messenger of God liberated her from a life of hell as a communal whore. She became a close companion and a scribe of revelation. He set the following precedent: free sex slaves and concubines, give them honor, dignity, and respect; educate them and raise their status in society.

93. When the Prophet Muhammad was at war with a people, he would free the slaves who came to him (Ahmad).

94. The Prophet Muhammad freed and married Safiyyah and Juwayriyyah. As Bukhari reported, "The Prophet... set free Sayiyyah and made her emancipation as her dowry." If Mariya the Copt ever existed, and the evidence suggests that she did not, then he freed and married her, as it is inconceivable that he would act against the command of the Qur'an to marry the enslaved women that one possessed (2:222). After all, he said "A man who owns a servant girl and mentors her, teaches her beautiful manners, educates her in the best way, then emancipates and marries her will have a double reward" (Bukhari). Why would he marry her if he was already having sex with her? Why buy the cow when he could get the milk for free?

Selective Evidence from the Sayings of the Prophet Muhammad

95. "I have forbidden injustice for Myself, and I have forbidden it among you, so do not oppress one another" said God in a sacred saying (Muslim).

96. The Prophet Muhammad said: "Protect yourselves from doing injustice" (Muslim)

97. The Prophet Muhammad said: "A Muslim should not oppress or be oppressed" (Bukhari and Muslim)

98. The Prophet Muhammad said: "Support the oppressed" (Bukhari).

99. The Prophet Muhammad cited God as saying: "Do not oppress one another" (Shirazi).

100. Slavery and concubinage damage the image of Islam, the Qur'an, the Prophet, the Imams, and Muslims.

101. In many traditions, the Prophet Muhammad condemned racism and insisted upon human equality (Kulayni, Ahmad, Khattabi, Majlisi).

102. The Prophet Muhammad said he would testify against those who sold free human beings on the Day of Judgment (Bukhari and Muslim).

103. The Prophet Muhammad said: "God will oppose a man who sells a free person" (Bukhari).

104. The Prophet Muhammad said: "God will forgive every sin except... selling a free person" (Majlisi).

105. The Prophet Muhammad and Khadijah freed all their slaves and encouraged others to do the same. The Messenger of God said, "Whoever frees a Muslim slave, then God will free every limb of his body from the Hellfire" (Bukhari).

106. The Prophet Muhammad said: "Do not cause harm or return harm," whoever harms others, God will harm him," and "Do not torture the creation of God."

107. The Prophet Muhammad said that "There is no *nikah* [sexual intercourse or marriage] without consent" (Bukhari, Muslim, Tirmidhi, Abu Dawud, Nasa'i, Hakim). As concubinage consists of coerced sexual relations, it cannot be said to be consensual. Promiscuous women might embrace it. Others might resign themselves to it. And yet others view it as sexual assault.

108. The Prophet Muhammad said: "If someone of good character and conduct proposes to your daughters, marry them. If you do not, there will be mischief and great corruption on Earth." (Kulayni and Tirmidhi). A man of good character does not enslave and sexually exploit women.

109. The Prophet Muhammad said: "Whoever wants to follow my Tradition, then marriage is my Tradition." ('Amili and Kulayni). It is the *sunnah* to marry; not to have sex with slave girls outside of marriage.

110. The Prophet Muhammad prohibited the castration and emasculation of enslaved boys and men (Abu Dawud, Nasa'i, Hakim). Since slavery and the creation of eunuchs is synonymous, the prohibition of the latter requires the prohibition of the former.

111. The Angel Gabriel told the Prophet Muhammad: "Verily, the worst of your *ummah* are those who sell human beings" (Saduq).

112. The Prophet Muhammad said: "The worst of people is the one who sells people" (Kulayni, Tusi, 'Amili, Saduq).

113. The Prophet Muhammad said: "Set the captives free" (Bukhari).

114. The last words of the Prophet Muhammad were: "fear God about those whom your right hands possess" (Ibn Majah).

Evidence from Imam 'Ali

115. Imam 'Ali said, "All people are born." "Do not be slaves for others," he stated, "since God has established you to be free."

116. Imam 'Ali banned the enslavement of the womenfolk of defeated foes, except for slaves captured in the enemy camp. He prohibited his fighters from offending the honor, modesty, and chastity of women (Morrow 2012: 329; Sistani 2015).

Evidence from Muslim Sects and Scholars

117. The Kharijites reportedly prohibited concubinage in general, or, at the very least, without the approval of the wife of the husband.

118. Atah ibn Abi Rabah (d. 732), an early Medinan scholar, believed that the *jihad* verses only applied to the wars waged by the Prophet Muhammad during his rule. He asserted that the universal rule was that it was only permitted to fight defensive wars.

119. Abu 'Ubayd (d. 838) noted in his *Kitab al-amwal* that the Prophet provided leaders with three options concerning captives of just *jihads*: pardon, ransom, or death. Slavery was not an option.

240 Islam & Slavery

120. The Mutazilites opposed slavery and concubinage. ʻAbd al-Jabbar, for example, viewed it as "inherently immoral and unbefitting of the loftiness of moral values."

121. Zaydi jurisprudence treats slavery as *makruh* or detestable. Jurists have the right to review all evidence and adjust *shariʻah* designations. Something *mustahab* or encouraged can be raised to the level of *wajib* or *fard* and vice versa. Likewise, something that is detestable, hateful, or reprehensible can be upgraded to *haram* or prohibited. The gentle, family-centered, temporary indentured servitude of prisoners of war that was practiced during the Prophet Muhammad's time might have been *makruh*; however, the brutal, inhumane, and dehumanizing type of slavery and concubinage that prevailed after his death and until the demise of the Ottoman Empire was most certainly *haram*.

122. ʻAli ibn Muhammad, the leader of the *Zanj* or Black Rebellion in Iraq (869-883), promised freedom, justice, and prosperity to tens of thousands of enslaved black Africans who were being worked to death in the marshes of the region. He freed slaves at every opportunity (Fahes 21). Due to a lack of doctrinal and intellectual depth, and no program for social reform, the leaders who followed him gave up on the ideals of the revolt and started to acquire slaves of their own (21). ʻAli ibn Muhammad, a self-proclaimed descendant of ʻAli and Fatimah, rose up against slavery. His aim was to apply the principles of Islam: justice, tolerance, and equality (21). The enslaved black African Muslims of Iraq simply wanted their freedom and to improve their socio-economic situation (21). Why take slave masters as religious and spiritual authorities? Why side with despotic and oppressive caliphs, imams, and sultans? Why not follow the example of abolitionist Muslim leaders?

123. The Qarmatians opposed slavery and concubinage. They abolished serfdom and paid wages to black African agricultural workers (Fahes 41-42). Widely viewed as heretics by other Muslim groups, they viewed the dominant forms of Islam as downright deviant when it came to slavery and concubinage. Nobody holds a monopoly on truth. On the issue of slavery and concubinage, they appear to have been in the right.

124. The *Epistles of the Brethren of Purity*, believed by some to be the philosophical foundation of the Qarmatians, contains "The Animals' Lawsuit Against Humanity," a fable that provides powerful arguments against slavery. Rather than attack the state religion directly, and risk obliteration, Fadi A. Fahes noted that groups like the Ismailis "resorted to an enigmatic dissemination of ideas" that "slowly cracked the halo of fear and the sanctity of applied Islamic practices" (47). It is not true that Muslim scholars did not oppose slavery. Due to the dangerous circumstances, they had to do so indirectly.

125. The legitimacy of aggressive as opposed to defensive *jihad* has been questioned by scholars since the early days of Islam. Some scholars suggested that the only legitimate *jihads* were those directed by the Prophet

Muhammad. Others included the first four caliphs. For Shiites, only their Imams had the right to declare *jihad* and all other wars were illegitimate. If such wars were Islamically illegal, so was the taking of slaves and concubines. As Sachiko Murata (b. 1943) and William C. Chittick (b. 1943) argue,

From the point of view of the strict application of Islamic teachings, most so-called *jihads* have not deserved the name. Any king (or dictator...) can declare a *jihad*. There were always a few of the religious authorities who would lend support to the king -- such as the scholar whom the king had appointed to be a chief preacher at the royal mosque. But there have usually been a good body of '*ulama*' who have not supported wars simply because kings declared them. Rather, they would only support those that followed the strict application of Islamic teachings. By these standards, it is probably safe to say that there have been few if any valid *jihads* in the past century, and perhaps not for the past several hundred years. (21-22)

Defensive wars were legitimate. And the most valid war of all was the *jihad* against slavery.

126. The 'Alawi-Nusayris, the Alevis, and the Bektashis, among other so-called Ghulat or semi-Ghulat groups, oppose polygyny and practice monogamy. Having sex slaves would not be countenanced in their communities. Although they are viewed as heretics by Sunnis and Twelver Shiites, these groups viewed their detractors as deviants who follow a corrupted form of Umayyad, 'Abbasid, Ottoman, or Safavid Islam. Truth is in the eye of the beholder.

127. Twelver Shiite jurisprudence views slave trading as a *makruh* occupation. After examining the evidence on the subject, jurists have the right to raise their standards and treat it as *haram*. Although there are traditions that claim that the twelfth Imam will reintroduce slavery and concubinage, there are others that insist that he will liberate all slaves. If Twelver Shiites were truly followers of the abolitionist Imam Muhammad al-Mahdi, they should have been the foremost in freeing the enslaved. Most of their jurists, with a few exceptions in our time, embraced the belief that the Mahdi was coming to kill, convert, and enslave.

128. Al-Hakim bi Amrillah (d. 1021), the Shiite Ismaili caliph of the Fatimids, prohibited slavery and concubinage, and emancipated all slaves for all times to come in the early eleventh century. While one may disagree with some of his other rulings and actions, and view the Ismaili faith in poor light, in matters of laws and morals, questions of creed are irrelevant and immaterial. The legal arguments made by al-Hakim were legitimate, and his abolition of slavery and liberation of enslaved people were historically unprecedented and worthy of praise and acclaim. He was a man ahead of his time.

129. Although the edict of al-Hakim had little impact in the Muslim world, the Druze, namely, the *Muwahhidun* or Unitarians, an off-shoot of Sevener Shiism, and the followers of caliph al-Hakim, outlawed slavery and concubinage in their communities in the tenth century. They may be considered by mainstream Muslims to be outside the fold of Islam, and to belong to an entirely different religion; however, that being said, their prohibition of slavery and concubinage, which are supported by Qur'anic verses, is to be commended.

130. According to numerous sources, 'Abd al-Qadir Kan (d. 1806), a religious leader from what is now Senegal, was the first person in modern times to abolish slavery and the slave trade in his Muslim state (Ware 116). Speaking of the slave trade, the British governor of Senegal in 1811 noted that it was "a commerce which the Prince ['Abd al-Qadir] always opposed as being contrary to the laws of his religion" (Ware 143). Not only did he free every *hafiz* or Walking Qur'an, but he extended this freedom to anyone who could read a single verse of the scripture (Ware 117).

131. The Ahmadiyyah, a revivalist Muslim movement, which is subject to irrational, unreasonable, and unconscionable hatred and violence from Sunnis and Shiites in Pakistan and beyond, have prohibited slavery and concubinage since their foundation. This fact should earn them accolades.

132. In 1841, the exportation of slaves out of Tunisia was outlawed.

133. In 1846, "the Sultan [of the Ottoman Empire] abolished the Istanbul slave market because it was contrary to the *shari'ah* and humanitarian principles" (Freamon 1998: 58).

134. In 1846, the Bey of Tunisia issued a new decree, freeing all slaves and definitively banning slavery. It stated that from that day forward, the children of slaves would be born free.

135. Tunisia was the first Muslim nation to abolish slavery. It did so before Denmark and France.

136. In 1847, an Ottoman *firman* abolished slavery in the Persian Gulf.

137. In 1851, the slave trade was outlawed in Iran. Mirza Ali Mohamed (1820-1850), the Persian founder of Babism, prohibited slavery in the strongest terms.

138. In 1854, an Ottoman decree proclaimed that, "man is the most noble of creatures God has formed, in making him free; selling people as animals, or articles of furniture, is contrary to the will of the Sovereign Creator" (Freamon 1998: 58).

139. In 1857, Sultan Abdulmejid I (1823-1861) issued a decree abolishing slavery throughout the Ottoman Empire, except for the *Hijaz*.

140. In 1875, the Bey of Tunisia reiterated the ban on slavery in an Anglo-Tunisian treaty.

141. In 1895, 'Abd al-Rahman Khan (d. 1901), the king of Afghanistan between 1880 and 1901, passed a law prohibiting slavery, trafficking, and castration.

Appendix 1   243

142. In 1882, Hasan I Morocco (d, 1894), declared that reducing free people to slavery, without legal right, was an impious act that would be neither ignored nor tolerated.

143. Alexander Russell Webb (1846-1916), who was appointed as the honorary consul of Turkey in the United States by Sultan Abdul Hamid II (1842-1918), decreed that "Slavery and concubinage are not allowed by the Koran" (51).

144. Ahmad ibn Khalid al-Nasiri (1835/1836-1897), a Moroccan abolitionist, insisted that the Qur'an prohibited slavery and that all human beings were born free. He denounced the traffic in black Muslim slaves.

145. 'Abd al-Rahman al-Kawakibi (c. 1854-c. 1902), the Syrian intellectual, argued that slavery could and should be abolished.

146. 'Ali Shah, a Twelver Shiite Sufi, and leader of the Nimatullahi Sufi Order of Iran, issued an edict in 1912 stating that "the purchase and sale of human beings are contrary to the dictates of religion and the practice of civilization."

147. In 1923, trafficking of slaves was officially abolished in Morocco (El Hamel 264). However, the ownership of slaves was not criminalized and the country never abolished slavery (264-265) In fact, "slavery in Morocco was never abolished by any decree from the royal authority" (306).

148. In 1923, all forms of slavery are outlawed in Ethiopia and Afghanistan.

149. In 1929, the Iranian Parliament passed the Slavery Abolition Act which declared that "no one shall be recognized as slave and every slave will be emancipated upon arrival at Iran's territorial soil or waters." It was Reza Shah Pahlavi (1878-1944), not the "grand ayatollahs," who prohibited slavery. Most of the mullahs were opposed to abolition.

150. In 1935, Mirza Bashir Ahmad, an Ahmadi scholar, published a treatise titled *Islam and Slavery*. He asserted that the teachings of Islam regarding slaves fell into two categories: 1) "the betterment of the condition of the existing slaves and measures for their gradual emancipation;" and 2) "steps for the permanent abolition of slavery" (4). Islam's emancipation program was "carried into effect under State supervision so that there could be no laxity or negligence in this respect" (74).

Bashir Ahmad also insisted that "emancipation through *mukatabat* did not depend upon the sweet will of the master; it was obligatory" 19). He notes that there was a massive attempt to emancipate slaves. According to his sources, the Prophet, 'A'ishah, 'Abbas, Hakim, 'Abd Allah ibn 'Umar, 'Abd al-Rahman ibn 'Awf, 'Uthman, and Dhu al-Kala al-Himyari alone liberated 32,320 enslaved human beings (25).

Islam, during the life of the Prophet, emancipated, as opposed to enslave, people. Had this example been emulated, millions of slaves would have been liberated. Alas, what followed was a "misguided age" which explains why slavery survived and even expanded in the Muslim world (41-42). Ignorant and worldly people "distorted and disfigured the noble teachings of Islam" (42). Not only did they follow the example of other nations, but "Muslims

244 Islam & Slavery

also abandoned the injunctions of Islam," reverting to the cruel ways of enslavement (42). Consequently,

It is… the imperative duty of Muslim governments and Muslim societies to devote themselves strenuously and whole-heartedly to the practical abolition of slavery and bring the world once more to that blessed goal to which the Holy Prophet of Islam and his companions desired to lead the world -- a goal of true freedom and true equality in the world. (42)

As Bashir Ahmad established, "Islam is strongly opposed to all forms of tyranny and transgression and is a powerful champion of the liberty and equality of man" (43). He also emphasized the fact that "nowhere in Islamic literature has it been laid down that it is permissible to enslave a free man" (44). And while prisoners could temporarily be deprived of their liberty, their condition, and that of their descendants was never permanent (47-60). As for masters, he argued that they could enter into common-law marriages with their female slaves without the performance of a formal ceremony (67).

150. In 1952, the shaykh of Kuwait expressed his desire to prohibit slavery.

151. In 1962, slavery is prohibited in Yemen.

152. In 1963, Malcolm X (d. 1965) delivered his famous speech on "The House Negro and the Field Negro." As he explained, the former looked out for the master. He kept the Field Negros in check. He received financial incentives from the slave master. He spoke like the master. He loved the master more than the master loved himself. If the master's house caught on fire, he would risk his life to put it out. Unlike the House Negro, who loved his master, the Field Negro hated the master. If he got sick, he would pray that he died. If his house caught on fire, he would pray for wind. Just as there were House Negros and Field Negros in Malcolm's time, there are plenty today. They are the Black Americans Muslims -- Sunnis, Shiites, and Sufis -- who are apologists for "Islamic" slavery. Give them some handouts, and some scholarships to study Islam, and they submissively surrender to those who enslaved their ancestors and their people. Some even insist that slavery is permitted by God for all times and places and cannot be prohibited. Some even defend its revival. And there are White House Slaves and Wannabe Masters egging them on.

153. In 1967, Mahmoud Mohamed Taha published *al-Risalah al-thaniyyah min al-Islam*, which would be translated as *The Second Message of Islam* in 1987, in which he argued that "slavery is not an original precept of Islam" since "Islam's original principle is freedom" (137). In his view,

It was neither possible, nor desirable, at that point, for the law to abolish slavery by a stroke of the pen. The needs of the enslaved individuals, as well as the social and economic needs of the community, necessitated the maintenance of the system, while developing it continuously, until every enslaved person would be emancipated. (138)

154. In 1981, slavery was outlawed in Mauritania.
155. In 1990, the Cairo Declaration of Human Rights in Islam asserted in article 11 that "Human beings are born free, and no one has the right to enslave, humiliate, oppress, or exploit them, and there can be no subjugation but to Allah, the Almighty" (Organization of the Islamic Conference 8).
156. In 1992, slavery was prohibited in Pakistan.
157. In 2007, in response to the continued existence of up to a million and a half black Muslim slaves in the nation, owned by Arab and Berber Muslims, Mauritania reiterated its abolition of slavery on Islamic grounds. As Boubacar Ould Messaoud (b. 1945), the leader of *SOS Esclaves*, commented,

Mauritania is an Islamic republic -- but Islam is not slavery. It was absolutely necessary to enshrine in law the condemnation of slavery by Islam. Respecting *shari'ah* would involve treating your slave as yourself, but that is impossible otherwise he would lose all usefulness. Therefore, the practice is not compatible with religious precepts. (Clémençot)

The deeply ingrained practice of slavery, however, has persisted in Mauritania, as it does in the Sudan, its last strongholds.
158. Rather than follow the illustrious example of caliph al-Hakim, the Nizari Ismailis only came out against slavery and concubinage in the twentieth century when their leader, Agha Khan III (r. 1885-1957), expressed his support for abolition.
159. The Nation of Islam, founded by Master W.D. Fard, on July 4, 1930, was vehemently opposed to slavery and concubinage. Whether he is viewed as a Prophet or God in Person, his views have divine weight in the eyes, minds, and hearts of the faithful who follow him. Elijah Muhammad was always adamantly against slavery, whether committed by Christians or Muslims. This is the only reasonable position that any black African, African American, or Afro descendant in the Americas can take.
According to the teachings of W.D. Fard, by embracing Slave Master Islam, black people have replaced one set of devils for another. They no longer belong to the 5% of "poor, righteous teachers." They are now followers of the 10%, "the rich; the slave-makers of the poor; who teach the poor lies... the Blood-Suckers of the Poor." They are followers of the Caucasian slave master, the Devil, and the Skunk of the Earth who is "One Hundred Percent Wicked." The Caucasoid category includes those who are Aryan, Semitic, and Hamitic. Europeans, Arabs, Imazighen, Persians, Turks, and others are considered to be "whites," or Caucasians.
As Master Fard taught, the Devil keeps blacks blind and ignorant so that he can master them. He desires "to make slaves out of all he can so that he can rob them and live in luxury." They have gone from life to mental death. True Islam, taught Fard, was based on "FREEDOM, JUSTICE and EQUALITY." He was emphatic that the Caucasian or Colored Devil could not be reformed.

246   Islam & Slavery

If that is the case, than neither can his Fake and Fraudulent Islam.

160. Muhammad Abu Zahra (1898-1974), the Egyptian authority on Islamic law, asserted that there was not a single verse of the Qur'an or a rigorously authenticated tradition of the Prophet Muhammad that mandated slavery (ElGendy). In the words of Brown, "Muhammad Abu Zahra summed it up: Islam would welcome a day when slavery was banned" (2017).

161. As 'Abbas al-'Aqqad (1889-1964), the Egyptian author asserted, "the Qur'an legitimizes emancipation and does not legitimize slavery" (ElGendy).

162. Ghulam Ahmed Perwez (1903-1985), a giant of a scholar, believed that slavery and concubinage were devoid of any Qur'anic basis.

163. Twelver Shiite scholars like Muhammad Baqir al-Sadr (d. 1980) and Morteza Muttahari (d. 1979) opposed slavery in their writings.

164. Ahmad Ghabal (d. 2012), the Iranian *mujtahid* believed that the abolition of slavery was consonant with the *shar'iat-i 'aqlani* or rule of reason (Ridgeon 176).

165. Mohammad-Hadi Ma'rifat (1931-2007), the Twelver Shiite Qur'anic commentator, advocated the idea of *naskh-i tamhidi* or preparatory abrogation (Ridgeon 35). As Ridgeon notes,

> He believed that some verses of the Qur'an (such as those related to the permissibility of slavery and the mistreatment of women) were incompatible with certain ethical goals. Therefore, although such institutions and practices were not abolished in the Qur'an, the ground was prepared by limiting their harm or practice, and so the eventual abrogation of these verses at a later stage (either by the Prophet himself of by the imams) was made much easier. (35-36)

166. Twelver Shiite scholars, and sources of emulation, including Muhammad Husayn Fadlullah (d. 2010) and Mostafa Mohaghegh-Damad (b. 1945) ruled that slavery and concubinage were prohibited. Yasser Awde, a Lebanese cleric, and student of Fadlullah, has also asserted that the claim that the Prophet took women as captives was a lie. However, he succumbs to the antisemitic trope that it was fabricated by Jews to corrupt the Islamic religion.

167. Twelver Shiite *mujtahids*, like Mohsen Kadivar (b. 1959), and Sunni jurists, like Bernard Freamon (b. 1947), have all published sophisticated scholarly refutations of slavery and concubinage. Kadivar relied on *naskh 'aqli*, abrogation by reason, to conclude that slavery is no longer legally authorized in Islam.

168. Sunni scholars, like Muhammad Yaqoubi (b. 1963), and the signatories to the *Open Letter to Baghdadi* have prohibited slavery and concubinage.

169. Modernist, reformist, progressive, and secular Muslim scholars all prohibit slavery and concubinage.

170. In 2012, Biram Dah Abeid (b. 1965), the leader of the Initiative for the Resurgence of the Abolitionist Movement, organized a protest in Nouakchott, the capital of Mauritania. After years of asking the government and the

Supreme Council for Fatwa and Grievances to prohibit slavery, this freedom fighter would ask no more. The IRA would take matters into their own hands and free slaves without the support of the so-called scholars of Islam. He showed some books of "Islamic" jurisprudence that legalize slavery and concubinage and declared:

Start your campaign against me. Say that I am against religion. Give money to your slaves and send them to say that everywhere -- that will not help you. We don't have to explain ourselves to them. We are not afraid and we don't need their money. Sometimes we have nothing but water for dinner. But we are not afraid. They are false Muslims, so they cannot evaluate our Islam. No one can have more conviction than us because we have the truth. If we die, it will be from the front, not the back. We will not run away...

These books justify selling people, they justify raping people. We will purify the religion, the faith, and the hearts of the Mauritanians. What the Prophet says was hidden by these books, which are not real words from God. These old books give a bad image of Islam. We have no choice but to take this step.

His bodyguard dropped the books into a box doused with lighter fluid and Abeid set them afire (Okeowo).

171. On December 2, 2014, at the Pontifical Academy of Sciences and Social Sciences at Vatican City, Mohammed Taqi al-Modaressi (b. 1945), an Iraqi Twelver Shiite source of emulation, signed the Joint Declaration of Religious Leaders against Slavery, along with Catholic, Anglican, Muslim, Hindu, Buddhist, Jewish, and Orthodox Christian leaders. He stated: "No one must take others as slaves, nor transgress their rights, be it in part or in whole, big or small" (End Slavery). He called for the creation of a permanent body, akin to UNICEF, that would devote itself to uprooting "the evil of slavery on a cultural level, and see criminals prosecuted and punished for forced labor and slavery" (End Slavery).

172. Although not absolute, as *ijma'* rarely is, there has been a large enough number of Muslim scholars who have opposed slavery and concubinage over the past century and a half to assert that there is a scholarly consensus against such practices. The problem at the present, writes Freamon, is that "There is little awareness, among jurists and among ordinary believers, of the legal history of slavery and trafficking in Muslim communities, and still less awareness that Islamic law principles are available to them in crafting an effort to end these practices" (2016: 305).

173. There has never been a time, since the dawn of Islam to its dusk, in which there were no Muslim abolitionists. There have always been Muslims who opposed and abhorred slavery and concubinage. Slavery was not synonymous with the Qur'an and true Islam. The institution did not go unchallenged. In

248   Islam & Slavery

fact, it was an inversion of Islamic principles. It took time for the moral minority to become the majority.

174. Scholarly consensus aside, the vast majority of Muslims worldwide are reportedly opposed to slavery and concubinage and find them to be morally abhorrent. The beliefs and practices of the majority of believers have an authoritative status. The consensus of the worldwide Muslim community condemns slavery and concubinage. As Shafi'i noted in his *Risalah*, the only true *ijma'* is that of the entire community, which includes scholars and lay people (Freamon 1998: 24). According to Freamon, "this new *ijma'* will recognize that the Qur'an and *sunnah* are, in fact, abolitionist texts in spirit and substance" (1998: 61). Although it is Johnny come lately, it is a tune all moral, freedom-loving, Muslims must sing. While it helps, a consensus against slavery does not suffice. Slavery, in all its dimensions, is complex, and its opposition requires a multi-pronged approach. What is more, a consensus against slavery is not a solution in and of itself as it was Islamic jurisprudence that produced the problem in the first place by permitting and regulating it. As the Sufi sages say, "If you want to go to hell, become a jurist." Rather than reflect the Qur'an, observes Cyrille Moreno al-'Ajami, Islamic law reflects the socio-political realities of its period (2020: 49).

175. In 2004, Muhammad Diakho, a black African Muslim jurist, published *L'esclavage en Islam* [*Slavery in Islam*], a powerful and persuasive jurisprudential treatise that provides a traditional Islamic rationale for the abolition and prohibition of slavery and concubinage.

176. In 2008, Malek Chebel (d. 2016) noted that Prophet Muhammad strongly opposed slavery. People, however, did not listen. As a result, Chebel estimates that Muslims enslaved twenty one to twenty two million human beings over the past fourteen hundred years and that there were approximately 2.5 million slaves across the Islamic world.

It is a disgrace that, as late as 2010, Chebel had to issue an "Appeal to the Conscience of Current Muslim Governments," urging them to view slavery, not as a taboo, but as a crime (491). He called upon them to take legal and theological action against slavery, noting that "universal principles must never be hindered by ethnic, ideological, or religious considerations (491). He asked them to take concrete political action against modern forms of slavery (491). He encouraged them to use the media to sensitize populations regularly regarding the reality of modern-day slavery and to help enslaved people escape from the vicious circle of misery (492). Finally, he urged that current slaves, and the descendants of slaves in the Muslim world, receive reparations to help them break from their ancestral chains and to integrate them fully integrate into society (492).

177. In Ahmad Qabel (1954-2012), the Iranian *mujtahid*, and advocate of rational *shari'ah*, emphasized "the impermissibility of a return to the practice of slavery and the religious unlawfulness of violations of the human right to

freedom" (52; Jahanbakhsh n. page).

178. In 2010, 'Ali al-Sistani, the Twelver Shiite religious authority was asked: "Is it permissible to enslave women belonging to infidels who make war [against us] without the permission of the legitimate ruler? Is it permissible to have sex with them before they surrender? And if someone bought or came to own a non-Muslim concubine, may he have sex with her?" He answered: "No, it is not allowed."

179. In 2014, Mohamed El Sadi, the spiritual leader of the Muslims in Malta, strongly condemned slavery. In his words, "Slavery used to be allowed in olden times, a long time ago; however, Islam moved away from this and wants to liberate all slaves and completely eliminate slavery. This is the goal of Islam" (Orland).

180. In 2015, Ajmal Masroor, a Bangladeshi-born British imam, broadcaster and politician, declared that "In Islam taking anyone as captive, mistreating them using them as sex slaves, torturing them and killing them is totally prohibited."

181. Writing in 2016, Abdullah Saeed, Rowan Gould, and Adis Duderija, asserted that,

The Qur'an commands us to end slavery, not increase it. Slavery has now been ended in Islam by consensus, in accordance with the will of God and His Prophet. The historical conditions that produced and sustained it should not be reproduced today. To do so is not to follow the example of the Prophet but to disobey it. (133)

182. In 2019, 'Ali al-Sistani, the Twelver Shiite religious authority, issued "Advice and Guidance to the Fighters on the Battlefield" in which he explicitly prohibited them from offending the honor and virtue of Muslim and non-Muslim women.

183. In 2016, Ahmed Subhy Mansour (b. 1949), the Qur'anist scholar, historian, and shaykh who received his doctorate from al-Azhar University, published *Slavery: A Fundamental Historical Overview* which provides a persuasive case against human bondage and concubinage. In 2018, he ruled that "Enslavement and slavery are prohibited in the Qur'an."

184. In 2016, Khaled Esseissah, the US-educated Mauritanian historian, argued that "Arab-Berber religious scholars have developed twisted interpretations of Islam, to justify the legality of the enslavement" of black people.

185. In 2019, Bernard K. Freamon, an African American Muslim jurist, published *Possessed by the Right Hand*, the first comprehensive legal history of slavery in Islam, providing a thorough case for prohibiting slavery and concubinage. In 2020, he published "Toward the Abolition of Slavery Under the Aegis of Islamic Law," in which he finds that "the emancipation of slaves is one of the highest priorities of the Islamic religion." Hence, "application of a robust prioritarian interpretation" of the Qur'an and *sunnah* "lead to the conclusion

250   Islam & Slavery

that abolition is the best way to accomplish the emancipatory result demanded by the text."

186. In 2020, Cyrille Moreno al-'Ajami, an Arabist who specializes in Qur'anic exegesis, published *Que dit vraiment le Coran?* [*What Does the Qur'an Really Say?*]. He stresses that the Qur'an approaches the abolition of slavery in a rational way. It reminded people that human beings were equal. It emphasized the inhumanity of subjecting human beings to slavery. It introduced measures to encourage manumission. It also prohibited the enslavement of prisoners of war. He insists that the Qur'an never mandated slavery. On the contrary, it established an emancipatory trajectory that was progressive and depended on the development of human consciousness. As he repeats, there is no humanity in inhumanity. It is therefore a dishonor and a disgrace to claim that the revealed message reflected the darkness of souls from the dark ages.

Although he believes that the Qur'an provided a program for the abolition of slavery, he refuses to believe that it tolerated the sexual abuse of female slaves by sexual predators. If the Qur'anic prohibition against concubinage was disregarded, it was through exegetical ruses. As he explains, macho, misogynistic, and sexist slavers misinterpreted the verses of the Qur'an to give themselves the right to preserve a degenerate and degrading practice that is an affront to human dignity. For al-'Ajami, "the Qur'an is not to blame; it is held hostage." If Muslims were the last to abolish slavery, it was due to their failure to respect the reforms instituted by the Qur'an (2020: 98-104)

187. In 2021, Liyakat Ali Takim, a Twelver Shiite academic, asserted that "the selling and purchase of humans is unethical and an affront to human values" (211).

188. In June of 2023, Reza Hosseini Nasab, an Iranian Twelver Shiite *marja* or source of emulation based in the Greater Toronto Area in Canada, was asked whether slavery and concubinage were permitted in Islam. He ruled that they were both prohibited.

189. In 2023, Biram Dah Abeid (b. 1965), the Mauritanian politician, advocate for the abolition of slavery, the recipient of the United Nations Prize in the Field of Human Rights, and one of the one hundred most influential people in the world according to *Time* magazine, expressed his unconditional support for my efforts to provide an Islamic basis for the abolition of slavery.

190. Slavery and concubinage oppose Natural Law or *fitrah*, which is the law of God within each and every one of us.

191. Slavery and sexual slavery and bondage violate three of the Ten Commandments: "Thou shalt not steal," "Thou shalt not commit adultery," and "Thou shalt not covet they neighbor's wife, nor his manservant, nor his maidservant."

192. The aforementioned evidence supporting the abolition of slavery and

Appendix I   251

concubinage in Islam barely scratches the surface. While there are traditions that can be used to support slavery and concubinage, there are just as many that can be used to oppose them. Citing them all would take volumes. Most, however, would be rejected by jurists as they insist that one cannot legislate ethics. Rather than hurl *hadith* back and forth in a futile battle, and argue about authenticity, which is not even the issue, as the real issue is the authorial enterprise, what is called for is a return to revelation, justice, and reason.

193. Some Muslims have been so wrong for far too long. The *ahl al-qur'an* followed the Qur'an and the Qur'an alone. The *ahl al-hadith* or *ahl al-sunnah* placed the *hadith* above the Qur'an and rejected reason. Their Shiite equivalent, the *ahl al-akhbar*, did the same. The *ahl al-bayt* insisted upon the Qur'an, the *sunnah* transmitted by the Imams, and reason. The *ahl al-kalam* placed reason above all else. The *ahl al-kalam*, *ahl al-ra'y*, *ahl al-'adl wa al-tawhid*, and *ahl al-istiqamah* focus on reason, divine unity, and divine justice.

194. When deriving rules and regulations, the best approach is one that relies on *'aql*, reason; *al-fitrah*, Natural Law; *'adl*, justice; *akhlaq*, ethics; *maqasid*; higher objectives; *tawhid*, divine unity; *maslahah*, the greater good; *'urf*, common practice; *zaman wa makan*, time and place; *la haraj*, avoiding difficulty; *la darar*, avoiding harm; *wahy*, revelation; and *hadith* or *sunnah*, so long as it agrees with all of the former.

195. It is an embarrassment to Islam that there are still Muslims who support the mass slavery and concubinage practiced by their predecessors and, in some cases, even their contemporaries. It is even more perplexing when black Muslim Uncle Toms, who descend from victims of the trans-Atlantic slave trade, do so themselves, coming to the defense of Muslims whose forefathers enslaved people in Africa, the Middle East, and Asia, keeping millions for themselves and selling millions of others to the merchant ships in an alliance that brought the worst of Muslims into an infernal alliance with the worst of Christians.

196. The Islamic legal and ethical ecosystem has always provided numerous instruments to abolish slavery and concubinage. In fact, it could be argued that the Qur'an and Islam offer more resources for emancipation and abolition than the Bible and Christianity.

197. Neither God, the Prophet, the Imams, nor Islam should be blamed for the sins and shortcomings of so-called Muslims who remained wide awake to wickedness or snoozed in the slumber of sin.

198. "Sleepers, wake up!" Truth is transcendent. Morals are absolute. Natural law is eternal, unchanging, and eternally valid. Muslims must break out of their boxes. They must burst the bubble of the universe. They must free their minds and souls from the shackles of man-made religion. They must stop taking their scholars as lords and gods. They should be slaves to God and God alone (3:79).

199. It is our divine and human duty to oppose any interpretation of Islam that

violates its principles of egalitarianism. Not only is another reading of the Qur'an possible, but it is also required. As Cyrille Moreno al-'Ajami argues, Islam, as a historical religion developed by men, has very little to do with the Qur'an as an original and primary source (2019).

200. In the final words of Muhammad, the Messenger of God: "The prayer, the prayer! And fear God with regard to those whom your right hands possess" (Abu Dawud, Ibn Majah, Nas'ai, Ahmad; Ahmad 74). He spoke these words in the presence of his wives, his daughter Fatimah, her children, Hasan and Husayn, the faithful *Muhajirin*, the loyal *Ansar*. However, his final thoughts and concerns were with the downtrodden slaves. They were the weightiest of words he ever uttered (Ahmad 74-75)

201. In the name of God and His Prophet: Emancipate the slaves! Free the slaves! Freedom, Justice, and Equality for all! After all, "Righteous is he who ... set slaves free" (Qur'an 2:177).

The Punishment for Slavery and Concubinage

During the rule of 'Ali, the first Imam, a group of men brought a man who had sold a free woman into slavery. The Imam cut off his hand (Kulayni, vol. 7, Book of Legal Penalties).

During the Imamate of Ja'far al-Sadiq, the sixth Imam was asked about a man who stole a free woman and sold her into slavery. He responded:

Four penalties (are applicable) -- as for the first one, so he is a thief, his hand would be cut; and the second if he had copulated with her, he would be whipped the penalty (*hadd*), and (a penalty) (*hadd*) upon the one who bought, if he had knowingly copulated with her, if he was married, stoning, and if he was not married, the penalty (*hadd*) of whipping; and if he had not known, then there is nothing upon him; and upon her, if she was coerced (forced), so there is nothing upon her, and if she had obeyed him, she would be whipped the penalty (*hadd*). (Kulayni, vol. 7, Book of Legal Penalties)

For 'Ali and Ja'far al-Sadiq, enslaving free human beings, which is precisely what was done by Muslim states and slavers throughout history, was an act of theft. Anyone who enslaves a person is to have a hand cut off according to Islamic law. According to the sixth Imam, anyone who has sexual intercourse with an enslaved female is to be whipped, if he is single, or stoned to death if he is married. Females who are forced to have sex are not to be punished. However, those who refuse to resist are to be punished. This tradition clearly establishes that sexual intercourse with enslaved women falls in the category of fornication or adultery. In subsequent traditions, however, the sixth Imam stresses, in no uncertain terms, that the punishment for forced intercourse, rape, and sexual assault, is death. Hence, men who have sex with enslaved, trafficked, and exploited females, be they slaves or prostitutes, should be condemned to death, life in prison, or severe punishment according to Islamic law.

These traditions stand in sharp contrast to those in which the Imams permitted Muslim men to purchase and sexually exploit free females who had been enslaved, and those that claim that they did so themselves.

"Woe to every sinful liar" (45:7); "Cursed be the liars" (51:10); "Aye! We have brought them the truth and verily they are the liars" (23:90); "Lo! Ye verily are liars!" (16:86); "It is only those who believe not in the signs of God who fabricate lies, and those! They are the liars" (16:105); "God guides not the liar" (39:3; 40:28). Truly, "God guides whom He pleases" (28:56).

Finally, in light of the carnage, suffering, and injustice they cause, slavery and concubinage are the very manifestation of "spreading corruption on earth" (2:11). In the words of the Qur'an,

> The punishment of those who wage war against God and His Messenger, and strive to spread corruption through the land is: execution, or crucifixion, or the cutting off of hands and feet from opposite sides, or exile from the land: that is their disgrace in this world, and a heavy punishment is theirs in the Hereafter. (5:33)

So let the punishment fit the crime. And "God is not unjust in the least" (8:51).

Appendix 2
Artistic Depictions of "Islamic" Slavery and Concubinage

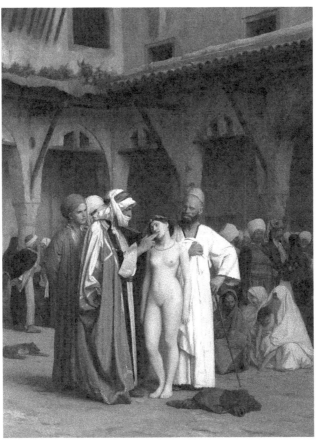

(Public Domain: "Slave Market" by Jean-Léon Gérôme, 1866)

(Public Domain: "The Slave Market" by Jean-Léon Gérôme, 1871)

Appendix 2

(Public Domain: "The Bulgarian Martyresses" by Konstantin Makovsky, 1877)

(Public Domain: "The Abduction of a Herzegovinian Woman" by Jaroslav Čermák, 1861)

Appendix 2

(Public Domain: "The Abduction" by Eduard Ansen Hofmann, 1820-1904)

(Public Domain: "The Slave Market" by Otto Pilny, 1910)

(Public Domain: "Abducted" by Eduard Ansen-Hofmann, 1820-1904)

(Public Domain: "Namona," by Henri Tanoux, 1883)

Appendix 2 261

(Public Domain: "The Bitter Draught of Slavery" by Ernest Norman, 1885)

(Public Domain: "A New Arrival" by Giulio Rosati, 1858-1917)

(Public Domain: "The New Slave Girl" by Eduard Ansen-Hofmann, 1820-1904)

Appendix 2

(Public Domain: "Examining Slaves" by Ettore Cercone, 1890)

(Public Domain: "Slave Dealer" by Otto Pliny, 1919)

264 Islam & Slavery

(Public Domain: "Slave Market" by Eduard Ansen-Hofmann, 1900)

Appendix 2 265

(Public Domain: "Slave Trade Negotiations" by Fabio Fabbi, 1861-1946)

(Public Domain: "New Arrival" by Eduard Ansen-Hofmann, 1820-1904)

(Public Domain: "The Serbian Concubine"
by Jean-Joseph Benjamin-Constant, 1876)

Appendix 2 267

(Public Domain: "Slave Market" by Émile Jean-Horace Vernet, 1836)

(Public Domain: "Harem Captive" by Eisenhut Ferencz, 1903)

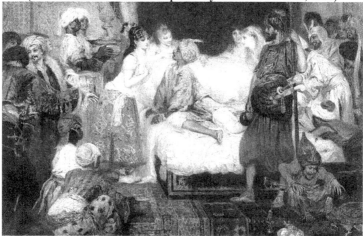
(Public Domain: "Scene from the Harem" by Fernand Cormon, 1877)

Appendix 3

Fatwa Prohibiting Slavery and Concubinage: The Shortest but Most Significant Edict in Islamic History

Question: Are slavery and concubinage permitted?
Answer: No!

Appendix 4

After Thoughts

Far too many Muslim scholars, academics, clerics, leaders, and activists that I have consulted over several decades stubbornly and obtusely insist that slavery and concubinage are permissible in Islam. They very much share the same view as Dr. Jonathan A.C. Brown, the Chair of the Saudi-funded Prince Alwaleed Bin Talal Center for Muslim-Christian Understanding at Georgetown University. This should come as no surprise since the fatwas issued in favor of slavery over the past fourteen hundred years greatly outnumber those against it. In fact, abolitionist edicts are infinitesimally small.

Be that as it may, how does a book that defends and justifies "Islamic" slavery and concubinage as divinely endorsed support the Center for Muslim-Christian Understanding's mission "to build bridges of mutual understanding between the Muslim world and the West and to enhance understanding of Muslims in the West?" By supporting the belief that Islam is slavery and slavery is Islam? Should Muslims and non-Muslims thank Brown for showing them "the real face of radical Islam" and the threat it poses? Perhaps they should. Thanks for the heads up.

If anything, Browns' book serves to reinforce anti-Islamic stereotypes and sentiments. In this "Woke New World," professors, even tenured, have been terminated from their employment for much less. Any criticism of Islam, however well-deserved, merited, and justified, is treated as an act of actual violence against Muslims. Academic freedom has long gone out the door. Professors lose their positions for failing to abide by the strictest, most radical, interpretations of Islam. In its fear to appear Islamophobic, the academy acts as the advocates of Islamists and extremists. Scholars have lost their positions for studying paintings of the Prophet Muhammad that were made lovingly by Muslim artists. The unimaginable has happened. In the Western world, non-Muslim administrators are applying the most extreme interpretations of Islamic law upon their faculty, favoring intolerant Islam, which they treat as normative, as opposed to tolerant Islam. From humble, respectful, seekers of knowledge, who thrived as a result of academic freedom, students have been turned into informers, denunciators, stool pigeons, and tattletales for the "Ministry of Truth."

Once upon a time, academia was dominated by Orientalists. By and large, they were loyal to their nations and cultures. Alas, thanks to foreign funding, and the weakening of Western civilization, it is now dominated to a large extent by Islamists, dual loyalists, fifth columnists, Muslim fundamentalists, self-hating suicidal liberals, and terrorist apologists. Hence, when it comes to defending "Islamic" slavery, Brown is not alone. Disturbingly, there is no shortage of like-minded people in his camp. They include people who present themselves as moderate and progressive Muslims as well as radical, dangerous, retrogrades who hold that Islamic laws regarding slavery and concubinage are immutable and that they can, and even should, be reimplemented and reinvigorated.

Many of my Muslim and non-Muslim colleagues and associates, some of whom I have known most of my life, are convinced that it is permissible to attack, kidnap, enslave, traffic, sell and buy human beings according to the Qur'an, the Prophet, the *sunnah*, and the *shari'ah*, including subjecting captive women to coerced sex. Such was the practice of the Prophet and the Imams, they insist. Some are so callous that they claim that being enslaved by Muslims is a blessing. All I can say is birds of a feather flock together and I am a metaphorical waterfowl hunter.

In my experience, which spans several decades, Islamic scholars and shaykhs who oppose slavery and concubinage, past, present, and future, are very much a minority. My "esteemed" teachers, including Sunni, Shiite, and Sufi *'ulama,'* all insisted that Muslim men had the right to rape female captives and prisoners. Only one, an African American shaykh, was adamant that it was *currently* forbidden for Muslim men to take concubines. As we say in Spanish, *mejor solo que mal acompañado* and *dime con quien andas y te diré quién eres.* "A man is judged by the company he keeps," wrote William J.H. Boetcker. Or as Johann Wolfgang von Goethe said, "Tell me with whom you associate, and I will tell you who you are." I support slave rebellions; not slave masters.

How any human being, especially blacks and women, could support slavery and concubinage is deeply disturbing. How anyone could embrace and defend such perverted practices is beyond belief. Such people have been brainwashed and need to be deprogrammed. They are in desperate need of psychological and spiritual therapy. They accuse abolitionists of being "apologists." As Bernard K. Freamon observes, "the positions taken by these scholars tend to be hopelessly doctrinal and parochial, offering little or no guidance for the Muslim who avows the abolition of slavery in Islam" (1998: 12).

Although some "orthodox" Muslim scholars, be they Sunni, Shiite or Sufi, oppose slavery, and support abolition, at least at the present time, many abolitionists cited in this work fall outside of the mainstream. They include Sunni and Shiite modernists and reformists, along with progressive Muslims, Islamic feminists, humanists, and secularists. They also include Qur'anists, Mutazilites, Qarmatians, Ahmadis, and members of minority sects, movements, and offshoots of Islam. This bodes bad for the imperial Islam of the oppressors and the claim it can be meaningfully reformed, modernized, and realigned with perennial ethical

Appendix 4

principles. For Cyrille Moreno al-'Ajami, reforming Islam requires reforming the Muslim:

> An uprising against authority in Islam is not actually possible, since the fluid structure, yet existing body assumes that you cannot materially face it. The orthodoxy has endogenous causes and clerics are its self-appointed guardians. They defend a mythological palace which cannot be attacked. Historically, any such attempt resulted in successful cases in a deep split and the creation of a new religion, as is the case of the "Reform" that did not reform, but whose suffering engendered Protestantism in its multiple branches. This is also the case for various revolts in the lands of Islam which gave birth to other Islams: Kharijism, Shiism, Ibadism, etc. But what reformer would claim to create a new Islam?
>
> If the clerics of Islam still apparently have moral weight on social attitudes, this does not mean that they have the power to shape them. They are rather their reflection.
>
> Orthodoxy is only an average definition resulting from a culture and a time of one or a number of societies which validate its content and formulation. In return, the guardians of the Temple speak on behalf of those who legitimized them and express what the majority wants. Thus it would be by changing the attitudes, i.e. the "habitus," that orthodoxy -- and consequently the custody of official scholars -- could be modified.
>
> Similarly, it would be wrong to conceive the conservative forms of Islam as marginal or outside of an Islamic reference (an Islam in capital letters then created by contrast as a pure entity and the paradigm to achieve the reform or a renewed effort thought). In reality, these expressions are an integral part of Islam, moreover, they are Islam. Islam is not a religion descended from heaven, but born from earth. This mix does not prohibit conducting the battle frontally, but it condemns the struggle to failure, because we cannot destroy what we want to deconstruct. (2013)

While the victory of moral, spiritual, rational, and civilizational Islam remains far on the horizon, it is heartening that many lay Muslims have become more morally evolved than their "religious" leaders who lag behind like relics. What is more, the worldwide community of Islam is starting to teem with new religious thinkers, most of them operating on the periphery or on the outside of Islamic universities and seminaries. They are particularly prevalent in Europe and North America, a reality that supports the prophecy that "The sun [of true Islam] will rise in the West."

I am deeply indebted to the committed and courageous Muslim scholars, leaders, writers, and activists who reviewed this work, and those who provided endorsements. I am especially grateful to Dr. Paul du Quenoy and Academica Press for publishing this potent piece of socially engaged scholarship. This is a difficult book to read. It was even more difficult to write. For Dr. Chouki El Hamel, "It is horrible but it is the naked truth." As Dr. Khaled Abou El Fadl acknowledges, "This is a truthful, honest, and painful book. Like all truth speaking books, it is challenging to read, but its criticisms are necessary and fair" (2023). Truth hurts. It hurts like hell. But "Behold! with every hardship comes ease" (94:5). After night, comes light. The Islam of Obscurantism must give way to an Islam of Illumination. After all, "God is the Light of the heavens and the earth" (24:35).

Works Cited

(URLs are truncated)

Abdullah, Aslam. "Islam Abolished Slavery, Jurisprudence Kept it Alive." *Muslim Mirror* (June 8, 2020). Internet: https://muslimmirror.com

Abdul-Samad, Lina. "Arabs, the N-Word and the A-Word are the Same." *Muslim Girl* (February 5, 2017). Internet: https://muslimgirl.com

Abou El Fadl, Khaled. "Endorsement." Personal correspondence. July 7, 2023.

---. "Slavery & Islam" Personal correspondence. June 26, 2023.

---. *Speaking in God's Name: Islamic Law, Authority and Women*. London: Oneworld Publications, 2013.

Abu-Izzeddin Nejla M. *The Druzes: A New Study of their History, Faith, and Society*. Leiden: E.J. Brill, 1993.

Afary, Janet. *Sexual Politics in Modern Iran*. Cambridge: Cambridge University Press, 2009.

Ahmad, Mirza Bashir. *Islam and Slavery*. Qadian: Mirza Wasim Ahmad, 1975.

'Ajami, Cyrille Moreno al-. *Que dit vraiment le Coran ?* Internet: https://www.alajami.fr

---. *Que dit vraiment le Coran ?* Paris: Erick Bonnier, 2020.

---. "Une autre lecture du Coran est possible." *Iqbal Hypotheses* (July 30, 2019). Internet: https://iqbal.hypotheses.org

---. "The Challenge for the Future is to Reform the Muslim." *Iqbal Hypotheses* (March 30, 2013). Internet:https://iqbalhypotheses.org

Akyol, Mustafa. *Reopening Muslim Minds: A Return to Reason, Freedom, and Tolerance*. New York: St. Martin's Essentials, 2022.

Ali, Mohammad. *The Position of Women in Islam: A Progressive View*. Albany: State University of New York Press, 2004.

Ali, S.V. Mir Ahmed. *The Holy Qur'an: With English Translation of the Arabic Text and Commentary according to the Version of the Holy Ahlul-Bait*. Elmhurst, NY: Tahrike Tarsile Qur'an, 1988.

Ali, Kecia. *Sexual Ethics and Islam: Feminist Reflections on Qur'an, Hadith, and Jurisprudence*. London: Oneworld Academic, 2017.

---. *Marriage and Slavery in Early Islam*. Harvard: Harvard University Press, 2010.

Ali, Syed Ameer. *The Personal Law of the Mahommedans, According to all the Schools*. London: W.H. Allen, 1880. Internet: https://archive.org

Ally, Shabbir. "Conclusion: Islam and Concubinage." *Let the Qur'an Speak*

(September 1, 2022). Internet: https://www.quranspeaks.com

'Amili, al-Hurr al-. *Wasa'il al-shi'ah*. Internet: http://lib.eshia.ir

Amini, Ibrahim. *Principles of Marriage Family Ethics*. Qum: Ansariyan, n. date.

Amrohi, Zafar Hasan. *Morals and Manners of the Holy Imams*. Trans. Athar Husayn S.H. Rizvi. Al-Islam.org. Internet: https://www.al-islam.org

Anello, Giancarlo. "The Concept of 'Contractual Citizenship' in the Charter of Medina (622 CE): A Contemporary Interpretation." *Islamochristiana, Journal of the PISAI Rome* (2021): 1-21. Internet: https://papers.ssrn.com

Ansary, Tamim. *Destiny Disrupted: A History of the World through Islamic Eyes*. New York: Public Affairs, 2009.

Anthony, Sean W. *Muhammad and the Empires of Faith: The Making of the Prophet of Islam*. Oakland: University of California Press, 2020.

Akyol, Mustafa. *Reopening Muslim Minds: A Return to Reason, Freedom, and Tolerance*. New York: St. Martin's Essentials, 2022.

---. *Why, as a Muslim, I Defend Liberty*. Washington DC: Cato Institute, 2021.

---. "Where Islam and Reason Meet." *Cato Institute* (April 15, 2021). Internet: https://www.cato.org

Arabiyya. "New Online Campaign Urges Americans to "Drop the A-Word." *Arabiyya News* (February 27, 2014). Internet: https://english.alarabiya.net

Asad, Muhammad. *The Message of the Qur'an*. London: The Book Foundation, 2012.

Asharis Assemble. "ISIS and the Theology of Rape: Rubbish Responses by Muslims." *Asharis Assemble* (August 21, 2015). Internet: https://asharis assemble.com

Awde, Yasser. "Opinion of Shaykh Yasser Awde." *Shia Reformers*. https://sites.google.com

'Ayyashi, Muhammad al- *Tafsir al-'Ayashi*. Internet: http://lib.eshia.ir

Azaiez, Mehdi, Gabriel Said Reynolds, Tommaso Tesei, and Hamza M. Zafer, eds. *The Qur'an Seminar Commentary / Le Qur'an Seminar. A Collaborative Study of 50 Qur'anic Passages / Commentaire collaboratif de 50 passages coraniques*. Berlin, Boston: De Gruyter, 2016. Internet: https://library.oapen. org

Azhar, al-. "Why Didn't Islam Abolish Slavery Immediately?" *Dar al-Ifta al-Missriyyah*. Internet: http://eng.dar-alifta.org

Azhar, Zahra, and Masoud Noori. "Shi'i Ideas of Slavery: A Study of the Qajar Era Before and After the Constitutional Revolution." *Journal of Islamic Law* 3.1 (2022). Internet: https://journalofislamiclaw.com

Azumah, John Allembillah. *The Legacy of Arab-Islam in Africa: A Quest for Inter-Religious Dialogue*. London: Oneworld Publications, 2021.

Bangash, Zafar. *Power Manifestations of the Sirah: Examining the Letters and Treaties of the Messenger of Allah*. Ed. Afeef Khan. Toronto: The Institute of Contemporary Islamic Thought, 2011.

Barlas, Asma. *Believing Women in Islam: Unreading Patriarchal Interpretations of the Qur'an*. Austin: University of Texas Press, 2019.

Barqi, Ahmad al-. *al-Mahasin / The Beauties*. Vol. 2. Book 6. Internet: https://hubeali.com/

Works Cited

Bauer, Karen. *Gender Hierarchy in the Qur'an: Medieval Interpretations, Modern Responses*. Cambridge: Cambridge University Press, 2017.

Bayindir, Abdulaziz. "Captivity, Slavery, and Concubinage According to the Qur'an." *Islam and Qur'an* (May 27, 2017). Internet : https://www.islamandquran.org

Bhatti, Faisal. "Broken *Hadiths*." *Medium* (March 10, 2020). Internet: https://medium.com

Bink, Stefan. *Thraldom: A History of Slavery in the Viking Age*. Cambridge: Oxford University Press, 2021.

Bano, Shadab. "Marriage and Concubinage in the Mughal Imperial Family." *Proceedings of the Indian History Congress* 60 (1999): 353-362. Internet: https://www.jstor.org

Bouknight, Sebastian, and Timothy Hucks. "Slavery Hidden in Plain Sight in Mauritania." *Inside Arabia* (January 30, 2019). Internet: https://insidearabia.com

Brown, Jonathan A.C. *Slavery & Islam*. London: Oneworld Academic, 2020.

---. "Apology without Apologetics." *Muslim Matters* (February 16, 2017). Internet: https://muslimmatters.org

Cannuyer, Christian. "Mariya, la concubine copte de Muhammad: réalité ou mythe?" *Acta Orientalia Belgica* 21 (2008): 251-264.

---. "Mariya, la concubine copte de Muhammad: réalité ou mythe?" *Solidarité-Orient* 253 (janvier-fevrier-mars 2010): 18-25. Internet: https://www.academia.edu

Catechism of the Catholic Church. 2nd ed. Rome: Libreria Editrice Vaticana, 2000. Internet: http://www.scborromeo.org

Chaudhry, Ayesha S. *Domestic Violence and the Islamic Tradition*. Oxford: Oxford University Press, 2013.

Chebel, Malek. *L'esclavage en terre d'Islam*. Domont: Pluriel, 2010.

---. "Le salut par l'abolition de l'esclavage." *Historia* (February 2008). Internet: https://www.historia.fr

Chesler, Phyllis. *Islamic Gender Apartheid: Exposing a Veiled War against Women*. Nashville: New English Review Press, 2017.

Chittick, William, trans. *The Psalms of Islam: al-Sahifat al-kamilat al-sajjadiyyah*. London: The Muhammadi Trust, 1987.

---. *As-Sahifa al-kamilah al-sajjadiyyah*. Al-Islam.org. Internet: https://www.al-islam.org

Clarence-Smith, William Gervase. "Islam and Slavery." *London School of Economics* (n. date). Internet: https://www.lse.ac.uk

---. "Slavery and Slave Trades in the Indian Ocean and Arab Worlds: Global Connections and Disconnections." *Proceedings from the 10th Annual Gilder Lehrman Center International Conference at Yale University* (Nov. 7-8, 2008). Internet: https://glc.yale.edu

---. *Islam and the Abolition of Slavery*. Oxford: Oxford University Press, 2006.

Clémençot, Julien. "La Mauritanie s'appuie sur l'islam pour criminaliser l'esclavage." *Afrik.com* (August 9, 2007). Internet: https://www.afrik.com

Considine, Craig. *People of the Book: Prophet Muhammad's Encounters with Christians*. London: Hurst, 2021.

---. *The Humanity of Muhammad: A Christian View*. Clifton, NJ: Blue Dome Press, 2020.

Cridem. "Boubacar Ould Messaoud: 'Je combats ma propre violence.'" *CRIDEM* (August 12, 2014). Internet: https://cridem.org

Crookston, Paul. "Professor Uses Lecture to Defend Islamic Slavery." *National Review* (February 15, 2017). Internet: https://www.nationalreview.com

Crowcroft, Barnaby. "Sanctioned by Sharia?" *Literary Review* (December 2019). Internet: https://literaryreview.co.uk

Dann, Michael. "Between History and Hagiography: The Mothers of the Imams in Imami Historical Memory." *Concubines and Courtesans: Women and Slavery in Islamic History*. Ed. Matthew S. Gordon and Kathryn A. Hain. Oxford: Oxford University Press, 2017. 244-264.

Dashti, 'Ali. *23 Years: A Study of the Prophetic Career of Mohammad*. Costa Mesa, CA: Mazda Publishers, 1994.

Dastghaib Shirazi, 'Abd al-Husayn. *82 Questions*. Trans. Athar Husayn S.H. Rizvi. *Al-Islam.org*. Internet: https://www.al-islam.org

Davis, Robert. *Christian Slaves, Muslim Masters: White Slavery in the Mediterranean, the Barbary Coast, and Italy, 1500-1800*. London: Palgrave Macmillan, 2003.

Diakho, Muhammad. *L'esclavage en Islam: entre les traditions arabes et les principes de l'Islam*. Paris: Les Éditions Albouraq, 2004.

Dibba, Abdullah. "How Islam Abolished Slavery, Leaving No Loopholes." *Al-Hakam* (June 10, 2020). Internet: https://www.alhakam.org

Esseissah, Khaled. "'Paradise is under the Feet of your Master.' The Construction of the Religious Basis of Racial Slavery in the Mauritanian Arab-Berber Community." *Journal of Black Studies* 47.1 (2016): 3-23. Internet: https://www.jstor.org

Elder, Larry. "Elder: Why Don't They Teach about the Arab-Muslim Slave Trade?" *The Toronto Sun* (Feb. 23, 2020). Internet: https://torontosun.com

ElGendy, Ayman. "Qur'ran Does Not Legitimize Slavery." *Egypt Independent* (December 26, 2018). Internet: http://www.egyptindependent.com

Eltahawy, Mona. "The Arab World's Dirty Little Secret." *New York Times* (November 10, 2008). Internet: http://www.nytimes.com

Eltis, David, and Stanley L. Engerman. *The Cambridge World History of Slavery. Vol. 3. AD 1420-1904*. Cambridge: Cambridge University Press, 2011.

Encyclopedia.Com. "Slavery and Abolition, Middle East." *Encyclopedia.com*. Internet: https://www.encyclopedia.com

End Slavery. "Address of Grand Ayatollah Mohammad Taqi al-Modarresi." *End Slavery* (2014). Internet: http://www.endslavery.va

Engineer, Asghar Ali. *Rights of Women in Islam*. 3rd ed. New Dehli: Sterling Publishers, 2004.

Fadlullah, Muhammad Husayn. "Fatwa on Slavery." Personal email from the Office of Grand Ayatullah Muhammad Husayn Fadlullah (April 2, 2023).

---. "Islam Today in the Dock." *Bayynat* (July 5, 2005). Internet: http://arabic.

bayynat.org.lb

Fahes, Fadi A. *Social Utopia in Tenth Century Islam: The Qarmatian Experiment*. Master of Arts thesis. Dominguez Hills, CA: California State University, 2018. Internet: https://scholarworks.calstate.edu

Faizer, Rizwi, ed. *The Life of Muhammad: al-Waqidi's* Kitab al-maghazi. Trans. Rizwi Faizer, Amal Ismail, and AbdulKader Tayob. London and New York: Routledge, 2011.

Fard, W.D. *The Supreme Wisdom Lessons*. Internet: https://www.ciphertheory.net

Farhat, Olfa. "Why Non-Black Arabs Should Never Use the N-Word." *Mille* (April 27, 2018). Internet: https://www.milleworld.com

Farid, Malik Ghulam. *The Holy Qur'an: Arabic Text with English Translation and Short Commentary*. London: Islam International Publications, 2006.

Fisher, Humphrey J. *Slavery in the History of Black Africa*. New York: New York University Press, 2001.

Flintoff, Corey. "Black Iraqis in Basra Face Racism." *Morning Edition: NPR News* (December 3, 2008). Internet: https://minorityrights.org

Floor, Willem. "BARDA and BARDA-DĀRI iv. From the Mongols to the Abolition of Slavery." *Encyclopædia Iranica*. Vol. III (2000): 768-774.

Freamon, Bernard K. *Possessed by the Right Hand: The Problem of Slavery in Islamic Law and Muslim Cultures*. Leiden: Brill, 2021.

---. "Jonathan A.C. Brown. *Slavery and Islam*. London: Oneworld Academic, 2019. 449 pp." *Journal of Islamic Ethics* 5 (2021) 331-352. Internet: https://brill.com

---. "Toward the Abolition of Slavery under the Aegis of Islamic Law." *The Comparative Jurist* (May 1, 2020). Internet: https://comparativejurist.org

---. "ISIS, Boko Haram, and the Human Right to Freedom from Slavery under Islamic Law." *Fordham International Law Journal* 39.2 (2016).

---. "Slavery, Freedom, and the Doctrine of Consensus in Islamic Jurisprudence." *Harvard Human Rights Journal* 11.1 (1998). Internet: https://papers.ssrn.com

Fregosi, Paul. *Jihad in the West: Muslim Conquests from the 7th to the 21st Centuries*. New York: Prometheus Books, 1998.

Gelgeç, Sevim. "*Ma Malakat Ayman* in the Context of Returning to the Ontological Understanding of Chastity." *The Journal of Tafsir Studies* 5.2 (October 2021). Internet: https://dergipark.org.tr

Gilliot, Claude. "Oralité et écriture dans la genèse, la transmission et la fixation du Coran." *Oralité & écriture dans la Bible & le Coran*. Ed. Philippe Cassuto and Pierre Larcher. Aix-en-Provence: PU Provence, 2014.

Gleissner, John Dewar. *Prison and Slavery: A Surprising Comparison*. Denver: Outskirts Press, 2010.

Gordon, Matthew S., and Kathryn A. Hain. *Concubines and Courtesans: Women and Slavery in Islamic History*. Oxford: Oxford University Press, 2017.

Gordon, Matthew. "Unhappy Offspring? Concubines and their Sons in Early Abbasid Society." *International Journal of Middle East Studies* (January 20, 2017). Internet: https://www.cambridge.org

Gray, Peter. "Sex, Slavery, and Islam: Ignoring the Elephant in the Room. *Altmuslimah* (September 20, 2011). Internet: https://www.altmuslimah.com

Guardian, The. "Prayer, Food, Sex and Water Parks in Iran's Holy City of Mashhad." *The Guardian* (May 7, 2015). Internet: https://www.the guardian.com

Hakami, 'Umarah ibn 'Ali al-. *Yaman: Its Early Medieval History*. Trans. Henry Cassels Kay. London: Edward Arnold, 1892.

Hakeem, Sayyid Mohammed Saeed al-. "Slavery." *Alhakeem.com*. Internet: https://www.alhakeem.com

Hain, Kathryn A. "Avenues to Social Mobility Available to Courtesans and Concubines." *Concubines and Courtesans: Women and Slavery in Islamic History*. Ed. Matthew S. Gordon and Kathryn A. Hain. Oxford: Oxford University Press, 2017. 324-337.

Hamel, Chouki El. *Black Morocco: A History of Slavery, Race, and Islam*. Cambridge: Cambridge University Press, 2013.

---. "Correspondence." (2023).

Hamid, Nasiruddin. "How Islam Abolished Slavery." *Light of Islam* (August 23, 2020). Internet: https://lightofislam.in

Hamoudi, Haider Ala. "The Problem of Slavery in Islamic Law: A Review of *Possessed by the Right Hand*, by Bernard Freamon." *Islamic Law Blog* (2020). Internet: https://islamiclaw.blog

---. "Sex and the Shari'a: Defining Gender Norms and Sexual Deviancy in Shi'i Islam." *Fordham International Law Journal* 39.1 (2015): 22-99. Internet: https://ir.lawnet.fordham.edu

Hanne, Olivier. "Le mariage coranique vu à travers l'Alcoran de Robert de Ketton." *Les stratégies matrimoniales (IXe-XIIIe siècle)*. Ed. Martin Aurell. Turnhout: Brepols, 2013: 267-290. Internet: https://halshs.archives-ouvertes.fr

Hanretta, Sean. "Islam and Emancipation." *African History* (April 20, 2022). Internet: http://oxfordre.com

Harrani, Hasan al- *Tuhaf al-Uqoul: The Masterpieces of the Intellects*. Trans. Badr Shahin. Qum: Ansariyan Publications, 2001.

Hassan, Riffat. "Human Right in the Qur'anic Perspective." *Windows of Faith: Muslim Women Scholar-Activists in North America*. Ed. Gisela Webb. Syracuse: Syracuse University Press, 2000. 241-248.

---. "What Does it Mean to be a Muslim Today?" *Cross Currents* (1990). Internet: http://www.crosscurrents.org

Hilali, Sulaym ibn Qays al-. *The Book of Sulaym*. Part III. Internet: https://hubeali.com

Hosseini Nasab, Reza. *Modern Islam*. Internet: http://www.hoseini.org

Hosni, Dina. *Female Youth in Contemporary Egypt: Post-Islamism and a New Politics of Visibility*. London: Taylor & Francis, 2022.

Howard, Barbara. "Exploring the Links between Slavery, Sex, and Scripture." *Brandeis Now* (October 29, 2010). Internet: https://www.brandeis.edu

Hub-e-Ali. *Tafsir Hub-e-Ali*. Hub-e-Ali. Internet: https://hubeali.com

Ibn al-Naqib al-Misri, Abu al-'Abbas Ahmad. *Reliance of the Traveler*. Trans.

Nuh Ha Mim Keller. Beltsville, MD: Amana Publications, 1994

Ibn Rashid, Ma'mar. *The Expeditions: An Early Biography of Muhammad*. Trans. Sean W. Anthony. New York and London: New York University Press, 2015.

Ibrahim, Raymond. "Islam's Hidden Role in the Transatlantic Slave Trade." *Middle East Forum* (February 6, 2020). Internet: https://www.meforum.org

---. "Raped and Ransacked in the Muslim World." *Raymond Ibrahim* (May 31, 2011). Internet: https://www.raymondibrahim.com

---. "Muslim Woman Seeks to Revive Institution of Sex-Slavery." *Middle East Forum* (June 6, 2011). Internet: https://www.meforum.org

Iddrisu, Abdulai. "A Study in Evil: The Slave Trade in Africa." *Religions* 2023 14.1. Internet: http://www.mdpi.com

International Republican Institute. *Living in the Shadows: The Enduring Marginalization of Black Iraqis*. Washington: International Republican Institute, 2020. Internet: https://www.iri.org

Islam, Yusuf. "The *Hoor al-Ayn* of Jannah Paradise." *Islam the True Religion of One God* (July 15, 2011). Internet: https://islamreligion1.wordpress.com

Islam, Joseph A. "Sexy Female Virgins for Men in Paradise? Really?" *The Qur'an and its Message* (January 24, 2014). Internet: http://quransmessage.com

---. "Sex with Slave Girls." *The Qur'an and its Message* (March 13, 2012). Internet: http://quransmessage.com

Jahanbakhsh, Forough. "Rational *Shari'ah*: Ahmad Qabel's Reformist Approach." *Religions* 2020 11.12. Internet: https://www.mdpi.com

Jaziri, 'Abd al-Rahman al-. *Islamic Jurisprudence According to the Four Sunni Schools*. Trans. Nancy Roberts. Louisville, KY: Fons Vitate, 2009.

Jebara, Mohamad. *Muhammad, The World-Changer: An Intimate Portrait*. New York: St. Martin's Essentials, 2021.

Jewish Virtual Library. "Concubine." *Jewish Virtual Library* (2008). Internet: https://www.jewishvirtuallibrary.org

Johnson, Heather. "There are Worse Things than Being Alone: Polygamy in Islam, Past, Present, and Future." *William & Mary Journal of Race, Gender, and Social Justice* 11.3 (2004-2005). Internet: https://scholarship.law.wm.edu

Jordac, George. *The Voice of Human Justice*. Trans. M. Fazal Haq. Qum: Ansariyan Publications, 1990.

Kadivar, Mohsen. "The Issue of Slavery in Contemporary Islam." *Iqra Online* (September 23, 2018). Internet: https://www.iqraonline.net

Karim, Kaleef K. "What Happened to the Captive Women in Awtas Incident?" *Discover the Truth* (June 23, 2016). Internet: https://discover-the-truth.com

Kaskas, Safi, and David Hungerford. *The Qur'an with References to the Bible*. Np: Bridges of Reconciliation, 2016.

Khadduri, Majid. *The Islamic Law of Nations: Shaybani's Siyar*. Baltimore: The John Hopkins Press, 1966.

Kılıçaslan, İbrahim. "Slavery & Islam." *İslam Araştırmaları Dergisi* 44 (2020): 263-285. Internet: https://dergipark.org.tr

Knight, Michael Muhammad. "Editing Homophobia out of the 'Islamic

Tradition.'" *Vice* (April 16, 2013). Internet: https://www.vice.com

Kulayni, Muhammad al-. *al-Kafi*. 8 volumes. Trans. Muhammad Sarwar. New York: The Islamic Seminary, 2015.

--- *al-Kafi*. Vol. 5. Internet: https://hubeali.com

---. *al-Kafi*. Internet: http://lib.eshia.ir

Kurzman, Charles. *Liberal Islam: A Source Book*. Oxford: Oxford University Press, 1998.

La Rue, George. "Slave Trades and Diaspora in the Middle East, 700 to 1900." *Oxford Research Encyclopedia* (May 26, 2021). Internet: https://oxfordre.com

Lal, K.S. *Muslim Slave System in Medieval India*. New Delhi: Aditya Prakashan, 1994. Internet: http://voiceofdharma.org

Lee, Umar. "Georgetown Professor Jonathan Brown Defends Slavery as Moral and Rape as Normal in Virginia Lecture." *Student Voices* (February 8, 2017). Internet: https://www.meforum.org

Levy, Reuben. *The Social Structure of Islam*. Cambridge: Cambridge University Press, 1957.

Lewis, Bernard. *Race and Slavery in the Middle East: An Historical Enquiry*. Oxford: Oxford University Press, 1990.

Loiaconi, Stephen. "Georgetown Professor under Fire for Statements on Islam and Rape, Slavery." *ABC News* (February 21, 2017). Internet: https://abc3340.com

Lumen Learning. *History of World Civilization II*. Internet: https://courses.lumen learning.com

Luxenberg, Christoph. *The Syro-Aramaic Reading of the Koran: A Contribution to the Decoding of the Language of the Koran*. Berlin: Schiler, 2007. Internet: https://ia803107.us.archive.org

Madelung, Wilfred. *The Succession to Muhammad: A Study of the Early Caliphate*. Cambridge: Cambridge University Press, 2004.

Mahajjah. "Narrators Who Have been Severely Impugned." *Mahajjah*. Internet: https://mahajjah.com

Majlisi, Muhammad Baqir. *Bihar al-Anwar*. Vol. 59. Internet: https://hubeali.com

---. *Hayat al-Qulub. Vol. 1. Stories of the Prophets. Al-Islam.org*. Internet: https://www.al-islam.org

--- *Haqqul Yaqeen: A Compendium of Twelver Shia Religious Beliefs*. Qum: Ansariyan, n.d.

Makarem Shirazi, Naser. "Slavery from the Perspective of Islam." *Makarem* (2019). Internet: https://www.makarem.ir

Mansour, Ahmed Subhy. "On Prohibition of Enslavement and Slavery in Islam." *Ahl al-Qur'an* (June 11, 2018). Internet: https://www.ahl-alquran.com

Mashayekhi, Ghodratullah. *A Divine Perspective on Rights*. Trans. Ali Peiravi and Lisa Zaynab Morgan. *Al-Islam.org*. Internet: https://www.al-islam.org

Massad, Joseph Andoni. *Desiring Arabs*. Chicago: University of Chicago Press, 2007. Internet: https://archive.org

Mathews, Nathaniel. "Responding to 'Hoteps:' Three Points on 'Islamic' Slavery." *Sapelo Square* (April 18, 2017). Internet: https://sapelosquare.com

Works Cited

283

---. "A Trajectory of Manumission: Examining the Issue of Slavery in Islam." *Sapelo Square* (April 18, 2017). Internet: https://sapelosquare.com

McLaughlin, Peter. *"Easy Meat:" Multiculturalism, Islam, and Child Sex Slavery.* UK: Law and Freedom Foundation, 2014. Internet: https://archive.org

MEMRI. "Leading Sunni Iraqi Cleric Khaled al-Mullah Criticizes ISIS Practices: The Times of Slavery are Over." *MEMRI* (July 1, 2016). Internet: https://www.memri.org

---. "Iraqi Ayatollah al-Haeri: People Who Will Oppose the Mahdi Will Become Slaves or Slave Girls, Who Can Be Lent Out to Friends." *MEMRI* (April 7, 2016). Internet: https://www.memri.org

Mernissi, Fatima. *The Veil and the Male Elite: A Feminist Interpretation of Women's Rights in Islam.* Trans. Mary Jo Lakeland. Reading, MA: Basic Books, 1991.

Mikva, Rachel S. *Dangerous Religious Ideas: The Deep Roots of Self-Critical Faith in Judaism, Christianity, and Islam.* Boston: Beacon Press, 2020

Milton, Giles. *White Gold.* London: Hodder & Stoughton, 2004.

Minority Rights Group International. "Black Iraqis." *Minority Rights* (Nov. 2017). Internet: https://minorityrights.org

Mir-Hosseini, Ziba. *Journeys Toward Gender Equality in Islam.* London: Oneworld Academic, 2022.

Mirza, K.A. *The Tragedy of Samarra.* Toronto: Q-Print, 1993.

Modarressi, Hossein. *Tradition and Survival: A Bibliographic Survey of Early Shiite Literature.* London: Oneworld Publications, 2003.

Morrow, John Andrew. *Controversies in Islam: Religious Law, Qur'anic Ethical Imperatives, and Higher Moral Objectives.* Cambridge-upon-Tyne: Cambridge Scholars Publishing, 2023.

---. *The Islamic Interfaith Initiative: No Fear Shall be Upon Them.* Newcastle upon Tyne: Cambridge Scholars Publishing, 2021.

---. *Shiism in the Maghrib and al-Andalus. Vol. 1. History.* Newcastle upon Tyne: Cambridge Scholars Publishing, 2021.

---. *The Messenger of Mercy: The Covenants of Coexistence from the Prophet of Pluralism.* New Delhi: Sanbun Publishers, 2021.

---. *The Most Controversial Qur'anic Verse: Why 4:34 Does Not Promote Violence Against Women.* Lanham, MD: Rowman & Littlefield, 2020.

---. *Islam and the People of the Book: Critical Studies on the Covenants of the Prophet.* 3 vols. Newcastle upon Tyne: Cambridge Scholars Publishing, 2017.

---, and Charles Upton. *The Words of God to the Prophet Muhammad: Forty Sacred Sayings.* Chicago: Kazi Publications, 2015.

---. *Islam and the People of the Book.* Vols. 1-3: Newcastle-upon-Tyne: Cambridge Scholars Publishing, 2017.

---. *The Covenants of the Prophet Muhammad with the Christians of the World.* Tacoma, WA: Angelico Press / Sophia Perennis, 2013.

---. *Islamic Insights: Writings and Review.* Qum: Ansariyan Publications, 2012.

Mufid, Shaykh al-. *Kitab al-irshad: The Book of Guidance into the Lives of the*

Twelve Imams. Trans. I.K.A. Howard. London: Muhammadi Trust, 1981.

Muhammad, Elijah. "The Coming of Allah." *Moslem World & the USA* (Oct-Nov-Dec 1956). Internet: https://transcription.si.edu

Muhammadin, Fajri Matahati. "Refuting Da'esh Properly: A Critical Review of the 'Letter to Baghdadi.'" *Journal of International Humanitarian Action* (July 29, 2016). Internet: https://jhumanitarianaction.springeropen.com

Mohaghegh Damad, Mostafa. "Revisiting Traditional *Fiqh* in Respect to New Daily Occurrences." *Iqra Online* (March 15, 2018). Internet: https://iqraonline.net

---. "The Role of Time and Social Welfare in the Modification of Legal Rulings." *Shiite Heritage: Essays on Classical and Modern Traditions*. Ed. Lynda Clarke. Binghamton, NY: Binghamton University / Global Academic Publishing, 2001. 213-222.

Mujahid, Abdul Malik. "Debunked: The Revival of Slavery." *WISE Muslim Women*. Internet: http://wisemuslimwomen.org

Murata, Sachiko, and William C. Chittick. *The Vision of Islam*. St. Paul, MN: Paragon House, 1994.

Muslim Skeptic Team. "Reviewing Yaqeen Institute: A Source of Certainty or Doubt?" *The Muslim Skeptic* (April 20, 2020). Internet: https://muslim skeptic.com

Nasr, Seyyed Hossein, ed. *The Study Qur'an*. New York: HarperOne, 2015.

Nategh, Amir. "Selling Sex to Survive in Iran." *BBC News* (March 17, 2022). Internet: https://www.bbc.com

National FGM Centre: "What is FGM?" *National FGM Centre*. Internet: https://nationalfgmcentre.org.uk

NBC News. "Al-Sadr Aide: Reward for Killing British Troops." *NBC News* (May 7, 2004). Internet: https://www.nbcnews.com

Nestby, Dag Hallvard. "How Could the Norwegian RE Subject Express the Presence of Human Rights Thinking in Islam?" *British Journal of Religious Education* (January 17, 2022). Internet: https://www.bing.com

Newman, Andrew J., ed. *Islamic Medical Wisdom*. Trans. Batool Isaphany. London: The Muhammadi Trust, 1991. Internet: https://www.al-islam.org

Nicolle, David. *Yarmuk 636 A.D. The Muslim Conquest of Syria*. London: Osprey Publishing, 1994.

Nu'man, al-Qadi al-. *The Pillars of Islam*. Vol. 1. Trans. Asaf A.A. Fyzee. Ed. Ismail Kurban Husein Poonawala. Oxford: Oxford University Press, 2006.

---. *The Pillars of Islam: Laws Pertaining to Human Intercourse*. Vol. 2. Trans. Asaf A.A. Fyzee. Ed. Ismail Kurban Husein Poonawala. Oxford: Oxford University Press, 2007.

Obeid, Anis. *The Druze: Their Faith in Tawhid*. Syracuse: Syracuse University Press, 2006.

Öhrnberg, Kaj. "Mariya al-Qibtiyya Unveiled." *Studia Orientalia* 55.14 (1984): 297-303.

Okeowo, Alexis. "Freedom Fighter: A Slaving Society and an Abolitionist Crusade." *The New Yorker* (September 1, 2014). Internet: https://www.new yorker.com

Open Letter to Baghdadi (2014). Internet: http://www.lettertobaghdadi.com

Organization of the Islamic Conference. *Cairo Declaration on Human Rights in Islam* (August 5, 1990). Internet: https://www.fmreview.org

Orland, Kevin. "Muslim Spiritual Leader in Malta Imam El Sadi Strongly Condemns ISIS." *The Independent* (December 17, 2014).

Osman, Rawand. *Female Personalities in the Qur'an and Sunna.* New York: Routledge, 2015.

Parwez, Ghulam Ahmad. *The Qur'anic Perspective on Apostasy, Slavery, and Concubines*. Lahore: Tolu-e-Islam Trust, no date. Internet: https://www.parwez.tv

Pavlu, George. "Recalling Africa's Harrowing Tale of its First Slavers -- The Arabs -- as UK Slave Trade Abolition is Commemorated." *New African* (March 27, 2018). Internet: https://newafricanmagazine.com

Pierce, Matthew. *Twelve Infallible Men: The Imams and the Making of Shiism.* Cambridge: Harvard University Press, 2016.

Pipes, Daniel. "Islamists Endorse Muslims Owning Slaves." *Daniel Pipes* (September 10, 2020). Internet: https://www.danielpipes.org

Powell, Eve Troutt. "African Slaves in Islamic Lands." *Afropop* (December 3, 2011). Internet: https://afropop.org

Powers, David S. *Muhammad is Not The Father of Any of Your Men: The Making of the Last Prophet*. Philadelphia: University of Pennsylvania Press, 2009.

Prima Qur'an. "Why I Now Follow the 'Ibadi School." *Prima Qur'an* (October 4, 2022). Internet: https://primaquran.com

Qabel, Ahmad. *Shari'at-e 'Aqlani: Maqalati dar Nesbat-i 'Aql va Shar'* (2012). Internet: http://www.ghabel.net

Quraishi-Landes, Asifa. "A Meditation on *Mahr*, Modernity, and Muslim Marriage Contract Law." *Feminism, Law, and Religion*. Ed. Marie A. Failinger, Elizabeth R. Schiltz, and Susan J. Stabile. London and New York: Routledge, 2016.

Qur'anic Path. "Does the Qur'an Allow Sex with Slaves / Concubines?" *Qur'anic Path*. Internet: https://quranicpath.com/misconceptions/concubines.html

Rahbari, Ladan. "Gendered and Ethnic Captivity and Slavery in Safavid Persia: A Literature Review." *Soc. Sci.* 2021, 10(1), 22; https://doi.org

Rahnema, Ali. *Shi'i Reformation in Iran: The Life and Theology of Shari'at Sangelaji*. London: Ashgate, 2015.

Rajaee, Farhang. *Islamism and Modernism: The Changing Discourse in Iran.* Austin: University of Texas Press, 2007.

Rashid, Qasim. *Extremist: A Response to Geert Wilders & Terrorists Everywhere.* Np: AyHa Publishing, 2014.

Reynolds, Gabriel Said. "Intertextuality, Doublets, and Orality in the Qur'an, with Attention to Suras 61 and 66." *Unlocking the Medinan Qur'an*. Ed. Nicolai Sinai. Leiden: Brill, 2022.

Ricks, Thomas. "Slaves and Slave trading in Shi'i Iran, AD 1500–1900." *Journal of Asian and African Studies* 36 (2001): 407-418. Internet: https://brill.com

Ridgeon, Llyod. *Hijab: Three Modern Iranian Seminarian Perspectives*. London:

Gingko, 2021.

Rizvi, Muhammad. *Marriage and Morals in Islam.* Vancouver: Islamic Educational Foundation, 1990.

Rizvi, Saeed Akhtar. *Slavery from Islamic and Christian Perspectives.* Vancouver: Vancouver Islamic Educational Foundation, 1987. Internet: https://www.al-islam.org

Rizvi, Saeed Akhtar. "Imam Hasan, The Myth of His Divorces." *Al-Islam.Org.* Internet: https://www.al-islam.org

Robinson, Majied. *Marriage in the Tribe of Muhammad: A Statistical Study of Early Arabic Genealogical Literature.* Berlin: De Gruyter, 2020.

Rodriguez, Junius P. *Chronology of World Slavery.* Santa Barbara: ABC-CLIO, 1999.

Rosenberg, Roger E. *Disagreeing with Malcolm.* Internet: https://www.academia.edu

Rosenblum, Amalia. "Visiting Dubai is like Standing on the Sidelines of a Gang Rape." *Haaretz* (November 30, 2020). Internet: https://www.haaretz.com

Saanei, Youself. "Interview." *Saanei* (2011). Internet: https://saanei.org

Sabio, Alfonso el. *Las siete partidas.* Internet: http://ficus.pntic.mec.es

Saduq, Shaykh al-. *'Illal al-shara'i.* Internet: http://lib.eshia.ir

Saeed, Abdullah, Rown Gould, and Adis Duderija. *Islamic Teachings on Contemporary Issues for Young Muslims.* Victoria: NCEIS, 2016.

Salem, Hazem Y. *Islamic Political Thought: Reviving a Rationalist Tradition.* Doctoral dissertation. Denver: University of Denver, 2013.

Segal, Ronald. *Islam's Black Slaves: The Other Black Diaspora.* New York: Farrar, Straus and Giroux, 2001.

Shahin, Sultan. "What is Wrong with 126 Moderate Ulema's 'Open Letter to 'Khalifa' Abu Bakr Al-Baghdadi,' and Why it Will Not Work? This Moderate Fatwa Does Not Leave any Leg for Moderate Islam to Stand On." *New Age Islam* (August 30, 2015). Internet: https://www.newageislam.com

Shaikh, Sa'diyya. *Sufi Narratives of Intimacy: Ibn 'Arabi, Gender, and Sexuality.* New Delhi: Munshiram Manoharlal Publishers, 2013.

Sherley, Anthony, Robert Sherley, and Thomas Sherley. *The Travelogue of the Sherley Brothers.* Translated by Avans. Tehran: Negah, 1983.

Shirazi, Makarem. "Slavery from the Perspective of Islam." *Makarem* (March 14, 2019). Internet: http://www.makarem.ir

Shoemaker, Stephen J. *Creating the Qur'an: A Historical-Critical Study.* Oakland: University of California, Press, 2022.

---. "Les vies de Muhammad." *Le Coran des historiens.* Vol. 1. Ed. Mohammad Ali Amir-Moezzi and Guillaume Dye. Paris: Le Cerf, 2019. 183-229.

Sistani, 'Ali al-. "Advice and Guidance to the Fighters on the Battlefields." *Sistani* (2015). Internet: https://www.sistani.org

---. "Ayatollah al-Sistani Prohibits the Enslavement and Rape of Women during a Military Campaign, and Forbids Sex with Non-Muslim Concubines." *Islamopediaonline.* (April 22, 2010). Internet: http://www.islamo pediaonline.org

Soroush, Abdolkarim. "Transcript of TV Interview with Dr. Soroush by Dariush

Sajjadi, Broadcast, Homa TV, 9 March 2006." Internet: http://www.drsoroush. com

Spencer, Robert. "Georgetown Prof. Jonathan Brown Now Says Islam Forbids Slavery and Rape, but in 2015 Said it Allowed Them." *Jihad Watch* (February 11, 2017). Internet: https://www.jihadwatch.org

Strauss, Valerie. "Georgetown Professor under Fire for Lecture about Slavery and Islam." *The Washington Post* (February 17, 2017). Internet: https://www. washingtonpost.com

Suleiman, Omar. "Exploring the Faith and Identity Criss of American Muslim Youth." *Yaqeen Institute* (March 3, 2017). Internet: https://yaqeeninstitute.org

---. "40 *Hadiths* on Social Justice." https://f.hubspotusercontent10.net

Tabarsi, Hasan al-. *Mishkat ul-Anwar fi ghurar il-akhbar: The Lamp Niche for the Best Traditions*. Trans. Lisa Zaynab Morgan and Ali Peiravi. Qum: Ansariyan Publications, 2007.

Tabataba'i, Muhammad Husayn. *Sunan an-Nabi: A Collection of Narrations on the Conduct and Customs of the Prophet Muhammad*. Trans. Tahir Ridha Jaffer. Qum: Ansariyan Publications, 2014.

Taha, Mahmoud Mohamed. *The Second Message of Islam*. Trans. Abdullahi Ahmed An-Na'im. Syracuse: Syracuse University Press, 1987.

Takim, Liyakat. *Shiism Revisited: Ijtihad & Reformation in Contemporary Times*. Oxford: Oxford University Press, 2022.

---. "Islamic Law and the Neoijtihadist Phenomenon." *Religions* 12.6 (2021). Internet: https://doi.org

Tracy, Larissa, ed. *Castration and Culture in the Middle Ages*. Cambridge: D.S. Brewer, 2013.

Tusi, Shaykh al-. *Tahdhib al-ahkam*. Internet: http://lib.eshia.ir

---. *al-Istibsar*. Internet: http://lib.eshia.ir

UN. "Migrant Workers in the Middle East often Exploited, UN Reports at Human Trafficking Conference." *UN News* (April 9, 2013). Internet: https://news.un.org

Urban, Elizabeth. *Conquered Populations in Early Islam: Non-Arabs, Slaves, and the Sons of Slave Mothers*. Edinburgh: Edinburgh University Press, 2020

---. "Hagar and Mariya: Early Islamic Models of Slave Motherhood." *Concubines and Courtesans: Women and Slavery in Islamic History*. Ed. Matthew S. Gordon and Kathryn A. Hain. Oxford: Oxford University Press, 2017. 225-243.

Valante, Mary A. "Castrating Monks: Vikings, the Slave Trade, and the Value of Eunuchs." *Castration and Culture in the Middle Ages*. Ed. Larissa Tracy. Cambridge: D.S. Brewer, 2013. 174-187.

Valeurs Actuelles. "En Ile-de-France, 93% des vols et 63% des agressions sexuelles dans les transports sont le fait d'étrangers." *Valeurs Actuelles* (December 21, 2020). Internet: https://www.valeursactuelles.com

Van Reeth, Jan M.F. "Sourate 33: *Al-Ahzab* (Les Factions). *Le Coran des historiens*. Vol. 2b. Ed. Mohammad Ali Amir-Moezzi and Guillaume Dye.

Paris: Éditions du Cerf, 2019. 1119-1147.

Wadud, Amina. *Qur'an and Woman: Rereading the Sacred Text from a Woman's Perspective.* Oxford: Oxford University Press, 1999.

Wallbank, T. Walter, et. al. *Civilization Past and Present.* Chicago: Scott, Foresman and Company, 1962.

Ware III, Rudolph T. *The Walking Qur'an: Islamic Education, Embodied Knowledge, and History in West Africa.* Chapel Hill: University of North Carolina Press, 2014.

Webb, Mohammed Alexander Russell. *Islam in America: A Brief Statement of Mohammedanism and an Outline of the American Islamic Propaganda.* New York: The Oriental Publishing Co., 1893.

Witztum, Joseph. "Q: 4:24 Revisited." *Islamic Law and Society* 16.1 (2009): 1-33. Internet: https://www.jstor.org

Yehoshua, Y., R. Green, and A. Agron. "Sex Slavery in the Islamic State: Practices, Social Media Discourses, and Justifications: Jabhat al-Nusra: ISIS is Taking our Women as Sex Slaves Too." *MEMRI* (August 17, 2015). Internet: https://www.memri.org

Yüksel, Edip. "Exposing Prof. Jonathan Brown." *YouTube* (June 14, 2019). Internet: https://www.youtube.com

Yüksel, Edip, Layth Saleh al-Shaiban, and Martha Shulte-Nafeh. *Qur'an: A Reformist Translation.* USA: Brainbow Press, 2007.

Yousuf. "Review of Dr. Jonathan Brown's Book on Slavery and Islam." *Yousuf Blog* (November 14, 2019). Internet: https://yousuf.blog

Zein, Ibrahim, and Ahmed El-Wakil. *The Covenants of the Prophet Muhammad: From Shared Historical Memory to Peaceful Co-Existence.* New York: Routledge, 2023.

Zouari, Fawzia. "Mohamed Talbi: 'L'islam est né laïc.'" *Jeune Afrique* (January 9, 2015). Internet: https://www.jeuneafrique.com

"Set the slaves free." (Qur'an 47:4)

Index

A

'A'ishah: 13, 39, 223, 243

'Abbasids: 23, 66, 84, 95, 122, 128, 162, 163, 169, 199, 227

'Abd al-Jabbar: 54, 182, 240

'Abd al-Rahman, Moulay: 30, 140

'Abdu, Muhammad: 56, 160, 193

Abdul-Jabbar, Kareem, 15

Abdullah, Aslam: 13, 17, 68

Abdullah, Fadel: 164

Abdulmejid, Sultan: 242

'Abd al-Muttalib: 213

'Abdul-Rahman III: 123

Abeid, Biram Dah: 170-171

'Abid: 198

Abou El Fadl, Khaled: 3, 167, 274

Abraham: xiv, 20, 21, 68, 221

Abu al-Jawza': 136

Abu Bakr: 15, 16, 137, 138, 198

Abu Zahra, Muhammad: 246

Abu Zayd, Nasr: 12

Abu-Izzeddin Nejla: 154

Abyssinia / Abyssinians: 6, 7, 9, 15, 42, 172

'Adl: 94, 185, 232, 251

Adult entertainers: 92, 117

Adultery: 6, 29, 32, 35, 38, 41, 44, 62, 78, 88, 89, 103, 110, 112-114, 156, 210, 216, 224, 233, 235, 250, 252

Afary, Janet: 42, 92

Afro-descendants: 130, 146, 173

Agha Khan III: 157, 245

Ahl al-'adl wa al-tawhid: 251

Ahl al-akhbar: 251

Ahl al-bayt: 76, 77, 84, 251

Ahl al-hadith: 251

Ahl al-harb: 31

Ahl al-istiqamah: 251

Ahl al-kalam: 251

Ahl al-ra'y: 251

Ahl al-sunnah: 107*, 251*

Ahmad, Bashir: 243-244

Ahmadiyyah: 36, 44, 45, 156, 157, 193, 211, 242, 243, 272

Ahmed, Leila: 87, 90-91, 154, 160, 210

'Ajami, Cyrille Moreno al-: 42, 54, 66, 90, 119, 132, 163, 165, 206, 209, 210, 248, 250, 252, 273

Akbar the Great: 123, 192

Akhlaq: 167, 182, 183, 185, 251

Alawis: 78, 241

Alcohol: 220

Alfonso the Wise: 51

Algeria: 99, 139, 145, 177, 222

Ali, Abdullah Yusuf: 25, 33

Ali, Kecia: 58, 72, 150

Ali, Maulvi Chiragh: 193

Ali, Mohammad: 43

Ali, Muhammad: 15

Ali, S.V. Mir Ahmed: 29, 234

Ali, Syed Ameer: 81

Amin, Qasim: 36

Amini, Ibrahim: 77

Ammar: 3, 107, 118

Amr bi al-ma'ruf: 115

Anal sex: 82

Andalus: 60, 81

Anello, Giancarlo: 176

Anglican Church: 51, 247

Ansary, Tamim: 221

Antibiotics: 130

292 Islam & Slavery

Apartheid: 51, 76, 179
Apologists: 7, 19, 49, 50, 63, 67, 78,
    87, 106, 108, 137, 174, 177, 222,
    223, 224, 244, 272
'Aqqad, 'Abbas al-: 246
'Aql: 185, 246, 251
Arab supremacy: 60, 207
Arabic: 60, 105, 205, 207-208, 216
Arafat, Yaser: 207
Aristocracy: 9
Armed Islamic Group: 145
'As, 'Amr ibn al-: 153, 227
Asad, Muhammad: 43, 45, 47
Ash'ari: 45
'Askari, Hasan al-: 78, 187, 188
Autonomy: 125, 226, 236
Awtas: 25, 27
'Ayni: 28
Azhar, al-: 62, 148, 150, 151, 249
Aztecs: 205
Azumah, John: 4, 8-9, 12, 39, 42-43,
    53, 64, 69, 73, 93, 102, 128, 130,
    136, 143, 152-153, 157, 160, 164,
    172, 174, 176, 178, 195, 201-202,
    203, 215, 221
Azzam, 'Abdullah: 217

B

Baba, Ahmad: 9
Badr: 15, 28
Baghavad Gita: 17
Baghdadi, Abu Bakr al- 175
Baha' al-Din: 155
Bangash, Zafar: 16
Bantu: 5, 7
Banu Makhzum: 137
Baqir al-Sadr, Muhammad: 193-94
Baqir, Muhammad al-: 77, 81, 84,
    88, 91, 186
Barakah: 13-15
Barbarity: 8
Barbary Coast: 177
Barqi: 186-188
Basra: 176
Bastards: 30

Bayindir, Abdulaziz: 196-197
Berbers: 69, 146
Bestiality: 4
Bhatti, Faisal: 189-190
Bible: xxi, 10, 20, 49-50, 71, 104,
    209, 214, 225, 251
Bigha': 35, 43, 235
Bigi, Jarullah: 193
Bilal: 9, 107, 137, 138, 226
Bilali, Salih: 59
Birr: 232
Black men: 42, 63, 103, 172, 178,
    179
Black women: 4, 5, 9, 42, 152, 179,
    215
Blasphemy: 52, 70, 107
Blind following: 34, 40, 111, 170
Blues: 217
Boko Haram: 145, 149, 211, 214,
    223
Bonhoeffer, Dietrich: 76
Booty: 22, 26, 36, 39-48, 127, 153-
    154, 170, 194, 221
Brazil: 67, 141, 173, 178
Breasts: 65, 92
Brethren of Purity: 240
Britain: 139, 141, 177
    'Abd: 146, 179
Brockopp, Jonathan: 43, 161
Brothels: xxi, 62, 123, 128, 220
Brown, Jack: 226
Buddhism: 59
Buffalo soldiers: 174
Bukhari: 201
Burayd: 5-6
Buti: 217
Buttocks: 5, 82, 92
Byzantines: 6, 26, 128
Byzantium: 5, 77

C

Cairo Declaration of Human Rights
    in Islam: 245
Calcutta: 62, 157
Cambodia: 217

Camel: 4-5
Cannibals: 8
Cannuyer, Christian: 21, 22
Captives: 16, 25-37, 50, 55, 63, 94, 106, 112, 117, 123, 136-137, 149-150, 156, 165-166, 169, 176, 196, 204, 222, 230, 232, 234, 236, 239, 246, 272
Casas, Bartolomé de las: 225
Castration: 92-93, 96, 127-133, 169, 173, 176, 178, 212, 215, 219, 225, 237, 239, 242
Casuistry: 157
Catechism: 51, 126
Cattle: 123
Caucasians: 33, 245
Celibacy: 58
Censorship: 17, 108
Chastity: 20, 28, 45, 46, 58, 78, 89, 99, 103, 119, 219, 234, 236, 239
Chaudhry, Ayesha: 115, 226
Chebel, Malek: 17, 33, 53, 56, 62-63, 68-69, 77, 116, 123, 130, 136, 138, 144, 155, 176, 179, 211, 215, 217, 225-226, 248
Chechnya: 149
Chetniks: 50
Chili sauce: 130
Chittick, William: 241
Chosroes: 21-22
Circassians: 22, 173
Circumcision: 170-171
Civil rights: 173
Civilizational collapse: 222
Clarence-Smith, William: 1, 36, 79, 81, 102, 116, 121, 123-124, 127, 133, 137, 140, 152, 154, 157, 159, 160, 164, 166, 168, 170, 176-177, 182, 186, 192, 194, 205, 208, 210, 211
Cleopatra: 22
Code Noir: 62
Coercion: 32, 60, 126, 154, 220
Colors: 3, 145, 230
Combattants: 31, 50, 53, 158

Comfort women: 228
Communism / communists: 139, 175
Compulsion: 119,
Constantinople: 55, 93
Copts: 12, 22
Corruption: 91, 112, 147, 166, 174, 229, 239
Corsairs: 177
Covenants of the Prophet: 32, 33, 175, 231
Cree: 87
Criminality: 230
Crimean Khanate: 50
Cuba: 141
Cum manu: 233

D

Daesh: 149, 175, 211, 223
Da'wah: 62
Dancers: 127, 215
Dar al-islam: 31, 93
Dashti, Ali: 220
Dastghaib Shirazi: 166, 191
David: 21, 50
Day of Judgment: 8, 13, 91, 131, 212, 225, 238
Day of Resurrection: 16-17
Daylam / Daylamites: 6
Death rate: 127, 129, 144, 177, 230
Deceit: 89, 231
Degeneracy: 56, 58, 91, 123, 198
Denialism: 10
Denmark: 141, 242
Devils' Advocate: 2, 159, 221
Dhimmah: 33
Diakho, Muhammad: 4, 8-9, 11, 16, 19, 27, 30-31, 34-35, 38, 40, 59, 62, 76, 78, 83, 92, 102, 115, 123-124, 132, 146, 164-165, 167-168, 198, 219, 227, 248
Dibba, Abdullah: 156
Disbelief: 11, 54, 72, 135, 139, 166
Discrimination: 51, 179, 196
Diversity: 3, 52, 105, 230

DNA of Islam: 2, 139, 211
Dolls: 91, 119
Donkey: 4-5
Donner, Fred: 138
Druze: 81, 154, 155, 157, 171, 192, 21, 242
Dubai: 144
Duderija, Adis: 249
Dutch Reformed Church: 51
Dye, Guillaum: 21

E

Egalitarianism: 137, 138, 252
Elder, Larry: 69
Emancipation: xxi, 14-15, 17, 47, 54-55, 68, 72, 87, 95-96, 98, 106, 108, 138,151, 164-165, 167-169, 174, 192-193, 195, 211, 233, 238, 243, 246, 249, 251
Emasculation: xxi, 63, 127-133, 170, 239
Endoparasitoid: 211
Enemies of God: 7, 8
Engineer, Asghar Ali: 44
Equality: 3, 7, 8, 15, 54, 57, 59, 60, 73, 84, 85, 96, 101, 136, 138, 147, 155, 167, 168, 201, 205, 206, 219, 226, 227, 228, 230, 237, 238, 240, 244, 245, 252
Eshkevari, Yousef: 161
Esseissah, Khaled: 249
Ethiopia / Ethiopian: 4, 5, 14, 64, 122, 243
Eunuchs: 51, 56, 96, 105, 127, 128, 129, 130, 132, 133, 174, 192, 212, 215, 230, 239
Excommunication: 135, 209, 214
Exotic entertainers: 127

F

Face-hugger: 211
Fadlullah, Muhammad Husayn: 84, 158, 246
Fahmy, Mansour: 36, 137
Farabi: 54

Fard, W.D.: 59-61, 67, 101, 156-157, 211, 227, 245
Farid, Malik Ghulam: 45
Farrakhan, Louis: 140, 212
Fatayat: 235
Fatimids: 102, 170, 241
Fawzan, Saleh al-: 149
Female genital mutilation: 57, 118, 150, 170, 171, 219, 225
Fetish: 125
Fifth columnists: 175, 272
First Nations: 205
Fitrah: 204, 250, 251
Fivers: 81, 87
Flies: 60
Forced labor: 14, 49, 144, 216, 224, 225, 247
France: 104, 141, 176, 222, 242
Freamon, Bernard: 9-10, 14-15, 28, 34, 36, 39-40, 54, 95-97 105-106, 117, 122-123, 127-128, 137-139, 143-145,147, 151, 152, 160, 165, 172, 176, 178-179, 192-196, 199, 203, 205, 208-209, 211, 242, 246-249, 272
Free women: 29, 31, 34, 37, 42, 79, 88, 94, 110, 138, 149
Frere, Henry: 137

G

Gelgeç, Sevim: 45
Gender inequality: 57
Genocide: 117, 170, 196, 217
Georgians: 33
Ghabal, Ahmad: 246
Ghazidadeh, Muhammad: 97
Ghiath-Ud-Din: 123
Ghulat: 84, 95, 241
Gilliot, Claude: 21
Gleissner, John Dewar: 177
Gnawa: 217
Golden Rule: 219, 237
Gordon, Matthew: 30, 143
Gradualism: 45
Gray, Peter: 146

Index

Greeks: 33, 136, 161
Grooming gangs: 93, 104

H

Haeri, Abdul-Karim: 82-83
Hagar: 20-21
Hajin: 161
Hakim, al- 3, 155, 241, 242, 245
Hakim, Sa'id al-: 97, 208
Hamel, Chouki El-: 8, 12, 23, 42-43,
    45-47, 67, 81, 90, 122-123, 128,
    140, 145, 152-155, 161, 176, 202,
    210, 215, 243, 274
Hamidullah, Muhammad: 174
Hamoudi, Haider Ala: 145
Hanafi: 171
Handmaids: 44
Hanut: 41
Harem: 122-123, 128-129, 159-160,
    178, 215, 229-230, 236
Harlotry: 35, 235
Harvesting children: 32
Hassan, Riffat: 136, 228
Hawazin: 27
Hawwari: 115
Heaven: 64-68, 95, 107, 122, 131,
    137, 273
Hell: 66, 95, 107, 122, 212, 248
Henna: 130
Heraclius: 21
Hidden Imam: 119, 163
Hinduism: 221
Hitler: 205
Hizb al-Tahrir: 99
Holocaust: 110, 177, 178, 205
Homosexuality: 112, 127, 128
Hosseini Nasab, Reza: 250
Hot oil: 130
Houris: 65-66
Hudaybiyyah: 15
Human rights: 46, 49, 101, 102, 141,
    171, 175, 180, 182, 185, 245, 250
Human sacrifice: 205

Human trafficking: 24, 33, 93, 104,
    108, 115, 118, 220, 222, 223
Hunayn: 25
Hurgronje, Christiaan: 137
Hurriyyah: 54
Huwayni, Abu Ishaq al-: 149
Hypocrisy / hypocrites: 1, 10, 11, 16,
    19, 42, 57, 71, 104, 108, 138, 163,
    201, 213, 225

I

'Ibadis: 54, 102, 154, 273
Iberians: 64, 171
Ibn 'Abidin: 11, 132
Ibn 'Amr: 136
Ibn 'Atiyyah: 115
Ibn al-Jawzi: 115
Ibn al-Naqib: 60
Ibn al-Nujaym: 78, 92, 115
Ibn al-Qasim: 77
Ibn Ghalid: 213
Ibn Hanbal: 3
Ibn Hibban: 3, 186
Ibn Khaldun: 8
Ibn Nusayr: 153
Ibn Sa'd: 27
Ibn Said: 59
Ibn Sayyid: 59
Ibn Sina: 8, 96
Ibn Sori: 59
Ibn Taymiyyah: 60, 122
Ibrahim: 20-23, 64
Iceland: 177
'Iddah: 30
Idrisi: 42
Ijma': 106, 111, 152, 174, 209, 218,
    247, 248
Ijtihad: 13, 76, 158, 205
Imamis: 54
Imazighen: 50, 153, 171, 173, 204,
    216, 245
Immorality: 35, 49, 114, 231, 235
Inaq: 28
Indecency: 91, 235

Indian Ocean: 102, 129, 140, 177
Indians: 6, 157
Infibulation: 170-171
Interfaith Harmony: 54
Invaders: 126, 171
Iranians: 141, 175
Iraqi, Fakhruddin al-: 58
Ireland: 177
Ishmael: 21
ISIS: 99, 106, 110, 112, 113, 145, 175, 198, 214, 221, 226
Islah: 196
Islam, Joseph: 33-34
Islamic Empire: 9, 102, 128, 152, 174
Islamic imperialism: 6, 80, 122, 175
Islamicity: 53, 102, 149
Islamists: 12, 19, 24, 59, 99, 118, 128, 145, 149, 205, 221-223, 271-272
Isma'il, Moulay: 123, 128, 145
Ismailis: 81, 82, 95, 157, 171, 240, 245
Israelites: 50, 232
Istishab: 124
Ithna-Asharis: 81, 86

J

Jaffer, Sadaf: 226
Jahiliyyah: 138, 147, 198, 227
Jahl: 73
Janjaweed: 152
Jassas: 115
Jaziri: 115
Jebara, Mohamad: 14, 41
Jekyll and Hyde: 86
Jesus: 10, 49, 61, 68, 136, 186, 187, 197, 202, 223
Jewish specialists: 130
Jim Crow: 67
Jizyah: 171
Johnson, Heather: 76
Judaism: 50, 59, 60, 123, 139, 220, 237

Jurisprudence: xiii, 9, 39, 40, 52, 57-58, 61, 68, 87, 90, 95, 102, 105, 107, 111, 131, 154, 163, 165, 166-168, 180, 195, 198, 199, 205-208, 210, 218-219, 228, 233, 240-241, 247-248
Juwariyyah: 37
Juwayni: 215

K

Kaabah: 4, 14, 130
Kadivar, Mohsen: 166, 167, 180, 186, 205, 218, 246
Kan, Abdul-Qadir: 55, 215, 242
Kanizes: 92
Karbala: 96, 179
Kasani: 115
Kaskas, Safi: 29
Kawakibi, 'Abd al-Rahman: 243
Kazim, Musa al-: 77, 79, 83-84, 93-94, 103, 186-189, 191
Khadijah: 14-15, 238
Khan, Ahmad: 164
Kharijites: 154, 239
Khassonké: 146
Khaybar: 27
Khayr: 232
Khazars: 6
Khomeini: 98, 102, 207-208
Khudri, Abu Sa'id al-
Khu'i, Abu al-Qasim al-: 93-94
Khums: 85, 87
Kishk, Muhammad Jalal: 131
Klansman Islam: 227
Kloran: 227
Knight, Michael Muhammad: 33
Kogi: 87
Krishna: 17
Ku Klux Klan: 187
Kufr: 11, 72, 73, 152, 172
Kuwait: 149, 244

L

La darar: 115, 185, 251
La haraj: 185, 251

Index

Lakota: 87
Lasciviousness: 35, 56, 107, 235
Lavigerie, Charles: 137
League of Nations: 141
Lee, Umar: 213
Lemmings: 10
Leo III: 123
Letter to al-Baghdadi: 148-149, 159, 196, 246
Levant: 145, 170, 177, 197
Lewdness: 35, 148, 235
Lewis, Bernard: 8, 121
Libertinism: 35, 235
Libi, Attyat Allah al-: 217
Libya: 179
Lincoln, Abraham: 220
Literalists: 192

M

Ma malakat aymanakum: 30, 34, 42, 43, 45-46, 105, 161-162
Ma'mun: 78
Madelung, Wilfred: 76
Maghili, Muhammad al-: 39, 139
Maghrib: 176
Mahdi: 55, 73, 78, 79, 82-83, 193, 241
Majid, Nurcholish: 73
Makarem Shirazi: 99, 160
Makruh: 87, 102, 105, 240, 241
Malê rebellion: 67
Malik: 9, 54, 72, 91, 107, 167, 171
Mallinké: 146
Mamluks: 129, 174
Mandinka: 146
Mankdim: 54
Mansour, Ahmed Subhy: 197-198, 249
Mansur: 23
Mao: 175
Maqasid: 185, 251
Maria the Jewess: 22
Mariya: 19-24
Ma'rifat, Mohammad-Hadi: 246

Marley, Bob: 217
Marmood, Yarrow: 59
Mary, the sister of Moses: 22
Mary Magdalene: 22
Mary, the Virgin: 22
Maryam: 22
Maslahah: 185, 232, 251
Masroor, Ajmal: 249
Masturbation: 89, 191
Materialism: 131, 230
Mathews, Nathaniel: 11, 55, 210, 218
Mauritania: 106-107, 139, 141, 146, 158, 173, 179, 222, 245, 246, 249, 250
Mawardi: 115
Mawdudi: 159
Mayas: 205
Mecca: 14, 28, 31, 37, 41, 60, 130, 137, 157, 163, 176, 195, 213
Medina: 12, 28, 37, 137, 162, 169, 170, 188, 207
Mernessi, Fatima: 91
Mesbah Yazdi: 97
Middle Passage: 177
Midianites: 50
Mikva, Rachel: 51-52
Milku al-yamin: 34, 35
Misogyny / misogynists: 10, 37, 57, 73, 82, 83, 86, 105, 118, 121, 210, 218, 223, 250
Modaressi, Mohammad: 247
Moderates: 13, 149
Modernists: 13, 157, 193, 211, 272
Mohaghegh-Damad, Mostafa: 158, 246
Monkeys: 118
Monogamy: 78, 80, 90, 91, 103, 155, 241
Monotheism / monotheists: xiii, 6, 60, 136, 194
Moral wrongs: 1, 11, 17, 214
Morocco: 12, 30, 42, 46, 53, 128, 145, 146, 153, 176, 193, 215, 217, 243

Moses: xiii-xiv, 49, 64, 68
Mossi: 146
Mu'allaq: 188
Mu'izz: 155
Muhammad, Elijah: 59-61, 67, 101, 211, 245
Muhammadin, Fajri: 148
Muhsinat : 44
Mujahid
Mujahid, Abdul Malik: 15, 166, 202-203, 211
Mujahidin: 217
Mujtahids: 72, 96, 205, 246
Mullah, Khaled al- : 204
munqati': 188
Muqallid: 119
Muqawqis: 19, 21, 22
Muqtadir: 128
Murata, Sachiko: 241
Mushrikin: 6, 52, 122
Musta'alis: 86, 171
Mustahab: 240
Mut'ah: 44, 90-91, 95, 103-104, 234
Mutairi, Salwa al-: 149
Mutawakkil: 123
Mutazilis: 54, 81, 155, 171, 182, 205, 211, 240, 273
Muttahari: 194, 246
Muwahhidun: 242
Muwalladun: 64

N

Na'im, Abdullahi an-: 139
Nahi 'an al-munkar: 232
Najaf: 96, 179
Nannies: 127, 215, 216
Naqi, 'Ali al-: 8, 60, 78, 188
Narjis: 78
Nasiri: 53, 193
Natural Law: 204, 250, 251
Nawawi: 28
Nazis: 205
Negro: 8, 174, 244
Negus: 6, 9
Netherlands: 141

New Testament: 52, 61
Nezahualcoyotl: 205
Nigeria: 99, 145, 193, 222
Nigger: 146, 216
Nikah: 35, 45, 114, 107
Nimatullahi: 157, 243
Nine-year-old girls: 13, 39, 57, 82, 126
Nizaris: 96, 156, 245
North Africa: 50, 73, 102, 117, 139, 172, 177, 209, 251
Nubia / Nubians: 6, 7, 42, 78, 153
Nusayris: 78, 90, 241
Nusrah: 217

O

Obeid, Anis: 155-156
Öhrnberg, Kaj: 20
Old Testament: 22, 61, 71
Omanis: 141
Oppression: 16, 60, 64, 95, 107, 108, 111, 138, 146, 229
Orientalists: 67, 136, 271-272
Orgies: 91
Orthodoxy: 40, 150, em272-273
Ottomans: 141, 169, 176, 213

P

Paganism: 92-93
Pahlavi, Reza Shah: 243
Pakistanis: 87, 104, 141, 173, 179
Parwez, Ghulam Ahmad: 166
Patriarchy: 73, 82, 104, 210
Peacemakers: 231
Pederasty / pederasts: 127, 131
Pedophilia / pedophiles: 93, 104, 108, 115, 118, 131, 132, 163, 204, 226
Penis: 4, 65, 129-130
People of the Book: 11, 28, 54, 148
Pepper: 130
Perfidy: 230
Persian Gulf: 144, 242
Peter: 23
Peul: 55, 146

Pharisees: 10, 143
Pharoah: 50, 68, 191, 232
Pierce, Matthew: 23
Pigs: 118
Pilegesh: 22
Pimps: 24, 41, 93, 103-108, 118, 126, 216, 222
Pirates: 154, 176-177
Plague: 177
Plantations: xxii, 30, 159, 174-175, 201, 208, 216, 224
Pol Pot: 175
Polygyny: 36, 50,57, 72, 76, 79, 80, 86, 90, 103, 104, 154, 163, 210, 241
Polynesian: 87
Polysemy: 52
Polytheism / polytheists: xiii, 6, 25, 28, 29, 31, 42, 68, 93, 122, 205
Pornography: 24, 64, 83, 104, 117, 220
Portugal: 141, 176
Powell, Eve Troutt: 173
Powers, David: 21
Pregnancy: 30-31, 82, 153
Pre-pubescent children: 17, 105, 210
Prostitution / prostitutes: xxi, 22, 24, 28, 30, 35, 40-41, 43-44, 78, 95, 104, 121, 123, 127, 128, 131, 144, 163, 177, 210, 215-216, 220, 235, 252
Purity: 78, 92, 236

Q

Qabel, Ahmad: 248-249
Qaradawi: 217
Qarmatians: 81, 84-86, 90, 154-155, 240, 272
Qatar: 144
Qays: 25
Qist: 232
Qum: 96
Qummi: 186
Qur'anists: 13, 86, 95, 197, 211, 272

Quraishi-Landes, Asifa: 204
Qurtubi: 28
Qutb, Sayyid: 36, 165, 193

R

Rabbis: 52, 72
Racism: 3, 7, 8, 9, 59, 60, 86, 101, 108, 131, 145, 146, 156, 168, 172, 173, 179, 210, 230, 238
Rahman, Fazlur: 160, 182
Rape: xxii, 26, 28, 33, 41, 50, 56, 62-63, 78, 80, 88-89, 104, 105-106, 109-115, 117-118, 132, 135, 144, 153-154, 163, 172, 176, 211-212, 215, 217, 222-223, 225, 231, 235, 252, 272
Rashid, Harun al-: 149
Rashid, Ma'mar al-: 27
Rashid, Qasim: 44
Rayhanah: 16, 37
Red Sea: 129, 176, 177
Reformists: 99, 149, 205, 211, 272
Reynolds, Gabriel Said: 20-21
Rida, 'Ali al-: 78, 94, 116
Rida, Rashid: 160, 164, 165
Righteousness: 3, 66, 73, 92, 165, 232, 233
Riqq: 50, 217, 221, 224
Rizvi, Muhammad: 77, 80,
Rizvi, Sa'eed Akhtar: 75, 158
Robinson, Majied: 161-162
Rodriguez, Junius: 99
Roman Catholic Church: 51, 62, 126
Romans: 22, 60, 83, 88, 93, 121, 170, 234
Rosenberg, Roger: 61
Rosenblum, Amalia: 144
Russians: 176
Rutter, Eldon: 137
Rwanda: 217

S

Sacred Feminine: 58
Sadat: 79

Sadi, Mohamed el-: 249
Sadiq, Ja'far al-: 81-85
Sadr, Muqtada: 97, 102, 122, 128, 169
Saduq: 186-187
Safavids: 215
Safiyyah: 16, 238
Sahara: 177-178
Salafis: 109, 110-114, 149, 202, 210, 213, 222-223
Saleh, Habib: 218
Saqabila: 6, 93
Sassanians: 161
Saudi Arabia: 123, 139, 148-149, 174
Saudi Arabia Committee of Fatwa: 148
Saudis: 141, 175
Schacht, Joseph: 195
Scott, John: 55
Secularists: 13, 139, 158, 272
Segal, Ronald: 76, 123, 130
Senegal: 11, 146, 215, 242
Senior Council of Clerics: 149
Sepúlvedas: 67
Seveners: 81, 84, 88
Sexism: 57, 59, 102, 108, 168, 210
Sexual assault: 28, 41, 63, 71, 81, 104, 106, 153, 239, 252
Shafi'i: 45, 72, 148, 167, 171, 174
Shafiq, Ahmad Bek: 56, 182
Shah, 'Ali: 158
Shahin, Sultan: 147
Shakespeare: 51-52
Shari'ah: 2, 10, 12, 29, 39, 54, 56, 58, 81-82, 96, 104-105, 106, 110, 116, 125, 139, 148, 151-152, 154, 163, 172, 175, 185, 194, 199, 204, 206, 209-210, 215-216, 217, 219, 223, 240, 242, 245, 248, 272
Shariati, 'Ali: 175
Sharr al-nas man ba'a al-nas: 185
Sheba: 22
Shem: 8
Shirin: 20
Shubayri Zanjani, Musa: 94
Sine manu: 233

Singers: 127
Sistani, 'Ali al-: 97, 249,
Slave markets: 170, 176, 178, 230
Slave Master Islam: 2, 59, 107, 175, 245
Slavery Convention: 141, 148,
Slavs: 6
Sodomy: 82
Soldiers: 63, 69, 80, 83, 109, 122, 152, 180, 192, 221, 224
Solomon: 50, 75
Soninke: 146
Sources of emulation: 157, 246
Spain: 63, 117, 141, 176
Stalin: 175
Submission: 56-57, 64, 122, 175, 193, 209
Sudan: 7, 9, 64, 146, 152, 158, 173, 179, 212, 222, 245
Sufis / Sufism: 84, 90, 102, 103, 107, 157, 223, 243, 244, 248, 272,
Suleiman, Omar: 50
Superiority: xiii, 3, 4, 9, 167
Suyuti: 115
Sweden: 141

T

Tabari: 27, 115, 172, 176
Taha, Mahmoud Mohamed: 153
Takfir: 1, 11, 213
Takim, Liyakat: 159, 163, 185, 250
Talmud: 217
Taoism: 220
Taqi, Muhammad al-: 78
Taqlid: 40, 119, 208
Taqwah: 232
Tassari: 38
Tawbah: 52
Temporary marriage: 29, 44, 77, 87, 91, 95, 103
Ten Commandments: 58, 250
Testicles: 127, 129, 130, 208
Theological trap: 1
Thirteenth Amendment: 141, 216
Thomas, Bertram: 137

Timbuktu: 9, 192
Titwani, Ahmad al-: 145
Tlemcen: 39
Torah: 52
Trans-Atlantic Slave Trade: 140, 170, 177, 179, 251
Trans-Saharan Slave Trade: 129, 140
Transsexuality: 128
Transgression: 244
Trauma: 14, 42, 62, 63, 117, 129, 130, 237
Treachery: 230
Treaties: 151, 204, 231
Trespassers: 229
Trimingham, J.S.: 171-172
Tripoli: 177
Tubman, Harriet: 88
Turks: 6, 12, 101, 127, 146, 164, 173, 245
Turpitude: 91
Tusi: 8, 29, 82, 83, 93, 96, 186, 239
Twelvers: 81, 84, 88, 188

U

Ulama': 96, 97, 106, 132, 193, 207, 216, 217, 241, 272
Umar: 13, 37, 91, 92, 117, 132, 137, 138, 165, 195, 198, 227, 243
Umayyads: 9, 60, 66, 162, 169, 199, 227
Umm walad: 23, 37, 103, 161
Uncle Tom: 67, 251
Underground Railroad: 88
Unitarians: 154, 242
United States: 30, 59, 63, 104, 114, 132, 141, 156, 157, 174, 178, 216, 225, 248
Universal Declaration of Human Rights: 141
Upton, Charles: 65
Urban, Elizabeth: 10, 21-23, 28, 162
Urethra: 130
'Urf: 103, 124, 185, 251
Ukrainians: 176

Usmani: 217
'Uthman: 3-4, 198

V

Vaginas: 65, 82, 83
Van Reeth, Jan: 21
Veiling: 84, 86
Vermont: 141
Virgins: 65, 82, 92, 132
Virtue: 92, 182, 249
Voltaire: xxi

W

Wadud, Amina: 91, 139, 160
Wahhabis: 201, 210, 213, 223
Wahidi: 136
Wahy: 251
Wajib: 158, 240
Ware, Rudolph T.: 9, 55, 106, 136, 137, 139, 146, 154, 172, 186, 191, 215-216, 242
Wasters: 229
Webb, Alexander: 91, 156, 243
Whataboutery: 226
White Muslims: 156, 201
White women: 65, 215
Whoredom: 34, 35, 43, 235
Wickedness: 8, 71, 251
Wife beating: 57
Wife-swapping: 82
Wilayat al-faqih: 97
Witztum, Joseph: 44
Wolof: 146
Wrongdoers: 229

X

X, Malcolm: 15, 59, 60-63, 67, 101, 144, 201, 244

Y

Yaqoubi, Muhammad: 159, 246
Yemenis: 141

Yüksel, Edip: xiii-xiv, 30, 42, 46, 68, 116, 198, 226

Z

Zahiris: 167, 233
Zaman wa makan: 185, 251
Zanj: 6, 7, 42, 145, 240
Zayd: 108
Zaydis: 81, 84, 86, 94
Zayn al-'Abidin: 6-7, 80, 84, 188
Zinah: 89, 95, 113, 153
Zombies: 62, 201
Zuhayli: 148
Zunayrah / Zinnirah: 107, 137-138, 237
Zwemer, Samuel: 137

Printed in the USA
CPSIA information can be obtained
at www.ICGtesting.com
JSHW011316240624
65298JS00020B/541/J